Course Booklet

CCNA Exploration
Accessing the WAN

Version 4.0

ciscopress.com

Cisco | Networking Academy
Mind Wide Open

CCNA Exploration Course Booklet Accessing the WAN, Version 4.0

Cisco Networking Academy

Copyright© 2010 Cisco Systems, Inc.

Published by:
Cisco Press
800 East 96th Street
Indianapolis, IN 46240 USA

All rights reserved. No part of this book may be reproduced or transmitted in any form or by any means, electronic or mechanical, including photocopying, recording, or by any information storage and retrieval system, without written permission from the publisher, except for the inclusion of brief quotations in a review.

Printed in the United States of America

First Printing   September 2009

Library of Congress Cataloging-in-Publication Data is available upon request

ISBN-13: 978-1-58713-255-1

ISBN-10: 1-58713-255-9

Warning and Disclaimer

This book is designed to provide information about accessing the WAN. Every effort has been made to make this book as complete and as accurate as possible, but no warranty or fitness is implied.

The information is provided on an "as is" basis. The authors, Cisco Press, and Cisco Systems, Inc. shall have neither liability nor responsibility to any person or entity with respect to any loss or damages arising from the information contained in this book or from the use of the discs or programs that may accompany it.

The opinions expressed in this book belong to the author and are not necessarily those of Cisco Systems, Inc.

Publisher
Paul Boger

Associate Publisher
Dave Dusthimer

Cisco Representative
Erik Ullanderson

Cisco Press Program Manager
Anand Sundaram

Executive Editor
Mary Beth Ray

Managing Editor
Patrick Kanouse

Project Editor
Bethany Wall

Editorial Assistant
Vanessa Evans

Cover Designer
Louisa Adair

Composition
Mark Shirar

This book is part of the Cisco Networking Academy® series from Cisco Press. The products in this series support and complement the Cisco Networking Academy curriculum. If you are using this book outside the Networking Academy, then you are not preparing with a Cisco trained and authorized Networking Academy provider.

For more information on the Cisco Networking Academy or to locate a Networking Academy, Please visit www.cisco.com/edu.

Trademark Acknowledgments

All terms mentioned in this book that are known to be trademarks or service marks have been appropriately capitalized. Cisco Press or Cisco Systems, Inc., cannot attest to the accuracy of this information. Use of a term in this book should not be regarded as affecting the validity of any trademark or service mark.

Feedback Information

At Cisco Press, our goal is to create in-depth technical books of the highest quality and value. Each book is crafted with care and precision, undergoing rigorous development that involves the unique expertise of members from the professional technical community.

Readers' feedback is a natural continuation of this process. If you have any comments regarding how we could improve the quality of this book, or otherwise alter it to better suit your needs, you can contact us through email at feedback@ciscopress.com. Please make sure to include the book title and ISBN in your message.

We greatly appreciate your assistance.

Americas Headquarters
Cisco Systems, Inc.
San Jose, CA

Asia Pacific Headquarters
Cisco Systems (USA) Pte. Ltd.
Singapore

Europe Headquarters
Cisco Systems International BV
Amsterdam, The Netherlands

Cisco has more than 200 offices worldwide. Addresses, phone numbers, and fax numbers are listed on the Cisco Website at **www.cisco.com/go/offices**.

CCDE, CCENT, Cisco Eos, Cisco HealthPresence, the Cisco logo, Cisco Lumin, Cisco Nexus, Cisco StadiumVision, Cisco TelePresence, Cisco WebEx, DCE, and Welcome to the Human Network are trademarks; Changing the Way We Work, Live, Play, and Learn and Cisco Store are service marks; and Access Registrar, Aironet, AsyncOS, Bringing the Meeting To You, Catalyst, CCDA, CCDP, CCIE, CCIP, CCNA, CCNP, CCSP, CCVP, Cisco, the Cisco Certified Internetwork Expert logo, Cisco IOS, Cisco Press, Cisco Systems, Cisco Systems Capital, the Cisco Systems logo, Cisco Unity, Collaboration Without Limitation, EtherFast, EtherSwitch, Event Center, Fast Step, Follow Me Browsing, FormShare, GigaDrive, HomeLink, Internet Quotient, IOS, iPhone, iQuick Study, IronPort, the IronPort logo, LightStream, Linksys, MediaTone, MeetingPlace, MeetingPlace Chime Sound, MGX, Networkers, Networking Academy, Network Registrar, PCNow, PIX, PowerPanels, ProConnect, ScriptShare, SenderBase, SMARTnet, Spectrum Expert, StackWise, The Fastest Way to Increase Your Internet Quotient, TransPath, WebEx, and the WebEx logo are registered trademarks of Cisco Systems, Inc. and/or its affiliates in the United States and certain other countries.

All other trademarks mentioned in this document or website are the property of their respective owners. The use of the word partner does not imply a partnership relationship between Cisco and any other company. (0812R)

Contents at a Glance

Introduction   1

Chapter 1   Introduction to WANs   5

Chapter 2   PPP   27

Chapter 3   Frame Relay   53

Chapter 4   Network Security   77

Chapter 5   ACLs   127

Chapter 6   Teleworker ServicesTeleworker Services   151

Chapter 7   IP Addressing Services   171

Chapter 8   Network Troubleshooting   207

Glossary   239

Contents

Introduction 1

Chapter 1 **Introduction to WANs** 5

Chapter Introduction 5

1.1 Providing Integrated Services to the Enterprise 5
    1.1.1 Introducing Wide Area Networks (WANs) 5
    1.1.2 The Evolving Enterprise 6
    1.1.3 The Evolving Network Model 8

1.2 WAN Technology Concepts 10
    1.2.1 WAN Technology Overview 11
    1.2.2 WAN Physical Layer Concepts 11
    1.2.3 WAN Data Link Layer Concepts 13
    1.2.4 WAN Switching Concepts 14

1.3 WAN Connection Options 16
    1.3.1 WAN Link Connection Options 16
    1.3.2 Dedicated Connection Link Options 17
    1.3.3 Circuit Switched Connection Options 17
    1.3.4 Packet Switched Connection Options 19
    1.3.5 Internet Connection Options 20

1.4 Chapter Labs 24
    1.4.1 Challenge Review 24

Chapter Summary 25

Chapter 2 **PPP** 27

Chapter Introduction 27

2.1 Serial Point-to-Point Links 27
    2.1.1 Introducing Serial Communications 27
    2.1.2 TDM 29
    2.1.3 Demarcation Point 31
    2.1.4 DTE and DCE 32
    2.1.5 HDLC Encapsulation 33
    2.1.6 Configuring HDLC Encapsulation 35
    2.1.7 Troubleshooting a Serial Interface 35

2.2 PPP Concepts 36
    2.2.1 Introducing PPP 36
    2.2.2 PPP Layered Architecture 37
    2.2.3 PPP Frame Structure 38
    2.2.4 Establishing a PPP Session 38
    2.2.5 Establishing a Link with LCP 39
    2.2.6 NCP Explained 40

2.3 Configuring PPP   41
2.3.1 PPP Configuration Options   41
2.3.2 PPP Configuration Commands   42
2.3.3 Verifying a Serial PPP Encapsulation Configuration   43
2.3.4 Troubleshooting PPP Encapsulation   43

2.4 Configuring PPP with Authentication   45
2.4.1 PPP Authentication Protocols   45
2.4.2 Password Authentication Protocol (PAP)   46
2.4.3 Challenge Handshake Authentication Protocol (CHAP)   46
2.4.4 PPP Encapsulation and Authentication Process   47
2.4.5 Configuring PPP with Authentication   48
2.4.6 Troubleshooting a PPP Configuration with Authentication   49

2.5 Chapter Labs   49
2.5.1 Basic PPP Configuration   49
2.5.2 Challenge PPP Configuration   50
2.5.3 Troubleshooting PPP Configuration   50

Chapter Summary   51

Chapter 3   Frame Relay   53

Introduction   53

3.1 Basic Frame Relay Concepts   53
3.1.1 Introducing Frame Relay   53
3.1.2 Virtual Circuits   56
3.1.3 Frame Relay Encapsulation   58
3.1.4 Frame Relay Topologies   59
3.1.5 Frame Relay Address Mapping   60

3.2 Configuring Frame Relay   63
3.2.1 Configuring Basic Frame Relay   63
3.2.2 Configuring Static Frame Relay Maps   64

3.3 Advanced Frame Relay Concepts   65
3.3.1 Solving Reachability Issues   65
3.3.2 Paying for Frame Relay   67
3.3.3 Frame Relay Flow Control   68

3.4 Configuring Advanced Frame Relay   69
3.4.1 Configuring Frame Relay Subinterfaces   69
3.4.2 Verifying Frame Relay Operation   71
3.4.3 Troubleshooting Frame Relay Configuration   72

3.5 Chapter Labs   73
3.5.1 Basic Frame Relay   73
3.5.2 Challenge Frame Relay Configuration   73
3.5.3 Troubleshooting Frame Relay   73

Chapter Summary   74

Chapter 4   Network Security   77

Chapter Introduction   77

4.1 Introduction to Network Security   77
4.1.1 Why is Network Security Important?   77
4.1.2 Common Security Threats   81
4.1.3 Types of Network Attacks   83
4.1.4 General Mitigation Techniques   90
4.1.5 The Network Security Wheel   93
4.1.6 The Enterprise Security Policy   95

4.2 Securing Cisco Routers   97
4.2.1 Router Security Issues   97
4.2.2 Applying Cisco IOS Security Features to Routers   99
4.2.3 Manage Router Security   99
4.2.4 Securing Remote Administrative Access to Routers   101
4.2.5 Logging Router Activity   104

4.3 Secure Router Network Services   105
4.3.1 Vulnerable Router Services and Interfaces   105
4.3.2 Securing Routing Protocols   107
4.3.3 Locking Down Your Router with Cisco Auto Secure   110

4.4 Using Cisco SDM   110
4.4.1 Cisco SDM Overview   110
4.4.2 Configuring Your Router to Support Cisco SDM   111
4.4.3 Starting Cisco SDM   111
4.4.4 The Cisco SDM Interface   111
4.4.5 Cisco SDM Wizards   113
4.4.6 Locking Down a Router with Cisco SDM   113

4.5 Secure Router Management   113
4.5.1 Maintaining Cisco IOS Software Images   113
4.5.2 Managing Cisco IOS Images   114
4.5.3 TFTP Managed Cisco IOS Images   116
4.5.4 Backing up and Upgrading Software Image   117
4.5.5 Recovering Software Images   118
4.5.6 Troubleshooting Cisco IOS Configurations   120
4.5.7 Recovering a Lost Router Password   122

4.6 Chapter Labs   124
4.6.1 Basic Security Configuration   124
4.6.2 Challenge Security Configuration   124
4.6.3 Troubleshooting Security Configuration   124

Chapter Summary   125

Chapter 5   ACLs   127

Introduction   127

5.1 Using ACLs to Secure Networks   127
    5.1.1 A TCP Conversation   127
    5.1.2 Packet Filtering   128
    5.1.3 What is an ACL?   129
    5.1.4 ACL Operation   130
    5.1.5 Types of Cisco ACLs   132
    5.1.6 How a Standard ACL Works   132
    5.1.7 Numbering and Naming ACLs   132
    5.1.8 Where to Place ACLs   133
    5.1.9 General Guidelines for Creating ACLs   134

5.2 Configuring Standard ACLs   134
    5.2.1 Entering Criteria Statements   134
    5.2.2 Configuring a Standard ACL   134
    5.2.3 ACL Wildcard Masking   135
    5.2.4 Applying Standard ACLs to Interfaces   138
    5.2.5 Editing Numbered ACLs   139
    5.2.6 Creating Standard Named ACLs   140
    5.2.7 Monitoring and Verifying ACLs   140
    5.2.8 Editing Named ACLs   141

5.3 Configuring Extended ACLs   141
    5.3.1 Extended ACLs   141
    5.3.2 Configuring Extended ACLs   142
    5.3.3 Applying Extended ACLs to Interfaces   143
    5.3.4 Creating Named Extended ACLs   143

5.4 Configure Complex ACLs   144
    5.4.1 What are Complex ACLs?   144
    5.4.2 Dynamic ACLs   144
    5.4.3 Reflexive ACLs   145
    5.4.4 Time-based ACLs   146
    5.4.5 Troubleshooting Common ACL Errors   146

5.5 Chapter Labs   148
    5.5.1 Basic Access Control Lists   148
    5.5.2 Access Control Lists Challenge   148
    5.5.3 Troubleshooting Access Control Lists   148

Chapter Summary   149

Chapter 6   **Teleworker ServicesTeleworker Services**   **151**

Chapter Introduction   151

6.1 Business Requirements for Teleworker Services   151
6.1.1 The Business Requirements for Teleworker Services   151

6.1.2 The Teleworker Solution   152

6.2 Broadband Services   153
6.2.1 Connecting Teleworkers to the WAN   153

6.2.2 Cable   154

6.2.3 DSL   156

6.2.4 Broadband Wireless   158

6.3 VPN Technology   161
6.3.1 VPNs and Their Benefits   161

6.3.2 Types of VPNs   162

6.3.3 VPN Components   163

6.3.4 Characteristics of Secure VPNs   163

6.3.5 VPN Tunneling   164

6.3.6 VPN Data Integrity   164

6.3.7 IPsec Security Protocols   167

Chapter Summary   169

Chapter 7   **IP Addressing Services**   **171**

Chapter Introduction   171

7.1 DHCP   171
7.1.1 Introducing DHCP   171

7.1.2 DHCP Operation   172

7.1.3 BOOTP and DHCP   173

7.1.4 Configuring a DHCP Server   176

7.1.5 Configuring a DHCP Client   178

7.1.6 DHCP Relay   178

7.1.7 Configuring a DHCP Server Using SDM   180

7.1.8 Troubleshooting DHCP   180

7.2 Scaling Networks with NAT   182
7.2.1 Private and Public IP Addressing   183

7.2.2 What is NAT?   183

7.2.3 Benefits and Drawbacks of Using NAT   186

7.2.4 Configuring Static NAT   187

7.2.5 Configuring Dynamic NAT   188

7.2.6 Configuring NAT Overload   188

7.2.7 Configuring Port Forwarding   189

7.2.8 Verifying and Troubleshooting NAT Configurations   190

7.3 IPv6   192

7.3.1 Reasons for Using IPv6   192

7.3.2 IPv6 Addressing   195

7.3.3 IPv6 Transition Strategies   198

7.3.4 Cisco IOS Dual Stack   198

7.3.5 IPv6 Tunneling   199

7.3.6 Routing Considerations with IPv6   200

7.3.7 Configuring IPv6 Addresses   201

7.3.8 Configuring RIPng with IPv6   202

7.3.9 Verifying and Troubleshooting RIPng   203

7.4 Chapter Labs   203

7.4.1 Basic DHCP and NAT Configuration   203

7.4.2 Challenge DHCP and NAT Configuration   203

7.4.3 Troubleshooting DHCP and NAT   203

Chapter Summary   205

Chapter 8   Network Troubleshooting   207

Chapter Introduction   207

8.1 Establishing the Network Performance Baseline   207

8.1.1 Documenting Your Network   207

8.1.2 Documenting Your Network   208

8.1.3 Why is Establishing a Network Baseline Important?   209

8.1.4 Steps for Establishing a Network Baseline   210

8.2 Troubleshooting Methodologies and Tools   211

8.2.1 A General Approach to Troubleshooting   211

8.2.2 Using Layered Models for Troubleshooting   212

8.2.3 General Troubleshooting Procedures   213

8.2.4 Troubleshooting Methods   213

8.2.5 Gathering Symptoms   214

8.2.6 Troubleshooting Tools   215

8.3 Common WAN Implementation Issues   217

8.3.1 WAN Communications   218

8.3.2 Steps in WAN Design   218

8.3.3 WAN Traffic Considerations   219

8.3.4 WAN Topology Considerations   219

8.3.5 WAN Bandwidth Considerations   220

8.3.6 Common WAN Implementation Issues   221

8.3.7 Case Study: WAN Troubleshooting from an ISP's Perspective   221

8.4 Network Troubleshooting 221

    8.4.1 Interpreting Network Diagrams to Identify Problems 221

    8.4.2 Physical Layer Troubleshooting 223

    8.4.3 Data Link Layer Troubleshooting 226

    8.4.4 Network Layer Troubleshooting 230

    8.4.5 Transport Layer Troubleshooting 231

    8.4.6 Application Layer Troubleshooting 233

8.5 Chapter Labs 236

    8.5.1 Troubleshooting Enterprise Networks 1 236

    8.5.2 Troubleshooting Enterprise Networks 2 236

    8.5.3 Troubleshooting Enterprise Networks 3 236

Chapter Summary 237

Glossary 239

Command Syntax Conventions

The conventions used to present command syntax in this book are the same conventions used in the IOS Command Reference. The Command Reference describes these conventions as follows:

- **Boldface** indicates commands and keywords that are entered literally as shown. In actual configuration examples and output (not general command syntax), boldface indicates commands that are manually input by the user (such as a **show** command).

- *Italic* indicates arguments for which you supply actual values.

- Vertical bars (|) separate alternative, mutually exclusive elements.

- Square brackets ([ ]) indicate an optional element.

- Braces ({ }) indicate a required choice.

- Braces within brackets ([{ }]) indicate a required choice within an optional element.

About this Course Booklet

Your Cisco Networking Academy Course Booklet is designed as a study resource you can easily read, highlight, and review on the go, wherever the Internet is not available or practical:

- The text is extracted directly, word-for-word, from the online course so you can highlight important points and take notes in the "Your Chapter Notes" section.

- Headings with the exact page correlations provide a quick reference to the online course for your classroom discussions and exam preparation.

- An icon system directs you to the online curriculum to take full advantage of the images, labs, Packet Tracer activities, and dynamic Flash-based activities embedded within the Networking Academy online course interface.

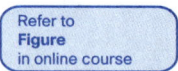
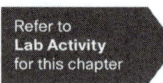

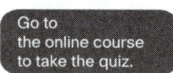

The Course Booklet is a basic, economical paper-based resource to help you succeed with the Cisco Networking Academy online course.

Course Introduction

Welcome

Welcome to the CCNA Exploration Accessing the WAN course. The goal of this course is to introduce you to fundamental networking concepts and technologies. These online course materials will assist you in developing the skills necessary to plan and implement small networks across a range of applications. The specific skills covered in each chapter are described at the start of each chapter.

More than just information

This computer-based learning environment is an important part of the overall course experience for students and instructors in the Networking Academy. These online course materials are designed to be used along with several other instructional tools and activities. These include:

- Class presentation, discussion, and practice with your instructor
- Hands-on labs that use networking equipment within the Networking Academy classroom
- Online scored assessments and a matching grade book
- Packet Tracer simulation tool
- Additional software for classroom activities

A global community

When you participate in the Networking Academy, you are joining a global community linked by common goals and technologies. Schools, colleges, universities and other entities in over 160 countries participate in the program. You can see an interactive network map of the global Networking Academy community at http://www.academynetspace.com.

The material in this course encompasses a broad range of technologies that facilitate how people work, live, play, and learn by communicating with voice, video, and other data. Networking and the Internet affect people differently in different parts of the world. Although we have worked with instructors from around the world to create these materials, it is important that you work with your instructor and fellow students to make the material in this course applicable to your local situation.

Keep in Touch

These online instructional materials, as well as the rest of the course tools, are part of the larger Networking Academy. The portal for the program is located at http://cisco.netacad.net. There you will obtain access to the other tools in the program such as the assessment server and student grade book), as well as informational updates and other relevant links.

Mind Wide Open®

An important goal in education is to enrich you, the student, by expanding what you know and can do. It is important to realize, however, that the instructional materials and the instructor can only *facilitate* the process. You must make the commitment yourself to learn new skills. Below are a few suggestions to help you learn and grow.

1. Take notes. Professionals in the networking field often keep Engineering Journals in which they write down the things they observe and learn. Taking notes is an important way to help your understanding grow over time.

2. Think about it. The course provides information both to change what you know and what you can do. As you go through the course, ask yourself what makes sense and what doesn't. Stop and ask questions when you are confused. Try to find out more about topics that interest you. If you are not sure why something is being taught, consider asking your instructor or a friend. Think about how the different parts of the course fit together.

3. Practice. Learning new skills requires practice. We believe this is so important to e-learning that we have a special name for it. We call it e-doing. It is very important that you complete the activities in the online instructional materials and that you also complete the hands-on labs and Packet Tracer® activities.

4. Practice again. Have you ever thought that you knew how to do something and then, when it was time to show it on a test or at work, you discovered that you really hadn't mastered it? Just like learning any new skill like a sport, game, or language, learning a professional skill requires patience and repeated practice before you can say you have truly learned it. The online instructional materials in this course provide opportunities for repeated practice for many skills. Take full advantage of them. You can also work with your instructor to extend Packet Tracer, and other tools, for additional practice as needed.

5. Teach it. Teaching a friend or colleague is often a good way to reinforce your own learning. To teach well, you will have to work through details that you may have overlooked on your first reading. Conversations about the course material with fellow students, colleagues, and the instructor can help solidify your understanding of networking concepts.

6. Make changes as you go. The course is designed to provide feedback through interactive activities and quizzes, the online assessment system, and through interactions with your instructor. You can use this feedback to better understand where your strengths and weaknesses are. If there is an area that you are having trouble with, focus on studying or practicing more in that area. Seek additional feedback from your instructor and other students.

Explore the world of networking

This version of the course includes a special tool called Packet Tracer 4.1®. Packet Tracer is a networking learning tool that supports a wide range of physical and logical simulations. It also provides visualization tools to help you to understand the internal workings of a network.

The Packet Tracer activities included in the course consist of network simulations, games, activities, and challenges that provide a broad range of learning experiences.

Create your own worlds

You can also use Packet Tracer to create your own experiments and networking scenarios. We hope that, over time, you consider using Packet Tracer – not only for experiencing the activities included in the course, but also to become an author, explorer, and experimenter.

The online course materials have embedded Packet Tracer activities that will launch on computers running Windows® operating systems, if Packet Tracer is installed. This integration may also work on other operating systems using Windows emulation.

Course Overview

The primary focus of this course is on accessing wide area networks (WAN). The goal is to develop an understanding of various WAN technologies to connect small- to medium-sized business networks.

The course introduces WAN converged applications and quality of service (QoS). It focuses on WAN technologies including PPP, Frame Relay, and broadband links. WAN security concepts are discussed in detail, including types of threats, how to analyze network vulnerabilities, general methods for mitigating common security threats and types of security appliances and applications. The course then explains the principles of traffic control and access control lists (ACLs) and describes how to implement IP addressing services for an Enterprise network, including how to configure NAT and DHCP. IPv6 addressing concepts are also discussed. During the course, you will learn how to use Cisco Router and Security Device Manager (SDM) to secure a router and implement IP addressing services. Finally, students learn how to detect, troubleshoot and correct common Enterprise network implementation issues.

The labs and Packet Tracer activities used in this course are designed to help you develop an understanding of how to configure routing operations while reinforcing the concepts learned in each chapter.

Chapter 1 Introduction to WANs - In Chapter 1, you will learn the fundamentals enterprise WANs, the technologies available to implement them, and the terminology used to discuss them. You will learn how the Cisco enterprise architecture provides integrated services over an enterprise network and how to select the appropriate WAN technology to meet different enterprise business requirements.

Chapter 2 PPP - Chapter 2 focuses on serial point-to-point communications and the Point-to-Point Protocol (PPP). Understanding how point-to-point communication links function to provide access to a WAN is important to an overall understanding of how WANs function. Various aspects of PPP are discussed including securing PPP using either Password Authentication Protocol (PAP) or the more effective Challenge Handshake Authentication Protocol (CHAP).

Chapter 3 Frame Relay - Chapter 3 focuses on the high-performance Frame Relay WAN protocol. You will learn how to implement Frame Relay for use between LANs over a WAN.

Chapter 4 Network Security - Chapter 4 introduces network security which has moved to the forefront of network management and implementation. The overall security challenge is to find a balance between two important requirements: the need to open networks to support evolving business opportunities, and the need to protect private, personal, and strategic business information. You will learn to identify security threats to enterprise networks and mitigation techniques. You will also learn how to configure basic router security, disable unused resources and interfaces. Finally you will learn to manage configurations and IOS files.

Chapter 5 ACLs - Chapter 5 builds on the concepts introduced in Chapter 4 and focuses on the application of ACLs. One of the most important skills a network administrator needs is mastery of access control lists (ACLs). You will learn how to create firewalls using standard and extended ACLs. Finally, you learn about advanced ACL features including dynamic, reflexive and timed ACLs.

Chapter 6 Teleworker Services - Chapter 6 discusses broadband technologies from a telecommuter's perspective. Specifically, you will learn about cable, DSL, and wireless broadband options. You will also explore how VPNs are utilized to secure broadband connections.

Chapter 7 IP Addressing Services - Chapter 7 discusses how a branch site can provide IP addressing services to users. You will identify teleworker requirements and recommend architectures for providing teleworking services. Specifically, you will learn how to configure a router to be a Dynamic Host Configuration Protocol (DHCP) server and how to integrate private addresses and Network Address Translation (NAT). You will finish with an overview of IPv6 and how to configure routers to exchange IPv6 routes using RIPng.

Chapter 8 Network Troubleshooting - Chapter 8 is the capstone chapter for this course. You will learn how to establish a network baseline and develop network documentation to help in network troubleshooting. You will also develop your network troubleshooting skills by reviewing troubleshooting methodology. You will learn to identify and troubleshoot common enterprise network implementation issues using a layered model approach.

CHAPTER 1

Introduction to WANs

Chapter Introduction

Refer to Figure in online course

When an enterprise grows to include branch offices, e-commerce services, or global operations, a single *LAN network* is no longer sufficient to meet its business requirements. Wide-area network (*WAN*) access has become essential for larger businesses today.

There are a variety of WAN technologies to meet the different needs of businesses and many ways to scale the network. Adding WAN access introduces other considerations, such as network security and *address* management. Consequently, designing a WAN and choosing the correct carrier network services is not a simple matter.

In this chapter, you will begin exploring some of the options available for designing enterprise WANs, the technologies available to implement them, and the terminology used to discuss them. You will learn about selecting the appropriate WAN technologies, services, and *devices* to meet the changing business requirements of an evolving enterprise. The activities and labs confirm and reinforce your learning.

Upon completion of this chapter, you will be able to identify and describe the appropriate WAN technologies to enable integrated WAN services over a multilocation *enterprise network*.

1.1 Providing Integrated Services to the Enterprise

1.1.1 Introducing Wide Area Networks (WANs)

Refer to Figure in online course

What is a WAN?

A WAN is a *data communications* network that operates beyond the geographic scope of a LAN.

WANs are different from LANs in several ways. While a LAN connects computers, peripherals, and other devices in a single building or other small geographic area, a WAN allows the transmission of data across greater geographic distances. In addition, an enterprise must subscribe to a WAN service provider to use WAN carrier network services. LANs are typically owned by the company or organization that uses them.

WANs use facilities provided by a service provider, or carrier, such as a telephone or cable company, to connect the locations of an organization to each other, to locations of other organizations, to external services, and to remote users. WANs generally carry a variety of traffic types, such as voice, data, and video.

Here are the three major characteristics of WANs:

- WANs generally connect devices that are separated by a broader geographical area than can be served by a LAN.

- WANs use the services of carriers, such as telephone companies, cable companies, satellite systems, and network providers.
- WANs use serial connections of various types to provide access to *bandwidth* over large geographic areas.

Why Are WANs Necessary?

LAN technologies provide both speed and cost-efficiency for the transmission of data in organizations over relatively small geographic areas. However, there are other business needs that require communication among remote sites, including the following:

- People in the regional or branch offices of an organization need to be able to communicate and share data with the central site.
- Organizations often want to share information with other organizations across large distances. For example, software manufacturers routinely communicate product and promotion information to distributors that sell their products to end users.
- Employees who travel on company business frequently need to access information that resides on their corporate networks.

In addition, home computer users need to send and receive data across increasingly larger distances. Here are some examples:

- It is now common in many households for consumers to communicate with banks, stores, and a variety of providers of goods and services via computers.
- Students do research for classes by accessing library indexes and publications located in other parts of their country and in other parts of the world.

Since it is obviously not feasible to connect computers across a country or around the world in the same way that computers are connected in a LAN with cables, different technologies have evolved to support this need. Increasingly, the *Internet* is being used as an inexpensive alternative to using an enterprise WAN for some applications. New technologies are available to businesses to provide security and privacy for their Internet communications and *transactions*. WANs used by themselves, or in concert with the Internet, allow organizations and individuals to meet their wide-area communication needs.

1.1.2 The Evolving Enterprise

Businesses and Their Networks

> Refer to Figure in online course

As companies grow, they hire more employees, open branch offices, and expand into global markets. These changes also influence their requirements for integrated services and drive their network requirements. In this topic, we will explore how company networks change to accommodate their changing business requirements.

Every business is unique and how an organization grows depends on many factors, such as the type of products or services the business sells, the management philosophy of the owners, and the economic climate of the country in which the business operates.

In slow economic times, many businesses focus on increasing their profitability by improving the efficiency of their existing operations, increasing employee productivity, and lowering operating costs. Establishing and managing networks can represent significant installation and operating expenses. To justify such a large expense, companies expect their networks to perform optimally and to be able to deliver an ever increasing array of services and applications to support productivity and profitability.

To illustrate, let us look at an example of a fictitious company called Span Engineering, and watch how its network requirements change as the company grows from a small local business into a global enterprise.

Click the tabs in the figure to see each growth stage and the associated network topology.

Small Office (Single LAN)

Span Engineering, an environmental consulting firm, has developed a special process for converting household waste into electricity and is developing a small pilot project for a municipal government in its local area. The company, which has been in business for four years, has grown to include 15 employees: six engineers, four computer-aided drawing (CAD) designers, a receptionist, two senior partners, and two office assistants.

Span Engineering's management is hoping that they will have full scale projects after the pilot project successfully demonstrates the feasibility of their process. Until then, the company must manage its costs carefully.

For their small office, Span Engineering uses a single LAN to share information between computers, and to share peripherals, such as a printer, a large-scale plotter (to print engineering drawings), and fax equipment. They have recently upgraded their LAN to provide inexpensive Voice over IP (*VoIP*) service to save on the costs of separate phone lines for their employees.

Connection to the Internet is through a common *broadband* service called Digital Subscriber Line (DSL), which is supplied by their local telephone service provider. With so few employees, bandwidth is not a significant problem.

The company cannot afford in-house information technology (IT) support staff, and uses support services purchased from the same service provider. The company also uses a hosting service rather than purchasing and operating its own *FTP* and *e-mail servers*. The figure shows an example of a small office and its network.

Campus (Multiple LANs)

Five years later, Span Engineering has grown rapidly. As the owners had hoped, the company was contracted to design and implement a full-sized waste conversion facility soon after the successful implementation of their first pilot plant. Since then, other projects have also been won in neighboring municipalities and in other parts of the country.

To handle the additional workload, the business has hired more staff and leased more office space. It is now a small to medium-sized business with several hundred employees. Many projects are being developed at the same time, and each requires a project manager and support staff. The company has organized itself into functional departments, with each department having its own organizational team. To meet its growing needs, the company has moved into several floors of a larger office building.

As the business has expanded, the network has also grown. Instead of a single small LAN, the network now consists of several subnetworks, each devoted to a different department. For example, all the engineering staff are on one LAN, while the marketing staff is on another LAN. These multiple LANs are joined to create a company-wide network, or campus, which spans several floors of the building.

The business now has in-house IT staff to support and maintain the network. The network includes servers for e-mail, data transfer and file storage, web-based productivity tools and applications, as well as for the company intranet to provide in-house documents and information to employees. In addition, the company has an extranet that provides project information only to designated customers.

Branch (WAN)

Another five years later, Span Engineering has been so successful with its patented process that demand for its services has skyrocketed, and new projects are now being built in other cities. To manage those projects, the company has opened small branch offices closer to the project sites.

This situation presents new challenges to the IT team. To manage the delivery of information and services throughout the company, Span Engineering now has a data center, which houses the various databases and servers of the company. To ensure that all parts of the business are able to access the same services and applications regardless of where the offices are located, the company now needs to implement a WAN.

For its branch offices that are in nearby cities, the company decides to use private dedicated *lines* through their local service provider. However, for those offices that are located in other countries, the Internet is now an attractive WAN connection option. Although connecting offices through the Internet is economical, it introduces security and privacy issues that the IT team must address.

Distributed (Global)

Span Engineering has now been in business for 20 years and has grown to thousands of employees distributed in offices worldwide. The cost of the network and its related services is now a significant expense. The company is now looking to provide its employees with the best network services at the lowest cost. Optimized network services would allow each employee to work at high efficiency.

To increase profitability, Span Engineering needs to reduce its operating expenses. It has relocated some of its office facilities to less expensive areas. The company is also encouraging teleworking and virtual teams. Web-based applications, including web-conferencing, e-learning, and online collaboration tools, are being used to increase productivity and reduce costs. Site-to-site and remote access Virtual Private Networks (VPNs) enable the company to use the Internet to connect easily and securely with employees and facilities around the world. To meet these requirements, the network must provide the necessary converged services and secure Internet WAN connectivity to remote offices and individuals.

As we have seen from this example, the network requirements of a company can change dramatically as the company grows over time. Distributing employees saves costs in many ways, but it puts increased demands on the network. Not only must a network meet the day-to-day operational needs of the business, but it needs to be able to adapt and grow as the company changes. Network designers and administrators meet these challenges by carefully choosing network technologies, protocols, and service providers, and by optimizing their networks using many of the techniques we teach in this series of courses. The next topic describes a network model for designing networks that can accommodate the changing needs of today's evolving businesses.

1.1.3 The Evolving Network Model

The Hierarchical Design Model

Refer to **Figure** in online course

The hierarchical network model is a useful high-level tool for designing a reliable network infrastructure. It provides a modular view of a network, making it easier to design and build a scalable network.

The Hierarchical Network Model

As you may recall from CCNA Exploration: LAN Switching and Wireless, the hierarchical network model divides a network into three layers:

- *Access layer-* Grants user access to network devices. In a network campus, the access layer generally incorporates switched LAN devices with *ports* that provide connectivity to workstations and servers. In the WAN environment, it may provide *teleworkers* or remote sites access to the corporate network across WAN technology.

- *Distribution layer-* Aggregates the *wiring closets*, using *switches* to *segment workgroups* and isolate network problems in a campus environment. Similarly, the distribution layer aggregates WAN connections at the edge of the campus and provides policy-based connectivity.

- *Core layer (also referred to as the backbone)* - A high-speed backbone that is designed to switch *packets* as fast as possible. Because the core is critical for connectivity, it must provide a high level of availability and adapt to changes very quickly. It also provides scalability and fast *convergence*.

Click Example *Topology* button in the figure.

The figure represents the Hierarchical Network Model in campus environments. The Hierarchical Network Model provides a modular framework that allows flexibility in network design, and facilitates ease of implementation and troubleshooting in the infrastructure. However, it is important to understand that the network infrastructure is only the foundation to a comprehensive architecture.

Networking technologies have advanced considerably in recent years, resulting in networks that are increasingly intelligent. The current network elements are more aware of traffic characteristics and can be configured to deliver specialized services based on such things as the types of data they carry, the priority of the data, and even the security needs. Although most of these various infrastructure services are outside the scope of this course, it is important to understand that they influence network design. In the next topic, we will explore the Cisco Enterprise Architecture, which expands upon the hierarchical model by making use of network intelligence to address the network infrastructure.

The Enterprise Architecture

As described earlier, different businesses need different types of networks, depending on how the business is organized and its business goals. Unfortunately, all too often networks grow in a haphazard way as new components are added in response to immediate needs. Over time, those networks become complex and expensive to manage. Because the network is a mixture of newer and older technologies, it can be difficult to support and maintain. Outages and poor performance are a constant source of trouble for *network administrators*.

To help prevent this situation, Cisco has developed a recommended architecture called the Cisco Enterprise Architecture that has relevance to the different stages of growth of a business. This architecture is designed to provide network planners with a roadmap for network growth as the business moves through different stages. By following the suggested roadmap, IT managers can plan for future network upgrades that will integrate seamlessly into the existing network and support the ever-growing need for services.

The following are some examples of the modules within the architecture that are relevant to the Span Engineering scenario described earlier:

- Enterprise Campus Architecture
- Enterprise Branch Architecture
- Enterprise Data Center Architecture
- Enterprise Teleworker Architecture

Modules in the Enterprise Architecture

The Cisco Enterprise Architecture consists of modules representing focused views that target each place in the network. Each module has a distinct network infrastructure with services and network applications that extend across the modules. The Cisco Enterprise Architecture includes the following modules.

Roll over each module in the figure.

Enterprise Campus Architecture

A campus network is a building or group of buildings connected into one enterprise network that consists of many LANs. A campus is generally limited to a fixed geographic area, but it can span several neighboring buildings, for example, an industrial complex or business park environment. In the Span Engineering example, the campus spanned multiple floors of the same building.

The Enterprise Campus Architecture describes the recommended methods to create a scalable network, while addressing the needs of campus-style business operations. The architecture is modular and can easily expand to include additional campus buildings or floors as the enterprise grows.

Enterprise Edge Architecture

This module offers connectivity to voice, video, and data services outside the enterprise. This module enables the enterprise to use Internet and partner resources, and provide resources for its customers. This module often functions as a liaison between the campus module and the other modules in the Enterprise Architecture. The Enterprise WAN and Metropolitan-Area Network (*MAN*) Architecture, which the technologies covered later in this course are relevant to, are considered part of this module.

Enterprise Branch Architecture

This module allows businesses to extend the applications and services found at the campus to thousands of remote locations and users or to a small group of branches. Much of this course focuses on the technologies that are often implemented in this module.

Enterprise Data Center Architecture

Data centers are responsible for managing and maintaining the many data systems that are vital to modern business operations. Employees, partners, and customers rely on data and resources in the data center to effectively create, collaborate, and interact. Over the last decade, the rise of Internet and web-based technologies has made the data center more important than ever, improving productivity, enhancing business processes, and accelerating change.

Enterprise Teleworker Architecture

Many businesses today offer a flexible work environment to their employees, allowing them to telecommute from home offices. To telecommute is to leverage the network resources of the enterprise from home. The teleworker module recommends that connections from home using broadband services such as cable *modem* or DSL connect to the Internet and from there to the corporate network. Because the Internet introduces significant security risks to businesses, special measures need to be taken to ensure that teleworker communications are secure and private.

Click the Example Topology button in the figure.

The figure shows an example of how these Enterprise Architecture modules can be used to build a business network topology.

Acitvity: Providing Integrated Services to the Enterprise

1.2 WAN Technology Concepts

1.2.1 WAN Technology Overview

WANs and the OSI Model

As described in relation to the *OSI* reference model, WAN operations focus primarily on Layer 1 and Layer 2. WAN access *standards* typically describe both *Physical layer* delivery methods and *Data Link layer* requirements, including *physical addressing*, *flow control*, and *encapsulation*. WAN access standards are defined and managed by a number of recognized authorities, including the International Organization for Standardization (*ISO*), the Telecommunication Industry Association (*TIA*), and the Electronic Industries Alliance (*EIA*).

The Physical layer (OSI Layer 1) protocols describe how to provide electrical, mechanical, operational, and functional connections to the services of a communications service provider.

The Data Link layer (OSI Layer 2) protocols define how data is encapsulated for transmission toward a remote location and the mechanisms for transferring the resulting *frames*. A variety of different technologies are used, such as *Frame Relay* and *ATM*. Some of these protocols use the same basic framing mechanism, High-Level Data Link Control (*HDLC*), an ISO standard, or one of its subsets or variants.

1.2.2 WAN Physical Layer Concepts

WAN Physical Layer Terminology

One primary difference between a WAN and a LAN is that a company or organization must subscribe to an outside WAN service provider to use WAN carrier network services. A WAN uses data links provided by carrier services to access the Internet and connect the locations of an organization to each other, to locations of other organizations, to external services, and to remote users. The WAN access Physical layer describes the physical connection between the company network and the service provider network. The figure illustrates the terminology commonly used to describe physical WAN connections, including:

- *Customer Premises Equipment (CPE)*- The devices and inside wiring located at the premises of the subscriber and connected with a telecommunication *channel* of a carrier. The subscriber either owns the CPE or leases the CPE from the service provider. A subscriber, in this context, is a company that arranges for WAN services from a service provider or carrier.

- *Data Communications Equipment (DCE)*- Also called *data circuit-terminating equipment*, the DCE consists of devices that put data on the local loop. The DCE primarily provides an *interface* to connect subscribers to a communication link on the WAN cloud.

- *Data Terminal Equipment (DTE)*- The customer devices that pass the data from a customer network or *host* computer for transmission over the WAN. The DTE connects to the local loop through the DCE.

- *Demarcation Point-* A point established in a building or complex to separate customer equipment from service provider equipment. Physically, the demarcation point is the cabling junction box, located on the customer premises, that connects the CPE wiring to the local loop. It is usually placed for easy access by a technician. The demarcation point is the place where the responsibility for the connection changes from the user to the service provider. This is very important because when problems arise, it is necessary to determine whether the user or the service provider is responsible for troubleshooting or repair.

- *Local Loop-* The copper or fiber telephone *cable* that connects the CPE at the subscriber site to the CO of the service provider. The local loop is also sometimes called the "last-mile."

- *Central Office (CO)*- A local service provider facility or building where local telephone cables link to long-haul, all-digital, fiber-optic *communications lines* through a system of switches and other equipment.

WAN Devices

WANs use numerous types of devices that are specific to WAN environments, including:

- *Modem-* Modulates an analog carrier signal to encode digital information, and also demodulates the carrier signal to decode the transmitted information. A voiceband modem converts the digital signals produced by a computer into voice frequencies that can be transmitted over the analog lines of the public telephone network. On the other side of the connection, another modem converts the sounds back into a *digital signal* for input to a computer or network connection. Faster modems, such as cable modems and DSL modems, transmit using higher broadband frequencies.

- *CSU/DSU-* Digital lines, such as *T1* or *T3* carrier lines, require a channel service unit (*CSU*) and a data service unit (*DSU*). The two are often combined into a single piece of equipment, called the CSU/DSU. The CSU provides termination for the digital signal and ensures connection integrity through error correction and line monitoring. The DSU converts the *T-carrier* line frames into frames that the LAN can interpret and vice versa.

- *Access server* - Concentrates dial-in and dial-out user communications. An access server may have a mixture of analog and digital interfaces and support hundreds of simultaneous users.

- *WAN switch-* A multiport internetworking device used in carrier networks. These devices typically switch traffic such as Frame Relay, ATM, or *X.25* , and operate at the Data Link layer of the OSI reference model. Public switched telephone network (*PSTN*) switches may also be used within the cloud for circuit-switched connections like Integrated Services Digital Network (*ISDN*) or analog dialup.

- *Router* - Provides *internetworking* and WAN access interface ports that are used to connect to the service provider network. These interfaces may be serial connections or other WAN interfaces. With some types of WAN interfaces, an external device such as a DSU/CSU or modem (analog, cable, or DSL) is required to connect the router to the local point of presence (*POP*) of the service provider.

- *Core router* - A router that resides within the middle or backbone of the WAN rather than at its periphery. To fulfill this role, a router must be able to support multiple *telecommunications* interfaces of the highest speed in use in the WAN core, and it must be able to forward IP packets at full speed on all of those interfaces. The router must also support the *routing* protocols being used in the core.

WAN Physical Layer Standards

WAN Physical layer *protocols* describe how to provide electrical, mechanical, operational, and functional connections for WAN services. The WAN Physical layer also describes the interface between the DTE and the DCE. The DTE/DCE interface uses various Physical layer protocols, including:

- *EIA/TIA-232* - This protocol allows signal speeds of up to 64 kb/s on a 25-pin D-connector over short distances. It was formerly known as *RS-232* . The *ITU-T V.24* specification is effectively the same.

- *EIA/TIA-449* /530- This protocol is a faster (up to 2 Mb/s) version of EIA/TIA-232. It uses a 36-pin D-connector and is capable of longer cable runs. There are several versions. This standard is also known as RS422 and *RS-423* .

- *EIA/TIA-612/613-* This standard describes the High-Speed Serial Interface (*HSSI*) protocol, which provides access to services up to 52 Mb/s on a 60-pin D-connector.

- *V.35* - This is the ITU-T standard for synchronous communications between a network access device and a packet network. Originally specified to support data rates of 48 kb/s, it now supports speeds of up to 2.048 Mb/s using a 34-pin rectangular connector.

- *X.21* - This protocol is an ITU-T standard for synchronous digital communications. It uses a 15-pin D-connector.

These protocols establish the codes and electrical parameters the devices use to communicate with each other. Choosing a protocol is largely determined by the service provider's method of facilitation.

Click the WAN Cable Connectors button in the figure to see the types of cable connectors associated with each Physical layer protocol.

1.2.3 WAN Data Link Layer Concepts

Data Link Protocols

In addition to Physical layer devices, WANs require Data Link layer protocols to establish the link across the communication line from the sending to the receiving device. This topic describes the common data link protocols that are used in today's enterprise networks to implement WAN connections.

Data Link layer protocols define how data is encapsulated for transmission to remote sites and the mechanisms for transferring the resulting frames. A variety of different technologies, such as ISDN, Frame Relay, or ATM, are used. Many of these protocols use the same basic framing mechanism, HDLC, an ISO standard, or one of its subsets or variants. ATM is different from the others, because it uses small fixed-size cells of 53*bytes* (48 bytes for data), unlike the other packet-switched technologies, which use variable-sized packets.

The most common WAN data-link protocols are:

- HDLC
- *PPP*
- Frame Relay
- ATM

ISDN and X.25 are older data-link protocols that are less frequently used today. However, ISDN is still covered in this course because of its use when provisioning VoIP network using PRI links. X.25 is mentioned to help explain the relevance of Frame Relay. As well, X.25 is still in use in developing countries where packet data networks (PDN) are used to transmit credit card and debit card transactions from retailers.

Note: Another Data Link layer protocol is the Multiprotocol Label Switching (MPLS) protocol. MPLS is increasingly being deployed by service providers to provide an economical solution to carry circuit-switched as well as packet-switched network traffic. It can operate over any existing infrastructure, such as IP, Frame Relay, ATM, or*Ethernet* . It sits between Layer 2 and Layer 3 and is sometimes referred to as a Layer 2.5 protocol. However, MPLS is beyond the scope of this course but is covered in the CCNP: Implementing Secure Converged Wide-area Networks.

WAN Encapsulation

Data from the*Network layer* is passed to the Data Link layer for delivery on a physical link, which is normally point-to-point on a WAN connection. The Data Link layer builds a frame around the Network layer data so that the necessary checks and controls can be applied. Each

WAN connection type uses a Layer 2 protocol to encapsulate a packet while it is crossing the WAN link. To ensure that the correct encapsulation protocol is used, the Layer 2 encapsulation type used for each router serial interface must be configured. The choice of encapsulation protocols depends on the WAN technology and the equipment. HDLC was first proposed in 1979 and for this reason, most framing protocols which were developed afterwards are based on it.

Click the Play button in the figure to view how WAN data-link protocols encapsulate traffic.

WAN Frame Encapsulation Formats

Examining the header portion of an HDLC frame will help identify common fields used by many WAN encapsulation protocols. The frame always starts and ends with an 8-*bit* flag field. The bit pattern is 01111110. The address field is not needed for WAN links, which are almost always point-to-point. The address field is still present and may be 1 or 2 bytes long. The control field is protocol dependent, but usually indicates whether the content of the data is control information or Network layer data. The control field is normally 1 byte.

Together the address and control fields are called the frame *header*. The encapsulated data follows the control field. Then a frame check sequence (*FCS*) uses the cyclic redundancy check (*CRC*) mechanism to establish a 2 or 4 byte field.

Several data-link protocols are used, including subsets and proprietary versions of HDLC. Both PPP and the Cisco version of HDLC have an extra field in the header to identify the Network layer protocol of the encapsulated data.

1.2.4 WAN Switching Concepts

Circuit Switching

A circuit-switched network is one that establishes a dedicated *circuit* (or channel) between *nodes* and terminals before the users may communicate.

As an example, when a subscriber makes a telephone call, the dialed number is used to set switches in the exchanges along the *route* of the call so that there is a continuous circuit from the caller to the called party. Because of the switching operation used to establish the circuit, the telephone system is called a circuit-switched network. If the telephones are replaced with modems, then the switched circuit is able to carry computer data.

The internal path taken by the circuit between exchanges is shared by a number of conversations. Time-division *multiplexing* (*TDM*) gives each conversation a share of the connection in turn. TDM assures that a fixed capacity connection is made available to the subscriber.

If the circuit carries computer data, the usage of this fixed capacity may not be efficient. For example, if the circuit is used to access the Internet, there is a burst of activity on the circuit while a web page is transferred. This could be followed by no activity while the user reads the page, and then another burst of activity while the next page is transferred. This variation in usage between none and maximum is typical of computer network traffic. Because the subscriber has sole use of the fixed capacity allocation, switched circuits are generally an expensive way of moving data.

PSTN and ISDN are two types of circuit-switching technology that may be used to implement a WAN in an enterprise setting.

Click the Play button in the figure to see how *circuit switching* works.

Packet Switching

In contrast to circuit switching, *packet switching* splits traffic data into packets that are routed over a shared network. Packet-switching networks do not require a circuit to be established, and they allow many pairs of nodes to communicate over the same channel.

The switches in a *packet-switched network* determine which link the packet must be sent on next from the addressing information in each packet. There are two approaches to this link determination, *connectionless* or *connection-oriented*.

- Connectionless systems, such as the Internet, carry full addressing information in each packet. Each switch must evaluate the address to determine where to send the packet.
- Connection-oriented systems predetermine the route for a packet, and each packet only has to carry an identifier. In the case of Frame Relay, these are called Data Link Connection Identifiers (*DLCIs*). The switch determines the onward route by looking up the identifier in tables held in memory. The set of entries in the tables identifies a particular route or circuit through the system. If this circuit is only physically in existence while a packet is traveling through it, it is called a virtual circuit (*VC*).

Because the internal links between the switches are shared between many users, the costs of packet switching are lower than those of circuit switching. *Delays* (*latency*) and variability of delay (*jitter*) are greater in packet-switched than in circuit-switched networks. This is because the links are shared, and packets must be entirely received at one switch before moving to the next. Despite the latency and jitter inherent in shared networks, modern technology allows satisfactory transport of voice and even video communications on these networks.

Click the Play button in the figure to see a packet switching example.

Server A is sending data to server B. As the packet traverses the provider network, it arrives at the second provider switch. The packet is added to the queue and forwarded after the other packets in the *queue* have been forwarded. Eventually, the packet reaches server B.

Virtual Circuits

Packet-switched networks may establish routes through the switches for particular end-to-end connections. These routes are called virtual circuits. A VC is a logical circuit created within a shared network between two network devices. Two types of VCs exist:

- *Permanent Virtual Circuit (PVC)*- A permanently established virtual circuit that consists of one mode: data transfer. PVCs are used in situations in which data transfer between devices is constant. PVCs decrease the bandwidth use associated with establishing and terminating VCs, but they increase costs because of constant virtual circuit availability. PVCs are generally configured by the service provider when an order is placed for service.
- *Switched Virtual Circuit (SVC)*- A VC that is dynamically established on demand and terminated when transmission is complete. Communication over an SVC consists of three phases: circuit establishment, data transfer, and circuit termination. The establishment phase involves creating the VC between the source and destination devices. Data transfer involves transmitting data between the devices over the VC, and the circuit termination phase involves tearing down the VC between the source and destination devices. SVCs are used in situations in which data transmission between devices is intermittent, largely to save costs. SVCs release the circuit when transmission is complete, which results in less expensive connection charges than those incurred by PVCs, which maintain constant virtual circuit availability.

Connecting to a Packet-Switched Network

To connect to a packet-switched network, a subscriber needs a local loop to the nearest location where the provider makes the service available. This is called the point-of-presence (POP) of the service. Normally this is a dedicated leased line. This line is much shorter than a leased line directly connected to the subscriber locations, and often carries several VCs. Because it is likely that not all the VCs require maximum demand simultaneously, the capacity of the *leased line* can be smaller than the sum of the individual VCs. Examples of packet- or cell-switched connections include:

- X.25
- Frame Relay
- ATM

Practice: WAN Technology Concepts

1.3 WAN Connection Options

1.3.1 WAN Link Connection Options

Many options for implementing WAN solutions are currently available. They differ in technology, speed, and cost. Familiarity with these technologies is an important part of network design and evaluation.

WAN connections can be either over a private infrastructure or over a public infrastructure, such as the Internet.

Private WAN Connection Options

Private WAN connections include both dedicated and switched communication link options.

Dedicated communication links

When permanent dedicated connections are required, point-to-point lines are used with various capacities that are limited only by the underlying physical facilities and the willingness of users to pay for these dedicated lines. A point-to-point link provides a pre-established WAN communications path from the customer premises through the provider network to a remote destination. Point-to-point lines are usually leased from a carrier and are also called leased lines.

Switched communication links

Switched communication links can be either circuit switched or packet switched.

- *Circuit-switched communication links-* Circuit switching dynamically establishes a dedicated virtual connection for voice or data between a sender and a receiver. Before communication can start, it is necessary to establish the connection through the network of the service provider. Examples of circuit-switched communication links are analog dialup (PSTN) and ISDN.

- *Packet-switched communication links-* Many WAN users do not make efficient use of the fixed bandwidth that is available with dedicated, switched, or permanent circuits because the data flow fluctuates. Communications providers have data networks available to more appropriately service these users. In packet-switched networks, the data is transmitted in labeled frames, cells, or packets. Packet-switched communication links include Frame Relay, ATM, X.25, and Metro Ethernet.

Public WAN Connection Options

Public connections use the global Internet infrastructure. Until recently, the Internet was not a viable networking option for many businesses because of the significant security risks and lack of adequate performance guarantees in an end-to end Internet connection. With the development of VPN technology, however, the Internet is now an inexpensive and secure option for connecting to teleworkers and remote offices where performance guarantees are not critical. Internet WAN connection links are through broadband services such as DSL, cable modem, and broadband wireless, and combined with VPN technology to provide privacy across the Internet.

1.3.2 Dedicated Connection Link Options

Leased Lines

When permanent dedicated connections are required, a point-to-point link is used to provide a pre-established WAN communications path from the customer premises through the provider network to a remote destination. Point-to-point lines are usually leased from a carrier and are called leased lines. This topic describes how enterprises use leased lines to provide a dedicated WAN connection.

Click the Line Types and Bandwidth button in the figure to view a list of the available leased line types and their *bit rate* capacities.

Leased lines are available in different capacities and are generally priced based on the bandwidth required and the distance between the two connected points.

Point-to-point links are usually more expensive than shared services such as Frame Relay. The cost of leased line solutions can become significant when they are used to connect many sites over increasing distances. However, there are times when the benefits outweigh the cost of the leased line. The dedicated capacity removes latency or jitter between the endpoints. Constant availability is essential for some applications such as VoIP or Video over IP.

A router serial port is required for each leased line connection. A CSU/DSU and the actual circuit from the service provider are also required.

Leased lines provide permanent dedicated capacity and are used extensively for building WANs. They have been the traditional connection of choice but have a number of disadvantages. Leased lines have a fixed capacity; however, WAN traffic is often variable leaving some of the capacity unused. In addition, each endpoint needs a separate physical interface on the router, which increases equipment costs. Any changes to the leased line generally require a site visit by the carrier.

Practice: WAN Technologies - Leased Lines

1.3.3 Circuit Switched Connection Options

Analog Dialup

When intermittent, low-volume data transfers are needed, modems and analog dialed telephone lines provide low capacity and dedicated switched connections. This topic describes the pros and cons of using analog dialup connection options, and identifies the types of business scenarios that benefit most from this type of option.

Traditional *telephony* uses a copper cable, called the local loop, to connect the telephone handset in the subscriber premises to the CO. The signal on the local loop during a call is a continuously varying electronic signal that is a translation of the subscriber voice, analog.

Traditional local loops can transport binary computer data through the voice telephone network using a modem. The modem modulates the *binary* data into an analog signal at the source and demodulates the analog signal to binary data at the destination. The physical characteristics of the local loop and its connection to the PSTN limit the rate of the signal to less than 56 kb/s.

For small businesses, these relatively low-speed dialup connections are adequate for the exchange of sales figures, prices, routine reports, and e-mail. Using automatic dialup at night or on weekends for large file transfers and data backup can take advantage of lower off-peak tariffs (line charges). Tariffs are based on the distance between the endpoints, time of day, and the duration of the call.

The advantages of modem and analog lines are simplicity, availability, and low implementation cost. The disadvantages are the low data rates and a relatively long connection time. The dedicated circuit has little delay or jitter for point-to-point traffic, but voice or video traffic does not operate adequately at these low bit rates.

Integrated Services Digital Network

Integrated Services Digital Network (ISDN) is a circuit-switching technology that enables the local loop of a PSTN to carry digital signals, resulting in higher capacity switched connections. ISDN changes the internal connections of the PSTN from carrying analog signals to time-division multiplexed (TDM) digital signals. TDM allows two or more signals or bit streams to be transferred as subchannels in one communication channel. The signals appear to transfer simultaneously, but physically are taking turns on the channel. A data block of subchannel 1 is transmitted during timeslot 1, subchannel 2 during timeslot 2, and so on. One TDM frame consists of one timeslot per subchannel. TDM is described in more detail in Chapter 2, PPP.

ISDN turns the local loop into a TDM digital connection. This change enables the local loop to carry digital signals that result in higher capacity switched connections. The connection uses 64 kb/s bearer channels (B) for carrying voice or data and a *signaling*, delta channel (D) for call setup and other purposes.

There are two types of ISDN interfaces:

- *Basic Rate Interface (BRI)*- ISDN is intended for the home and small enterprise and provides two 64 kb/s *B channels* and a 16 kb/s *D channel*. The BRI D channel is designed for control and often underused, because it has only two B channels to control. Therefore, some providers allow the D channel to carry data at low bit rates, such as X.25 connections at 9.6 kb/s.

- *Primary Rate Interface (PRI)*- ISDN is also available for larger installations. PRI delivers 23 B channels with 64 kb/s and one D channel with 64 kb/s in North America, for a total bit rate of up to 1.544 Mb/s. This includes some additional overhead for *synchronization*. In Europe, Australia, and other parts of the world, ISDN PRI provides 30 B channels and one D channel, for a total bit rate of up to 2.048 Mb/s, including synchronization overhead. In North America, PRI corresponds to a T1 connection. The rate of international PRI corresponds to an *E1* or J1 connection.

For small WANs, the BRI ISDN can provide an ideal connection mechanism. BRI has a *call setup time* that is less than a second, and the 64 kb/s B channel provides greater capacity than an analog modem link. If greater capacity is required, a second B channel can be activated to provide a total of 128 kb/s. Although inadequate for video, this permits several simultaneous voice conversations in addition to data traffic.

Another common application of ISDN is to provide additional capacity as needed on a leased line connection. The leased line is sized to carry average traffic loads while ISDN is added during peak demand periods. ISDN is also used as a backup if the leased line fails. ISDN tariffs are based on a per-B channel basis and are similar to those of analog voice connections.

With PRI ISDN, multiple B channels can be connected between two endpoints. This allows for videoconferencing and high-bandwidth data connections with no latency or jitter. However, multiple connections can be very expensive over long distances.

Note: Although ISDN is still an important technology for telephone service provider networks, it is declining in popularity as an Internet connection option with the introduction of high-speed DSL and other broadband services.

Practice: WAN Technologies - Circuit Switching

1.3.4 Packet Switched Connection Options

Common Packet Switching WAN Technologies

> Refer to **Figure** in online course

The most common packet-switching technologies used in today's enterprise WAN networks include Frame Relay, ATM, and legacy X.25.

Click the X.25 button in the figure.

X.25

X.25 is a legacy Network layer protocol that provides subscribers with a *network address* . Virtual circuits can be established through the network with call request packets to the target address. The resulting SVC is identified by a channel number. Data packets labeled with the channel number are delivered to the corresponding address. Multiple channels can be active on a single connection.

Typical X.25 applications are point-of-sale card readers. These readers use X.25 in dialup mode to validate transactions on a central computer. For these applications, the low bandwidth and high latency are not a concern, and the low cost makes X.25 affordable.

X.25 link speeds vary from 2400 b/s up to 2 Mb/s. However, public networks are usually low capacity with speeds rarely exceeding above 64 kb/s.

X.25 networks are now in dramatic decline being replaced by newer Layer 2 technologies such as Frame Relay, ATM, and ADSL. However, they are still in use in many portions of the developing world, where there is limited access to newer technologies.

Click the Frame Relay button in the figure.

Frame Relay

Although the network layout appears similar to X.25, Frame Relay differs from X.25 in several ways. Most importantly, it is a much simpler protocol that works at the Data Link layer rather than the Network layer. Frame Relay implements no error or flow control. The simplified handling of frames leads to reduced latency, and measures taken to avoid frame build-up at intermediate switches help reduce jitter. Frame Relay offers data rates up to 4 Mb/s, with some providers offering even higher rates.

Frame Relay VCs are uniquely identified by a DLCI, which ensures bidirectional communication from one DTE device to another. Most Frame Relay connections are PVCs rather than SVCs.

Frame Relay provides permanent, shared, medium-bandwidth connectivity that carries both voice and data traffic. Frame Relay is ideal for connecting enterprise LANs. The router on the LAN needs only a single interface, even when multiple VCs are used. The short-leased line to the Frame Relay network edge allows cost-effective connections between widely scattered LANs.

Frame Relay is described in more detail in Chapter 3, "Frame Relay."

Click the ATM button in the figure.

ATM

Asynchronous Transfer Mode (*ATM*) technology is capable of transferring voice, video, and data through private and public networks. It is built on a *cell* -based architecture rather than on a frame-based architecture. ATM cells are always a fixed length of 53 bytes. The ATM cell contains a 5 byte ATM header followed by 48 bytes of ATM payload. Small, fixed-length cells are well suited for carrying voice and video traffic because this traffic is intolerant of delay. Video and voice traffic do not have to wait for a larger data packet to be transmitted.

The 53 byte ATM cell is less efficient than the bigger frames and packets of Frame Relay and X.25. Furthermore, the ATM cell has at least 5 bytes of overhead for each 48-byte *payload* . When the cell is carrying segmented Network layer packets, the overhead is higher because the ATM switch must be able to reassemble the packets at the destination. A typical ATM line needs almost 20 percent greater bandwidth than Frame Relay to carry the same volume of Network layer data.

ATM was designed to be extremely scalable and can support link speeds of T1/E1 to OC-12 (622 Mb/s) and higher.

ATM offers both PVCs and SVCs, although PVCs are more common with WANs. And as with other shared technologies, ATM allows multiple VCs on a single leased-line connection to the network edge.

Practice: WAN Technologies - Packet Switching

1.3.5 Internet Connection Options

Broadband Services

Broadband connection options are typically used to connect telecommuting employees to a corporate site over the Internet. These options include cable, DSL, and wireless.

Click the DSL button in the figure.

DSL

DSL technology is an always-on connection technology that uses existing twisted-pair telephone lines to transport high-bandwidth data, and provides IP services to subscribers. A DSL modem converts an Ethernet signal from the user device to a DSL signal, which is transmitted to the central office.

Multiple DSL subscriber lines are multiplexed into a single, high-capacity link using a DSL access multiplexer (DSLAM) at the provider location. DSLAMs incorporate TDM technology to aggregate many subscriber lines into a single *medium*, generally a T3 (DS3) connection. Current DSL technologies use sophisticated *coding* and *modulation* techniques to achieve data rates of up to 8.192 Mb/s.

There is a wide variety of DSL types, standards, and emerging standards. DSL is now a popular choice for enterprise IT departments to support home workers. Generally, a subscriber cannot choose to connect to an enterprise network directly, but must first connect to an ISP, and then an IP connection is made through the Internet to the enterprise. Security risks are incurred in this process, but can be mediated with security measures.

Click the Cable Modem button in the figure.

Cable Modem

Coaxial cable is widely used in urban areas to distribute television signals. Network access is available from some *cable television* networks. This allows for greater bandwidth than the conventional telephone local loop.

Cable modems provide an always-on connection and a simple installation. A subscriber connects a computer or LAN router to the cable modem, which translates the digital signals into the broadband frequencies used for transmitting on a cable television network. The local cable TV office, which is called the cable headend, contains the computer system and databases needed to provide Internet access. The most important component located at the *headend* is the cable modem termination system (CMTS), which sends and receives digital cable modem signals on a cable network and is necessary for providing Internet services to cable subscribers.

Cable modem subscribers must use the ISP associated with the service provider. All the local subscribers share the same cable bandwidth. As more users join the service, available bandwidth may be below the expected rate.

Click the Broadband Wireless button in the figure.

Broadband Wireless

Wireless technology uses the unlicensed radio spectrum to send and receive data. The unlicensed spectrum is accessible to anyone who has a wireless router and wireless technology in the device they are using.

Until recently, one limitation of wireless access has been the need to be within the local transmission *range* (typically less than 100 feet) of a wireless router or a wireless modem that has a wired connection to the Internet. The following new developments in broadband wireless technology are changing this situation:

- *Municipal WiFi-* Many cities have begun setting up municipal wireless networks. Some of these networks provide high-speed Internet access for free or for substantially less than the price of other broadband services. Others are for city use only, allowing police and fire departments and other city employees to do certain aspects of their jobs remotely. To connect to a municipal WiFi, a subscriber typically needs a wireless modem, which provides a stronger radio and directional antenna than conventional wireless *adapters*. Most service providers provide the necessary equipment for free or for a fee, much like they do with DSL or cable modems.

- *WiMAX-* Worldwide *Interoperability* for *Microwave* Access (WiMAX) is a new technology that is just beginning to come into use. It is described in the *IEEE* standard 802.16. WiMAX provides high-speed broadband service with wireless access and provides broad coverage like a cell phone network rather than through small WiFi hotspots. WiMAX operates in a similar way to WiFi, but at higher speeds, over greater distances, and for a greater number of users. It uses a network of WiMAX towers that are similar to cell phone towers. To access a WiMAX network, subscribers must subscribe to an ISP with a WiMAX tower within 10 miles of their location. They also need a WiMAX-enabled computer and a special *encryption* code to get access to the base station.

- *Satellite Internet-* Typically used by rural users where cable and DSL are not available. A satellite dish provides two-way (upload and download) data communications. The upload speed is about one-tenth of the 500 kb/s download speed. Cable and DSL have higher download speeds, but satellite systems are about 10 times faster than an analog modem. To access satellite Internet services, subscribers need a satellite dish, two modems (uplink and downlink), and coaxial cables between the dish and the modem.

DSL, cable, and wireless broadband services are described in more detail in Chapter 6, "Teleworker Services."

VPN Technology

Security risks are incurred when a teleworker or remote office uses broadband services to access the corporate WAN over the Internet. To address security concerns, broadband services provide capabilities for using Virtual Private Network (VPN) connections to a VPN server, which is typically located at the corporate site.

A VPN is an encrypted connection between private networks over a public network such as the Internet. Instead of using a dedicated Layer 2 connection such as a leased line, a VPN uses virtual connections called VPN tunnels, which are routed through the Internet from the private network of the company to the remote site or employee host.

VPN Benefits

Benefits of VPN include the following:

- *Cost savings-* VPNs enable organizations to use the global Internet to connect remote offices and remote users to the main corporate site, thus eliminating expensive dedicated WAN links and modem banks.

- *Security-* VPNs provide the highest level of security by using advanced encryption and *authentication* protocols that protect data from unauthorized access.

- *Scalability-* Because VPNs use the Internet infrastructure within ISPs and devices, it is easy to add new users. Corporations are able to add large amounts of capacity without adding significant infrastructure.

- *Compatibility with broadband technology-* VPN technology is supported by broadband service providers such as DSL and cable, so mobile workers and telecommuters can take advantage of their home high-speed Internet service to access their corporate networks. Business-grade, high-speed broadband connections can also provide a cost-effective solution for connecting remote offices.

Types of VPN Access

There are two types of VPN access:

- *Site-to-site VPNs-* Site-to-site VPNs connect entire networks to each other, for example, they can connect a branch office network to a company headquarters network, as shown in the figure. Each site is equipped with a VPN gateway, such as a router, *firewall*, VPN concentrator, or security appliance. In the figure, a remote branch office uses a site-to-site-VPN to connect with the corporate head office.

- *Remote-access VPNs-* Remote-access VPNs enable individual hosts, such as telecommuters, mobile users, and extranet consumers, to access a company network securely over the Internet. Each host typically has VPN*client* software loaded or uses a web-based client.

Click the Remote Access VPN button or the Site-to-Site VPN button in the figure to see an example of each type of VPN connection.

Refer to Figure in online course

Metro Ethernet

Metro Ethernet is a rapidly maturing networking technology that broadens Ethernet to the public networks run by telecommunications companies. IP-aware Ethernet switches enable service providers to offer enterprises converged voice, data, and video services such as IP telephony, video streaming, imaging, and data storage. By extending Ethernet to the metropolitan area, companies can provide their remote offices with reliable access to applications and data on the corporate headquarters LAN.

Benefits of Metro Ethernet include:

- *Reduced expenses and administration-* Metro Ethernet provides a switched, high-bandwidth Layer 2 network capable of managing data, voice, and video all on the same infrastructure. This characteristic increases bandwidth and eliminates expensive conversions to ATM and Frame Relay. The technology enables businesses to inexpensively connect numerous sites in a metropolitan area to each other and to the Internet.

- *Easy integration with existing networks-* Metro Ethernet connects easily to existing Ethernet LANs, reducing installation costs and time.

- *Enhanced business productivity-* Metro Ethernet enables businesses to take advantage of productivity-enhancing IP applications that are difficult to implement on TDM or Frame Relay networks, such as hosted IP communications, VoIP, and streaming and broadcast video.

> Refer to **Figure** in online course

Choosing a WAN Link Connection

Now that we have looked at the variety of WAN connection options, how do you choose the best technology to meet the requirements of a specific business? The figure compares the advantages and disadvantages of the WAN connection options that we have discussed in this chapter. This information is a good start. In addition, to help in the decision-making process, here are some questions to ask yourself when choosing a WAN connection option.

What is the purpose of the WAN?

Do you want to connect local branches in the same city area, connect remote branches, connect to a single branch, connect to customers, connect to business partners, or some combination of these? If the WAN is for providing authorized customers or business partners limited access to the company intranet, what is the best option?

What is the geographic scope?

Is it local, regional, global, one-to-one (single branch), one-to-many branches, many-to-many (distributed)? Depending on the range, some WAN connection options may be better than others.

What are the traffic requirements?

Traffic requirements to consider include:

- Traffic type (data only, VoIP, video, large files, streaming files) determines the quality and performance requirements. For example, if you are sending a lot of voice or streaming video traffic, ATM may be the best choice.

- Traffic volumes depending on type (voice, video, or data) for each destination determine the bandwidth capacity required for the WAN connection to the ISP.

- Quality requirements may limit your choices. If your traffic is highly sensitive to latency and jitter, you can eliminate any WAN connection options that cannot provide the required quality.

- Security requirements (data integrity, confidentiality, and security) is an important factor if the traffic is of a highly confidential nature or if provides essential services, such as emergency response.

Should the WAN use a private or public infrastructure?

A private infrastructure offers the best security and confidentiality, whereas the public Internet infrastructure offers the most flexibility and lowest ongoing expense. Your choice depends on the purpose of the WAN, the types of traffic it carries, and available operating budget. For example, if the purpose is to provide a nearby branch with high-speed secure services, a private dedicated or switched connection may be best. If the purpose is to connect many remote offices, an public WAN using the Internet may be the best choice. For distributed operations, a combination of options may be the solution.

For a private WAN, should it be dedicated or switched?

Real-time, high-volume transactions have special requirements that could favor a dedicated line, such as traffic flowing between the data center and the corporate head office. If you are connecting to a local single branch, you could use a dedicated leased line. However, that option would become very expensive for a WAN connecting multiple offices. In that case, a switched connection might be better.

For a public WAN, what type of VPN access do you need?

If the purpose of the WAN is to connect a remote office, a site-to-site VPN may be the best choice. To connect teleworkers or customers, remote-access VPNs are a better option. If the WAN is serving a mixture of remote offices, teleworkers, and authorized customers, such as a global company with distributed operations, a combination of VPN options may be required.

Which connection options are available locally?

In some areas, not all WAN connection options are available. In this case, your selection process is simplified, although the resulting WAN may provide less than optimal performance. For example, in a rural or remote area, the only option may be broadband satellite Internet access.

What is the cost of the available connection options?

Depending on the option you choose, the WAN can be a significant ongoing expense. The cost of a particular option must be weighed against how well it meets your other requirements. For example, a dedicated leased line is the most expensive option, but the expense may be justified if it is critical to ensure secure transmission of high volumes of real-time data. For less demanding applications, a cheaper switched or Internet connection option may be more suitable.

As you can see, there are many important factors to consider when choosing an appropriate WAN connection. Following the guidelines described above, as well as those described by the Cisco Enterprise Architecture, you should now be able to choose an appropriate WAN connection to meet the requirements of different business scenarios.

Activity: Using Appropriate WAN in the ECNM

1.4 Chapter Labs

1.4.1 Challenge Review

In this lab, you will review basic routing and switching concepts. Try to do as much on your own as possible. Refer back to previous material when you cannot proceed on your own.

Note: Configuring three separate routing protocols-*RIP*, OSPF, and *EIGRP*-to route the same network is emphatically not a best practice. It should be considered a worst practice and is not something that would be done in a production network. It is done here so that you can review the major routing protocols before proceeding, and see a dramatic illustration of the concept of *administrative distance*.

Chapter Summary

A WAN is a data communications network that operates beyond the geographic scope of a LAN.

As companies grow, adding more employees, opening branch offices, and expanding into global markets, their requirements for integrated services change. These business requirements drive their network requirements.

The Cisco Enterprise Architecture expands upon the Hierarchical Design Model by further dividing the enterprise network into physical, logical, and functional areas.

Implementation of a Cisco Enterprise Architecture provides a secure, robust network with high availability that facilitates the deployment of converged networks.

WANs operate in relation to the OSI reference model, primarily on Layer 1 and Layer 2.

Devices that put data on the local loop are called data circuit-terminating equipment, or data communications equipment (DCE). The customer devices that pass the data to the DCE are called data terminal equipment (DTE). The DCE primarily provides an interface for the DTE into the communication link on the WAN cloud.

The physical demarcation point is the place where the responsibility for the connection changes from the enterprise to the service provider.

Data Link layer protocols define how data is encapsulated for transmission to remote sites and the mechanisms for transferring the resulting frames.

A circuit-switching network establishes a dedicated circuit (or channel) between nodes and terminals before the users may communicate.

A packet-switching network splits traffic data into packets that are routed over a shared network. Packet-switching networks do not require a circuit to be established and allow many pairs of nodes to communicate over the same channel.

A point-to-point link provides a pre-established WAN communications path from the customer premises through the provider network to a remote destination. Point-to-point links use leased lines to provide a dedicated connection.

Circuit-switching WAN options include analog dialup and ISDN. Packet-switching WAN options include X.25, Frame Relay, and ATM. ATM transmits data in 53-byte cells rather than frames. ATM is most suited to video traffic.

Internet WAN connection options include broadband services, such as DSL, cable modem or broadband wireless, and Metro Ethernet. VPN technology enables businesses to provide secure teleworker access through the Internet over broadband services.

This activity covers many of the skills you acquired in the first three Exploration courses. Skills include building a network, applying an addressing scheme, configuring routing, VLANs, STP and VTP, and testing connectivity. You should review those skills before proceeding. In addition, this activity provides you an opportunity to review the basics of the Packet Tracer program. Packet Tracer is integrated throughout this course. You must know how to navigate the Packet Tracer environment to complete this course. Use the tutorials if you need a review of Packet Tracer fundamentals. The tutorials are located in the Packet Tracer Help menu.

Detailed instructions are provided within the activity as well as in the PDF link below.

Activity Instructions (PDF)

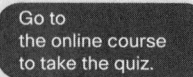

Chapter Quiz

Take the chapter quiz to test your knowledge.

Your Chapter Notes

CHAPTER 2

PPP

Chapter Introduction

This chapter starts your exploration of WAN technologies by introducing point-to-point communications and the Point-to-Point Protocol (*PPP*).

One of the most common types of WAN connection is the point-to-point connection. Point-to-point connections are used to connect LANs to service provider WANs, and to connect LAN segments within an Enterprise network. A LAN-to-WAN point-to-point connection is also referred to as a serial connection or leased-line connection, because the lines are leased from a carrier (usually a telephone company) and are dedicated for use by the company leasing the lines. Companies pay for a continuous connection between two remote sites, and the line is continuously active and available. Understanding how point-to-point communication links function to provide access to a WAN is important to an overall understanding of how WANs function.

Point-to-Point Protocol (PPP) provides multiprotocol LAN-to-WAN connections handling *TCP/IP*, Internetwork Packet Exchange (*IPX*), and *AppleTalk* simultaneously. It can be used over *twisted pair*, fiber-optic lines, and satellite transmission. PPP provides transport over ATM, Frame Relay, ISDN and optical links. In modern networks, security is a key concern. PPP allows you to authenticate connections using either Password Authentication Protocol (*PAP*) or the more effective Challenge Handshake Authentication Protocol (*CHAP*). These are taught in the fourth section.

In this chapter you will also learn the key concepts of serial communications, and how to configure and troubleshoot a PPP serial connection on a Cisco router.

2.1 Serial Point-to-Point Links

2.1.1 Introducing Serial Communications

How Does Serial Communication Work?

You know that most PCs have both serial and parallel ports. You also know that electricity can only move at one speed. One way to get bits to move faster through a wire is to compress the data so that less bits are necessary and then require less time on the wire, or transmit the bits simultaneously. Computers make use of relatively short parallel connections between interior components, but use a serial *bus* to convert signals for most external communications.

Let's compare serial and parallel communications.

Click the Serial and Parallel button to view the animation.

- With a serial connection, information is sent across one wire, one data bit at a time. The 9-pin serial connector on most PCs uses two loops of wire, one in each direction, for data communication, plus additional wires to control the flow of information. In any given direction, data is still flowing over a single wire.

- A parallel connection sends the bits over more wires simultaneously. In the case of the 25-pin parallel port on your PC, there are eight data-carrying wires to carry 8 bits simultaneously. Because there are eight wires to carry the data, the parallel link theoretically transfers data eight times faster than a serial connection. So based on this theory, a parallel connection sends a byte in the time a serial connection sends a bit.

This explanation brings up some questions. What is meant by theoretically faster? If parallel is faster than serial, is parallel more suitable for connecting to a WAN? In reality, it is often the case that serial links can be clocked considerably faster than parallel links, and they achieve a higher data rate, because of two factors that affect parallel communications: clock skew and crosstalk *interference* .

Click the Clock Skew button in the figure.

In a parallel connection, it is wrong to assume that the 8 bits leaving the sender at the same time arrive at the receiver at the same time. Rather, some of the bits get there later than others. This is known as clock skew. Overcoming clock skew is not trivial. The receiving end must synchronize itself with the transmitter and then wait until all the bits have arrived. The process of reading, waiting, latching, waiting for clock signal, and transmitting the 8 bits adds time to the transmission. In parallel communications, a latch is a data storage system used to store information in sequential logic systems. The more wires you use and the farther the connection reaches, compounds the problem and adds delay. The need for clocking slows *parallel transmission* well below theoretical expectations.

This is not a factor with serial links, because most serial links do not need clocking. Serial connections require fewer wires and cables. They occupy less space and can be better isolated from interference from other wires and cables.

Click the Interference button in the figure.

Parallel wires are physically bundled in a parallel cable, and signals can imprint themselves on each other. The possibility of crosstalk across the wires requires more processing, especially at higher frequencies. The serial buses on computers, including routers, compensate for crosstalk before transmitting the bits. Since serial cables have fewer wires, there is less crosstalk, and network devices transmit serial communications at higher, more efficient frequencies.

In most cases, serial communications are considerably cheaper to implement. Serial communications use fewer wires, cheaper cables, and fewer connector pins.

Serial Communication Standards

All long-haul communications and most computer networks use serial connections, because the cost of cable and synchronization difficulties make parallel connections impractical. The most significant advantage is simpler wiring. Also, serial cables can be longer than parallel cables, because there is much less interaction (crosstalk) among the *conductors* in the cable. In this chapter, we will confine our consideration of serial communications to those connecting LANs to WANs.

The figure is a simple representation of a serial communication. Data is encapsulated by the communications protocol used by the sending router. The encapsulated frame is sent on a *physical medium* to the WAN. There are various ways to traverse the WAN, but the receiving router uses the same communications protocol to de-encapsulate the frame when it arrives.

There are many different serial communication standards, each one using a different signaling method. There are three key serial communication standards affecting LAN-to-WAN connections:

- *RS-232 -* Most serial ports on personal computers conform to the RS-232C or newer *RS-422* and RS-423 standards. Both 9-pin and 25-pin connectors are used. A serial port is a general-purpose interface that can be used for almost any type of device, including modems, mice, and printers. Many network devices use RJ-45 connectors that also conform to the RS-232 standard. The figure shows an example of an RS-232 connector.

- *V.35* - Typically used for modem-to-multiplexer communication, this ITU standard for high-speed, synchronous data exchange combines the bandwidth of several telephone circuits. In the U.S., V.35 is the interface standard used by most routers and DSUs that connect to T1 carriers. V.35 cables are high-speed serial assemblies designed to support higher data rates and connectivity between DTEs and DCEs over digital lines. There is more on DTEs and DCEs later in this section.

- *HSSI* - A High-Speed Serial Interface (HSSI) supports transmission rates up to 52 Mb/s. Engineers use HSSI to connect routers on LANs with WANs over high-speed lines such as T3 lines. Engineers also use HSSI to provide high-speed connectivity between LANs, using *Token Ring* or Ethernet. HSSI is a DTE/DCE interface developed by Cisco Systems and T3plus Networking to address the need for high-speed communication over WAN links.

Click the RS-232 button in the figure.

As well as using different signaling methods, each of these standards uses different types of cables and connectors. Each standard plays a different role in a LAN-to-WAN topology. While this course does not examine the details of V.35 and HSSI pinning schemes, a quick look at a 9-pin RS-232 connector used to connect a PC to a modem helps illustrate the concept. A later topic looks at V.35 and HSSI cables.

- Pin 1 - Data Carrier Detect (DCD) indicates that the carrier for the transmit data is ON.
- Pin 2 - The receive pin (RXD) carries data from the serial device to the computer.
- Pin 3 - The transmit pin (TxD) carries data from the computer to the serial device.
- Pin 4 - Data Terminal Ready (*DTR*) indicates to the modem that the computer is ready to transmit.
- Pin 5 - Ground.
- Pin 6 - Data Set Ready (*DSR*) is similar to DTR. It indicates that the Dataset is ON.
- Pin 7 - The RTS pin requests clearance to send data to a modem.
- Pin 8 - The serial device uses the Clear to Send (*CTS*) pin to acknowledge the RTS signal of the computer. In most situations, RTS and CTS are constantly ON throughout the communication session.
- Pin 9 - An auto answer modem uses the Ring Indicator (RI) to signal receipt of a telephone ring signal.

The DCD and RI pins are only available in connections to a modem. These two lines are used rarely because most modems transmit status information to a PC when a carrier signal is detected (when a connection is made to another modem) or when the modem receives a ring signal from the telephone line.

2.1.2 TDM

Time Division Multiplexing

Bell Laboratories invented time-division multiplexing (*TDM*) to maximize the amount of voice traffic carried over a medium. Before multiplexing, each telephone call required its own physical link. This was an expensive and unscalable solution. TDM divides the bandwidth of a single link into separate channels or time slots. TDM transmits two or more channels over the same link by allocating a different time interval (time slot) for the transmission of each channel. In effect, the channels take turns using the link.

TDM is a Physical layer concept. It has no regard for the nature of the information that is being multiplexed onto the output channel. TDM is independent of the Layer 2 protocol that has been used by the input channels.

TDM can be explained by an analogy to highway traffic. To transport traffic from four roads to another city, you can send all the traffic on one lane if the feeding roads are equally serviced and the traffic is synchronized. So, if each of the four roads puts a car onto the main highway every four seconds, the highway gets a car at the rate of one each second. As long as the speed of all the cars is synchronized, there is no collision. At the destination, the reverse happens and the cars are taken off the highway and fed to the local roads by the same synchronous mechanism.

This is the principle used in synchronous TDM when sending data over a link. TDM increases the capacity of the *transmission link* by slicing time into smaller intervals so that the link carries the bits from multiple input sources, effectively increasing the number of bits transmitted per second. With TDM, the transmitter and the receiver both know exactly which signal is being sent.

In our example, a multiplexer (MUX) at the transmitter accepts three separate signals. The MUX breaks each signal into segments. The MUX puts each segment into a single channel by inserting each segment into a timeslot.

A MUX at the receiving end reassembles the TDM stream into the three separate *data streams* based only on the timing of the arrival of each bit. A technique called bit interleaving keeps track of the number and sequence of the bits from each specific transmission so that they can be quickly and efficiently reassembled into their original form upon receipt. Byte interleaving performs the same functions, but because there are eight bits in each byte, the process needs a bigger or longer time slot.

Statistical Time Division Multiplexing

In another analogy, compare TDM to a train with 32 railroad cars. Each car is owned by a different freight company, and every day the train leaves with the 32 cars attached. If one of the companies has cargo to send, the car is loaded. If the company has nothing to send, the car remains empty but stays on the train. Shipping empty containers is not very efficient. TDM shares this inefficiency when traffic is intermittent, because the time slot is still allocated even when the channel has no data to transmit.

Statistical time-division multiplexing (*STDM*) was developed to overcome this inefficiency. STDM uses a variable time slot length allowing channels to compete for any free slot space. It employs a *buffer* memory that temporarily stores the data during periods of peak traffic. STDM does not waste high-speed line time with inactive channels using this scheme. STDM requires each transmission to carry identification information (a channel identifier).

TDM Examples - ISDN and SONET

An example of a technology that uses synchronous TDM is ISDN. ISDN basic rate (BRI) has three channels consisting of two 64 kb/s B-channels (B1 and B2), and a 16 kb/s D-channel. The TDM has nine timeslots, which are repeated in the sequence shown in the figure.

On a larger scale, the telecommunications industry uses the *SONET* or SDH standard for optical transport of TDM data. SONET, used in North America, and SDH, used elsewhere, are two closely related standards that specify interface parameters, rates, framing formats, multiplexing methods, and management for synchronous TDM over fiber.

Click the SONET button in the figure.

The figure displays an example of statistical TDM. SONET/SDH takes n bit streams, multiplexes them, and optically modulates the signal, sending it out using a light emitting device over fiber with a bit rate equal to (incoming bit rate) x n. Thus traffic arriving at the SONET multiplexer from four places at 2.5 Gb/s goes out as a single stream at 4 x 2.5 Gb/s, or 10 Gb/s. This principle is illustrated in the figure, which shows an increase in the bit rate by a factor of four in time slot T.

Click the DS0 button in the figure.

The original unit used in multiplexing telephone calls is 64 kb/s, which represents one phone call. It is referred to as a *DS-0 or DS0* (digital signal level zero). In North America, 24 DS0 units are multiplexed using TDM into a higher bit-rate signal with an aggregate speed of 1.544 Mb/s for transmission over T1 lines. Outside North America, 32 DS0 units are multiplexed for E1 transmission at 2.048 Mb/s.

The signal level hierarchy for multiplexing telephone calls is shown in the table. As an aside, while it is common to refer to a 1.544 Mb/s transmission as a T1, it is more correct to refer to it as DS1.

Click the T-Carrier Hierarchy button in the figure.

T-carrier refers to the bundling of DS0s. For example, a T1 = 24 DS0s, a T1C = 48 DS0s (or 2 T1s), and so on. The figure shows a sample T-carrier infrastructure hierarchy. E-Carrier Hierarchy is similar.

2.1.3 Demarcation Point

Demarcation Point

Prior to deregulation in North America and other countries, telephone companies owned the local loop, including the wiring and equipment on the premises of the customers. Deregulation forced telephone companies to unbundle their local loop infrastructure to allow other suppliers to provide equipment and services. This led to a need to delineate which part of the network the telephone company owned and which part the customer owned. This point of delineation is the demarcation point, or demarc. The demarcation point marks the point where your network interfaces with the network owned by another organization. In telephone terminology, this is the interface between customer-premises equipment (CPE) and network service provider equipment. The demarcation point is the point in the network where the responsibility of the service provider ends.

The example presents an ISDN scenario. In the United States, a service provider provides the local loop into the customer premises, and the customer provides the active equipment such as the channel service unit/data service unit (CSU/DSU) on which the local loop is terminated. This termination often occurs in a telecommunications closet, and the customer is responsible for maintaining, replacing, or repairing the equipment. In other countries, the network terminating unit (NTU) is provided and managed by the service provider. This allows the service provider to actively manage and troubleshoot the local loop with the demarcation point occurring after the NTU. The customer connects a CPE device, such as a router or *Frame Relay access device*, to the NTU using a V.35 or RS-232 serial interface.

2.1.4 DTE and DCE

DTE-DCE

From the point of view of connecting to the WAN, a serial connection has a DTE device at one end of the connection and a DCE device at the other end. The connection between the two DCE devices is the WAN service provider transmission network. In this case:

- The CPE, which is generally a router, is the DTE. The DTE could also be a terminal, computer, printer, or fax machine if they connect directly to the service provider network.

- The DCE, commonly a modem or CSU/DSU, is the device used to convert the user data from the DTE into a form acceptable to the WAN service provider transmission link. This signal is received at the remote DCE, which decodes the signal back into a sequence of bits. The remote DCE then signals this sequence to the remote DTE.

The Electronics Industry Association (EIA) and the International Telecommunication Union Telecommunications Standardization Sector (ITU-T) have been most active in the development of standards that allow DTEs to communicate with DCEs. The EIA refers to the DCE as data communication equipment, while the ITU-T refers to the DCE as data circuit-terminating equipment.

Cable Standards

Originally, the concept of DCEs and DTEs was based on two types of equipment: terminal equipment that generated or received data, and communication equipment that only relayed data. In the development of the RS-232 standard, there were reasons why 25-pin RS-232 connectors on these two types of equipment needed to be wired differently. These reasons are no longer significant, but we are left with two different types of cables: one for connecting a DTE to a DCE, and another for connecting two DTEs directly to each other.

The DTE/DCE interface for a particular standard defines the following specifications:

- Mechanical/physical - Number of pins and connector type
- Electrical - Defines voltage levels for 0 and 1
- Functional - Specifies the functions that are performed by assigning meanings to each of the signaling lines in the interface
- Procedural - Specifies the sequence of events for transmitting data

Click the Null Modem button in the figure.

The original RS-232 standard only defined the connection of DTEs with DCEs, which were modems. However, if you want to connect two DTEs, such as two computers or two routers in the lab, a special cable called a null modem eliminates the need for a DCE. In other words, the two devices can be connected without a modem. A null modem is a communication method to directly connect two DTEs, such as a computer, terminal, or printer, using a RS-232 serial cable. With a *null modem* connection, the transmit (Tx) and receive (Rx) lines are crosslinked as shown in the figure. Cisco devices support the EIA/TIA-232, EIA/TIA-449, V.35, X.21, and EIA/TIA-530 serial standards.

Click the DB-60 button in the figure.

The cable for the DTE to DCE connection is a shielded serial transition cable. The router end of the shielded serial transition cable may be a DB-60 connector, which connects to the DB-60 port on a serial WAN interface card. The other end of the serial transition cable is available with the connector appropriate for the standard that is to be used. The WAN provider or the CSU/DSU usually dictates this cable type.

Click the Smart Serial button in the figure.

To support higher port densities in a smaller form factor, Cisco has introduced a Smart Serial cable. The router interface end of the Smart Serial cable is a 26-pin connector that is significantly more compact than the DB-60 connector.

Click the Router-to-Router button in the figure.

When using a null modem, keep in mind that synchronous connections require a clock signal. An external device can generate the signal, or one of the DTEs can generate the clock signal. When a DTE and DCE are connected, the serial port on a router is the DTE end of the connection by default, and the clock signal is typically provided by a CSU/DSU or similar DCE device. However, when using a null modem cable in a router-to-router connection, one of the serial interfaces must be configured as the DCE end to provide the clock signal for the connection.

Parallel to Serial Conversion

The terms DTE and DCE are relative with respect to what part of a network you are observing. RS-232C is the recommended standard (RS) describing the physical interface and protocol for relatively low-speed, serial data communication between computers and related devices. The EIA originally defined RS-232C for teletypewriter devices. The DTE is the RS-232C interface that a computer uses to exchange data with a modem or other serial device. The DCE is the RS-232C interface that a modem or other serial device uses in exchanging data with the computer.

For instance, your PC typically uses an RS-232C interface to communicate and exchange data with connected serial devices such as a modem. Your PC also has a Universal Asynchronous Receiver/Transmitter (*UART*) chip on the motherboard. Since the data in your PC flows along parallel circuits, the UART chip converts the groups of bits in parallel to a serial stream of bits. To work faster, a UART chip has buffers so it can cache data coming from the system bus while it processes data going out the serial port. The UART is the DTE *agent* of your PC and communicates with the modem or other serial device, which, in accordance with the RS-232C standard, has a complementary interface called the DCE interface.

2.1.5 HDLC Encapsulation

WAN Encapsulation Protocols

On each WAN connection, data is encapsulated into frames before crossing the WAN link. To ensure that the correct protocol is used, you need to configure the appropriate Layer 2 encapsulation type. The choice of protocol depends on the WAN technology and the communicating equipment. The more common WAN protocols and where they are used is shown in the figure, following are short descriptions:

- **HDLC -** The default encapsulation type on point-to-point connections, dedicated links, and circuit-switched connections when the link uses two Cisco devices. HDLC is now the basis for synchronous PPP used by many servers to connect to a WAN, most commonly the Internet.

- **PPP -** Provides router-to-router and host-to-network connections over synchronous and asynchronous circuits. PPP works with several Network layer protocols, such as IP and IPX. PPP also has built-in security mechanisms such as PAP and CHAP. Most of this chapter deals with PPP.

- *Serial Line Internet Protocol (SLIP)* - A standard protocol for point-to-point serial connections using TCP/IP. SLIP has been largely displaced by PPP.

- *X.25/Link Access Procedure, Balanced (LAPB)* - ITU-T standard that defines how connections between a DTE and DCE are maintained for remote terminal access and computer communications in public data networks. X.25 specifies LAPB, a Data Link layer protocol. X.25 is a predecessor to Frame Relay.

- *Frame Relay* - Industry standard, switched, Data Link layer protocol that handles multiple virtual circuits. Frame Relay is a next generation protocol after X.25. Frame Relay eliminates some of the time-consuming processes (such as error correction and flow control) employed in X.25. The next chapter is devoted to Frame Relay.

- *ATM* - The international standard for *cell relay* in which devices send multiple service types (such as voice, video, or data) in fixed-length (53-byte) cells. Fixed-length cells allow processing to occur in hardware, thereby reducing transit delays. ATM takes advantages of high-speed transmission *media* such as *E3*, SONET, and T3.

HDLC Encapsulation

HDLC is a synchronous Data Link layer *bit-oriented protocol* developed by the International Organization for Standardization (*ISO*). The current standard for HDLC is ISO 13239. HDLC was developed from the Synchronous Data Link Control (*SDLC*) standard proposed in the 1970s. HDLC provides both connection-oriented and connectionless service.

HDLC uses synchronous *serial transmission* to provide error-free communication between two points. HDLC defines a Layer 2 framing structure that allows for flow control and error control through the use of acknowledgments. Each frame has the same format, whether it is a data frame or a control frame.

When you want to transmit frames over synchronous or asynchronous links, you must remember that those links have no mechanism to mark the beginnings or ends of frames. HDLC uses a frame delimiter, or flag, to mark the beginning and the end of each frame.

Cisco has developed an extension to the HDLC protocol to solve the inability to provide multiprotocol support. Although Cisco HDLC (also referred to as cHDLC) is proprietary, Cisco has allowed many other network equipment vendors to implement it. Cisco HDLC frames contain a field for identifying the network protocol being encapsulated. The figure compares HDLC to Cisco HDLC.

Click the HDLC Frame Types button in the figure.

HDLC defines three types of frames, each with a different control field format. The following descriptions summarize the fields illustrated in the figure.

Flag - The flag field initiates and terminates error checking. The frame always starts and ends with an 8-bit flag field. The bit pattern is 01111110. Because there is a likelihood that this pattern occurs in the actual data, the sending HDLC system always inserts a 0 bit after every five 1s in the data field, so in practice the flag sequence can only occur at the frame ends. The receiving system strips out the inserted bits. When frames are transmitted consecutively, the end flag of the first frame is used as the start flag of the next frame.

Address - The address field contains the HDLC address of the secondary station. This address can contain a specific address, a group address, or a *broadcast address*. A primary address is either a communication source or a destination, which eliminates the need to include the address of the primary.

Control - The control field uses three different formats, depending on the type of HDLC frame used:

- *Information (I) frame:* I-frames carry upper layer information and some control information. This frame sends and receives *sequence numbers*, and the poll final (P/F) bit performs flow and error control. The send sequence number refers to the number of the frame to be sent next. The receive sequence number provides the number of the frame to be received next. Both sender and receiver maintain send and receive sequence numbers. A *primary station* uses the P/F bit to tell the secondary whether it requires an immediate response. A secondary station uses the P/F bit to tell the primary whether the current frame is the last in its current response.

- *Supervisory (S) frame:* S-frames provide control information. An S-frame can request and suspend transmission, report on status, and acknowledge receipt of I-frames. S-frames do not have an information field.

- *Unnumbered (U) frame:* U-frames support control purposes and are not sequenced. A U-frame can be used to initialize secondaries. Depending on the function of the U-frame, its control field is 1 or 2 bytes. Some U-frames have an information field.

Protocol - (only used in Cisco HDLC) This field specifies the protocol type encapsulated within the frame (e.g. 0x0800 for IP).

Data - The data field contains a path information unit (PIU) or exchange identification (*XID*) information.

Frame check sequence (FCS) - The FCS precedes the ending flag delimiter and is usually a cyclic redundancy check (CRC) calculation remainder. The CRC calculation is redone in the receiver. If the result differs from the value in the original frame, an error is assumed.

2.1.6 Configuring HDLC Encapsulation

Configuring HDLC Encapsulation

Cisco HDLC is the default encapsulation method used by Cisco devices on synchronous serial lines.

You use Cisco HDLC as a point-to-point protocol on leased lines between two Cisco devices. If you are connecting to a non-Cisco device, use synchronous PPP.

If the default encapsulation method has been changed, use the `encapsulation hdlc` command in privileged mode to re-enable HDLC.

There are two steps to enable HDLC encapsulation:

Step 1. Enter the interface configuration mode of the serial interface.

Step 2. Enter the `encapsulation hdlc` command to specify the encapsulation protocol on the interface.

2.1.7 Troubleshooting a Serial Interface

The output of the `show interfaces serial` command displays information specific to serial interfaces. When HDLC is configured, "Encapsulation HDLC" should be reflected in the output, as highlighted in the figure.

Click the Possible States button in the figure.

The `show interface serial` command returns one of five possible states. You can identify any of the following five possible problem states in the interface status line:

Click the Status button in the figure.

- Serial x is down, line protocol is down
- Serial x is up, line protocol is down
- Serial x is up, line protocol is up (looped)
- Serial x is up, line protocol is down (disabled)
- Serial x is administratively down, line protocol is down

Click the Controllers button in the figure.

The `show controllers` command is another important diagnostic tool when troubleshooting serial lines. The output indicates the state of the interface channels and whether a cable is attached to the interface. In the figure, serial interface 0/0 has a V.35 DCE cable attached. The command syntax varies, depending on the platform. *Cisco 7000* series routers use a cBus controller card for connecting serial links. With these routers, use the `show controllers cbus` command.

If the electrical interface output is shown as **UNKNOWN** instead of **V.35**, **EIA/TIA-449**, or some other electrical interface type, the likely problem is an improperly connected cable. A problem with the internal wiring of the card is also possible. If the electrical interface is unknown, the corresponding display for the `show interfaces serial <x>` command shows that the interface and line protocol are down.

In this activity, you will practice troubleshooting serial interfaces. Detailed instructions are provided within the activity as well as in the PDF link below.

Activity Instructions (PDF)

Complex Flash: Identifying WAN Technology Components and Concepts

2.2 PPP Concepts

2.2.1 Introducing PPP

What is PPP?

Recall that HDLC is the default serial encapsulation method when you connect two Cisco routers. With an added protocol type field, the Cisco version of HDLC is proprietary. Thus, Cisco HDLC can only work with other Cisco devices. However, when you need to connect to a non-Cisco router, you should use PPP encapsulation.

PPP encapsulation has been carefully designed to retain compatibility with most commonly used supporting hardware. PPP encapsulates data frames for transmission over Layer 2 physical links. PPP establishes a direct connection using serial cables, phone lines, trunk lines, cellular telephones, specialized radio links, or fiber-optic links. There are many advantages to using PPP, including the fact that it is not proprietary. Moreover, it includes many features not available in HDLC:

- The link quality management feature monitors the quality of the link. If too many errors are detected, PPP takes the link down.
- PPP supports PAP and *CHAP* authentication. This feature is explained and practiced in a later section.

PPP contains three main components:

- HDLC protocol for encapsulating *datagrams* over point-to-point links.
- Extensible Link Control Protocol (*LCP*) to establish, configure, and test the data link connection.
- Family of Network Control Protocols (*NCPs*) for establishing and configuring different Network layer protocols. PPP allows the simultaneous use of multiple Network layer protocols. Some of the more common NCPs are Internet Protocol Control Protocol, Appletalk Control Protocol, *Novell IPX* Control Protocol, Cisco Systems Control Protocol, *SNA* Control Protocol, and Compression Control Protocol.

2.2.2 PPP Layered Architecture

PPP Architecture

A layered architecture is a logical model, design, or blueprint that aids in communication between interconnecting layers. The figure maps the layered architecture of PPP against the Open System Interconnection (OSI) model. PPP and OSI share the same Physical layer, but PPP distributes the functions of LCP and NCP differently.

At the Physical layer, you can configure PPP on a range of interfaces, including:

- Asynchronous serial
- Synchronous serial
- HSSI
- ISDN

PPP operates across any DTE/DCE interface (RS-232-C, RS-422, RS-423, or V.35). The only absolute requirement imposed by PPP is a duplex circuit, either dedicated or switched, that can operate in either an asynchronous or synchronous bit-serial mode, transparent to PPP link layer frames. PPP does not impose any restrictions regarding transmission rate other than those imposed by the particular DTE/DCE interface in use.

Most of the work done by PPP is at the data link and Network layers by the LCP and NCPs. The LCP sets up the PPP connection and its parameters, the NCPs handle higher layer protocol configurations, and the LCP terminates the PPP connection.

PPP Architecture - Link Control Protocol Layer

The LCP is the real working part of PPP. The LCP sits on top of the Physical layer and has a role in establishing, configuring, and testing the data-link connection. The LCP establishes the point-to-point link. The LCP also negotiates and sets up control options on the WAN data link, which are handled by the NCPs.

The LCP provides automatic configuration of the interfaces at each end, including:

- Handling varying limits on packet size
- Detecting common misconfiguration errors
- Terminating the link
- Determining when a link is functioning properly or when it is failing

PPP also uses the LCP to agree automatically on encapsulation formats (authentication, compression, error detection) as soon as the link is established.

PPP Architecture - Network Control Protocol Layer

Point-to-point links tend to worsen many problems with the current family of network protocols. For instance, assignment and management of *IP addresses*, which is a problem even in LAN environments, is especially difficult over circuit-switched point-to-point links (such as dialup modem servers). PPP addresses these issues using NCPs.

PPP permits multiple Network layer protocols to operate on the same communications link. For every Network layer protocol used, PPP uses a separate NCP. For example, IP uses the IP Control Protocol (IPCP), and IPX uses the Novell IPX Control Protocol (IPXCP).

Click the Network Layer button in the figure.

NCPs include functional fields containing standardized codes (PPP protocol field numbers shown in the figure) to indicate the Network layer protocol that PPP encapsulates. Each NCP manages the specific needs required by its respective Network layer protocols. The various NCP components encapsulate and negotiate options for multiple Network layer protocols. Using NCPs to configure the various Network layer protocols is explained and practiced later in this chapter.

2.2.3 PPP Frame Structure

PPP Frame Structure

A PPP frame has six fields as shown in the figure.

Roll your mouse over each field for an explanation of what each one contains and does.

The LCP can negotiate modifications to the standard PPP frame structure.

2.2.4 Establishing a PPP Session

Establishing a PPP Session

The figure shows the three phases of establishing a PPP session:

- *Phase 1: Link establishment and configuration negotiation -* Before PPP exchanges any Network layer datagrams (for example, IP), the LCP must first open the connection and negotiate configuration options. This phase is complete when the receiving router sends a configuration-acknowledgment frame back to the router initiating the connection.

- *Phase 2: Link quality determination (optional) -* The LCP tests the link to determine whether the link quality is sufficient to bring up Network layer protocols. The LCP can delay transmission of Network layer protocol information until this phase is complete.

- *Phase 3: Network layer protocol configuration negotiation -* After the LCP has finished the link quality determination phase, the appropriate NCP can separately configure the Network layer protocols, and bring them up and take them down at any time. If the LCP closes the link, it informs the Network layer protocols so that they can take appropriate action.

The link remains configured for communications until explicit LCP or NCP frames close the link, or until some external event occurs (for example, an inactivity timer expires or a user intervenes). The LCP can terminate the link at any time. This is usually done when one of the routers requests termination, but can happen because of a physical event, such as the loss of a carrier or the expiration of an idle-period timer.

2.2.5 Establishing a Link with LCP

LCP Operation

LCP operation includes provisions for link establishment, link maintenance and link termination. LCP operation uses three classes of LCP frames to accomplish the work of each of the LCP phases:

- Link-establishment frames establish and configure a link (Configure-Request, Configure-*Ack*, Configure-*Nak*, and Configure-Reject)
- Link-maintenance frames manage and debug a link (Code-Reject, Protocol-Reject, Echo-Request, Echo-Reply, and Discard-Request)
- Link-termination frames terminate a link (Terminate-Request and Terminate-Ack)

The first phase of LCP operation is link establishment. This phase must complete successfully, before any Network layer packets can be exchanged. During link establishment, the LCP opens the connection and negotiates the configuration parameters.

Click the Link Negotiation button in the figure.

The link establishment process starts with the initiating device sending a Configure-Request frame to the responder. The Configure-Request frame includes a variable number of configuration options needed to set up on the link. In other words, the initiator has sent a "wish list" to the responder.

The initiator's wish list includes options for how it wants the link created, including protocol or authentication parameters. The responder processes the wish list, and if it is acceptable responds with a Configure-Ack *message*. After receiving the Configure-Ack message, the process moves on to the authentication stage.

If the options are not acceptable or not recognized the responder sends a Configure-Nak or Configure-Reject. If a Configure-Ack is received, the operation of the link is handed over to the NCP. If either a Configure-Nak or Configure-Reject message is sent to the requester, the link is not established. If the negotiation fails, the initiator needs to restart the process with new options.

During link maintenance, LCP can use messages to provide feedback and test the link.

- Code-Reject and Protocol-Reject - These frame types provide feedback when one device receives an invalid frame due to either an unrecognized LCP code (LCP frame type) or a bad protocol identifier. For example, if an un-interpretable packet is received from the peer, a Code-Reject packet is sent in response.
- Echo-Request, Echo-Reply, and Discard-Request - These frames can be used for testing the link.

After the transfer of data at the Network layer completes, the LCP terminates the link. In the figure, notice that the NCP only terminates the Network layer and NCP link. The link remains open until the LCP terminates it. If the LCP terminates the link before the NCP, the NCP *session* is also terminated.

PPP can terminate the link at any time. This might happen because of the loss of the carrier, authentication failure, link quality failure, the expiration of an idle-period timer, or the administrative closing of the link. The LCP closes the link by exchanging Terminate packets. The device initiating the shutdown sends a Terminate-Request message. The other device replies with a Terminate-Ack. A termination request indicates that the device sending it needs to close the link. When the link is closing, PPP informs the Network layer protocols so that they may take appropriate action.

LCP Packet

The figure shows the fields in an LCP packet.

Roll over each field and read the description.

Each LCP packet is a single LCP message consisting of an LCP code field identifying the type of LCP packet, an identifier field so that requests and replies can be matched, and a length field indicating the size of the LCP packet and LCP packet type-specific data.

Click the LCP Codes button in the figure.

Each LCP packet has a specific function in the exchange of configuration information depending on its packet type. The code field of the LCP packet identifies the packet type according to the table.

PPP Configuration Options

PPP can be configured to support various functions including:

- Authentication using either PAP or CHAP
- Compression using either Stacker or Predictor
- Multilink which combines two or more channels to increase the WAN bandwidth

These options are discussed in more detail in the next section.

Click the LCP Option Field button in the figure.

To negotiate the use of these PPP options, the LCP link-establishment frames contain Option information in the Data field of the LCP frame. If a configuration option is not included in an LCP frame, the default value for that configuration option is assumed.

This phase is complete when a configuration acknowledgment frame has been sent and received.

2.2.6 NCP Explained

NCP Process

After the link has been initiated, the LCP passes control to the appropriate NCP. Although initially designed for *IP datagrams*, PPP can carry data from many types of Network layer protocols by using a modular approach in its implementation. It can also carry two or more Layer 3 protocols simultaneously. Its modular model allows the LCP to set up the link and then hand the details of a network protocol to a specific NCP. Each network protocol has a corresponding NCP. Each NCP has a corresponding RFC. There are NCPs for IP, IPX, AppleTalk, and many others. NCPs use the same packet format as the LCPs.

After the LCP has configured and authenticated the basic link, the appropriate NCP is invoked to complete the specific configuration of the Network layer protocol being used. When the NCP has successfully configured the Network layer protocol, the network protocol is in the open state on the established LCP link. At this point, PPP can carry the corresponding Network layer protocol packets.

IPCP Example

As an example of how the NCP layer works, IP, which is the most common Layer 3 protocol, is used. After LCP has established the link, the routers exchange IPCP messages, negotiating options specific to the protocol. IPCP is responsible for configuring, enabling, and disabling the IP modules on both ends of the link.

IPCP negotiates two options:

- Compression - Allows devices to negotiate an *algorithm* to compress *TCP* and IP headers and save bandwidth. Van Jacobson TCP/IP header compression reduces the size of the TCP/IP headers to as few as 3 bytes. This can be a significant improvement on slow serial lines, particularly for interactive traffic.

- IP-Address - Allows the initiating device to specify an IP address to use for routing IP over the PPP link, or to request an IP address for the responder. Dialup network links commonly use the IP address option.

When the NCP process is complete, the link goes into the open state and LCP takes over again. Link traffic consists of any possible combination of LCP, NCP, and Network layer protocol packets. The figure shows how LCP messages can then be used by either device to manage or debug the link.

Complex Flash: Identifying PPP Concepts and Processes

2.3 Configuring PPP

2.3.1 PPP Configuration Options

PPP Configuration Options

In the previous section, you were introduced to LCP options you can configure to meet specific WAN connection requirements. PPP may include the following LCP options:

- *Authentication* - Peer routers exchange authentication messages. Two authentication choices are Password Authentication Protocol (PAP) and Challenge Handshake Authentication Protocol (CHAP). Authentication is explained in the next section.

- *Compression* - Increases the effective *throughput* on PPP connections by reducing the amount of data in the frame that must travel across the link. The protocol decompresses the frame at its destination. Two compression protocols available in Cisco routers are Stacker and Predictor.

- *Error detection* - Identifies fault conditions. The Quality and Magic Number options help ensure a reliable, loop-free data link. The Magic Number field helps in detecting links that are in a looped-back condition. Until the Magic-Number Configuration Option has been successfully negotiated, the Magic-Number must be transmitted as zero. Magic numbers are generated randomly at each end of the connection.

- *Multilink* - Cisco *IOS* Release 11.1 and later supports multilink PPP. This alternative provides *load balancing* over the router interfaces that PPP uses. Multilink PPP (also referred to as MP, MPPP, MLP, or Multilink) provides a method for spreading traffic across multiple physical WAN links while providing packet *fragmentation* and *reassembly*, proper sequencing, multivendor interoperability, and load balancing on inbound and outbound traffic. Multilink is not covered in this course.

- *PPP Callback* - To enhance security, Cisco IOS Release 11.1 and later offers callback over PPP. With this LCP option, a Cisco router can act as a callback client or a callback server. The client makes the initial call, requests that the server call it back, and terminates its initial call. The callback router answers the initial call and makes the return call to the client based on its configuration statements. The command is **ppp callback [accept | request]**.

When options are configured, a corresponding field value is inserted into the LCP option field.

2.3.2 PPP Configuration Commands

PPP Configuration Commands

Before you actually configure PPP on a serial interface, we will look at the commands and the syntax of these commands as shown in the figure. This series of examples shows you how to configure PPP and some of the options.

Example 1: Enabling PPP on an Interface

To set PPP as the encapsulation method used by a serial or ISDN interface, use the `encapsulation ppp` interface configuration command.

The following example enables PPP encapsulation on serial interface 0/0/0:

```
R3#configure terminal
 R3(config)#interface serial 0/0/0
 R3(config-if)#encapsulation ppp
```

The `encapsulation ppp` command has no arguments, however, you must first configure the router with an IP *routing protocol* to use PPP encapsulation. You should recall that if you do not configure PPP on a Cisco router, the default encapsulation for serial interfaces is HLDC.

Example 2: Compression

You can configure point-to-point software compression on serial interfaces after you have enabled PPP encapsulation. Because this option invokes a software compression process, it can affect system performance. If the traffic already consists of compressed files (.zip, .tar, or .mpeg, for example), do not use this option. The figure shows the command syntax for the `compress` command.

To configure compression over PPP, enter the following commands:

```
R3(config)#interface serial 0/0/0
 R3(config-if)#encapsulation ppp
 R3(config-if)#compress [predictor | stac]
```

Example 3: Link Quality Monitoring

Recall from our discussion on LCP phases that LCP provides an optional link quality determination phase. In this phase, LCP tests the link to determine whether the link quality is sufficient to use Layer 3 protocols. The command `ppp quality` *percentage* ensures that the link meets the quality requirement you set; otherwise, the link closes down.

The percentages are calculated for both incoming and outgoing directions. The outgoing quality is calculated by comparing the total number of packets and bytes sent to the total number of packets and bytes received by the destination node. The incoming quality is calculated by comparing the total number of packets and bytes received to the total number of packets and bytes sent by the destination node.

If the link quality percentage is not maintained, the link is deemed to be of poor quality and is taken down. Link Quality Monitoring (LQM) implements a time lag so that the link does not bounce up and down.

This example configuration monitors the data dropped on the link and avoids frame looping:

```
R3(config)#interface serial 0/0/0
 R3(config-if)#encapsulation ppp
 R3(config-if)#ppp quality 80
```

Use the `no ppp quality` command to disable LQM.

Example 4: Load Balancing Across Links

Multilink PPP (also referred to as MP, MPPP, MLP, or Multilink) provides a method for spreading traffic across multiple physical WAN links while providing packet fragmentation and reassembly, proper sequencing, multivendor interoperability, and load balancing on inbound and outbound traffic.

MPPP allows packets to be fragmented and sends these fragments simultaneously over multiple point-to-point links to the same remote address. The multiple physical links come up in response to a user-defined load threshold. MPPP can measure the load on just inbound traffic, or on just outbound traffic, but not on the combined load of both inbound and outbound traffic.

The following commands perform load balancing across multiple links:

```
Router(config)#interface serial 0/0/0
 Router(config-if)#encapsulation ppp
 Router(config-if)#ppp multilink
```

The **multilink** command has no arguments. To disable PPP multilink, use the **no ppp multilink** command.

2.3.3 Verifying a Serial PPP Encapsulation Configuration

Verifying PPP Encapsulation Configuration

Refer to Figure in online course

Use the `show interfaces serial` command to verify proper configuration of HDLC or PPP encapsulation. The command output in the figure shows a PPP configuration.

When you configure HDLC, the output of the `show interfaces serial` command should show "encapsulation HDLC". When you configure PPP, you can check its LCP and NCP states.

Click the Commands button in the figure.

The figure summarizes commands used when verifying PPP.

2.3.4 Troubleshooting PPP Encapsulation

Troubleshooting the Serial Encapsulation Configuration

Refer to Figure in online course

By now you are aware that **debug** command is used for troubleshooting and is accessed from privileged *exec* mode of the command line interface. Debug displays information about various router operations and the related traffic generated or received by the router, as well as any error messages. It is a very useful and informative tool, but you must always remember that Cisco IOS treats debug as a high priority task. It can consume a significant amount of resources, and the router is forced to process-switch the packets being debugged. Debug must not be used as a monitoring tool-it is meant to be used for a short period of time for troubleshooting. When troubleshooting a serial connection, you use the same approach as you have used in other configuration tasks.

Use the **debug ppp** command to display information about the operation of PPP. The figure shows the command syntax. The **no** form of this command disables debugging output.

Output of the `debug ppp packet` Command

Refer to Figure in online course

A good command to use when troubleshooting serial interface encapsulation is the **debug ppp packet** command. The example in the figure is output from the **debug ppp packet** command as seen from the Link Quality Monitor (LQM) side of the connection. This display example depicts packet exchanges under normal PPP operation. This is only a partial listing, but enough to get you ready for the practice lab.

Look at each line in the output and match it to the meaning of the field. Use the following to guide your examination of the output.

- PPP - PPP debugging output.

- Serial2 - Interface number associated with this debugging information.
- (o), O - The detected packet is an output packet.
- (i), I - The detected packet is an input packet.
- lcp_slqr() - Procedure name; running LQM, send a Link Quality Report (LQR).
- lcp_rlqr() - Procedure name; running LQM, received an LQR.
- input (C021) - Router received a packet of the specified packet type (in *hexadecimal*). A value of C025 indicates packet of type LQM.
- state = OPEN - PPP state; normal state is OPEN.
- magic = D21B4 - Magic Number for indicated node; when output is indicated, this is the Magic Number of the node on which debugging is enabled. The actual Magic Number depends on whether the packet detected is indicated as I or O.
- datagramsize = 52 - Packet length including header.
- code = ECHOREQ(9) - Identifies the type of packet received in both string and hexadecimal form.
- len = 48 - Packet length without header.
- id = 3 - ID number per Link Control Protocol (LCP) packet format.
- pkt type 0xC025 - Packet type in hexadecimal; typical packet types are C025 for LQM and C021 for LCP.
- LCP ECHOREQ (9) - Echo Request; value in parentheses is the hexadecimal representation of the LCP type.
- LCP ECHOREP (A) - Echo Reply; value in parentheses is the hexadecimal representation of the LCP type.

Output of the `debug ppp negotiation` Command

The figure shows the output of the `debug ppp negotiation` command in a normal negotiation, where both sides agree on NCP parameters. In this case, protocol type IP is proposed and acknowledged. Taking the output a line or two at a time:

The first two lines indicate that the router is trying to bring up the LCP and will use the indicated negotiation options (Quality Protocol and Magic Number). The value fields are the values of the options themselves. C025/3E8 translates to Quality Protocol LQM. 3E8 is the reporting period (in hundredths of a second). 3D56CAC is the value of the Magic Number for the router.

```
ppp: sending CONFREQ, type = 4 (CI_QUALITYTYPE), value = C025/3E8
 ppp: sending CONFREQ, type = 5 (CI_MAGICNUMBER), value = 3D56CAC
```

The next two lines indicate that the other side negotiated for options 4 and 5 and that it requested and acknowledged both. If the responding end does not support the options, the responding node sends a CONFREJ. If the responding end does not accept the value of the option, it sends a CONFNAK with the value field modified.

```
ppp: received config for type = 4 (QUALITYTYPE) acked
 ppp: received config for type = 5 (MAGICNUMBER) value = 3D567F8 acked (ok)
```

The next three lines indicate that the router received a CONFACK from the responding side and displays accepted option values. Use the rcvd id field to verify that the CONFREQ and CONFACK have the same id field.

```
PPP Serial2: state = ACKSENT fsm_rconfack(C021): rcvd id 5
 ppp: config ACK received, type = 4 (CI_QUALITYTYPE), value = C025
```

```
ppp: config ACK received, type = 5 (CI_MAGICNUMBER), value = 3D56CAC
```
The next line indicates that the router has IP routing enabled on this interface and that the IPCP NCP negotiated successfully.
```
ppp: ipcp_reqci: returning CONFACK (ok)
```
Output of the `debug ppp error` Command

You can use the **debug ppp error** command to display protocol errors and error statistics associated with PPP connection negotiation and operation. These messages might appear when the Quality Protocol option is enabled on an interface that is already running PPP. The figure shows an example.

Look at each line in the output and match it to the meaning of the field. Use the following to guide your examination of the output.

- PPP - PPP debugging output.

- Serial3(i) - Interface number associated with this debugging information; indicates that this is an input packet.

- rlqr receive failure - Receiver does not accept the request to negotiate the Quality Protocol option.

- myrcvdiffp = 159 - Number of packets received over the time period specified.

- peerxmitdiffp = 41091 - Number of packets sent by the remote node over this period.

- myrcvdiffo = 2183 - Number of octets received over this period.

- peerxmitdiffo = 1714439 - Number of octets sent by the remote node over this period.

- threshold = 25 - Maximum error percentage acceptable on this interface. You calculate this percentage using the threshold value entered in the **ppp quality** *percentage* interface configuration command. A value of 100 minus number is the maximum error percentage. In this case, a number of 75 was entered. This means that the local router must maintain a minimum 75 percent non-error percentage, or the PPP link closes down.

- OutLQRs = 1 - Current send LQR sequence number of the local router.

- LastOutLQRs = 1 - Last sequence number that the remote node side has seen from the local node.

In this activity, you will practice changing the encapsulation on serial interfaces. Detailed instructions are provided within the activity as well as in the PDF link below.

Activity Instructions (PDF)

2.4 Configuring PPP with Authentication

2.4.1 PPP Authentication Protocols

PAP Authentication Protocol

PPP defines an extensible LCP that allows negotiation of an authentication protocol for authenticating its peer before allowing Network layer protocols to transmit over the link. *RFC* 1334 defines two protocols for authentication, as shown in the figure.

PAP is a very basic two-way process. There is no encryption-the username and password are sent in plain text. If it is accepted, the connection is allowed. CHAP is more secure than PAP. It involves a three-way exchange of a shared secret. The process is described later in this section.

The authentication phase of a PPP session is optional. If used, you can authenticate the peer after the LCP establishes the link and choose the authentication protocol. If it is used, authentication takes place before the Network layer protocol configuration phase begins.

The authentication options require that the calling side of the link enter authentication information. This helps to ensure that the user has the permission of the network administrator to make the call. Peer routers exchange authentication messages.

2.4.2 Password Authentication Protocol (PAP)

One of the many features of PPP is that it performs Layer 2 authentication in addition to other layers of authentication, encryption, access control, and general security procedures.

Initiating PAP

PAP provides a simple method for a remote node to establish its identity using a two-way handshake. PAP is not interactive. When the `ppp authentication pap` command is used, the username and password are sent as one LCP data package, rather than the server sending a login prompt and waiting for a response. The figure shows that after PPP completes the link establishment phase, the remote node repeatedly sends a username-password pair across the link until the sending node acknowledges it or terminates the connection.

Click the Completing PAP button in the figure.

At the receiving node, the username-password is checked by an authentication server that either allows or denies the connection. An accept or reject message is returned to the requester.

PAP is not a strong authentication protocol. Using PAP, you send passwords across the link in clear text and there is no protection from playback or repeated trial-and-error attacks. The remote node is in control of the frequency and timing of the login attempts.

Nonetheless, there are times when using PAP can be justified. For example, despite its shortcomings, PAP may be used in the following environments:

- A large installed base of client applications that do not support CHAP
- Incompatibilities between different vendor implementations of CHAP
- Situations where a plaintext password must be available to simulate a login at the remote host

2.4.3 Challenge Handshake Authentication Protocol (CHAP)

Challenge Handshake Authentication Protocol (CHAP)

Once authentication is established with PAP, it essentially stops working. This leaves the network vulnerable to attack. Unlike PAP, which only authenticates once, CHAP conducts periodic challenges to make sure that the remote node still has a valid password value.

After the PPP link establishment phase is complete, the local router sends a challenge message to the remote node.

Click the Responding CHAP button in the figure.

The remote node responds with a value calculated using a one-way hash function, which is typically Message Digest 5 (*MD5*) based on the password and challenge message.

Click the Completing CHAP button in the figure.

The local router checks the response against its own calculation of the expected hash value. If the values match, the initiating node acknowledges the authentication. Otherwise, it immediately terminates the connection.

CHAP provides protection against playback attack by using a variable challenge value that is unique and unpredictable. Because the challenge is unique and random, the resulting hash value is also unique and random. The use of repeated challenges limits the time of exposure to any single attack. The local router or a third-party authentication server is in control of the frequency and timing of the challenges.

2.4.4 PPP Encapsulation and Authentication Process

PPP Encapsulation and Authentication Process

Refer to Figure in online course

You can use a flowchart to help understand the PPP authentication process when configuring PPP. The flowchart provides a visual example of the logic decisions made by PPP.

For example, if an incoming PPP request requires no authentication, then PPP progresses to the next level. If an incoming PPP request requires authentication, then it can be authenticated using either the local database or a security server. As illustrated in the flowchart, successful authentication progresses to the next level, while an authentication failure will disconnect and drop the incoming PPP request.

Click the CHAP Example button and click the play button for an animated example.

Follow the steps as the animation progresses. Router R1 wishes to establish an authenticated PPP CHAP connection with Router R2.

Step 1. R1 initially negotiates the link connection using LCP with router R2 and the two systems agree to use CHAP authentication during the PPP LCP negotiation.

Step 2. Router R2 generates an ID and a random number and sends that plus its username as a CHAP challenge packet to R1.

Step 3. R1 will use the username of the challenger (R2) and cross reference it with its local database to find its associated password. R1 will then generate a unique MD5 hash number using the R2's username, ID, random number and the shared secret password.

Step 4. Router R1 then sends the challenge ID, the hashed value, and its username (R1) to R2.

Step 5. R2 generates it own hash value using the ID, the shared secret password, and the random number it originally sent to R1.

Step 6. R2 compares its hash value with the hash value sent by R1. If the values are the same, R2 sends a link established response to R1.

If the authentication failed, a CHAP failure packet is built from the following components:

- 04 = CHAP failure message type
- id = copied from the response packet
- "Authentication failure" or some such text message, which is meant to be a user-readable explanation

Note that the shared secret password must be identical on R1 and R2.

2.4.5 Configuring PPP with Authentication

The ppp authentication Command

To specify the order in which the CHAP or PAP protocols are requested on the interface, use the **ppp authentication** interface configuration command, as shown in the figure. Use the **no** form of the command to disable this authentication.

After you have enabled CHAP or PAP authentication, or both, the local router requires the remote device to prove its identity before allowing data traffic to flow. This is done as follows:

- PAP authentication requires the remote device to send a name and password to be checked against a matching entry in the local username database or in the remote *TACACS/TACACS+* database.

- CHAP authentication sends a challenge to the remote device. The remote device must encrypt the challenge value with a shared secret and return the encrypted value and its name to the local router in a response message. The local router uses the name of the remote device to look up the appropriate secret in the local username or remote TACACS/TACACS+ database. It uses the looked-up secret to encrypt the original challenge and verify that the encrypted values match.

Note: AAA/TACACS is a dedicated server used to authenticate users. AAA stands for "authentication, authorization and accounting". TACACS clients send a query to a TACACS authentication server. The server can authenticate the user, authorize what the user can do and track what the user has done.

You may enable PAP or CHAP or both. If both methods are enabled, the first method specified is requested during link negotiation. If the peer suggests using the second method or simply refuses the first method, the second method is tried. Some remote devices support CHAP only and some PAP only. The order in which you specify the methods is based on your concerns about the ability of the remote device to correctly negotiate the appropriate method as well as your concern about data line security. PAP usernames and passwords are sent as clear-text strings and can be intercepted and reused. CHAP has eliminated most of the known security holes.

Configuring PPP Authentication

The procedure outlined in the graphic describes how to configure PPP encapsulation and PAP/CHAP authentication protocols. Correct configuration is essential, because PAP and CHAP use these parameters to authenticate.

Click the PAP Example button in the figure.

The figure is an example of a two-way PAP authentication configuration. Both routers authenticate and are authenticated, so the PAP authentication commands mirror each other. The PAP username and password that each router sends must match those specified with the **username** *name* **password** *password* command of the other router.

PAP provides a simple method for a remote node to establish its identity using a two-way handshake. This is done only on initial link establishment. The hostname on one router must match the username the other router has configured. The passwords do not have to match.

Click the CHAP Example button in the figure.

CHAP periodically verifies the identity of the remote node using a three-way handshake. The hostname on one router must match the username the other router has configured. The passwords must also match. This occurs on initial link establishment and can be repeated any time after the link has been established. The figure is an example of a CHAP configuration.

2.4.6 Troubleshooting a PPP Configuration with Authentication

Troubleshooting a PPP Configuration with Authentication

Authentication is a feature that needs to be implemented correctly or the security of your serial connection may be compromised. Always verify your configuration with the `show interfaces serial` command, in the same way as you did without authentication.

Never assume your authentication configuration works without testing it. Debugging allows you to confirm your configuration and correct any deficiencies. The command for debugging PPP authentication is `debug ppp authentication`.

The figure shows an example output of the `debug ppp authentication` command. The following is an interpretation of the output:

Line 1 says that the router is unable to authenticate on interface Serial0 because the peer did not send a name.

Line 2 says the router was unable to validate the CHAP response because USERNAME 'pioneer' was not found.

Line 3 says no password was found for 'pioneer'. Other possible responses at this line might have been no name received to authenticate, unknown name, no secret for given name, short MD5 response received, or MD5 compare failed.

In the last line, the code = 4 means a failure has occurred. Other code values are as follows:

- 1 = Challenge
- 2 = Response
- 3 = Success
- 4 = Failure

id = 3 is the ID number per LCP packet format.

len = 48 is the packet length without the header.

PPP encapsulation allows for two different types of authentication: PAP (Password Authentication Protocol) and CHAP (Challenge Handshake Authentication Protocol). PAP uses a clear-text password, while CHAP invokes a one-way hash that provides more security than PAP. In this activity, you will configure both PAP and CHAP as well as review OSPF routing configuration. Detailed instructions are provided within the activity as well as in the PDF link below.

Activity Instructions (PDF)

2.5 Chapter Labs

2.5.1 Basic PPP Configuration

In this lab, you will learn how to configure PPP encapsulation on serial links using the network shown in the topology diagram. You will also learn how to restore serial links to their default HDLC encapsulation. Pay special attention to what the output of the router looks like when you intentionally break PPP encapsulation. This will assist you in the Troubleshooting lab associated with this chapter. Finally, you will configure PPP PAP authentication and PPP CHAP authentication.

> Refer to **Packet Tracer Activity** for this chapter

This activity is a variation of Lab 2.5.1. Packet Tracer may not support all the tasks specified in the hands-on lab. This activity should not be considered equivalent to completing the hands-on lab. Packet Tracer is not a substitute for a hands-on lab experience with real equipment.

Detailed instructions are provided within the activity as well as in the PDF link below.

Activity Instructions (PDF)

2.5.2 Challenge PPP Configuration

> Refer to **Lab Activity** for this chapter

In this lab, you will learn how to configure PPP encapsulation on serial links using the network shown in the topology diagram. You will also configure PPP CHAP authentication. If you need assistance, refer back to the Basic PPP Configuration lab, but try to do as much on your own as possible.

> Refer to **Packet Tracer Activity** for this chapter

This activity is a variation of Lab 2.5.2. Packet Tracer may not support all the tasks specified in the hands-on lab. This activity should not be considered equivalent to completing the hands-on lab. Packet Tracer is not a substitute for a hands-on lab experience with real equipment.

Detailed instructions are provided within the activity as well as in the PDF link below.

Activity Instructions (PDF)

2.5.3 Troubleshooting PPP Configuration

> Refer to **Lab Activity** for this chapter

The routers at your company were configured by an inexperienced network engineer. Several errors in the configuration have resulted in connectivity issues. Your boss has asked you to troubleshoot and correct the configuration errors and document your work. Using your knowledge of PPP and standard testing methods, find and correct the errors. Make sure that all of the serial links use PPP CHAP authentication, and that all of the networks are reachable.

> Refer to **Packet Tracer Activity** for this chapter

This activity is a variation of Lab 2.5.3. Packet Tracer may not support all the tasks specified in the hands-on lab. This activity should not be considered equivalent to completing the hands-on lab. Packet Tracer is not a substitute for a hands-on lab experience with real equipment.

Detailed instructions are provided within the activity as well as in the PDF link below.

Activity Instructions (PDF)

Chapter Summary

On completing this chapter you can describe in conceptual and practical terms why serial point-to-point communications are used to connect your LAN to your service provider WAN, rather than using parallel connections that might intuitively seem faster. You can explain how multiplexing allows efficient communications and maximize the amount of data that can be passed over a communications link. You learned the functions of key components and protocols of serial communications, and can configure a serial interface with HDLC encapsulation on a Cisco router.

This provided a good basis for comprehending PPP including its features, components and architectures. You can explain how a PPP session is established using the functions of the LCP and NCPs. You learned the syntax of the configuration commands and use of various options required to configure a PPP connection, as well as how to use PAP or CHAP to ensure a secure connection. The steps required for verification and troubleshooting were described. You are now ready to confirm your knowledge in the lab where you will configure your router to use PPP to connect to a WAN.

In this activity, you will design an addressing scheme, configure routing and VLANs, and configure PPP with CHAP. Detailed instructions are provided within the activity as well as in the PDF link below.

Activity Instructions (PDF)

Chapter Quiz

Take the chapter quiz to test your knowledge.

Your Chapter Notes

CHAPTER 3

Frame Relay

Introduction

Frame Relay is a high-performance WAN protocol that operates at the physical and Data Link layers of the OSI reference model.

Eric Scace, an engineer at Sprint International, invented Frame Relay as a simpler version of the X.25 protocol to use across Integrated Services Digital Network (ISDN) interfaces. Today, it is used over a variety of other network interfaces as well. When Sprint first implemented Frame Relay in its public network, they used StrataCom switches. Cisco's acquisition of StrataCom in 1996 marked their entry into the carrier market.

Network providers commonly implement Frame Relay for voice and data as an encapsulation technique, used between LANs over a WAN. Each end user gets a private line (or leased line) to a Frame Relay node. The Frame Relay network handles the transmission over a frequently changing path transparent to all end users.

Frame Relay has become one of the most extensively used WAN protocols, primarily because it is inexpensive compared to dedicated lines. In addition, configuring user equipment in a Frame Relay network is very simple. Frame Relay connections are created by configuring CPE routers or other devices to communicate with a service provider Frame Relay switch. The service provider configures the Frame Relay switch, which helps keep end-user configuration tasks to a minimum.

This chapter describes Frame Relay and explains how to configure Frame Relay on a Cisco router.

3.1 Basic Frame Relay Concepts

3.1.1 Introducing Frame Relay

Frame Relay: An Efficient and Flexible WAN Technology

Frame Relay has become the most widely used WAN technology in the world. Large enterprises, governments, ISPs, and small businesses use Frame Relay, primarily because of its price and flexibility. As organizations grow and depend more and more on reliable data transport, traditional leased-line solutions are prohibitively expensive. The pace of technological change, and mergers and acquisitions in the networking industry, demand and require more flexibility.

Frame Relay reduces network costs by using less equipment, less complexity, and an easier implementation. Moreover, Frame Relay provides greater bandwidth, reliability, and resiliency than private or leased lines. With increasing globalization and the growth of one-to-many branch office topologies, Frame Relay offers simpler network architecture and lower cost of ownership.

Using an example of a large enterprise network helps illustrate the benefits of using a Frame Relay WAN. In the example shown in the figure, Span Engineering has five campuses across North America. Like most organizations, Span's bandwidth requirements do not fit "a one size fits all" solution.

The first thing to consider is the bandwidth requirement of each site. Working out from the headquarters, the Chicago to New York connection requires a maximum speed of 256 kb/s. Three other sites need a maximum speed of 48 kb/s connecting to the headquarters, while the connection between the New York and Dallas branch offices requires only 12 kb/s.

Before Frame Relay became available, Span leased *dedicated lines*.

Click the Dedicated Lines button in the figure.

Using leased lines, each Span site is connected through a switch at the local telephone company's central office (CO) through the local loop, and then across the entire network. The Chicago and New York sites each use a dedicated T1 line (equivalent to 24 DS0 channels) to connect to the switch, while other sites use ISDN connections (56 kb/s). Because the Dallas site connects with both New York and Chicago, it has two locally leased lines. The network providers have provided Span with one DS0 between the respective COs, except for the larger pipe connecting Chicago to New York, which has four DS0s. DS0s are priced differently from region to region, and usually are offered at a fixed price. These lines are truly dedicated in that the network provider reserves that line for Span's own use. There is no sharing, and Span is paying for the end-to-end circuit regardless of how much bandwidth it uses.

A dedicated line provides little practical opportunity for a one-to-many connection without getting more lines from the network provider. In the example, almost all communication must flow through the corporate headquarters, simply to reduce the cost of additional lines.

If you examine what each site requires in terms of bandwidth, you notice a lack of efficiency:

- Of the 24 DS0 channels available in the T1 connection, the Chicago site only uses seven. Some carriers offer fractional T1 connections in increments of 64 kb/s, but this requires a specialized multiplexer at the customer end to channelize the signals. In this case, Span has opted for the full T1 service.
- Similarly, the New York site only uses five of its available 24 DS0s.
- Because Dallas needs to connect to Chicago and New York, there are two lines connecting through the CO to each site.

The leased-line design also limits flexibility. Unless circuits are already installed, connecting new sites typically requires new circuit installations and takes considerable time to implement. From a network *reliability* point of view, imagine the additional costs in money and complexity of adding spare and redundant circuits.

Click the Frame Relay button in the figure.

Span's Frame Relay network uses permanent virtual circuits (PVCs). A PVC is the logical path along an originating Frame Relay link, through the network, and along a terminating Frame Relay link to its ultimate destination. Compare this to the physical path used by a dedicated connection. In a network with Frame Relay access, a PVC uniquely defines the path between two endpoints. The concept of virtual circuits is discussed in more detail later in this section.

Span's Frame Relay solution provides both cost effectiveness and flexibility.

Cost Effectiveness of Frame Relay

Frame Relay is a more cost-effective option for two reasons. First, with dedicated lines, customers pay for an end-to-end connection. That includes the local loop and the network link. With Frame Relay, customers only pay for the local loop, and for the bandwidth they purchase from the network provider. Distance between nodes is not important. While in a dedicated-line model, customers use dedicated lines provided in increments of 64 kb/s, Frame Relay customers can define their virtual circuit needs in far greater granularity, often in increments as small as 4 kb/s.

The second reason for Frame Relay's cost effectiveness is that it shares bandwidth across a larger base of customers. Typically, a network provider can service 40 or more 56 kb/s customers over one T1 circuit. Using dedicated lines would require more DSU/CSUs (one for each line) and more complicated routing and switching. Network providers save because there is less equipment to purchase and maintain.

The Flexibility of Frame Relay

A virtual circuit provides considerable flexibility in network design. Looking at the figure, you can see that Span's offices all connect to the Frame Relay cloud over their respective local loops. What happens in the cloud is really of no concern at this time. All that matters is that when any Span office wants to communicate with any other Span office, all it needs to do is connect to a virtual circuit leading to the other office. In Frame Relay, the end of each connection has a number to identify it called a Data Link Connection Identifier (DLCI). Any station can connect with any other simply by stating the address of that station and DLCI number of the line it needs to use. In a later section, you will learn that when Frame Relay is configured, all the data from all the configured DLCIs flows through the same port of the router. Try to picture the same flexibility using dedicated lines. Not only is it complicated, but it also requires considerably more equipment.

Click the Cost button in the figure.

The table shows a representative cost comparison for comparable ISDN and Frame Relay connections. While initial costs for Frame Relay are higher than for ISDN, the monthly cost is considerably lower. Frame Relay is easier to manage and configure than ISDN. In addition, customers can increase their bandwidth as their needs grow in the future. Frame Relay customers pay only for the bandwidth they need. With Frame Relay, there are no hourly charges, while ISDN calls are metered and can result in unexpectedly high monthly charges from the telephone company if a full-time connection is maintained.

The next few topics will expand your understanding of Frame Relay by defining the key concepts introduced in the example.

Refer to
Figure
in online course

The Frame Relay WAN

In the late 1970s and into the early 1990s, the WAN technology joining the end sites was typically using the X.25 protocol. Now considered a legacy protocol, X.25 was a very popular packet switching technology because it provided a very reliable connection over unreliable cabling infrastructures. It did so by including additional error control and flow control. However, these additional features added overhead to the protocol. Its major application was for processing credit card authorization and for automatic teller machines. This course mentions X.25 only for historical purposes.

When you build a WAN, regardless of the transport you choose, there is always a minimum of three basic components, or groups of components, connecting any two sites. Each site needs its own equipment (DTE) to access the telephone company's CO serving the area (DCE). The third component sits in the middle, joining the two access points. In the figure, this is the portion supplied by the Frame Relay backbone.

Frame Relay has lower overhead than X.25 because it has fewer capabilities. For example, Frame Relay does not provide error correction, modern WAN facilities offer more reliable connection services and a higher degree of reliability than older facilities. The Frame Relay node simply drops packets without notification when it detects errors. Any necessary error correction, such as retransmission of data, is left to the endpoints. This makes propagation from customer end to customer end through the network very fast.

Frame Relay handles volume and speed efficiently by combining the necessary functions of the data link and Network layers into one simple protocol. As a data link protocol, Frame Relay provides access to a network, delimits and delivers frames in proper order, and recognizes transmission errors through a standard Cyclic Redundancy Check. As a network protocol, Frame Relay provides multiple logical connections over a single physical circuit and allows the network to route data over those connections to its intended destinations.

Frame Relay operates between an end-user device, such as a LAN *bridge* or router, and a network. The network itself can use any transmission method that is compatible with the speed and efficiency that Frame Relay applications require. Some networks use Frame Relay itself, but others use digital circuit switching or ATM cell relay systems. The figure shows a circuit-switching backbone as indicated by the Class 4/5 switches. The remaining graphics in this section show more contemporary packet-switching Frame Relay backbones.

Frame Relay Operation

The connection between a DTE device and a DCE device consists of both a Physical layer component and a link layer component:

- The physical component defines the mechanical, electrical, functional, and procedural specifications for the connection between the devices. One of the most commonly used Physical layer interface specifications is the RS-232 specification.

- The link layer component defines the protocol that establishes the connection between the DTE device, such as a router, and the DCE device, such as a switch.

When carriers use Frame Relay to interconnect LANs, a router on each LAN is the DTE. A serial connection, such as a T1/E1 leased line, connects the router to the Frame Relay switch of the carrier at the nearest point-of-presence (POP) for the carrier. The Frame Relay switch is a DCE device. Network switches move frames from one DTE across the network and deliver frames to other DTEs by way of DCEs. Computing equipment that is not on a LAN may also send data across a Frame Relay network. The computing equipment uses a Frame Relay access device (*FRAD*) as the DTE. The FRAD is sometimes referred to as a Frame Relay assembler/dissembler and is a dedicated appliance or a router configured to support Frame Relay. It is located on the customer's premises and connects to a switch port on the service provider's network. In turn, the service provider interconnects the Frame Relay switches.

3.1.2 Virtual Circuits

Virtual Circuits

The connection through a Frame Relay network between two DTEs is called a virtual circuit (VC). The circuits are virtual because there is no direct electrical connection from end to end. The connection is logical, and data moves from end to end, without a direct electrical circuit. With VCs, Frame Relay shares the bandwidth among multiple users and any single site can communicate with any other single site without using multiple dedicated physical lines.

There are two ways to establish VCs:

- SVCs, switched virtual circuits, are established dynamically by sending signaling messages to the network (CALL SETUP, DATA TRANSFER, IDLE, CALL TERMINATION).

- PVCs, permanent virtual circuits, are preconfigured by the carrier, and after they are set up, only operate in DATA TRANSFER and IDLE modes. Note that some publications refer to PVCs as private VCs.

Click the Play button in the figure.

In the figure, there is a VC between the sending and receiving nodes. The VC follows the path A, B, C, and D. Frame Relay creates a VC by storing input-port to output-port mapping in the memory of each switch and thus links one switch to another until a continuous path from one end of the circuit to the other is identified. A VC can pass through any number of intermediate devices (switches) located within the Frame Relay network.

The question you may ask at this point is, "How are the various nodes and switches identified?"

Click the Local Significance button in the figure.

VCs provide a bidirectional communication path from one device to another. VCs are identified by DLCIs. DLCI values typically are assigned by the Frame Relay service provider (for example, the telephone company). Frame Relay DLCIs have local significance, which means that the values themselves are not unique in the Frame Relay WAN. A DLCI identifies a VC to the equipment at an endpoint. A DLCI has no significance beyond the single link. Two devices connected by a VC may use a different DLCI value to refer to the same connection.

Locally significant DLCIs have become the primary method of addressing, because the same address can be used in several different locations while still referring to different connections. Local addressing prevents a customer from running out of DLCIs as the network grows.

Click the Idenfiying VCs button and click the Play button in the figure.

This is the same network as presented in the previous figure, but this time, as the frame moves across the network, Frame Relay labels each VC with a DLCI. The DLCI is stored in the address field of every frame transmitted to tell the network how the frame should be routed. The Frame Relay service provider assigns DLCI numbers. Usually, DLCIs 0 to 15 and 1008 to 1023 are reserved for special purposes. Therefore, service providers typically assign DLCIs in the range of 16 to 1007.

In this example, the frame uses DLCI 102. It leaves the router (R1) using Port 0 and VC 102. At switch A, the frame exits Port 1 using VC 432. This process of VC-port mapping continues through the WAN until the frame reaches its destination at DLCI 201, as shown in the figure. The DLCI is stored in the address field of every frame transmitted.

Refer to Figure in online course

Multiple VCs

Frame Relay is statistically multiplexed, meaning that it transmits only one frame at a time, but that many logical connections can co-exist on a single physical line. The Frame Relay Access Device (FRAD) or router connected to the Frame Relay network may have multiple VCs connecting it to various endpoints. Multiple VCs on a single physical line are distinguished because each VC has its own DLCI. Remember that the DLCI has only local significance and may be different at each end of a VC.

The figure shows an example of two VCs on a single access line, each with its own DLCI, attaching to a router (R1).

This capability often reduces the equipment and network complexity required to connect multiple devices, making it a very cost-effective replacement for a *mesh* of access lines. With this configuration, each endpoint needs only a single access line and interface. More savings arise as the capacity of the access line is based on the average bandwidth requirement of the VCs, rather than on the maximum bandwidth requirement.

Click the Span's DLCIs button in the figure.

For example, Span Engineering has five locations, with its headquarters in Chicago. Chicago is connected to the network using five VCs and each VC is given a DLCI. To see Chicago's respective DLCI mappings, click on the location in the table.

Cost Benefits of Multiple VCs

Recall the earlier example of how Span Engineering evolved from a dedicated-line network to a Frame Relay network. Specifically, look at the table comparing the cost of a single Frame Relay connection compared to a similar sized ISDN connection. Note that with Frame Relay, customers pay for the bandwidth they use. In effect, they pay for a Frame Relay port. When they increase the number of ports, as has been described above, they pay for more bandwidth. But will they pay for more equipment? The short answer is "no" because the ports are virtual. There is no change to the physical infrastructure. Compare this to purchasing more bandwidth using dedicated lines.

3.1.3 Frame Relay Encapsulation

The Frame Relay Encapsulation Process

Refer to Figure in online course

Frame Relay takes data packets from a Network layer protocol, such as IP or IPX, encapsulates them as the data portion of a Frame Relay frame, and then passes the frame to the Physical layer for delivery on the wire. To understand how this works, it is helpful to understand how it relates to the lower levels of the OSI model.

The figure shows how Frame Relay encapsulates data for transport and moves it down to the Physical layer for delivery.

First, Frame Relay accepts a packet from a Network layer protocol such as IP. It then wraps it with an address field that contains the DLCI and a *checksum*. Flag fields are added to indicate the beginning and end of the frame. The flag fields mark the start and end of the frame and are always the same. The flags are represented either as the hexadecimal number 7E or as the binary number 01111110. After the packet is encapsulated, Frame Relay passes the frame to the Physical layer for transport.

Click the Frame Format button in the figure.

The CPE router encapsulates each Layer 3 packet inside a Frame Relay header and *trailer* before sending it across the VC. The header and trailer are defined by the Link Access Procedure for Frame Relay (*LAPF*) Bearer Services specification, ITU Q.922-A. Specifically, the Frame Relay header (address field) contains the following:

- DLCI - The 10-bit DLCI is the essence of the Frame Relay header. This value represents the virtual connection between the DTE device and the switch. Each virtual connection that is multiplexed onto the physical channel is represented by a unique DLCI. The DLCI values have local significance only, which means that they are unique only to the physical channel on which they reside. Therefore, devices at opposite ends of a connection can use different DLCI values to refer to the same virtual connection.

- Extended Address (EA) - If the value of the EA field is 1, the current byte is determined to be the last DLCI octet. Although current Frame Relay implementations all use a two-octet DLCI, this capability does allow longer DLCIs in the future. The eighth bit of each byte of the Address field indicates the EA.

- C/R - Follows the most significant DLCI in the Address field. The C/R bit is not generally used by Frame Relay.

- *Congestion* Control - Contains 3 bits that control the Frame Relay congestion-notification mechanisms. The *FECN*, *BECN*, and *DE* bits are the last three bits in the Address field. Congestion control is discussed in a later topic.

The Physical layer is typically EIA/TIA-232, 449 or 530, V.35, or X.21. The Frame Relay frame is a subset of the HDLC frame type. Therefore, it is delimited with flag fields. The 1-byte flag uses the bit pattern 01111110. The FCS determines whether any errors in the Layer 2 address field occurred during transmission. The FCS is calculated prior to transmission by the sending node, and the result is inserted in the FCS field. At the distant end, a second FCS value is calculated and compared to the FCS in the frame. If the results are the same, the frame is processed. If there is a difference, the frame is discarded. Frame Relay does not notify the source when a frame is discarded. Error control is left to the upper layers of the OSI model.

3.1.4 Frame Relay Topologies

When more than two sites are to be connected, you must consider the topology of the connections between them. A topology is the map or visual layout of the Frame Relay network. You need to consider the topology from several perspectives to understand the network and the equipment used to build the network. Complete topologies for design, implementation, operation, and maintenance include overview maps, logical connection maps, functional maps, and address maps showing the detailed equipment and channel links.

Cost-effective Frame Relay networks link dozens and even hundreds of sites. Considering that a corporate network might span any number of service providers and include networks from acquired businesses differing in basic design, documenting topologies can be a very complicated process. However, every network or network segment can be viewed as being one of three topology types: star, *full mesh*, or *partial mesh*.

Star Topology (Hub and Spoke)

The simplest WAN topology is a star, as shown in the figure. In this topology, Span Engineering has a central site in Chicago that acts as a *hub* and hosts the primary services. Notice that Span has grown and recently opened an office in San Jose. Using Frame Relay made this expansion relatively easy.

Connections to each of the five remote sites act as spokes. In a star topology, the location of the hub is usually chosen by the lowest leased-line cost. When implementing a star topology with Frame Relay, each remote site has an access link to the Frame Relay cloud with a single VC.

Click the FR Star button in the figure.

This shows the star topology in the context of a Frame Relay cloud. The hub at Chicago has an access link with multiple VCs, one for each remote site. The lines going out from the cloud represent the connections from the Frame Relay service provider and terminate at the customer premises. These are typically lines ranging in speed from 56,000 bps to E-1 (2.048 Mb/s) and faster. One or more DLCI numbers are assigned to each line endpoint. Because Frame Relay costs are not distance related, the hub does not need to be in the geographical center of the network.

Full Mesh Topology

This figure represents a full mesh topology using dedicated lines. A full mesh topology suits a situation in which the services to be accessed are geographically dispersed and highly reliable access to them is required. A full mesh topology connects every site to every other site. Using leased-line interconnections, additional serial interfaces and lines add costs. In this example, 10 dedicated lines are required to interconnect each site in a full mesh topology.

Click FR Full Mesh on the figure.

Using Frame Relay, a network designer can build multiple connections simply by configuring additional VCs on each existing link. This software upgrade grows the star topology to a full mesh topology without the expense of additional hardware or dedicated lines. Since VCs use *statistical multiplexing*, multiple VCs on an access link generally make better use of Frame Relay than single VCs. The figure shows how Span has used four VCs on each link to scale its network without adding new hardware. Service providers will charge for the additional bandwidth, but this solution is usually more cost effective than using dedicated lines.

Partial Mesh Topology

For large networks, a full mesh topology is seldom affordable because the number of links required increases dramatically. The issue is not with the cost of the hardware, but because there is a theoretical limit of less than 1,000 VCs per link. In practice, the limit is less than that.

For this reason, larger networks are generally configured in a partial mesh topology. With partial mesh, there are more interconnections than required for a star arrangement, but not as many as for a full mesh. The actual pattern is dependant on the data flow requirements.

3.1.5 Frame Relay Address Mapping

Before a Cisco router is able to transmit data over Frame Relay, it needs to know which local DLCI maps to the Layer 3 address of the remote destination. Cisco routers support all Network layer protocols over Frame Relay, such as IP, IPX, and AppleTalk. This address-to-DLCI mapping can be accomplished either by static or dynamic mapping.

Inverse ARP

The Inverse Address Resolution Protocol, also called Inverse ARP, obtains Layer 3 addresses of other stations from Layer 2 addresses, such as the DLCI in Frame Relay networks. It is primarily used in Frame Relay and ATM networks, where Layer 2 addresses of VCs are sometimes obtained from Layer 2 signaling, and the corresponding Layer 3 addresses must be available before these VCs can be used. Whereas ARP resolves Layer 3 addresses to Layer 2 addresses, Inverse ARP does the opposite.

Dynamic Mapping

Dynamic *address mapping* relies on Inverse ARP to resolve a next *hop* network *protocol address* to a local DLCI value. The Frame Relay router sends out Inverse ARP requests on its PVC to discover the protocol address of the remote device connected to the Frame Relay network. The router uses the responses to populate an address-to-DLCI mapping table on the Frame Relay router or access server. The router builds and maintains this mapping table, which contains all resolved Inverse ARP requests, including both dynamic and static mapping entries.

The figure shows the output of the `show frame-relay map` command. You can see that the interface is up and that the destination IP address is 10.1.1.2. The DLCI identifies the logical connection being used to reach this interface. This value is displayed in three ways: its decimal value (102), its hexadecimal value (0x66), and its value as it would appear on the wire (0x1860). This is a static entry, not a dynamic entry. The link is using Cisco encapsulation as opposed to *IETF* encapsulation.

On Cisco routers, Inverse ARP is enabled by default for all protocols enabled on the physical interface. Inverse ARP packets are not sent out for protocols that are not enabled on the interface.

Click the Static Mapping button in the figure.

The user can choose to override dynamic Inverse ARP mapping by supplying a manual static mapping for the next hop protocol address to a local DLCI. A static map works similarly to dynamic Inverse ARP by associating a specified next hop protocol address to a local Frame Relay DLCI. You cannot use Inverse ARP and a map statement for the same DLCI and protocol.

An example of using static address mapping is a situation in which the router at the other side of the Frame Relay network does not support dynamic Inverse ARP for a specific network protocol. To provide accessibility, a static mapping is required to complete the remote Network layer address to local DLCI resolution.

Another example is on a hub-and-spoke Frame Relay network. Use static address mapping on the spoke routers to provide spoke-to-spoke reachability. Because the spoke routers do not have direct connectivity with each other, dynamic Inverse ARP would not work between them. Dynamic Inverse ARP relies on the presence of a direct point-to-point connection between two ends. In this case, dynamic Inverse ARP only works between hub and spoke, and the spokes require static mapping to provide reachability to each other.

Configuring Static Mapping

Establishing static mapping depends on your network needs. Here are the various commands to use:

To map between a next hop protocol address and DLCI *destination address*, use this command:
`frame-relay map protocol` *protocol-address dlci* [broadcast] [`ietf`] [`cisco`].

Use the keyword `ietf` when connecting to a non-Cisco router.

You can greatly simplify the configuration for the *Open Shortest Path First* (OSPF) protocol by adding the optional `broadcast` keyword when doing this task.

The figure provides an example of static mapping on a Cisco router. In this example, static address mapping is performed on interface serial 0/0/0, and the Frame Relay encapsulation used on DLCI 102 is CISCO. As seen in the configuration steps, static mapping of the address using the `frame-relay map` command allows users to select the type of Frame Relay encapsulation used on a per-VC basis. Static mapping configuration is discussed in more detail in the next section.

Local Management Interface (*LMI*)

A review of networking history will help you to understand the role played by the Local Management Interface (LMI). The Frame Relay design provides packet-switched data transfer with minimum end-to-end delays. The original design omits anything that might contribute to delay.

When vendors implemented Frame Relay as a separate technology rather than as one component of ISDN, they decided that there was a need for DTEs to dynamically acquire information about the status of the network. However, the original design did not include this feature. A consortium of Cisco, Digital Equipment Corporation (DEC), Northern Telecom, and StrataCom extended the Frame Relay protocol to provide additional capabilities for complex internetworking environments. These extensions are referred to collectively as the LMI.

Basically, the LMI is a keepalive mechanism that provides status information about Frame Relay connections between the router (DTE) and the Frame Relay switch (DCE). Every 10 seconds or so, the end device polls the network, either requesting a dumb sequenced response or channel status information. If the network does not respond with the requested information, the user device may consider the connection to be down. When the network responds with a FULL STATUS response, it includes status information about DLCIs that are allocated to that line. The end device can use this information to determine whether the logical connections are able to pass data.

The figure shows the output of the `show frame-relay lmi` command. The output shows the LMI type used by the Frame Relay interface and the counters for the LMI status exchange sequence, including errors such as LMI timeouts.

It is easy to confuse the LMI and encapsulation. The LMI is a definition of the messages used between the DTE (R1) and the DCE (the Frame Relay switch owned by the service provider). Encapsulation defines the headers used by a DTE to communicate information to the DTE at the other end of a VC. The switch and its connected router care about using the same LMI. The switch does not care about the encapsulation. The endpoint routers (DTEs) do care about the encapsulation.

LMI Extensions

In addition to the Frame Relay protocol functions for transferring data, the Frame Relay specification includes optional LMI extensions that are extremely useful in an internetworking environment. Some of the extensions include:

- *VC status messages* - Provide information about PVC integrity by communicating and synchronizing between devices, periodically reporting the existence of new PVCs and the deletion of already existing PVCs. VC status messages prevent data from being sent into *black holes* (PVCs that no longer exist).

- *Multicasting* - Allows a sender to transmit a single frame that is delivered to multiple recipients. Multicasting supports the efficient delivery of routing protocol messages and *address resolution* procedures that are typically sent to many destinations simultaneously.

- *Global addressing* - Gives connection identifiers global rather than local significance, allowing them to be used to identify a specific interface to the Frame Relay network. Global addressing makes the Frame Relay network resemble a LAN in terms of addressing, and ARPs perform exactly as they do over a LAN.

- *Simple flow control* - Provides for an XON/XOFF flow control mechanism that applies to the entire Frame Relay interface. It is intended for those devices whose higher layers cannot use the congestion notification bits and need some level of flow control.

Click the LMI Identifiers button in the figure.

The 10-bit DLCI field supports 1,024 VC identifiers: 0 through 1023. The LMI extensions reserve some of these identifiers, thereby reducing the number of permitted VCs. LMI messages are exchanged between the DTE and DCE using these reserved DLCIs.

There are several LMI types, each of which is incompatible with the others. The LMI type configured on the router must match the type used by the service provider. Three types of LMIs are supported by Cisco routers:

- Cisco - Original LMI extension
- Ansi - Corresponding to the *ANSI* standard T1.617 Annex D
- q933a - Corresponding to the ITU standard Q933 Annex A

Starting with *Cisco IOS software* release 11.2, the default LMI autosense feature detects the LMI type supported by the directly connected Frame Relay switch. Based on the LMI status messages it receives from the Frame Relay switch, the router automatically configures its interface with the supported LMI type acknowledged by the Frame Relay switch.

If it is necessary to set the LMI type, use the **frame-relay lmi-type [cisco | ansi | q933a]** interface configuration command. Configuring the LMI type, disables the autosense feature.

When manually setting up the LMI type, you must configure the *keepalive interval* on the Frame Relay interface to prevent status exchanges between the router and the switch from timing out. The LMI status exchange messages determine the status of the PVC connection. For example, a large mismatch in the keepalive interval on the router and the switch can cause the switch to declare the router dead.

By default, the keepalive time interval is 10 seconds on Cisco serial interfaces. You can change the keepalive interval with the **keepalive** interface configuration command.

Refer to Figure in online course

Setting the LMI type and configuring the keepalive are practiced in a following activity.

LMI Frame Format

LMI messages are carried in a variant of LAPF frames. The address field carries one of the reserved DLCIs. Following the DLCI field are the control, protocol discriminator, and call reference fields that do not change. The fourth field indicates the LMI message type.

Status messages help verify the integrity of logical and physical links. This information is critical in a routing environment because routing protocols make decisions based on link integrity.

Using LMI and Inverse ARP to Map Addresses

LMI status messages combined with Inverse ARP messages allow a router to associate Network layer and Data Link layer addresses.

Click the LMI 1 button and play to watch how the LMI process begins.

In this example, when R1 connects to the Frame Relay network, it sends an LMI status inquiry message to the network. The network replies with an LMI status message containing details of every VC configured on the access link.

Periodically, the router repeats the status inquiry, but subsequent responses include only status changes. After a set number of these abbreviated responses, the network sends a full status message.

Click the LMI 2 button and play to see the next stage.

If the router needs to map the VCs to Network layer addresses, it sends an Inverse ARP message on each VC. The Inverse ARP message includes the Network layer address of the router, so the remote DTE, or router, can also perform the mapping. The Inverse ARP reply allows the router to make the necessary mapping entries in its address-to-DLCI map table. If several Network layer protocols are supported on the link, Inverse ARP messages are sent for each one.

Activity: Basic Frame Relay Concepts

3.2 Configuring Frame Relay

3.2.1 Configuring Basic Frame Relay

Frame Relay Configuration Tasks

Frame Relay is configured on a Cisco router from the Cisco IOS command-line interface (*CLI*). This section outlines the required steps to enable Frame Relay on your network, as well as some of the optional steps that you can use to enhance or customize your configuration.

The figure shows the basic setup model used for this discussion. Later in this section, additional hardware will be added to the diagram to help explain more complex configuration tasks. In this section, you will configure the Cisco routers as Frame Relay access devices, or DTE, connected directly to a dedicated Frame Relay switch, or DCE.

The figure shows a typical Frame Relay configuration and lists the steps to follow. These are explained and practiced in this chapter.

Enable Frame Relay Encapsulation

This first figure, displays how Frame Relay has been configured on the serial interfaces. This involves assigning an IP address, setting the encapsulation type, and allocating bandwidth. The figure shows routers at each end of the Frame Relay link with the configuration scripts for routers R1 and R2.

Step 1. Setting the IP Address on the Interface

On a Cisco router, Frame Relay is most commonly supported on synchronous serial interfaces. Use the `ip address` command to set the IP address of the interface. You can see that R1 has been assigned 10.1.1.1/24, and R2 has been assigned IP address 10.1.1.2/24.

Step 2. Configuring Encapsulation

The `encapsulation frame-relay` interface configuration command enables Frame Relay encapsulation and allows Frame Relay processing on the supported interface. There are two encapsulation options to choose from, and these are described below.

Step 3. Setting the Bandwidth

Use the `bandwidth` command to set the bandwidth of the serial interface. Specify bandwidth in kb/s. This command notifies the routing protocol that bandwidth is statically configured on the link. The EIGRP and OSPF routing protocols use the bandwidth value to calculate and determine the *metric* of the link.

Step 4. Setting the LMI Type (optional)

This is an optional step as Cisco routers autosense the LMI type. Recall that Cisco supports three LMI types: Cisco, ANSI Annex D, and Q933-A Annex A and that the default LMI type for Cisco routers is cisco.

Encapsulation Options

Recall that the default encapsulation type on a serial interface on a Cisco router is the Cisco proprietary version of HDLC. To change the encapsulation from HDLC to Frame Relay, use the `encapsulation frame-relay [cisco | ietf]` command. The **no** form of the `encapsulation frame-relay` command removes the Frame Relay encapsulation on the interface and returns the interface to the default HDLC encapsulation.

The default Frame Relay encapsulation enabled on supported interfaces is the Cisco encapsulation. Use this option if connecting to another Cisco router. Many non-Cisco devices also support this encapsulation type. It uses a 4-byte header, with 2 bytes to identify the DLCI and 2 bytes to identify the packet type.

The IETF encapsulation type complies with RFC 1490 and RFC 2427. Use this option if connecting to a non-Cisco router.

Click the Verifying Configuration button in the figure.

This output of the `show interfaces serial` command verifies the configuration.

3.2.2 Configuring Static Frame Relay Maps

Configuring a Static Frame Relay Map

Cisco routers support all Network layer protocols over Frame Relay, such as IP, IPX, and AppleTalk, and the address-to-DLCI mapping can be accomplished either by dynamic or static address mapping.

Dynamic mapping is performed by the Inverse ARP feature. Because Inverse ARP is enabled by default, no additional command is required to configure dynamic mapping on an interface.

Static mapping is manually configured on a router. Establishing static mapping depends on your network needs. To map between a next hop protocol address and a DLCI destination address, use the `frame-relay map` *protocol protocol-address dlci* `[broadcast]` command.

Using the Broadcast Keyword

Frame Relay, ATM, and X.25 are nonbroadcast multiaccess (*NBMA*) networks. NBMA networks allow only data transfer from one computer to another over a VC or across a switching device. NBMA networks do not support multicast or broadcast traffic, so a single packet cannot reach all destinations. This requires you to broadcast to replicate the packets manually to all destinations.

Some routing protocols may require additional additional configuration options. For example, RIP, EIGRP and OSPF require additional configurations to be supported on NBMA networks.

Because NBMA does not support broadcast traffic, using the **broadcast** keyword is a simplified way to forward *routing updates*. The **broadcast** keyword allows broadcasts and multicasts over the PVC and, in effect, turns the broadcast into a *unicast* so that the other node gets the routing updates.

In the example configuration, R1 uses the `frame-relay map` command to map the VC to R2.

Click the Parameters button in the figure.

The figure shows how to use the keywords when configuring static address maps.

Click the Verify button in the figure.

To verify the Frame Relay mapping, use the `show frame-relay map` command.

In this activity, you will configure two static Frame Relay maps on each router to reach two other routers. Although the LMI type is autosensed on the routers, you will statically assign the type by manually configuring the LMI. Detailed instructions are provided within the activity as well as in the PDF link below.

Activity Instructions (PDF)

3.3 Advanced Frame Relay Concepts

3.3.1 Solving Reachability Issues

Split Horizon

By default, a Frame Relay network provides NBMA connectivity between remote sites. NBMA clouds usually use a hub-and-spoke topology. Unfortunately, a basic routing operation based on the split horizon principle can cause reachability issues on a Frame Relay NBMA network.

Recall that split horizon is a technique used to prevent a routing loop in networks using distance vector routing protocols. Split horizon updates reduce routing loops by preventing a routing update received on one interface to be forwarded out the same interface.

The figure shows R2, a spoke router, sending a broadcast routing update to R1, the hub router.

Routers that support multiple connections over a single physical interface have many PVCs terminating on a single interface. R1 must replicate broadcast packets, such as routing update broadcasts, on each PVC to the remote routers. The replicated broadcast packets can consume bandwidth and cause significant latency to user traffic. The amount of broadcast traffic and the number of VCs terminating at each router should be evaluated during the design phase of a Frame Relay network. Overhead traffic, such as routing updates, can affect the delivery of critical user data, especially when the delivery path contains low-bandwidth (56 kb/s) links.

Click the Split Horizon Problem button in the figure.

R1 has multiple PVCs on a single physical interface, so the split horizon rule prevents R1 from *forwarding* that routing update through the same physical interface to other remote spoke routers (R3).

Disabling split horizon may seem to be a simple solution because it allows routing updates to be forwarded out the same physical interface from which they came. However, only IP allows you to disable split horizon; IPX and AppleTalk do not. Also, disabling split horizon increases the chance of routing loops in any network. Split horizon could be disabled for physical interfaces with a single PVC.

The next obvious solution to solve the split horizon problem is to use a fully meshed topology. However, this is expensive because more PVCs are required. The preferred solution is to use subinterfaces, which is explained in the next topic.

Frame Relay Subinterfaces

Frame Relay can partition a physical interface into multiple virtual interfaces called subinterfaces. A subinterface is simply a logical interface that is directly associated with a physical interface. Therefore, a Frame Relay subinterface can be configured for each of the PVCs coming into a physical serial interface.

To enable the forwarding of broadcast routing updates in a Frame Relay network, you can configure the router with logically assigned subinterfaces. A partially meshed network can be divided into a number of smaller, fully meshed, point-to-point networks. Each point-to-point *subnetwork* can be assigned a unique network address, which allows packets received on a physical interface to be sent out the same physical interface because the packets are forwarded on VCs in different subinterfaces.

Frame Relay subinterfaces can be configured in either point-to-point or multipoint mode:

- Point-to-point - A single point-to-point subinterface establishes one PVC connection to another physical interface or subinterface on a remote router. In this case, each pair of the point-to-point routers is on its own subnet, and each point-to-point subinterface has a single DLCI. In a point-to-point environment, each subinterface is acting like a point-to-point interface. Typically, there is a separate subnet for each point-to-point VC. Therefore, routing update traffic is not subject to the split horizon rule.

- Multipoint - A single multipoint subinterface establishes multiple PVC connections to multiple physical interfaces or subinterfaces on remote routers. All the participating interfaces are in the same subnet. The subinterface acts like an NBMA Frame Relay interface, so routing update traffic is subject to the split horizon rule. Typically, all multipoint VCs belong to the same subnet.

The figure illustrates two types of subinterfaces supported by Cisco routers.

In split horizon routing environments, routing updates received on one subinterface can be sent out another subinterface. In a subinterface configuration, each VC can be configured as a point-to-point connection. This allows each subinterface to act similarly to a leased line. Using a Frame Relay point-to-point subinterface, each pair of the point-to-point routers is on its own subnet.

The `encapsulation frame-relay` command is assigned to the physical interface. All other configuration items, such as the Network layer address and DLCIs, are assigned to the subinterface.

You can use multipoint configurations to conserve addresses. This can be especially helpful if *Variable Length Subnet Masking* is not being used. However, multipoint configurations may not work properly given the broadcast traffic and split horizon considerations. The point-to-point subinterface option was created to avoid these issues.

Roll over Point-to-Point subinterface and Multipoint subinterface in the figure for summary descriptions.

Configuring subinterfaces is explained and practiced in the next section.

3.3.2 Paying for Frame Relay

Key Terminology

Refer to Figure in online course

Service providers build Frame Relay networks using very large and very powerful switches, but as a customer, your devices only see the switch interface of the service provider. Customers are usually not exposed to the inner workings of the network, which may be built on very high-speed technologies, such as T1, T3, SONET, or ATM.

From a customer's point of view then, Frame Relay is an interface and one or more PVCs. Customers simply buy Frame Relay services from a service provider. However, before considering how to pay for Frame Relay services, there are some key terms and concepts to learn, as illustrated in the figure:

- *Access rate or port speed* - From a customer's point of view, the service provider provides a serial connection or access link to the Frame Relay network over a leased line. The speed of the line is the access speed or port speed. Access rate is the rate at which your access circuits join the Frame Relay network. These are typically at 56 kb/s, T1 (1.536 Mb/s), or Fractional T1 (a multiple of 56 kb/s or 64 kb/s). Port speeds are clocked on the Frame Relay switch. It is not possible to send data at higher than port speed.

- *Committed Information Rate (CIR)* - Customers negotiate CIRs with service providers for each PVC. The CIR is the amount of data that the network receives from the access circuit. The service provider guarantees that the customer can send data at the CIR. All frames received at or below the CIR are accepted.

A great advantage of Frame Relay is that any network capacity that is being unused is made available or shared with all customers, usually at no extra charge. This allows customers to "burst" over their CIR as a bonus. Bursting is explained in the next topic.

Click the Example button in the figure.

In this example, aside from any CPE costs, the customer pays for three Frame Relay cost components as follows:

- Access or port speed: The cost of the access line from the DTE to the DCE (customer to service provider). This line is charged based on the port speed that has been negotiated and installed.

- PVC: This cost component is based on the PVCs. Once a PVC is established, the additional cost to increase CIR is typically small and can be done in small (4 kb/s) increments.

- CIR: Customers normally choose a CIR lower than the port speed or access rate. This allows them to take advantage of bursts.

In the example, the customer is paying for the following:

- An access line with a rate of 64 kb/s connecting their DCE to the DCE of the service provider through serial port S0/0/0.

- Two virtual ports, one at 32 kb/s and the other at 16 kb/s.

- A CIR of 48 kb/s across the entire Frame Relay network. This is usually a flat charge and not connected to the distance.

Oversubscription

Service providers sometimes sell more capacity than they have on the assumption that not everyone will demand their entitled capacity all of the time. This oversubscription is analogous to airlines selling more seats than they have in the expectation that some of the booked customers will not show up. Because of oversubscription, there will be instances when the sum of CIRs from multiple PVCs to a given location is higher than the port or access channel rate. This can cause traffic issues, such as congestion and dropped traffic.

Bursting

A great advantage of Frame Relay is that any network capacity that is being unused is made available or shared with all customers, usually at no extra charge.

Using the previous example, the figure shows an access rate on serial port S0/0/0 of router R1 to be 64 kb/s. This is higher than the combined CIRs of the two PVCs. Under normal circumstances, the two PVCs should not transmit more than 32 kb/s and 16 kb/s, respectively. As long as the amount of data the two PVCs are sending does not exceed its CIR, it should get through the network.

Because the physical circuits of the Frame Relay network are shared between subscribers, there will often be time where there is excess bandwidth available. Frame Relay can allow customers to dynamically access this extra bandwidth and "burst" over their CIR for free.

Bursting allows devices that temporarily need additional bandwidth to borrow it at no extra cost from other devices not using it. For example, if PVC 102 is transferring a large file, it could use any of the 16 kb/s not being used by PVC 103. A device can burst up to the access rate and still expect the data to get through. The duration of a burst transmission should be short, less than three or four seconds.

Various terms are used to describe burst rates including the Committed Burst Information Rate (CBIR) and Excess Burst (*BE*) size.

The CBIR is a negotiated rate above the CIR which the customer can use to transmit for short burst. It allows traffic to burst to higher speeds, as available network bandwidth permits. However, it cannot exceed the port speed of the link. A device can burst up to the CBIR and still expect the data to get through. The duration of a burst transmission should be short, less than three or four seconds. If long bursts persist, then a higher CIR should be purchased.

For example, DLCI 102 has a CIR of 32 kb/s with an additional CBIR of 16 kb/s for a total of up to 48 kb/s. Frames submitted at this level are marked as Discard Eligible (*DE*) in the frame header, indicating that they may be dropped if there is congestion or there is not enough capacity in the network. Frames within the negotiated CIR are not eligible for discard (DE = 0). Frames above the CIR have the DE bit set to 1, marking it as eligible to be discarded, should the network be congested.

The BE is the term used to describe the bandwidth available above the CBIR up to the access rate of the link. Unlike the CBIR, it is not negotiated. Frames may be transmitted at this level but will most likely be dropped.

Click the Bursting button in the figure.

The figure illustrates the relationship between the various bursting terms.

3.3.3 Frame Relay Flow Control

Frame Relay reduces network overhead by implementing simple congestion-notification mechanisms rather than explicit, per-VC flow control. These congestion-notification mechanisms are the Forward Explicit Congestion Notification (*FECN*) and the Backward Explicit Congestion Notification (*BECN*).

To help understand the mechanisms, the graphic showing the structure of the Frame Relay frame is presented for review. FECN and BECN are each controlled by a single bit contained in the frame header. They let the router know that there is congestion and that the router should stop transmission until the condition is reversed. BECN is a direct notification. FECN is an indirect one.

The frame header also contains a Discard Eligibility (DE) bit, which identifies less important traffic that can be dropped during periods of congestion. DTE devices can set the value of the DE bit to 1 to indicate that the frame has lower importance than other frames. When the network becomes congested, DCE devices discard the frames with the DE bit set to 1 before discarding those that do not. This reduces the likelihood of critical data being dropped during periods of congestion.

In periods of congestion, the provider's Frame Relay switch applies the following logic rules to each incoming frame based on whether the CIR is exceeded:

- If the incoming frame does not exceed the CIR, the frame is passed.
- If an incoming frame exceeds the CIR, it is marked DE.
- If an incoming frame exceeds the CIR plus the BE, it is discarded.

Click the Queuing button in the figure and click play in the animation.

Frames arriving at a switch are queued or buffered prior to forwarding. As in any queuing system, it is possible that there will be an excessive buildup of frames at a switch. This causes delays. Delays lead to unnecessary retransmissions that occur when higher level protocols receive no acknowledgment within a set time. In severe cases, this can cause a serious drop in network throughput. To avoid this problem, Frame Relay incorporates a flow control feature.

The figure shows a switch with a filling queue. To reduce the flow of frames to the queue, the switch notifies DTEs of the problem using the Explicit Congestion Notification bits in the frame address field.

- The FECN bit, indicated by the "F" in the figure, is set on every frame that the upstream switch *receives* on the congested link.
- The BECN bit, indicated by the "B" in the figure, is set on every frame that the switch *places* onto the congested link to the downstream switch.

DTEs receiving frames with the ECN bits set are expected to try to reduce the flow of frames until the congestion clears.

If the congestion occurs on an internal trunk, DTEs may receive notification even though they are not the cause of the congestion.

Activity: Advance Frame Relay Concepts

3.4 Configuring Advanced Frame Relay

3.4.1 Configuring Frame Relay Subinterfaces

Recall that using Frame Relay subinterfaces ensures that a single physical interface is treated as multiple virtual interfaces to overcome split horizon rules. Packets received on one virtual interface can be forwarded to another virtual interface, even if they are configured on the same physical interface.

Subinterfaces address the limitations of Frame Relay networks by providing a way to subdivide a partially meshed Frame Relay network into a number of smaller, fully meshed (or point-to-point) subnetworks. Each subnetwork is assigned its own *network number* and appears to the protocols as if it were reachable through a separate interface. Point-to-point subinterfaces can be unnumbered for use with IP, reducing the addressing burden that might otherwise result.

To create a subinterface, use the `interface serial` command. Specify the port number, followed by a period (.) and the subinterface number. To make troubleshooting easier, use the DLCI as the subinterface number. You must also specify whether the interface is point-to-point or point-to-multipoint using either the `multipoint` or `point-to-point` keyword because there is no default. These keywords are defined in the figure.

The following command creates a point-to-point subinterface for PVC 103 to R3: R1(config-if)#`interface serial 0/0/0.103 point-to-point`.

Click the DLCI button in the figure.

If the subinterface is configured as point-to-point, the local DLCI for the subinterface must also be configured to distinguish it from the physical interface. The DLCI is also required for multipoint subinterfaces for which Inverse ARP is enabled. It is not required for multipoint subinterfaces configured with static maps.

The Frame Relay service provider assigns the DLCI numbers. These numbers range from 16 to 991, and usually have only local significance. The range varies depending on the LMI used.

The `frame-relay interface-dlci` command configures the local DLCI on the subinterface. For example: R1(config-subif)#`frame-relay interface-dlci 103`.

Note: Unfortunately, altering an exiting Frame Relay subinterface configuration may fail to provide the expected result. In these situations, it may be necessary to save the configuration and reload the router.

Refer to
Figure
in online course

Configuring Subinterfaces Example

In the figure, R1 has two point-to-point subinterfaces. The s0/0.0.102 subinterface connects to R2, and the s0/0/0.103 subinterface connects to R3. Each subinterface is on a different subnet.

To configure subinterfaces on a physical interface, the following steps are required:

Step 1. Remove any Network layer address assigned to the physical interface. If the physical interface has an address, frames are not received by the local subinterfaces.

Step 2. Configure Frame Relay encapsulation on the physical interface using the `encapsulation frame-relay` command.

Step 3. For each of the defined PVCs, create a logical subinterface. Specify the port number, followed by a period (.) and the subinterface number. To make troubleshooting easier, it is suggested that the subinterface number matches the DLCI number.

Step 4. Configure an IP address for the interface and set the bandwidth.

At this point, we will configure the DLCI. Recall that the Frame Relay service provider assigns the DLCI numbers.

Step 5. Configure the local DLCI on the subinterface using the `frame-relay interface-dlci` command.

3.4.2 Verifying Frame Relay Operation

> Refer to
> **Figure**
> in online course

Frame Relay is generally a very reliable service. Nonetheless, there are times when the network performs at less than expected levels and troubleshooting is necessary. For example, users may report slow and intermittent connections across the circuit. Circuits may go down. Regardless of the reason, network outages are very expensive in terms of lost productivity. A recommended best practice is to verify your configuration before problems appear.

In this topic, you will step though a verification procedure to ensure everything is working correctly before you launch your configuration on a live network.

Verify Frame Relay Interfaces

After configuring a Frame Relay PVC and when troubleshooting an issue, verify that Frame Relay is operating correctly on that interface using the **show interfaces** command.

Recall that with Frame Relay, the router is normally considered a DTE device. However, a Cisco router can be configured as a Frame Relay switch. In such cases, the router becomes a DCE device when it is configured as a Frame Relay switch.

The **show interfaces** command displays how the encapsulation is set up, along with useful Layer 1 and Layer 2 status information, including:

- LMI type
- LMI DLCI
- Frame Relay DTE/DCE type

The first step is always to confirm that the interfaces are properly configured. The figure shows a sample output for the **show interfaces** command. Among other things, you can see details about the encapsulation, the DLCI on the Frame Relay-configured serial interface, and the DLCI used for the LMI. You should confirm that these values are the expected values. If not, you may need to make changes.

Click on the LMI button in the figure to verify LMI performance.

The next step is to look at some LMI statistics using the **show frame-relay lmi** command. In the output, look for any non-zero "Invalid" items. This helps isolate the problem to a Frame Relay communications issue between the carrier's switch and your router.

The figure displays a sample output that shows the number of status messages exchanged between the local router and the local Frame Relay switch.

Now look at the statistics for the interface.

Click the PVC Status button in the figure to verify PVC status.

Use the **show frame-relay pvc** [**interface** *interface*] [**dlci**] command to view PVC and traffic statistics. This command is also useful for viewing the number of BECN and FECN packets received by the router. The PVC status can be active, inactive, or deleted.

The **show frame-relay pvc** command displays the status of all the PVCs configured on the router. You can also specify a particular PVC. Click PVC Status in th figure to see a sample output of the **show frame-relay pvc 102** command.

Once you have gathered all the statistics, use the **clear counters** command to reset the statistics counters. Wait 5 or 10 minutes after clearing the counters before issuing the **show** commands again. Note any additional errors. If you need to contact the carrier, these statistics help in resolving the issues.

A final task is to confirm whether the **frame-relay inverse-arp** command resolved a remote IP address to a local DLCI. Use the **show frame-relay map** command to display the current map entries and information about the connections.

Click the Inverse ARP button in the figure.

The output shows the following information:

- 10.140.1.1 is the IP address of the remote router, dynamically learned via the Inverse ARP process.
- 100 is the decimal value of the local DLCI number.
- 0x64 is the hex conversion of the DLCI number, 0x64 = 100 decimal.
- 0x1840 is the value as it would appear on the wire because of the way the DLCI bits are spread out in the address field of the Frame Relay frame.
- Broadcast/multicast is enabled on the PVC.
- PVC status is active.

To clear dynamically created Frame Relay maps that are created using Inverse ARP, use the **clear frame-relay-inarp** command. **Click the Clear Maps button** to see an example of this step.

3.4.3 Troubleshooting Frame Relay Configuration

If the verification procedure indicates that your Frame Relay configuration is not working properly, you need to troubleshoot the configuration.

Use the **debug frame-relay lmi** command to determine whether the router and the Frame Relay switch are sending and receiving LMI packets properly.

Look at the figure and examine the output of an LMI exchange.

- "out" is an LMI status message sent by the router.
- "in" is a message received from the Frame Relay switch.
- A full LMI status message is a "type 0" (not shown in the figure).
- An LMI exchange is a "type 1".
- "dlci 100, status 0x2" means that the status of DLCI 100 is active (not shown in figure).

When an Inverse ARP request is made, the router updates its map table with three possible LMI connection states. These states are active state, inactive state, and deleted state

- ACTIVE States indicates a successful end-to-end (DTE to DTE) circuit.
- INACTIVE State indicates a successful connection to the switch (DTE to DCE) without a DTE detected on the other end of the PVC. This can occur due to residual or incorrect configuration on the switch.
- DELETED State indicates that the DTE is configured for a DLCI the switch does not recognize as valid for that interface.

The possible values of the status field are as follows:

- 0x0 - The switch has this DLCI programmed, but for some reason it is not usable. The reason could possibly be the other end of the PVC is down.
- 0x2 - The Frame Relay switch has the DLCI and everything is operational.
- 0x4 - The Frame Relay switch does not have this DLCI programmed for the router, but that it was programmed at some point in the past. This could also be caused by the DLCIs being reversed on the router, or by the PVC being deleted by the service provider in the Frame Relay cloud.

Simulation: Configuring Frame Relay Point-to-Point Subinterfaces

3.5 Chapter Labs

3.5.1 Basic Frame Relay

In this lab, you will learn how to configure Frame Relay encapsulation on serial links using the network shown in the topology diagram. You will also learn how to configure a router as a Frame Relay switch. There are both Cisco standards and Open standards that apply to Frame Relay. You will learn both. Pay special attention in the lab section in which you intentionally break the Frame Relay configurations. This will help you in the Troubleshooting lab associated with this chapter.

3.5.2 Challenge Frame Relay Configuration

In this lab, you will configure Frame Relay using the network shown in the topology diagram. If you need assistance, refer to the Basic Frame Relay lab. However, try to do as much on your own as possible.

3.5.3 Troubleshooting Frame Relay

In this lab, you will practice troubleshooting a misconfigured Frame Relay environment. Load or have your instructor load the configurations below into your routers. Locate and repair all errors in the configurations and establish end-to-end connectivity. Your final configuration should match the topology diagram and addressing table.

Chapter Summary

Frame Relay provides greater bandwidth, reliability, and resiliency than private or leased lines. Frame Relay has reduced network costs by using less equipment, less complexity, and by providing easier implementation. For these reasons, Frame Relay has become the most widely used WAN technology in the world.

A Frame Relay connection between a DTE device at the LAN edge and a DCE device at the carrier edge has a link layer component and a physical layer component. Frame Relay takes data packets and encapsulates them in a Frame Relay frame, and then passes the frame to the Physical layer for delivery on the wire. The connection across the carrier network is a VC identified by a DLCI. Multiple VCs can be multiplexed using a FRAD. Frame Relay networks usually use a partial mesh topology optimized to the data flow requirements of the carrier's customer base.

Frame Relay uses Inverse ARP to map DCLIs to the IP addresses of remote locations. Dynamic address mapping relies on Inverse ARP to resolve a next hop network protocol address to a local DLCI value. The Frame Relay router sends out Inverse ARP requests on its PVC to discover the protocol address of the remote device connected to the Frame Relay network. DTE Frame Relay routers use the LMI to provide status information about their connection with the DCE Frame Relay switch. LMI extensions provide additional internetworking information.

The first two tasks in configuring Frame Relay on a Cisco router are to enable Frame Relay encapsulation on the interface and then configure either static of dynamic mapping. After this, there are a number of optional tasks that can be completed as required including configuring the LMI, VCs, `traffic shaping` and customizing Frame Relay on your network. Monitoring maintaining Frame Relay connections is the final task.

Frame Relay configuration must consider the split horizon problem which arises when multiple VCs converge on a single physical interface. Frame Relay can partition a physical interface into multiple virtual interfaces called subinterfaces. Subinterface configuration was also explained and practiced.

The configuration of Frame Relay is affected by the way in which service providers charge for connections using units of access rates and committed information rates (CIR). An advantage of these charging schemes is that unused network capacity is available or shared with all customers, usually at no extra charge. This allows users to burst traffic for short periods.

Configuring flow control in a Frame Relay network is also affected by service provider charging schemes. You can configure queuing and shape traffic according to the CIR. DTEs can be configured to control congestion in the network by adding BECN and FECN bits to frame addresses. DTEs can also be configured to set a discard eligible bit indicting that the frame may be discarded in preference to other frames if congestion occurs. Frames that are sent in excess of the CIR are marked as "discard eligible" (DE) which means they can be dropped should congestion occur within the frame relay network.

Finally, once having configured Frame Relay, you learned how to verify and troubleshoot the connections.

This activity allows you to practice a variety of skills, including configuring Frame Relay, PPP with CHAP, static and default routing, VTP, and VLAN. Because there are close to 150 graded components in this activity, you may not see the completion percentage increase every time you configure a graded command. You can always click **Check Results** and **Assessment Items** to see if you correctly entered a graded command. Detailed instructions are provided within the activity as well as in the PDF link below.

Activity Instructions (PDF)

> Go to the online course to take the quiz.

Chapter Quiz

Take the chapter quiz to test your knowledge.

Your Chapter Notes

CHAPTER 4

Network Security

Chapter Introduction

Security has moved to the forefront of *network management* and implementation. The overall security challenge is to find a balance between two important requirements: the need to open networks to support evolving business opportunities, and the need to protect private, personal, and strategic business information.

The application of an effective security policy is the most important step that an organization can take to protect its network. It provides guidelines about the activities to be carried out and the resources to be used to secure an organization's network.

Layer 2 security is not discussed in this chapter. For information about Layer 2 LAN security measures, refer to the CCNA Exploration: LAN Switching and Wireless course.

4.1 Introduction to Network Security

4.1.1 Why is Network Security Important?

Why is Network Security Important?

Computer networks have grown in both size and importance in a very short time. If the security of the network is compromised, there could be serious consequences, such as loss of privacy, theft of information, and even legal liability. To make the situation even more challenging, the types of potential threats to network security are always evolving.

As e-business and Internet applications continue to grow, finding the balance between being isolated and open is critical. In addition, the rise of mobile commerce and wireless networks demands that security solutions become seamlessly integrated, more transparent, and more flexible.

In this chapter you are going to be taken on a whirlwind tour of the world of network security. You will learn about different types of threats, the development of organizational security policies, mitigation techniques, and Cisco IOS software tools to help secure networks. The chapter ends with a look at managing Cisco IOS software images. Although this may not seem like a security issue, Cisco IOS software images and configurations can be deleted. Devices compromised in this way pose security risks.

The Increasing Threat to Security

Over the years, network attack tools and methods have evolved. As shown in the figure, in 1985 an attacker had to have sophisticated computer, programming, and networking knowledge to make use of rudimentary tools and basic attacks. As time went on, and attackers' methods and tools improved, attackers no longer required the same level of sophisticated knowledge. This has effectively lowered the entry-level requirements for attackers. People who previously would not have participated in computer crime are now able to do so.

As the types of threats, attacks, and exploits have evolved, various terms have been coined to describe the individuals involved. Some of the most common terms are as follows:

- *White hat-* An individual who looks for vulnerabilities in systems or networks and then reports these vulnerabilities to the owners of the system so that they can be fixed. They are ethically opposed to the abuse of computer systems. A white hat generally focuses on securing IT systems, whereas a black hat (the opposite) would like to break into them.

- *Hacker-* A general term that has historically been used to describe a computer programming expert. More recently, this term is often used in a negative way to describe an individual that attempts to gain unauthorized access to network resources with malicious intent.

- *Black hat-* Another term for individuals who use their knowledge of computer systems to break into systems or networks that they are not authorized to use, usually for personal or financial gain. A cracker is an example of a black hat.

- *Cracker-* A more accurate term to describe someone who tries to gain unauthorized access to network resources with malicious intent.

- *Phreaker-* An individual who manipulates the phone network to cause it to perform a function that is not allowed. A common goal of phreaking is breaking into the phone network, usually through a payphone, to make free long distance calls.

- *Spammer-* An individual who sends large quantities of unsolicited e-mail messages. Spammers often use viruses to take control of home computers and use them to send out their bulk messages.

- *Phisher-* Uses e-mail or other means to trick others into providing sensitive information, such as credit card numbers or passwords. A phisher masquerades as a trusted party that would have a legitimate need for the sensitive information.

Think Like a Attacker

The attacker's goal is to compromise a network target or an *application* running within a network. Many attackers use this seven-step process to gain information and state an attack.

Step 1. Perform footprint analysis (reconnaissance). A company webpage can lead to information, such as the IP addresses of servers. From there, an attacker can build a picture of the security profile or "footprint" of the company.

Step 2. Enumerate information. An attacker can expand on the footprint by monitoring network traffic with a packet sniffer such as Wireshark, finding information such as version numbers of FTP servers and mail servers. A cross-reference with vulnerability databases exposes the applications of the company to potential exploits.

Step 3. Manipulate users to gain access. Sometimes employees choose passwords that are easily crackable. In other instances, employees can be duped by talented attackers into giving up sensitive access-related information.

Step 4. Escalate privileges. After attackers gain basic access, they use their skills to increase their network privileges.

Step 5. Gather additional passwords and secrets. With improved access privileges, attackers use their talents to gain access to well-guarded, sensitive information.

Step 6. Install backdoors. Backdoors provide the attacker with a way to enter the system without being detected. The most common backdoor is an open listening TCP or *UDP* port.

Step 7. Leverage the compromised system. After a system is compromised, an attacker uses it to stage attacks on other hosts in the network.

Types of Computer Crime

As security measures have improved over the years, some of the most common types of attacks have diminished in frequency, while new ones have emerged. Conceiving of network security solutions begins with an appreciation of the complete scope of computer crime. These are the most commonly reported acts of computer crime that have network security implications:

- Insider abuse of network access
- Virus
- Mobile device theft
- Phishing where an organization is fraudulently represented as the sender
- Instant messaging misuse
- Denial of service
- Unauthorized access to information
- *Bots* within the organization
- Theft of customer or employee data
- Abuse of wireless network
- System penetration
- Financial fraud
- Password sniffing
- Key logging
- Website defacement
- Misuse of a public web application
- Theft of proprietary information
- Exploiting the *DNS* server of an organization
- Telecom fraud
- Sabotage

Note: In certain countries, some of these activities may not be a crime, but are still a problem.

Open versus Closed Networks

The overall security challenge facing network administrators is balancing two important needs: keeping networks open to support evolving business requirements and protecting private, personal, and strategic business information.

Network security models follow a progressive scale from open-any service is permitted unless it is expressly denied-to restrictive-services are denied by default unless deemed necessary. In the case of the open network, the security risks are self-evident. In the case of the closed network, the rules for what are permitted are defined in the form of a policy by an individual or group in the organization.

A change in access policy may be as simple as asking a network administrator to enable a service. Depending on the company, a change could require an amendment to the enterprise security policy before the administrator is allowed to enable the service. For example, a security policy could disallow the use of instant messaging (IM) services, but demand from employees may cause the company to change the policy.

An extreme alternative for managing security is to completely close a network from the outside world. A closed network provides connectivity only to trusted known parties and sites. A closed network does not allow a connection to public networks. Because there is no outside connectivity, networks designed in this way are considered safe from outside attacks. However, internal threats still exist. A closed network does little to prevent attacks from within the enterprise.

Developing a Security Policy

The first step any organization should take to protect its data and itself from a liability challenge is to develop a security policy. A policy is a set of principles that guide decision-making processes and enable leaders in an organization to distribute authority confidently. RFC2196 states that a "security policy is a formal statement of the rules by which people who are given access to an organization's technology and information assets must abide." A security policy can be as simple as a brief Acceptable Use Policy for network resources, or it can be several hundred pages long and detail every element of connectivity and associated policies.

A security policy meets these goals:

- Informs users, staff, and managers of their obligatory requirements for protecting technology and information assets
- Specifies the mechanisms through which these requirements can be met
- Provides a baseline from which to acquire, configure, and audit computer systems and networks for compliance with the policy

Assembling a security policy can be daunting if it is undertaken without guidance. For this reason, the International Organization for Standardization (ISO) and the International Electrotechnical Commission (*IEC*) have published a security standard document called ISO/IEC 27002. This document refers specifically to information technology and outlines a code of practice for information security management.

ISO/IEC 27002 is intended to be a common basis and practical guideline for developing organizational security standards and effective security management practices. The document consists of 12 sections:

- Risk assessment
- Security policy
- Organization of information security
- Asset management
- Human resources security
- Physical and environmental security
- Communications and operations management
- Access control
- Information systems acquisition, development, and maintenance
- Information security incident management
- Business continuity management
- Compliance

This chapter focuses on the security policy section. To read about all the sections, visit http://en.wikipedia.org/wiki/ISO/IEC_27002. The development of the network security policy document is discussed in topic 4.1.5 "The Network Security Wheel" and topic 4.1.6 "The Enterprise Security Policy."

4.1.2 Common Security Threats

Vulnerabilities

When discussing network security, three common factors are vulnerability, threat, and attack.

Vulnerability is the degree of weakness which is inherent in every network and device. This includes routers, switches, desktops, servers, and even security devices.

Threats are the people interested and qualified in taking advantage of each security weakness. Such individuals can be expected to continually search for new exploits and weaknesses.

The threats use a variety of tools, scripts, and programs to launch attacks against networks and network devices. Typically, the network devices under attack are the endpoints, such as servers and desktop computers.

There are three primary vulnerabilities or weaknesses:

- Technological weaknesses
- Configuration weaknesses
- Security policy weaknesses

Click the Technology button in the figure.

Computer and network technologies have intrinsic security weaknesses. These include TCP/IP protocol, operating system, and network equipment weaknesses.

Click the Configuration button in the figure.

Network administrators or network engineers need to learn what the configuration weaknesses are and correctly configure their computing and network devices to compensate.

Click the Policy button in the figure.

Security risks to the network exist if users do not follow the security policy. Some common security policy weaknesses and how those weaknesses are exploited are listed in the figure.

Threats to Physical Infrastructure

When you think of network security, or even computer security, you may imagine attackers exploiting software vulnerabilities. A less glamorous, but no less important, class of threat is the physical security of devices. An attacker can deny the use of network resources if those resources can be physically compromised.

The four classes of physical threats are:

- *Hardware threats-* Physical damage to servers, routers, switches, cabling plant, and workstations

- *Environmental threats-* Temperature extremes (too hot or too cold) or humidity extremes (too wet or too dry)

- *Electrical threats-* Voltage *spikes*, insufficient supply voltage (brownouts), unconditioned power (noise), and total power loss

- *Maintenance threats-* Poor handling of key electrical components (*electrostatic discharge*), lack of critical spare parts, poor cabling, and poor labeling

Some of these issues must be dealt with in an organizational policy. Some of them are subject to good leadership and management in the organization. The consequences of bad luck can wreak havoc in a network if the physical security is not sufficiently prepared.

Here are some ways to mitigate physical threats:

- Hardware threat mitigation
- Environmental threat mitigation
- Electrical threat mitigation
- Mechanical threat mitigation

Click the Hardware button in the figure.

Hardware threat mitigation

Lock the wiring closet and only allow access to authorized personnel. Block access through any dropped ceiling, raised floor, window, ductwork, or point of entry other than the secured access point. Use electronic access control, and log all entry attempts. Monitor facilities with security cameras.

Click the Environmental button in the figure.

Environmental threat mitigation

Create a proper operating environment through temperature control, humidity control, positive air flow, remote environmental alarming, and recording and monitoring.

Click the Electrical button in the figure.

Electrical threat mitigation

Limit electrical supply problems by installing UPS systems and generator sets, following a preventative maintenance plan, installing redundant power supplies, and performing remote alarming and monitoring.

Click the Maintenance button in the figure.

Maintenance threat mitigation

Maintenance-related threat mitigation-Use neat cable runs, label critical cables and components, use electrostatic discharge procedures, stock critical spares, and control access to *console* ports.

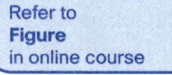

Threats to Networks

Earlier in this chapter the common computer crimes that have implications for network security were listed. These crimes can be grouped into four primary classes of threats to networks:

Unstructured Threats

Unstructured threats consist of mostly inexperienced individuals using easily available hacking tools, such as shell scripts and password crackers. Even unstructured threats that are only executed with the intent of testing an attacker's skills can do serious damage to a network. For example, if a company website is hacked, the reputation of the company may be damaged. Even if the website is separated from the private information that sits behind a protective firewall, the public does not know that. What the public perceives is that the site might not be a safe environment to conduct business.

Structured Threats

Structured threats come from individuals or groups that are more highly motivated and technically competent. These people know system vulnerabilities and use sophisticated hacking techniques to penetrate unsuspecting businesses. They break into business and government computers to commit fraud, destroy or alter records, or simply to create havoc. These groups are often involved with the major fraud and theft cases reported to law enforcement agencies. Their hacking is so complex and sophisticated that only specially trained investigators understand what is happening.

In 1995, Kevin Mitnick was convicted of accessing interstate computers in the United States for criminal purposes. He broke into the California Department of Motor Vehicles database, routinely took control of New York and California telephone switching hubs, and stole credit card numbers. He inspired the 1983 movie "War Games."

External Threats

External threats can arise from individuals or organizations working outside of a company who do not have authorized access to the computer systems or network. They work their way into a network mainly from the Internet or dialup access servers. External threats can vary in severity depending on the expertise of the attacker-either amateurish (unstructured) or expert (structured).

Internal Threats

Internal threats occur when someone has authorized access to the network with either an account or physical access. Just as for external threats, the severity of an internal threat depends on the expertise of the attacker.

Social Engineering

The easiest hack involves no computer skill at all. If an intruder can trick a member of an organization into giving over valuable information, such as the location of files or passwords, the process of hacking is made much easier. This type of attack is called social engineering, and it preys on personal vulnerabilities that can be discovered by talented attackers. It can include appeals to the ego of an employee, or it can be a disguised person or faked document that causes someone to provide sensitive information.

Phishing is a type of social engineering attack that involves using e-mail or other types of messages in an attempt to trick others into providing sensitive information, such as credit card numbers or passwords. The phisher masquerades as a trusted party that has a seemingly legitimate need for the sensitive information.

Frequently, phishing scams involve sending out spam e-mails that appear to be from known online banking or auction sites. The figure shows a replica of such an e-mail. The actual company used as the lure in this example has been changed. These e-mails contain hyperlinks that appear to be legitimate, but actually take users to a fake website set up by the phisher to capture their information. The site appears to belong to the party that was faked in the e-mail. When the user enters the information, it is recorded for the phisher to use.

Phishing attacks can be prevented by educating users and implementing reporting guidelines when they receive suspicious e-mail. Administrators can also block access to certain web sites and configure filters that block suspicious e-mail.

4.1.3 Types of Network Attacks

Types of Network Attacks

There are four primary classes of attacks.

Reconnaissance

Reconnaissance is the unauthorized discovery and mapping of systems, services, or vulnerabilities. It is also known as information gathering and, in most cases, it precedes another type of attack.

Reconnaissance is similar to a thief casing a neighborhood for vulnerable homes to break into, such as an unoccupied residence, easy-to-open doors, or open windows.

Access

System access is the ability for an intruder to gain access to a device for which the intruder does not have an account or a password. Entering or accessing systems usually involves running a hack, script, or tool that exploits a known vulnerability of the system or application being attacked.

Denial of Service

Denial of service (DoS) is when an attacker disables or corrupts networks, systems, or services with the intent to deny services to intended users. DoS attacks involve either crashing the system or slowing it down to the point that it is unusable. But DoS can also be as simple as deleting or corrupting information. In most cases, performing the attack involves simply running a hack or script. For these reasons, DoS attacks are the most feared.

Worms, Viruses, and Trojan Horses

Malicious software can be inserted onto a host to damage or corrupt a system, replicate itself, or deny access to networks, systems, or services. Common names for this type of software are worms, viruses, and Trojan horses.

Reconnaissance Attacks

Reconnaissance attacks can consist of the following:

- Internet information queries
- *Ping* sweeps
- Port scans
- Packet sniffers

External attackers can use Internet tools, such as the nslookup and whois utilities, to easily determine the IP address space assigned to a given corporation or entity. After the IP address space is determined, an attacker can then ping the publicly available IP addresses to identify the addresses that are active. To help automate this step, an attacker may use a ping sweep tool, such as fping or gping, which systematically pings all network addresses in a given range or subnet. This is similar to going through a section of a telephone book and calling each number to see who answers.

When the active IP addresses are identified, the intruder uses a port scanner to determine which network services or ports are active on the live IP addresses. A port scanner is software, such as Nmap or Superscan, that is designed to search a network host for open ports. The port scanner queries the ports to determine the application type and version, as well as the type and version of operating system (OS) running on the target host. Based on this information, the intruder can determine if a possible vulnerability that can be exploited exists. As shown in the figure, a network exploration tool such as Nmap can be used to conduct host discovery, port scanning, version detection, and OS detection. Many of these tools are available and easy to use.

Internal attackers may attempt to "eavesdrop" on network traffic.

Network snooping and packet sniffing are common terms for eavesdropping. The information gathered by eavesdropping can be used to pose other attacks to the network.

Two common uses of eavesdropping are as follows:

- *Information gathering-* Network intruders can identify usernames, passwords, or information carried in a packet.

- *Information theft-* The theft can occur as data is transmitted over the internal or external network. The network intruder can also steal data from networked computers by gaining unauthorized access. Examples include breaking into or eavesdropping on financial institutions and obtaining credit card numbers.

An example of data susceptible to eavesdropping is *SNMP* version 1 *community strings*, which are sent in clear text. SNMP is a management protocol that provides a means for network devices to collect information about their status and to send it to an administrator. An intruder could eavesdrop on SNMP queries and gather valuable data on network equipment configuration. Another example is the capture of usernames and passwords as they cross a network.

A common method for eavesdropping on communications is to capture TCP/IP or other protocol packets and decode the contents using a *protocol analyzer* or similar utility. An example of such a program is Wireshark, which you have been using extensively throughout the Exploration courses. After packets are captured, they can be examined for vulnerable information.

Three of the most effective methods for counteracting eavesdropping are as follows:

- Using switched networks instead of hubs so that traffic is not forwarded to all endpoints or network hosts.
- Using encryption that meets the data security needs of the organization without imposing an excessive burden on system resources or users.
- Implementing and enforcing a policy directive that forbids the use of protocols with known susceptibilities to eavesdropping. For example, SNMP version 3 can encrypt community strings, so a company could forbid using SNMP version 1, but permit SNMP version 3.

Encryption provides protection for data susceptible to eavesdropping attacks, password crackers, or manipulation. Almost every company has transactions that could have negative consequences if viewed by an eavesdropper. Encryption ensures that when sensitive data passes over a medium susceptible to eavesdropping, it cannot be altered or observed. *Decryption* is necessary when the data reaches the destination host.

One method of encryption is called payload-only encryption. This method encrypts the payload section (data section) after a User Datagram Protocol (*UDP*) or TCP header. This enables Cisco IOS routers and switches to read the Network layer information and forward the traffic as any other IP packet. Payload-only encryption allows flow switching and all access-list features to work with the encrypted traffic just as they would with plain text traffic, thereby preserving desired quality of service (*QoS*) for all data.

Refer to **Figure** in online course

Access Attacks

Access attacks exploit known vulnerabilities in authentication services, FTP services, and web services to gain entry to web accounts, confidential databases, and other sensitive information.

Password Attacks

Password attacks can be implemented using a packet sniffer to yield user accounts and passwords that are transmitted as clear text. Password attacks usually refer to repeated attempts to log in to a shared resource, such as a server or router, to identify a user account, password, or both. These repeated attempts are called dictionary attacks or brute-force attacks.

To conduct a dictionary attack, attackers can use tools such as L0phtCrack or Cain. These programs repeatedly attempt to log in as a user using words derived from a dictionary. Dictionary attacks often succeed because users have a tendency to choose simple passwords that are short, single words or are simple variations that are easy to predict, such as adding the number 1 to a word.

Another password attack method uses rainbow tables. A rainbow table is precomputed series of passwords which is constructed by building chains of possible plaintext passwords. Each chain is developed by starting with a randomly selected "guess" of the plaintext password and then successively applying variations on it. The attack software will apply the passwords in the rainbow table until it solves the password. To conduct a rainbow table attack, attackers can use a tool such as L0phtCrack.

A brute-force attack tool is more sophisticated because it searches exhaustively using combinations of character sets to compute every possible password made up of those characters. The downside is that more time is required for completion of this type of attack. Brute-force attack tools have been known to solve simple passwords in less than a minute. Longer, more complex passwords may take days or weeks to resolve.

Password attacks can be mitigated by educating users to use complex passwords and specifying minimum password lengths. Brute-force attacks could be mitigated by restricting the number of failed login attempts. However, a brute-force attack can also be performed offline. For example, if an attacker snoops an encrypted password, either through eavesdropping or by accessing a configuration file, the attacker could then attempt to resolve the password without actually being connected to the host.

Trust Exploitation

The goal of a trust exploitation attack is to compromise a trusted host, using it to stage attacks on other hosts in a network. If a host in a network of a company is protected by a firewall (inside host), but is accessible to a trusted host outside the firewall (outside host), the inside host can be attacked through the trusted outside host.

The means used by attackers to gain access to the trusted outside host as well as the details of trust exploitation are not discussed in this chapter. For information about trust exploitation, refer to the course Networking Academy Network Security course.

Trust exploitation-based attacks can be mitigated through tight constraints on trust levels within a network, for example, private VLANs can be deployed in public-service segments where multiple public servers are available. Systems on the outside of a firewall should never be absolutely trusted by systems on the inside of a firewall. Such trust should be limited to specific protocols and should be authenticated by something other than an IP address, where possible.

Port Redirection

A port redirection attack is a type of trust exploitation attack that uses a compromised host to pass traffic through a firewall that would otherwise be blocked.

Consider a firewall with three interfaces and a host on each interface. The host on the outside can reach the host on the public services segment, but not the host on the inside. This publicly accessible segment is commonly referred to as a demilitarized zone (DMZ). The host on the public services segment can reach the host on both the outside and the inside. If attackers were able to compromise the public services segment host, they could install software to redirect traffic from the outside host directly to the inside host. Although neither communication violates the rules implemented in the firewall, the outside host has now achieved connectivity to the inside host through the port redirection process on the public services host. An example of a utility that can provide this type of access is netcat.

Port redirection can be mitigated primarily through the use of proper trust models, which are network specific (as mentioned earlier). When a system is under attack, a host-based intrusion detection system (IDS) can help detect an attacker and prevent installation of such utilities on a host.

Man-in-the-Middle Attack

A man-in-the-middle (MITM) attack is carried out by attackers that manage to position themselves between two legitimate hosts. The attacker may allow the normal transactions between hosts to occur, and only periodically manipulate the conversation between the two.

There are many ways that an attacker gets position between two hosts. The details of these methods are beyond the scope of this course, but a brief description of one popular method, the transparent *proxy*, helps illustrate the nature of MITM attacks.

In a transparent proxy attack, an attacker may catch a victim with a phishing e-mail or by defacing a website. Then the *URL* of a legitimate website has the attackers URL added to the front of it (prepended). For instance http:www.legitimate.com becomes http:www.attacker.com/http://www.legitimate.com.

Step 1. When a victim requests a webpage, the host of the victim makes the request to the host of the attacker's.

Step 2. The attacker's host receives the request and fetches the real page from the legitimate website.

Step 3. The attacker can alter the legitimate webpage and apply any transformations to the data they want to make.

Step 4. The attacker forwards the requested page to the victim.

Other sorts of MITM attacks are potentially even more harmful. If attackers manage to get into a strategic position, they can steal information, hijack an ongoing session to gain access to private network resources, conduct DoS attacks, corrupt transmitted data, or introduce new information into network sessions.

WAN MITM attack mitigation is achieved by using VPN tunnels, which allow the attacker to see only the encrypted, undecipherable text. LAN MITM attacks use such tools as ettercap and ARP poisoning. Most LAN MITM attack mitigation can usually be mitigated by configuring port security on LAN switches.

DoS Attacks

> Refer to Figure in online course

DoS attacks are the most publicized form of attack and also among the most difficult to eliminate. Even within the attacker community, DoS attacks are regarded as trivial and considered bad form, because they require so little effort to execute. But because of their ease of implementation and potentially significant damage, DoS attacks deserve special attention from security administrators.

DoS attacks take many forms. Ultimately, they prevent authorized people from using a service by consuming system resources. The following are some examples of common DoS threats:

Click the Ping of Death button in the figure.

A ping of death attack gained popularity back in the late 1990s. It took advantage of vulnerabilities in older operating systems. This attack modified the IP portion of a ping packet header to indicate that there is more data in the packet than there actually was. A ping is normally 64 or 84 bytes, while a ping of death could be up to 65,536 bytes. Sending a ping of this size may crash an older target computer. Most networks are no longer susceptible to this type of attack.

Click the SYN Flood button in the figure.

A SYN flood attack exploits the TCP three-way handshake. It involves sending multiple SYN requests (1,000+) to a targeted server. The server replies with the usual SYN-ACK response, but the malicious host never responds with the final ACK to complete the handshake. This ties up the server until it eventually runs out of resources and cannot respond to a valid host request.

Other types of DoS attacks include:

- *E-mail bombs* - Programs send bulk e-mails to individuals, lists, or domains, monopolizing e-mail services.
- *Malicious applets* - These attacks are Java, JavaScript, or ActiveX programs that cause destruction or tie up computer resources.

DDos Attacks

Distributed DoS (DDoS) attacks are designed to saturate network links with illegitimate data. This data can overwhelm an Internet link, causing legitimate traffic to be dropped. DDoS uses attack methods similar to standard DoS attacks, but operates on a much larger scale. Typically, hundreds or thousands of attack points attempt to overwhelm a target.

Click the DDoS button in the figure.

Typically, there are three components to a DDoS attack.

- There is a Client who is typically a person who launches the attack.
- A Handler is a compromised host that is running the attacker program and each Handler is capable of controlling multiple Agents
- An Agent is a compromised host that is running the attacker program and is responsible for generating a stream of packets that is directed toward the intended victim

Examples of DDoS attacks include the following:

- SMURF attack
- Tribe flood network (TFN)
- Stacheldraht
- MyDoom

Click the Smurf Attack button in the figure.

The Smurf attack uses spoofed broadcast ping messages to flood a target system. It starts with an attacker sending a large number of ICMP echo requests to the network broadcast address from valid spoofed source IP addresses. A router could perform the Layer 3 broadcast-to-Layer 2 broadcast function, most hosts will each respond with an ICMP echo reply, multiplying the traffic by the number of hosts responding. On a multi-access broadcast network, there could potentially be hundreds of machines replying to each echo packet.

For example, assume that the network has 100 hosts and that the attacker has a high performance T1 link. The attacker sends a 768 kb/s stream of ICMP echo requests packets with a spoofed *source address* of the victim to the broadcast address of a targeted network (referred to as a bounce site). These ping packets hit the bounce site on the broadcast network of 100 hosts, and each of them takes the packet and responds to it, creating 100 outbound ping replies. A total of 76.8 megabits per second (*Mb/s*) of bandwidth is used outbound from the bounce site after the traffic is multiplied. This is then sent to the victim or the spoofed source of the originating packets.

Turning off directed broadcast capability in the network infrastructure prevents the network from being used as a bounce site. Directed broadcast capability is now turned off by default in Cisco IOS software since version 12.0.

DoS and DDoS attacks can be mitigated by implementing special anti-spoof and anti-DoS *access control lists*. ISPs can also implement traffic rate, limiting the amount of nonessential traffic that crosses network segments. A common example is to limit the amount of ICMP traffic that is allowed into a network, because this traffic is used only for diagnostic purposes.

Details of the operation of these attacks is beyond the scope of this course. For more information, refer to the Networking Academy Network Security course.

Malicious Code Attacks

The primary vulnerabilities for end-user workstations are worm, virus, and Trojan horse attacks.

A worm executes code and installs copies of itself in the memory of the infected computer, which can, in turn, infect other hosts.

A virus is malicious software that is attached to another program for the purpose of executing a particular unwanted function on a workstation.

A Trojan horse is different from a worm or virus only in that the entire application was written to look like something else, when in fact it is an attack tool.

Worms

The anatomy of a worm attack is as follows:

- *The enabling vulnerability-* A worm installs itself by exploiting known vulnerabilities in systems, such as naive end users who open unverified executable attachments in e-mails.

- *Propagation mechanism-* After gaining access to a host, a worm copies itself to that host and then selects new targets.

- *Payload-* Once a host is infected with a worm, the attacker has access to the host, often as a privileged user. Attackers could use a local exploit to escalate their privilege level to administrator.

Typically, worms are self-contained programs that attack a system and try to exploit a specific vulnerability in the target. Upon successful exploitation of the vulnerability, the worm copies its program from the attacking host to the newly exploited system to begin the cycle again. In January 2007, a worm infected the popular MySpace community. Unsuspecting users enabled propagation of the worm, which began to replicate itself on user sites with the defacement "w0rm.EricAndrew".

Worm attack mitigation requires diligence on the part of system and network administration staff. Coordination between system administration, network engineering, and security operations personnel is critical in responding effectively to a worm incident. The following are the recommended steps for worm attack mitigation:

- *Containment-* Contain the spread of the worm in and within the network. Compartmentalize uninfected parts of the network.

- *Inoculation-* Start patching all systems and, if possible, scanning for vulnerable systems.

- *Quarantine-* Track down each infected machine inside the network. Disconnect, remove, or block infected machines from the network.

- *Treatment-* Clean and patch each infected system. Some worms may require complete core system reinstallations to clean the system.

Viruses and Trojan Horses

A virus is malicious software that is attached to another program to execute a particular unwanted function on a workstation. An example is a program that is attached to command.com (the primary interpreter for Windows systems) and deletes certain files and infects any other versions of command.com that it can find.

A Trojan horse is different only in that the entire application was written to look like something else, when in fact it is an attack tool. An example of a Trojan horse is a software application that runs a simple game on a workstation. While the user is occupied with the game, the Trojan horse mails a copy of itself to every address in the user's address book. The other users receive the game and play it, thereby spreading the Trojan horse to the addresses in each address book.

A virus normally requires a delivery mechanism-a vector-such as a zip file or some other executable file attached to an e-mail, to carry the virus code from one system to another. The key element that distinguishes a computer worm from a computer virus is that human interaction is required to facilitate the spread of a virus.

These kinds of applications can be contained through the effective use of antivirus software at the user level, and potentially at the network level. Antivirus software can detect most viruses and many Trojan horse applications and prevent them from spreading in the network. Keeping up to date with the latest developments in these sorts of attacks can also lead to a more effective posture toward these attacks. As new virus or Trojan applications are released, enterprises need to keep current with the latest versions of antivirus software.

Sub7, or subseven, is a common Trojan horse that installs a backdoor program on user systems. It is popular for both unstructured and structured attacks. As an unstructured threat, inexperienced attackers can use the program to cause mouse cursers to disappear. As a structured threat, crackers can use it to install keystroke loggers (programs that record all user keystrokes) to capture sensitive information.

4.1.4 General Mitigation Techniques

Host and Server Based Security

Device Hardening

When a new operating system is installed on a computer, the security settings are set to the default values. In most cases, this level of security is inadequate. There are some simple steps that should be taken that apply to most operating systems:

- Default usernames and passwords should be changed immediately.
- Access to system resources should be restricted to only the individuals that are authorized to use those resources.
- Any unnecessary services and applications should be turned off and uninstalled, when possible.

Section 4.2 "Securing Cisco Routers" describes device hardening in more detail.

It is critical to protect network hosts, such as workstation PCs and servers. These hosts need to be secured as they are added to the network, and should be updated with security patches as these updates become available. Additional steps can be taken to secure these hosts. Antivirus, firewall, and intrusion detection are valuable tools that can be used to secure network hosts. Because many business resources may be contained on a single file server, it is especially important for servers to be accessible and available.

Antivirus Software

Install host antivirus software to protect against known viruses. Antivirus software can detect most viruses and many Trojan horse applications, and prevent them from spreading in the network.

Antivirus software does this in two ways:

- It scans files, comparing their contents to known viruses in a virus dictionary. Matches are flagged in a manner defined by the end user.
- It monitors suspicious processes running on a host that might indicate infection. This monitoring may include data captures, port monitoring, and other methods.

Most commercial antivirus software uses both of these approaches.

Click the Antivirus button in the figure.

Update antivirus software vigilantly.

Personal Firewall

Personal computers connected to the Internet through a dialup connection, DSL, or cable modems are as vulnerable as corporate networks. Personal firewalls reside on the PC of the user and attempt to prevent attacks. Personal firewalls are not designed for LAN implementations, such as appliance-based or server-based firewalls, and they may prevent network access if installed with other networking clients, services, protocols, or adapters.

Click the Personal Firewalls button in the figure.

Some personal firewall software vendors include McAfee, Norton, Symantec, and Zone Labs.

Operating System Patches

The most effective way to mitigate a worm and its variants is to download security updates from the operating system vendor and patch all vulnerable systems. This is difficult with uncontrolled user systems in the local network, and even more troublesome if these systems are remotely connected to the network via a virtual private network (VPN) or remote access server (RAS). Administering numerous systems involves the creation of a standard software image (operating system and accredited applications that are authorized for use on deployed client systems) that is deployed on new or upgraded systems. These images may not contain the latest patches, and the process of continually remaking the image to integrate the latest patch may quickly become administratively time-consuming. Pushing patches out to all systems requires that those systems be connected in some way to the network, which may not be possible.

One solution to the management of critical security patches is to create a central patch server that all systems must communicate with after a set period of time. Any patches that are not applied to a host are automatically downloaded from the patch server and installed without user intervention.

In addition to performing security updates from the OS vendor, determining which devices are exploitable can be simplified by the use of security auditing tools that look for vulnerabilities.

Click the OS Patches button in the figure.

> Refer to Figure in online course

Intrusion Detection and Prevention

Intrusion detection systems (IDS) detect attacks against a network and send logs to a management console. Intrusion prevention systems (IPS) prevent attacks against the network and should provide the following active defense mechanisms in addition to detection:

- *Prevention-* Stops the detected attack from executing.

- *Reaction-* Immunizes the system from future attacks from a malicious source.

Either technology can be implemented at a network level or host level, or both for maximum protection.

Host-based Intrusion Detection Systems

Host-based intrusion is typically implemented as inline or passive technology, depending on the vendor.

Passive technology, which was the first generation technology, is called a host-based intrusion detection system (HIDS). HIDS sends logs to a management console after the attack has occurred and the damage is done.

Inline technology, called a host-based intrusion prevention system (HIPS), actually stops the attack, prevents damage, and blocks the propagation of worms and viruses.

Active detection can be set to shut down the network connection or to stop impacted services automatically. Corrective action can be taken immediately. Cisco provides HIPS using the Cisco Security Agent software.

HIPS software must be installed on each host, either the server or desktop, to monitor activity performed on and against the host. This software is referred to as agent software. The agent software performs the intrusion detection analysis and prevention. Agent software also sends logs and alerts to a centralized management/policy server.

The advantage of HIPS is that it can monitor operating system processes and protect critical system resources, including files that may exist only on that specific host. This means it can notify network managers when some external process tries to modify a system file in a way that may include a hidden back door program.

The figure illustrates a typical HIPS deployment. Agents are installed on publicly accessible servers and corporate mail and application servers. The agent reports events to a central console server located inside the corporate firewall. As an alternative, agents on the host can send logs as e-mail to an administrator.

Refer to Figure in online course

Common Security Appliances and Applications

Security is a top consideration whenever planning a network. In the past, the one device that would come to mind for network security was the firewall. A firewall by itself is no longer adequate for securing a network. An integrated approach involving firewall, intrusion prevention, and VPN is necessary.

An integrated approach to security, and the necessary devices to make it happen, follows these building blocks:

Threat control-Regulates network access, isolates infected systems, prevents intrusions, and protects assets by counteracting malicious traffic, such as worms and viruses. Devices that provide threat control solutions are:

- Cisco ASA 5500 Series Adaptive Security Appliances
- Integrated Services Routers (ISR)
- Network Admission Control
- Cisco Security Agent for Desktops
- Cisco Intrusion Prevention Systems

Secure communications-Secures network endpoints with VPN. The devices that allow an organization to deploy VPN are Cisco ISR routers with Cisco IOS VPN solution, and the Cisco 5500 ASA and Cisco Catalyst 6500 switches.

Network admission control (*NAC*)-Provides a roles-based method of preventing unauthorized access to a network. Cisco offers a NAC appliance.

Cisco IOS Software on Cisco Integrated Services Routers (ISRs)

Cisco provides many of the required security measures for customers within the Cisco IOS software. Cisco IOS software provides built-in Cisco IOS Firewall, IPsec, SSL VPN, and IPS services.

Cisco ASA 5500 Series Adaptive Security Appliance

At one time, the PIX firewall was the one device that a secure network would deploy. The PIX has evolved into a platform that integrates many different security features, called the Cisco Adaptive Security Appliance (ASA). The Cisco ASA integrates firewall, voice security, SSL and IPsec VPN, IPS, and content security services in one device.

Cisco IPS 4200 Series Sensors

For larger networks, an inline intrusion prevention system is provided by the Cisco IPS 4200 series sensors. This sensor identifies, classifies, and stops malicious traffic on the network.

Cisco NAC Appliance

The Cisco NAC appliance uses the network infrastructure to enforce security policy compliance on all devices seeking to access network computing resources.

Cisco Security Agent (CSA)

Cisco Security Agent software provides threat protection capabilities for server, desktop, and point-of-service (POS) computing systems. CSA defends these systems against targeted attacks, spyware, rootkits, and day-zero attacks.

In-depth coverage of these appliances is beyond the scope of this course. Refer to the CCNP: Implementing Secure Converged Wide-area Networks and the Network Security 1 and 2 courses for more information.

4.1.5 The Network Security Wheel

Most security incidents occur because system administrators do not implement available countermeasures, and attackers or disgruntled employees exploit the oversight. Therefore, the issue is not just one of confirming that a technical vulnerability exists and finding a countermeasure that works, it is also critical to verify that the countermeasure is in place and working properly.

To assist with the compliance of a security policy, the Security Wheel, a continuous process, has proven to be an effective approach. The Security Wheel promotes retesting and reapplying updated security measures on a continuous basis.

To begin the Security Wheel process, first develop a security policy that enables the application of security measures. A security policy includes the following:

- Identifies the security objectives of the organization.
- Documents the resources to be protected.
- Identifies the network infrastructure with current maps and inventories.

- Identifies the critical resources that need to be protected, such as research and development, finance, and human resources. This is called a risk analysis.

The security policy is the hub upon which the four steps of the Security Wheel are based. The steps are secure, monitor, test, and improve.

Step 1. Secure

Secure the network by applying the security policy and implementing the following security solutions:

- `Threat defense`
  - *Stateful inspection and packet filtering-* Filter network traffic to allow only valid traffic and services.

Note: Stateful inspection refers to a firewall keeping information on the state of a connection in a state table so that it can recognize changes in the connection that could mean an attacker is attempting to hijack a session or otherwise manipulate a connection.

  - *Intrusion prevention systems-* Deploy at the network and host level to actively stop malicious traffic.
  - *Vulnerability patching-* Apply fixes or measures to stop the exploitation of known vulnerabilities.
  - *Disable unnecessary services-* The fewer services that are enabled, the harder it is for attackers to gain access.

Secure connectivity

- *VPNs-* Encrypt network traffic to prevent unwanted disclosure to unauthorized or malicious individuals.
- *Trust and identity-* Implement tight constraints on trust levels within a network. For example, systems on the outside of a firewall should never be absolutely trusted by systems on the inside of a firewall.
- *Authentication-* Give access to authorized users only. One example of this is using one-time passwords.
- *Policy enforcement-* Ensure that users and end devices are in compliance with the corporate policy.

Step 2. Monitor

Monitoring security involves both active and passive methods of detecting security violations. The most commonly used active method is to audit host-level log files. Most operating systems include auditing functionality. System administrators must enable the audit system for every host on the network and take the time to check and interpret the log file entries.

Passive methods include using IDS devices to automatically detect intrusion. This method requires less attention from network security administrators than active methods. These systems can detect security violations in real time and can be configured to automatically respond before an intruder does any damage.

An added benefit of network monitoring is the verification that the security measures implemented in step 1 of the Security Wheel have been configured and are working properly.

Step 3. Test

In the testing phase of the Security Wheel, the security measures are proactively tested. Specifically, the functionality of the security solutions implemented in step 1 and the system auditing and intrusion detection methods implemented in step 2 are verified. Vulnerability assessment tools such as SATAN, Nessus, or Nmap are useful for periodically testing the network security measures at the network and host level.

Step 4. Improve

The improvement phase of the Security Wheel involves analyzing the data collected during the monitoring and testing phases. This analysis contributes to developing and implementing improvement mechanisms that augment the security policy and results in adding items to step 1. To keep a network as secure as possible, the cycle of the Security Wheel must be continually repeated, because new network vulnerabilities and risks are emerging every day.

With the information collected from the monitoring and testing phases, IDSs can be used to implement improvements to the security. The security policy should be adjusted as new security vulnerabilities and risks are discovered.

4.1.6 The Enterprise Security Policy

What is a Security Policy?

A security policy is a set of guidelines established to safeguard the network from attacks, both from inside and outside a company. Forming a policy starts with asking questions. How does the network help the organization achieve its vision, mission, and strategic plan? What implications do business requirements have on network security, and how do those requirements get translated into the purchase of specialized equipment and the configurations loaded onto devices?

A security policy benefits an organization in the following ways:

- Provides a means to audit existing network security and compare the requirements to what is in place.
- Plan security improvements, including equipment, software, and procedures.
- Defines the roles and responsibilities of the company executives, administrators, and users.
- Defines which behavior is and is not allowed.
- Defines a process for handling network security incidents.
- Enables global security implementation and enforcement by acting as a standard between sites.
- Creates a basis for legal action if necessary.

A security policy is a living document, meaning that the document is never finished and is continuously updated as technology and employee requirements change. It act as a bridge between management objectives and specific security requirements.

Functions of a Security Policy

A comprehensive security policy fulfills these essential functions:

- Protects people and information
- Sets the rules for expected behavior by users, system administrators, management, and security personnel
- Authorizes security personnel to monitor, probe, and investigate

- Defines and authorizes the consequences of violations

The security policy is for everyone, including employees, contractors, suppliers, and customers who have access to the network. However, the security policy should treat each of these groups differently. Each group should only be shown the portion of the policy appropriate to their work and level of access to the network.

For example, an explanation for why something is being done is not always necessary. You can assume that the technical staff already know why a particular requirement is included. Managers are not likely to be interested in the technical aspects of a particular requirement; they may want just a high-level overview or the principle supporting the requirement. However, when end users know why a particular security control has been included, they are more likely to comply with the policy. Therefore, one document is not likely to meet the needs of the entire audience in a large organization.

Components of a Security Policy

The SANS Institute (http://www.sans.org) provides guidelines developed in cooperation with a number of industry leaders, including Cisco, for developing comprehensive security policies for organizations large and small. Not all organizations need all of these policies.

The following are general security policies that an organization may invoke:

- *Statement of authority and scope-* Defines who in the organization sponsors the security policy, who is responsible for implementing it, and what areas are covered by the policy.

- *Acceptable use policy (AUP)-* Defines the acceptable use of equipment and computing services, and the appropriate employee security measures to protect the organization corporate resources and proprietary information.

- *Identification and authentication policy-* Defines which technologies the company uses to ensure that only authorized personnel have access to its data.

- *Internet access policy-* Defines what the company will and will not tolerate with respect to the use of its Internet connectivity by employees and guests.

- *Campus access policy-* Defines acceptable use of campus technology resources by employees and guests.

- *Remote access policy-* Defines how remote users can use the remote access infrastructure of the company.

- *Incident handling procedure-* Specifies who will respond to security incidents, and how they are to be handled.

In addition to these key security policy sections, some others that may be necessary in certain organizations include:

- *Account access request policy-* Formalizes the account and access request process within the organization. Users and system administrators who bypass the standard processes for account and access requests can lead to legal action against the organization.

- *Acquisition assessment policy-* Defines the responsibilities regarding corporate acquisitions and defines the minimum requirements of an acquisition assessment that the information security group must complete.

- *Audit policy-* Defines audit policies to ensure the integrity of information and resources. This includes a process to investigate incidents, ensure conformance to security policies, and monitor user and system activity where appropriate

- *Information sensitivity policy-* Defines the requirements for classifying and securing information in a manner appropriate to its sensitivity level.
- *Password policy-* Defines the standards for creating, protecting, and changing strong passwords.
- *Risk assessment policy-* Defines the requirements and provides the authority for the information security team to identify, assess, and remediate risks to the information infrastructure associated with conducting business.
- *Global web server policy-* Defines the standards required by all web hosts.

With the extensive use of e-mail, an organization may also want to have policies specifically related to e-mail, such as:

- *Automatically forwarded e-mail policy-* Documents the policy restricting automatic e-mail forwarding to an external destination without prior approval from the appropriate manager or director.
- *E-mail policy-* Defines content standards to prevent tarnishing the public image of the organization.
- *Spam policy-* Defines how spam should be reported and treated.

Remote access policies might include:

- *Dial-in access policy-* Defines the appropriate dial-in access and its use by authorized personnel.
- *Remote access policy-* Defines the standards for connecting to the organization network from any host or network external to the organization.
- *VPN security policy-* Defines the requirements for VPN connections to the network of the organization.

It should be noted that users who defy or violate the rules in a security policy may be subject to disciplinary action, up to and including termination of employment.

Activity Page

4.2 Securing Cisco Routers

4.2.1 Router Security Issues

The Role of Routers in Network Security

You know that you can build a LAN by connecting devices with basic Layer 2 LAN switches. You can then use a router to route traffic between different networks based on Layer 3 IP addresses.

Router security is a critical element in any security deployment. Routers are definite targets for network attackers. If an attacker can compromise and access a router, it can be a potential aid to them. Knowing the roles that routers fulfill in the network helps you understand their vulnerabilities.

Routers fulfill the following roles:

- Advertise networks and filter who can use them.
- Provide access to network segments and subnetworks.

Routers are Targets

Because routers provide gateways to other networks, they are obvious targets, and are subject to a variety of attacks. Here are some examples of various security problems:

- Compromising the access control can expose network configuration details, thereby facilitating attacks against other network components.
- Compromising the route tables can reduce performance, deny network communication services, and expose sensitive data.
- Misconfiguring a router traffic *filter* can expose internal network components to scans and attacks, making it easier for attackers to avoid detection.

Attackers can compromise routers in different ways, so there is no single approach that network administrators can use to combat them. The ways that routers are compromised are similar to the types of attacks you learned about earlier in this chapter, including trust exploitation attacks, IP *spoofing*, session hijacking, and MITM attacks.

Note: This section focuses on securing routers. Most of the best practices discussed can also be used to secure switches. However, this section does not cover Layer 2 threats, such as *MAC address flooding* attacks and STP attacks, because these are covered in CCNA Exploration: LAN Switching and Wireless.

Securing Your Network

Securing routers at the network perimeter is an important first step in securing the network.

Think about router security in terms in these categories:

- Physical security
- Update the router IOS whenever advisable
- Backup the router configuration and IOS
- Harden the router to eliminate the potential abuse of unused ports and services

To provide physical security, locate the router in a locked room that is accessible only to authorized personnel. It should also be free of any electrostatic or magnetic interference, and have controls for temperature and humidity. To reduce the possibility of DoS due to a power failure, install an uninterruptible power supply (*UPS*) and keep spare components available.

Physical devices used to connect to the router should be stored in a locked facility, or they should remain in the possession of a trustworthy individual so that they are not compromised. A device that is left in the open could have Trojans or some other sort of executable file stored on it.

Provision the router with the maximum amount of memory possible. Availability of memory can help protect against some DoS attacks, while supporting the widest range of security services.

The security features in an operating system evolve over time. However, the latest version of an operating system may not be the most stable version available. To get the best security performance from your operating system, use the latest stable release that meets the feature requirements of your network.

Always have a backup copy of a configuration and IOS on hand in case a router fails. Keep a secure copy of the router operating system image and router configuration file on a *TFTP* server for backup purposes.

Harden the router to make it as secure as possible. A router has many services enabled by default. Many of these services are unnecessary and may be used by an attacker for information gathering or exploitation. You should harden your router configuration by disabling unnecessary services.

4.2.2 Applying Cisco IOS Security Features to Routers

Before you configure security features on a router, you need a plan for all the Cisco IOS security configuration steps.

The figure shows the steps to safeguard a router. The first five steps are discussed in this chapter. Though access control lists (ACLs) are discussed in the next chapter, they are a critical technology and must be configured to control and filter network traffic.

4.2.3 Manage Router Security

Basic router security consists of configuring passwords. A strong password is the most fundamental element in controlling secure access to a router. For this reason, strong passwords should always be configured.

Good password practices include the following:

- Do not write passwords down and leave them in obvious places such as your desk or on your monitor.

- Avoid dictionary words, names, phone numbers, and dates. Using dictionary words makes the passwords vulnerable to dictionary attacks.

- Combine letters, numbers, and symbols. Include at least one lowercase letter, uppercase letter, digit, and special character.

- Deliberately misspell a password. For example, **Smith** can be spelled as **Smyth** or can also include numbers such as **5mYth**. Another example could be **Security** spelled as **5ecur1ty**.

- Make passwords lengthy. The best practice is to have a minimum of eight characters. You can enforce the minimum length using a feature that is available on Cisco IOS routers, discussed later in this topic.

- Change passwords as often as possible. You should have a policy defining when and how often the passwords must be changed. Changing passwords frequently provides two advantages. This practice limits the window of opportunity in which a hacker can crack a password and limits the window of exposure after a password has been compromised.

Note: Password-leading spaces are ignored, but all spaces after the first character are not ignored.

Passphrases

A recommended method for creating strong complex passwords is to use passphrases. A passphrase is basically a sentence or phrase that serves as a more secure password. Make sure that the phrase is long enough to be hard to guess but easy to remember and type accurately.

Use a sentence, quote from a book, or song lyric that you can easily remember as the basis of your strong password or passphrase. The figure provides examples of passphrases.

By default, Cisco IOS software leaves passwords in plain text when they are entered on a router. This is not secure since anyone walking behind you when you are looking at a router configuration could snoop over your shoulder and see the password.

Using the **enable password** command or the **username** *username* **password** *password* command would result in these passwords being displayed when looking at the running configuration.

For example:

```
R1(config)# username Student password cisco123
R1(config)# do show run | include username
username Student password 0 cisco123
R1(config)#
```

The **0** displayed in the running configuration, indicates that password is not hidden.

For this reason, all passwords should be encrypted in a configuration file. Cisco IOS provides two password protection schemes:

- Simple encryption called a type 7 scheme. It uses the Cisco-defined encryption algorithm and will hide the password using a simple encryption algorithm.
- Complex encryption called a type 5 scheme. It uses a more secure MD5 hash.

The type 7 encryption can be used by the **enable password**, **username**, and **line password** commands including vty, line console, and aux port. It does not offer very much protection as it only hides the password using a simple encryption algorithm. Although not as secure as the type 5 encryption, it is still better than no encryption.

To encrypt passwords using type 7 encryption, use the **service password-encryption** global configuration command as displayed in the figure. This command prevents passwords that are displayed on the screen from being readable.

For example:

```
R1(config)# service password-encryption
R1(config)# do show run | include username
username Student password 7 03075218050061
R1(config)#
```

The **7** displayed in the running configuration indicates that password is hidden. In the figure, you can see the line console password is now hidden.

Click the Configure Password button in the figure.

Cisco recommends that Type 5 encryption be used instead of Type 7 whenever possible. MD5 encryption is a strong encryption method. It should be used whenever possible. It is configured by replacing the keyword **password** with **secret**.

Therefore, to protect the privileged EXEC level as much as possible, always configure the **enable secret** command as shown in the figure. Also make sure that the secret password is unique and does not match any other user password.

A router will always use the secret password over the enable password. For this reason, the **enable password** command should never be configured as it may give away a system password.

Note: If you forget the privileged EXEC password, then you will have to perform the password recovery procedure. This procedure is covered later in this chapter.

The local database usernames should be also configured using the **username** *username* **secret** *password* global configuration command. For example:

```
R1(config)# username Student secret cisco
  R1(config)# do show run | include username
 username Student secret 5 $1$z245$lVSTJzuYgdQDJiacwP2Tv/
R1(config)#
```

Note: Some processes may not be able to use type 5 encrypted passwords. For example PAP uses clear text passwords and cannot use MD5 encrypted passwords.

Click the Password Length button in the figure.

Cisco IOS Software Release 12.3(1) and later allow administrators to set the minimum character length for all router passwords using the `security passwords min-length` global configuration command, as shown in the figure. This command provides enhanced security access to the router by allowing you to specify a minimum password length, eliminating common passwords that are prevalent on most networks, such as "lab" and "cisco."

This command affects any new user passwords, enable passwords and secrets, and line passwords created after the command was executed. The command does not affect existing router passwords.

4.2.4 Securing Remote Administrative Access to Routers

Securing Administrative Access to Routers

Network administrators can connect to a router or switch locally or remotely. Local access through the console port is the preferred way for an administrator to connect to a device to manage it because it is secure. As companies get bigger and the number of routers and switches in the network grows, the administrator workload to connect to all the devices locally can become overwhelming.

Remote administrative access is more convenient than local access for administrators that have many devices to manage. However, if it is not implemented securely, an attacker could collect valuable confidential information. For example, implementing remote administrative access using *Telnet* can be very insecure because Telnet forwards all network traffic in clear text. An attacker could capture network traffic while an administrator is logged in remotely to a router and sniff the administrator passwords or router configuration information. Therefore, remote administrative access must be configured with additional security precautions.

To secure administrative access to routers and switches, first you will secure the administrative lines (VTY, AUX), then you will configure the network device to encrypt traffic in an SSH tunnel.

Remote Administrative Access with Telnet and SSH

Having remote access to network devices is critical for effectively managing a network. Remote access typically involves allowing Telnet, Secure Shell (SSH), HTTP, HTTP Secure (HTTPS), or SNMP connections to the router from a computer on the same internetwork as the router.

If remote access is required, your options are as follows:

- Establish a dedicated management network. The management network should include only identified administration hosts and connections to infrastructure devices. This could be accomplished using a management VLAN or by using an additional physical network to connect the devices to.

- Encrypt all traffic between the administrator computer and the router. In either case, a packet filter can be configured to only allow the identified administration hosts and protocol to access the router. For example, only permit the administration host IP address to initiate an SSH connection to the routers in the network.

Remote access not only applies to the VTY line of the router, it also applies to the TTY lines and the auxiliary (AUX) port. TTY lines provide asynchronous access to a router using a modem. Although less common than they once were, they still exist in some installations. Securing these ports is even more important than securing local terminal ports.

The best way to protect a system is to ensure that appropriate controls are applied on all lines, including VTY, TTY, and AUX lines.

Administrators should make sure that logins on all lines are controlled using an authentication mechanism, even on machines that are supposed to be inaccessible from untrusted networks. This is especially important for VTY lines and for lines connected to modems or other remote access devices.

Logins may be completely prevented on any line by configuring the router with the **login** and **no password** commands. This is the default configuration for VTYs, but not for TTYs and the AUX port. Therefore, if these lines are not required, ensure that they are configured with the **login** and **no password** command combination.

Click Config in the Prevent Logins button to view an example.

Controlling VTYs

By default, all VTY lines are configured to accept any type of remote connection. For security reasons, VTY lines should be configured to accept connections only with the protocols actually needed. This is done with the **transport input** command. For example, a VTY that was expected to receive only Telnet sessions would be configured with **transport input telnet**, and a VTY permitting both Telnet and SSH sessions would have **transport input telnet ssh** configured.

Click the VTY Access button in the figure.

The first configuration example displays how to configure the VTY to only accept Telnet and SSH connections, while the second example displays how to configure the VTY to only accept SSH connections. If the Cisco IOS image on a router supports SSH, it is strongly advisable to enable only that protocol.

A Cisco IOS device has a limited number of VTY lines, usually five. When all of the VTYs are in use, no more additional remote connections can be established. This creates the opportunity for a DoS attack. If an attacker can open remote sessions to all the VTYs on the system, the legitimate administrator may not be able to log in. The attacker does not have to log in to do this. The sessions can simply be left at the login prompt.

One way of reducing this exposure is to configure the last VTY line to accept connections only from a single, specific administrative workstation, whereas the other VTYs can accept connections from any address in a corporate network. This ensures that at least one VTY line is available to the administrator. To implement this, ACLs, along with the **ip access-class** command on the last VTY line, must be configured. This implementation is discussed in Chapter 5.

Another useful tactic is to configure VTY timeouts using the **exec-timeout** command. This prevents an idle session from consuming the VTY indefinitely. Although its effectiveness against deliberate attacks is relatively limited, it provides some protection against sessions accidentally left idle. Similarly, enabling TCP keepalives on incoming connections by using the **service tcp-keepalives-in** command can help guard against both malicious attacks and orphaned sessions caused by remote system crashes.

Click the Secure VTY button in the figure.

The configuration displays how to set the executive timeout to 3 minutes and enable TCP keepalives.

Implementing SSH to Secure Remote Administrative Access

Traditionally, remote administrative access on routers was configured using Telnet on TCP port 23. However, Telnet was developed in the days when security was not an issue. For this reason, all Telnet traffic is forwarded in plain text.

SSH has replaced Telnet as the best practice for providing remote router administration with connections that support strong privacy and session integrity. SSH uses port TCP 22. It provides functionality that is similar to that of an outbound Telnet connection, except that the connection is encrypted. With authentication and encryption, SSH allows for secure communications over an insecure network.

Not all Cisco IOS images support SSH. Only cryptographic images can. Typically, these images have image IDs of k8 or k9 in their image names. Image names are discussed in Section 5.

The SSH terminal-line access feature enables administrators to configure routers with secure access and perform the following tasks:

- Connect to a router that has multiple terminal lines connected to consoles or serial ports of other routers, switches, and devices.
- Simplify connectivity to a router from anywhere by securely connecting to the *terminal server* on a specific line.
- Allow modems attached to routers to be used for dial-out securely.
- Require authentication to each of the lines through a locally defined username and password, or a security server such as a TACACS+ or RADIUS server.

Cisco routers are capable of acting as the SSH client and server. By default, both of these functions are enabled on the router when SSH is enabled. As a client, a router can SSH to another router. As a server, a router can accept SSH client connections.

> Refer to **Figure** in online course

Configuring SSH Security

To enable SSH on the router, the following parameters must be configured:

- Hostname
- *Domain* name
- Asymmetrical keys
- Local authentication

Optional configuration parameters include:

- Timeouts
- Retries

The following steps configure SSH on a router.

Step 1: Set router parameters

Configure the router hostname with the **hostname** *hostname* command from configuration mode.

Step 2: Set the domain name

A domain name must exist to enable SSH. In this example, enter the **ip domain-name** command from global configuration mode.

Step 3: Generate asymmetric keys

You need to create a key that the router uses to encrypt its SSH management traffic with the **crypto key** *generate rsa* command from configuration mode. The router responds with a message showing the naming convention for the keys. Choose the size of the key modulus in the range of 360 to 2048 for your General Purpose Keys. Choosing a key modulus greater than 512 may take a few minutes. As a best practice, Cisco recommends using a minimum modulus length of 1024.

You should be aware that a longer modulus takes longer to generate and to use, but it offers stronger security.

You can learn more about the `crypto key` command in the Network Security course.

Step 4: Configure local authentication and vty

You must define a local user and assign SSH communication to the vty lines as shown in the figure.

Step 5: Configure SSH timeouts (optional)

Timeouts provide additional security for the connection by terminating lingering, inactive connections. Use the command `ip ssh time-out` *seconds* and the command `authentication-retries` *integer* to enable timeouts and authentication retries. Set the SSH timeout to 15 seconds and the amount of retries to 2.

To connect to a router configured with SSH, you have to use an SSH client application such as PuTTY or TeraTerm. You must be sure to choose the SSH option and that it uses TCP port 22.

Click the Use SSH button in the figure.

Using TeraTerm to connect securely to the R2 router with SSH, once the connection is initiated, the R2 displays a username prompt, followed by a password prompt. Assuming that the correct credentials are provided, TeraTerm displays the router R2 user EXEC prompt.

Complex Flash Activity

4.2.5 Logging Router Activity

Logs allow you to verify that a router is working properly or to determine whether the router has been compromised. In some cases, a log can show what types of probes or attacks are being attempted against the router or the protected network.

Configuring logging (syslog) on the router should be done carefully. Send the router logs to a designated log host. The log host should be connected to a trusted or protected network or an isolated and dedicated router interface. Harden the log host by removing all unnecessary services and accounts. Routers support different levels of logging. The eight levels range from 0, emergencies indicating that the system is unstable, to 7 for debugging messages that include all router information.

Logs can be forwarded to a variety of locations, including router memory or a dedicated syslog server. A syslog server provides a better solution because all network devices can forward their logs to one central station where an administrator can review them. An example of a syslog server application is Kiwi Syslog Daemon.

Also consider sending the logs to a second storage device, for example, to write-once media or a dedicated printer, to deal with worst-case scenarios (for example, a compromise of the log host).

The most important thing to remember about logging is that logs must be reviewed regularly. By checking over the logs regularly, you can gain a feeling for the normal behavior of your network. A sound understanding of normal operation and its reflection in the logs helps you identify abnormal or attack conditions.

Accurate time stamps are important to logging. Time stamps allow you to trace network attacks more credibly. All routers are capable of maintaining their own time of day, but this is usually not sufficient. Instead, direct the router to at least two different reliable time servers to ensure the accuracy and availability of time information. A Network Time Protocol (NTP) server may have to be configured to provide a synchronized time source for all devices. Configuring this option is beyond the scope of this course.

For example:

```
R2(config)#service timestamps ?
  debug Timestamp debug messages
  log Timestamp log messages
  <cr>
R2(config)#service timestamps
```
Later in this chapter you will learn about the **debug** command. Output from the **debug** command can also be sent to logs.

4.3 Secure Router Network Services

4.3.1 Vulnerable Router Services and Interfaces

Vulnerable Router Services and Interfaces

Cisco routers support a large number of network services at Layers 2, 3, 4, and 7, as described in the figure. Some of these services are *Application layer* protocols that allow users and host processes to connect to the router. Others are automatic processes and settings intended to support legacy or specialized configurations that pose security risks. Some of these services can be restricted or disabled to improve security without degrading the operational use of the router. General security practice for routers should be used to support only the traffic and protocols a network needs.

Most of the services listed in this section are usually not required. The table in the figure describes general vulnerable router services and lists best practices associated to those services.

Turning off a network service on the router itself does not prevent it from supporting a network where that protocol is employed. For example, a network may require TFTP services to backup configuration files and IOS images. This service is typically provided by a dedicated TFTP server. In certain instances, a router could also be configured as a TFTP server. However, this is very unusual. Therefore, in most cases the TFTP service on the router should be disabled.

In many cases, Cisco IOS software supports turning a service off entirely, or restricting access to particular network segments or sets of hosts. If a particular portion of a network needs a service but the rest does not, the restriction features should be employed to limit the scope of the service.

Turning off an automatic network feature usually prevents a certain kind of network traffic from being processed by the router, or prevents it from traversing the router. For example, IP source routing is a little-used feature of IP that can be utilized in network attacks. Unless it is required for the network to operate, IP source routing should be disabled.

Note: CDP is leveraged in some IP Phone implementations. This needs to be considered before broadly disabling the service.

There are a variety of commands that are required to disable services. The **show running-config** output in the figure provides a sample configuration of various services which has been disabled.

Services which should typically be disabled are listed below. These include:

- Small services such as echo, discard, and chargen - Use the **no service tcp-small-servers** or **no service udp-small-servers** command.
- *BOOTP* - Use the **no ip bootp server** command.
- Finger - Use the **no service finger** command.
- HTTP - Use the **no ip http server** command.
- SNMP - Use the **no snmp-server** command.

It is also important to disable services that allow certain packets to pass through the router, send special packets, or are used for remote router configuration. The corresponding commands to disable these services are:

- Cisco Discovery Protocol (*CDP*) - Use the `no cdp run` command.
- Remote configuration - Use the `no service config` command.
- Source routing - Use the `no ip source-route` command.
- Classless routing - Use the `no ip classless` command.

The interfaces on the router can be made more secure by using certain commands in interface configuration mode:

- Unused interfaces - Use the `shutdown` command.
- No SMURF attacks - Use the `no ip directed-broadcast` command.
- *Ad hoc* routing - Use the `no ip proxy-arp` command.

SNMP, NTP, and DNS Vulnerabilities

The figure describes three management services which should also be secured. The methods for disabling or tuning the configurations for these services are beyond the scope of this course. These services are covered in the CCNP: Implementing Secure Converged Wide-area Network course.

The descriptions and guidelines to secure these services are listed below.

SNMP

SNMP is the standard Internet protocol for automated remote monitoring and administration. There are several different versions of SNMP with different security properties. Versions of SNMP prior to version 3 shuttle information in clear text. Normally, SNMP version 3 should be used.

NTP

Cisco routers and other hosts use NTP to keep their time-of-day clocks accurate. If possible, network administrators should configure all routers as part of an NTP hierarchy, which makes one router the master timer and provides its time to other routers on the network. If an NTP hierarchy is not available on the network, you should disable NTP.

Disabling NTP on an interface does not prevent NTP messages from traversing the router. To reject all NTP messages at a particular interface, use an access list.

DNS

Cisco IOS software supports looking up hostnames with the Domain Name System (DNS). DNS provides the mapping between names, such as central.mydomain.com to IP addresses, such as 14.2.9.250.

Unfortunately, the basic DNS protocol offers no authentication or integrity assurance. By default, name queries are sent to the broadcast address 255.255.255.255.

If one or more *name servers* are available on the network, and it is desirable to use names in Cisco IOS commands, explicitly set the name server addresses using the global configuration command `ip name-server` *addresses*. Otherwise, turn off DNS name resolution with the command `no ip domain-lookup`. It is also a good idea to give the router a name, using the command `hostname`. The name given to the router appears in the prompt.

4.3.2 Securing Routing Protocols

Routing Protocol Authentication Overview

As a network administrator, you have to be aware that your routers are at risk from attack just as much as your end-user systems. Anyone with a packet sniffer such as Wireshark can read information propagating between routers. In general, routing systems can be attacked in two ways:

- Disruption of peers
- Falsification of routing information

Disruption of peers is the less critical of the two attacks because routing protocols heal themselves, making the disruption last only slightly longer than the attack itself.

A more subtle class of attack targets the information carried within the routing protocol. Falsified routing information may generally be used to cause systems to misinform (lie to) each other, cause a DoS, or cause traffic to follow a path it would not normally follow. The consequences of falsifying routing information are as follows:

Step 1. Redirect traffic to create routing loops as shown in the figure

Step 2. Redirect traffic so it can be monitored on an insecure link

Step 3. Redirect traffic to discard it

A straightforward way to attack the routing system is to attack the routers running the routing protocols, gain access to the routers and inject false information. Be aware that anyone "listening" can capture routing updates.

Click the Play button in the figure to view an animation of a routing loop attack.

The animation shows an example of an attack that creates a routing loop. An attacker has been able to connect directly to the link between routers R2 and R3. The attacker injects false routing information destined to router R1 only, indicating that R3 is the preferred destination to the 192.168.10.10/32 host route. Although R1 has a *routing table* entry to the directly connected 192.168.10.0/24 network, it will add the injected route to its routing table because of the longer *subnet mask*. A route with a longer matching subnet mask is considered to be superior to a route with a shorter subnet mask. Consequently when a router receives a packet it will select the longer subnet mask because it is a more precise route to the destination.

When PC3 sends a packet to PC1 (192.168.10.10/24), R1 will not forward the packet to the PC1 host. Instead it will route the packet to router R3, because, as far as it is concerned, the best path to 192.168.10.10/32 is through R3. When R3 gets the packet, it will look in its routing table and forward the packet back to R1, which creates the loop.

The best way to protect routing information on the network is to authenticate routing protocol packets using message digest algorithm 5 (MD5). An algorithm like MD5 allows the routers to compare signatures that should all be the same.

Click the Protect Update button in the figure.

The figure shows how each router in the update chain creates a signature. The three components of such a system include:

Step 1. Encryption algorithm, which is generally public knowledge

Step 2. Key used in the encryption algorithm, which is a secret shared by the routers authenticating their packets

Step 3. Contents of the packet itself

Click the Operation button in the figure.

Click Play to view an animation.

In the animation we see how each router authenticates the routing information. Generally, the originator of the routing information produces a signature using the key and routing data it is about to send as inputs to the encryption algorithm. The routers receiving this routing data can then repeat the process using the same key, the data it has received, and the same routing data. If the signature the receiver computes is the same as the signature the sender computes, the data and key must be the same as the sender transmitted, and the update is authenticated.

RIPv2, EIGRP, OSPF, *IS-IS*, and *BGP* all support various forms of MD5 authentication.

Configuring RIPv2 with Routing Protocol Authentication

The topology in the figure is displaying a network configured with RIPv2 routing protocol. RIPv2 supports routing protocol authentication. To secure routing updates each router must be configured to support authentication. The steps to secure RIPv2 updates are as follows:

Step 1. Prevent RIP routing update propagation

Step 2. Prevent unauthorized reception of RIP updates

Step 3. Verify the operation of RIP routing

Prevent RIP Routing Update Propagation

You need to prevent an intruder listening on the network from receiving updates to which they are not entitled. You do this by forcing all interfaces on the router into passive mode, and then bringing up only those interfaces that are required for sending and receiving RIP updates. An interface in passive mode receives updates but does not send updates. You must configure passive mode interfaces on all the routers in the network.

Click the Config button then Step 1.

The figure shows the configuration commands to control which interfaces will participate in the routing updates. Routing updates should never be advertised on interfaces which are not connected to other routers. For example, the LAN interfaces on router R1 do not connect to other routers and therefore should not advertise routing updates. Only the S0/0/0 interface on router R1 should advertise routing updates.

In the screen output, the `passive-interface default` command disables routing advertisements on all interfaces. This also includes the S0/0/0 interface. The `no passive-interface s0/0/0` command enables the S0/0/0 interface to send and receive RIP updates.

Click the Topology button then Step 2.

Prevent Unauthorized Reception of RIP Updates

In the figure the intruder is prevented from intercepting RIP updates because MD5 authentication has been enabled on routers, R1, R2 and R3; the routers that are participating in the RIP updates.

Click the Config button then Step 2.

The output shows the commands to configure routing protocol authentication on router R1. Routers R2 and R3 also need to be configured with these commands on the appropriate interfaces.

The example shows commands to create a key chain named RIP_KEY. Although multiple key can be considered our example only shows one key. Key 1 is configured to contain a key string called cisco. The key string is similar to a password and routers exchanging authentication keys must configured with the same key string. Interface S0/0/0 is configured to support MD5 authentication. The RIP_KEY chain and the routing update, are processed using the MD5 algorithm to produce a unique signature.

Once R1 is configured, the other routers will receive routing updates with a unique signature and consequently will no longer be able to decipher the updates from R1. This condition will remain until each router in the network is configured with routing protocol authentication.

Click the Topology button then Step 3.

Verify the Operation of RIP Routing

After you have configured all the routers in the network you need to verify the operation of RIP routing in the network.

Click the Config button then Step 3.

Using the `show ip route` command the output confirms that router R1 has authenticated with the other routers and has been able to acquire the routes from the routers R2 and R3.

Overview of Routing Protocol Authentication for EIGRP and OSPF

Routing protocol authentication should also be configured for other routing protocols such as EIGRP and OSPF. For details on routing protocol authentication for EIGRP and OSPF, refer to CCNP2: Implementing Secure Converged Wide-area Networks.

Click the EIGRP button in the figure.

EIGRP

The figure shows the commands used to configure routing protocol authentication for EIGRP on router R1. These commands are very similar to the ones you used for RIPv2 MD5 authentication. The steps to configure EIGRP routing protocol authentication on router R1 are as follows:

Step 1. The top highlighted area shows how to create a key chain to be used by all routers in your network. These commands create a key chain named EIGRP_KEY and places your terminal in keychain configuration mode, a key number of 1 and a key string value of cisco.

Step 2. The bottom highlighted area shows how to enable MD5 authentication in EIGRP packets traversing an interface.

Click the OSPF button in the figure.

OSPF

The figure shows the commands used to configure routing protocol authentication for OSPF on router R1 on interface S0/0/0. The first command specifies the key that will be used for MD5 authentication. The next command enables MD5 authentication.

This activity covers both OSPF simple authentication and OSPF MD5 (message digest 5) authentication. You can enable authentication in OSPF to exchange routing update information in a secure manner. With simple authentication, the password is sent in clear-text over the network. Simple authentication is used when devices within an *area* cannot support the more secure MD5 authentication. With MD5 authentication, the password is not sent over the network. MD5 is considered the most secure OSPF authentication mode. When you configure authentication, you must configure an entire area with the same type of authentication. In this activity, you will configure simple authentication between R1 and R2, and MD5 authentication between R2 and R3.

Detailed instructions are provided within the activity as well as in the PDF link below.

Activity Instructions (PDF)

4.3.3 Locking Down Your Router with Cisco Auto Secure

Cisco AutoSecure uses a single command to disable non-essential system processes and services, eliminating potential security threats. You can configure AutoSecure in privileged EXEC mode using the **auto secure** command in one of these two modes:

- *Interactive mode* - This mode prompts you with options to enable and disable services and other security features. This is the default mode.
- *Non-interactive mode* - This mode automatically executes the auto secure command with the recommended Cisco default settings. This mode is enabled with the no-interact command option.

Click the Router Output button in the figure.

Perform AutoSecure on a Cisco Router

The screen output shows a partial output from a Cisco AutoSecure configuration. To start the process of securing a router issue the **auto secure** command. Cisco AutoSecure will ask you for a number of items including :

- Interface specifics
- Banners
- Passwords
- SSH
- IOS firewall features

Note: The Cisco Router and Security Device Manager (SDM) provides a similar feature as the Cisco AutoSecure command. This feature is described in the "Using Cisco SDM" section.

4.4 Using Cisco SDM

4.4.1 Cisco SDM Overview

What is Cisco SDM?

The Cisco Router and Security Device Manager (SDM) is an easy-to-use, web-based device-management tool designed for configuring LAN, WAN, and security features on Cisco IOS software-based routers.

The figure shows the main screen of SDM. The interface helps network administrators of small- to medium-sized businesses perform day-to-day operations. It provides easy-to-use smart wizards, automates router security management, and assists through comprehensive online help and tutorials.

Cisco SDM supports a wide range of Cisco IOS software releases. It ships preinstalled by default on all new Cisco integrated services routers. If it is not preinstalled, you will have to install it. The SDM files can be installed on the router, a PC, or on both. An advantage of installing SDM on the PC is that it saves router memory, and allows you to use SDM to manage other routers on the network. If Cisco SDM is pre-installed on the router, Cisco recommends using Cisco SDM to perform the initial configuration.

Cisco SDM Features

Cisco SDM simplifies router and security configuration through the use of several intelligent wizards to enable efficient configuration of key router virtual private network (VPN) and Cisco IOS firewall parameters. This capability permits administrators to quickly and easily deploy, configure, and monitor Cisco access routers.

Cisco SDM smart wizards guide users step-by-step through router and security configuration workflow by systematically configuring LAN and WAN interfaces, firewall, IPS, and VPNs.

Cisco SDM smart wizards can intelligently detect incorrect configurations and propose fixes, such as allowing DHCP traffic through a firewall if the WAN interface is DHCP-addressed. Online help embedded within Cisco SDM contains appropriate background information, in addition to step-by-step procedures to help users enter correct data in Cisco SDM.

4.4.2 Configuring Your Router to Support Cisco SDM

Cisco SDM should be installed on all new Cisco routers. If you have a router that is already in use but that does not have Cisco SDM, you can install and run it without disrupting network traffic. Before you can install it on an operational router, you must ensure that a few configuration settings are present in the router configuration file. The figure shows a topology in which the system administrator will install Cisco SDM on router R1.

To configure Cisco SDM on a router already in use, without disrupting network traffic, follow these steps:

Step 1. Access the router's Cisco CLI interface using Telnet or the console connection

Step 2. Enable the HTTP and HTTPS servers on the router

Step 3 Create a user account defined with privilege level 15 (enable privileges).

Step 4 Configure SSH and Telnet for local login and privilege level 15.

Click the Router Output button in the figure.

The screen output shows an example of the configuration needed to ensure you can install and run Cisco SDM on a production router without disrupting network traffic.

4.4.3 Starting Cisco SDM

Cisco SDM is stored in the router *flash memory*. It can also be stored on a local PC. To launch the Cisco SDM use the HTTPS protocol and put the IP address of the router into the *browser*. The figure shows the browser with an address of https://198.162.20.1 and the launch page for Cisco SDM. The http:// prefix can be used if SSL is not available. When the username and password dialog box appears (not shown), enter a username and password for the privileged (privilege level 15) account on the router. After the launch page appears a signed Cisco SDM Java applet appears which must remain open while Cisco SDM is running. Because it is a signed Cisco SDM Java applet you may be prompted to accept a certificate. The certificate security alert appears in the bottom right of the figure.

Note: The sequence of login steps may vary depending on if you run Cisco SDM from a personal computer, or directly from a Cisco ISR router.

4.4.4 The Cisco SDM Interface

Cisco SDM Home Page Overview

After Cisco SDM has started and you have logged in, the first page displayed is the Overview page.

This page displays the router model, total amount of memory, the versions of flash, IOS, and SDM, the hardware installed, and a summary of some security features, such as firewall status and the number of active VPN connections.

Specifically, it provides basic information about the router hardware, software, and configuration:

- Menu bar - The top of the screen has a typical menu bar with File, Edit, View, Tools, and Help menu items.

- Tool bar - Below the menu bar, it has the SDM wizards and modes you can select.

- Router information - The current mode is displayed on the left side under the tool bar.

Note: The menu bar, tool bar, and current mode are always displayed at the top of each screen. The other areas of the screen change based upon the mode and function you are performing.

- Configuration overview - Summarizes the configuration settings. To view the running configuration, click the **View Running Config** button.

About Your Router Area

Refer to Figure in online course

When you click the buttons in the figure, you will be able to see the details associated with each of the following *GUI* elements:

About Your Router - The area of the Cisco SDM home page that shows you basic information about the router hardware and software, and includes the following elements:

- Host Name - This area shows the configured hostname for the router, which is RouterX

- Hardware - This area shows the router model number, the available and total amount of *RAM*, and the amount of Flash memory available.

- Software - This area describes the Cisco IOS software and Cisco SDM versions running on the router.

- The Feature Availability bar, found across the bottom of the About Your Router tab, shows the features available in the Cisco IOS image that the router is using. If the indicator beside each feature is green, the feature is available. If it is red it is not available. Check marks show that the feature is configured on the router. In the figure, Cisco SDM shows that IP, firewall, VPN, IPS, and NAC are available, but only IP is configured.

Configuration Overview Area

Refer to Figure in online course

The figure shows the configuration overview area of the Cisco SDM home page. When you click the buttons in the figure, you will be able to see the details associated with each of the following GUI elements:

- *Interfaces and Connections* - This area displays interface-related and connection-related information, including the number of connections that are up and down, the total number of LAN and WAN interfaces that are present in the router, and the number of LAN and WAN interfaces currently configured on the router. It also displays DHCP information.

- *Firewall Policies* - This area displays firewall-related information, including if a firewall is in place, the number of trusted (inside) interfaces, untrusted (outside) interfaces, and DMZ interfaces. It also displays the name of the interface to which a firewall has been applied, whether the interface is designated as an inside or an outside interface, and if the *NAT* rule has been applied to this interface.

- *VPN* - This area displays VPN-related information, including the number of active VPN connections, the number of configured site-to-site VPN connections, and the number of active VPN clients.

- *Routing -* This area displays the number of static routes and which routing protocols are configured.

4.4.5 Cisco SDM Wizards

Cisco SDM provides a number of wizards to help you configure a Cisco ISR router. Once a task is selected from the task area in the Cisco SDM GUI, the task pane allows you to select a wizard. The figure shows various Cisco SDM GUI screens for the Basic NAT wizard. NAT is discussed later in the IP Addressing Services sections course.

Check http://www.cisco.com/go/sdm for the latest information about the Cisco SDM wizards and the interfaces they support.

4.4.6 Locking Down a Router with Cisco SDM

The Cisco SDM one-step lockdown wizard implements almost all of the security configurations that Cisco AutoSecure offers. The one-step lockdown wizard is accessed from the Configure GUI interface by clicking the Security Audit task. The one-step lockdown wizard tests your router configuration for potential security problems and automatically makes any necessary configuration changes to correct any problems found.

Do not assume that the network is secure simply because you executed a one-step lockdown. In addition, not all the features of Cisco AutoSecure are implemented in Cisco SDM. AutoSecure features that are implemented differently in Cisco SDM include the following:

- Disables SNMP, and does not configure SNMP version 3.
- Enables and configures SSH on crypto Cisco IOS images
- Does not enable Service Control Point or disable other access and *file transfer* services, such as FTP.

Click the buttons in the figure to explore the steps of the Cisco one-step lockdown wizard.

4.5 Secure Router Management

4.5.1 Maintaining Cisco IOS Software Images

Periodically, the router requires updates to be loaded to either the operating system or the configuration file. These updates are necessary to fix known security vulnerabilities, support new features that allow more advanced security policies, or improve performance.

Note: It is not always a good idea to upgrade to the very latest version of Cisco IOS software. Many times that release is not stable.

There are certain guidelines that you must follow when changing the Cisco IOS software on a router. Changes are classified as either updates or upgrades. An update replaces one release with another without upgrading the feature set. The software might be updated to fix a bug or to replace a release that is no longer supported. Updates are free.

An upgrade replaces a release with one that has an upgraded feature set. The software might be upgraded to add new features or technologies, or replace a release that is no longer supported. Upgrades are not free. Cisco.com offers guidelines to assist in determining which method applies.

Cisco recommends following a four-phase migration process to simplify network operations and management. When you follow a repeatable process, you can also benefit from reduced costs in operations, management, and training. The four phases are:

- *Plan-* Set goals, identify resources, profile network hardware and software, and create a preliminary schedule for migrating to new releases.
- *Design-* Choose new Cisco IOS releases and create a strategy for migrating to the releases.
- *Implement-* Schedule and execute the migration.
- *Operate-* Monitor the migration progress and make backup copies of images that are running on your network.

There are a number of tools available on Cisco.com to aid in migrating Cisco IOS software. You can use the tools to get information about releases, feature sets, platforms, and images. The following tools do not require a Cisco.com login:

- *Cisco IOS Reference Guide-* Covers the basics of the Cisco IOS software family
- *Cisco IOS software technical documents-* Documentation for each release of Cisco IOS software
- *Cisco Feature Navigator-* Finds releases that support a set of software features and hardware, and compares releases

The following tools require valid Cisco.com login accounts:

- *Download Software-* Cisco IOS software downloads
- *Bug Toolkit-* Searches for known software fixes based on software version, feature set, and keywords
- *Software Advisor-* Compares releases, matches Cisco IOS software and Cisco Catalyst OS features to releases, and finds out which software release supports a given hardware device
- *Cisco IOS Upgrade Planner-* Finds releases by hardware, release, and feature set, and downloads images of Cisco IOS software

For a complete listing of tools available on Cisco.com, go to http://www.cisco.com/en/US/support/tsd_most_requested_tools.html.

4.5.2 Managing Cisco IOS Images

Cisco IOS File Systems and Devices

The availability of the network can be at risk if a router configuration or operating system is compromised. Attackers who gain access to infrastructure devices can alter or delete configuration files. They can also upload incompatible IOS images or delete the IOS image. The changes are invoked automatically or invoked once the device is rebooted.

To mitigate against these problems, you have to be able to save, back up, and restore configuration and IOS images. To do so, you learn how to carry out a few file management operations in Cisco IOS software.

Cisco IOS devices provide a feature called the Cisco IOS Integrated File System (IFS). This system allows you to create, navigate, and manipulate directories on a Cisco device. The directories available depend on the platform.

For instance, the figure displays the output of the `show file systems` command which lists all of the available file systems on a Cisco 1841 router. This command provides insightful information such as the amount of available and free memory, the type of file system and its permissions. Permissions include read only (ro), write only (wo), and read and write (rw).

Although there are several file systems listed, of interest to us will be the tftp, flash and *nvram* file systems. The remainder of the file systems listed are beyond the scope of this course.

Network file systems include using FTP, trivial FTP (TFTP), or Remote Copy Protocol (*RCP*). This course focuses on TFTP.

Notice that the flash file system also has an asterisks preceding it which indicates that this is the current default file system. Recall that the bootable IOS is located in flash, therefore the pound symbol (#) appended to the flash listing indicates that this is a bootable disk.

Click the Flash button in the figure.

This figure lists the content of the current default file system, which in this case is flash as was indicated by the asterisks preceding the listing in the previous figure. There are several files located in flash, but of specific interest is the last listing. that is the file image name of the current IOS running in RAM.

Click the NVRAM button in the figure.

To view the contents of NVRAM, you must change the current default file system using the `cd` change directory command. The `pwd` present working directory command verifies that we are located in the NVRAM directory. Finally, the `dir` command lists the contents of NVRAM. Although there are several configuration files listed, of specific interest to us is the startup-configuration file.

URL Prefixes for Cisco Devices

When a network administrator wants to move files around on a computer, the operating system offers a visible file structure to specify sources and destinations. Administrators do not have visual cues when working at a router CLI. The show file systems command in the previous topic displayed the various file systems available on the Cisco 1841 platform.

File locations are specified in Cisco IFS using the URL convention. The URLs used by Cisco IOS platforms look similar to the format you know from the web.

For instance, the TFTP example in the figure is: tftp://192.168.20.254/configs/backup-config.

- The expression "tftp:" is called the prefix.
- Everything after the double-slash (//) defines the location.
- 192.168.20.254 is the location of the TFTP server.
- "configs" is the master directory.
- "backup-config" is the filename.

The URL prefix specifies the file system. Scroll over the various buttons in the figure to view common prefixes and syntax associated to each.

Commands for Managing Configuration Files

Good practice for maintaining system availability is to ensure you always have backup copies of the startup configuration files and IOS image files. The Cisco IOS software `copy` command is used to move configuration files from one component or device to another, such as RAM, NVRAM, or a TFTP server. The figure highlights the command syntax.

The following provides examples of common **copy** command use. The examples list two methods to accomplish the same tasks. The first example is a simple syntax and the second example provides a more explicit example.

Copy the running configuration from RAM to the startup configuration in NVRAM:

R2# `copy running-config startup-config`
 R2# `copy system:running-config nvram:startup-config`

Copy the running configuration from RAM to a remote location:

R2# `copy running-config tftp:`
 R2# `copy system:running-config tftp:`

Copy a configuration from a remote source to the running configuration:

R2# `copy tftp: running-config`
 R2# `copy tftp: system:running-config`

Copy a configuration from a remote source to the startup configuration:

R2# `copy tftp: startup-config`
 R2# `copy tftp: nvram:startup-config`

Cisco IOS File Naming Conventions

The Cisco IOS image file is based on a special naming convention. The name for the Cisco IOS image file contains multiple parts, each with a specific meaning. It is important that you understand this naming convention when upgrading and selecting an IOS.

For example, the filename in the figure is explained as follows:

The first part, **c1841**, identifies the platform on which the image runs. In this example, the platform is a Cisco 1841.

The second part, **ipbase**, specifies the feature set. In this case, "ipbase" refers to the basic IP internetworking image. Other feature set possibilities include:

i - Designates the IP feature set

j - Designates the enterprise feature set (all protocols)

s - Designates a PLUS feature set (extra queuing, manipulation, or translations)

56i - Designates 56-bit IPsec *DES* encryption

3 - Designates the firewall/IDS

k2 - Designates the 3DES IPsec encryption (168 bit)

The third part, **mz**, indicates where the image runs and if the file is compressed. In this example, "mz" indicates that the file runs from RAM and is compressed.

The fourth part, **12.3-14.T7**, is the version number.

The final part, **bin**, is the file extension. The .bin extension indicates that this is a binary executable file.

4.5.3 TFTP Managed Cisco IOS Images

Using TFTP Servers to Manage IOS Images

Production internetworks usually span wide areas and contain multiple routers. It is an important task of an administrator to routinely upgrade Cisco IOS images whenever exploits and vulnerabilities are discovered. It is also a sound practice to ensure that all of your platforms are running the same version of Cisco IOS software whenever possible. Finally, for any network, it is always prudent to retain a backup copy of the Cisco IOS software image in case the system image in the router becomes corrupted or accidentally erased.

Widely distributed routers need a source or backup location for Cisco IOS software images. Using a network TFTP server allows image and configuration uploads and downloads over the network. The network TFTP server can be another router, a workstation, or a host system.

As any network grows, storage of Cisco IOS software images and configuration files on the central TFTP server enables control of the number and revision level of Cisco IOS images and configuration files that must be maintained.

Before changing a Cisco IOS image on the router, you need to complete these tasks:

- Determine the memory required for the update and, if necessary, install additional memory.
- Set up and test the file transfer capability between the administrator host and the router.
- Schedule the required downtime, normally outside of business hours, for the router to perform the update.

When you are ready to do the update, carry out these steps:

- Shut down all interfaces on the router not needed to perform the update.
- Back up the current operating system and the current configuration file to a TFTP server.
- Load the update for either the operating system or the configuration file.
- Test to confirm that the update works properly. If the tests are successful, you can then re-enable the interfaces you disabled. If the tests are not successful, back out the update, determine what went wrong, and start again.

A great challenge for *network operators* is to minimize the downtime after a router has been compromised and the operating software and configuration data have been erased from persistent storage. The operator must retrieve an archived copy (if one exists) of the configuration and restore a working image to the router. Recovery must then be performed for each affected router, which adds to the total network downtime.

Bear in mind that the Cisco IOS software resilient configuration feature enables a router to secure and maintain a working copy of the running operating system image and configuration so that those files can withstand malicious attempts to erase the contents of persistent storage (NVRAM and flash).

4.5.4 Backing up and Upgrading Software Image

Backing Up IOS Software Image

Basic management tasks include saving backups of your configuration files as well as downloading and installing upgraded configuration files when directed. A software backup image file is created by copying the image file from a router to a network TFTP server.

To copy a Cisco IOS image software from flash memory to the network TFTP server, you should follow these suggested steps.

Click the Topology and Config buttons in the figure as you progress through each step.

Step 1. Ping the TFTP server to make sure you have access to it.

Step 2. Verify that the TFTP server has sufficient disk space to accommodate the Cisco IOS software image. Use the `show flash:` command on the router to determine the size of the Cisco IOS image file.

The `show flash:` command is an important tool to gather information about the router memory and image file. It can determine the following:

- Total amount of flash memory on the router
- Amount of flash memory available
- Name of all the files stored in the flash memory

With steps 1 and 2 completed, now back up the software image.

Step 3. Copy the current system image file from the router to the network TFTP server, using the `copy flash: tftp:` command in privileged EXEC mode. The command requires that you to enter the IP address of the remote host and the name of the source and destination system image files.

During the copy process, exclamation points (!) indicate the progress. Each exclamation point signifies that one UDP segment has successfully transferred.

Upgrading IOS Software Images

Upgrading a system to a newer software version requires a different system image file to be loaded on the router. Use the `copy tftp: flash:` command to download the new image from the network TFTP server.

Click the Config button in the figure.

The command prompts you for the IP address of the remote host and the name of the source and destination system image file. Enter the appropriate filename of the update image just as it appears on the server.

After these entries are confirmed, the `Erase flash:` prompt appears. Erasing flash memory makes room for the new image. Erase flash memory if there is not sufficient flash memory for more than one Cisco IOS image. If no free flash memory is available, the erase routine is required before new files can be copied. The system informs you of these conditions and prompts for a response.

Each exclamation point (!) means that one UDP segment has successfully transferred.

Note: Make sure that the Cisco IOS image loaded is appropriate for the router platform. If the wrong Cisco IOS image is loaded, the router could be made unbootable, requiring ROM monitor (ROMmon) intervention.

In this activity, you will configure access to a TFTP server and upload a newer, more advanced Cisco IOS image. Although Packet Tracer simulates upgrading the Cisco IOS image on a router, it does not simulate backing up a Cisco IOS image to the TFTP server. In addition, although the image you are upgrading to is more advanced, this Packet Tracer simulation will not reflect the upgrade by enabling more advanced commands. The same Packet Tracer command set will still be in effect.

Detailed instructions are provided within the activity as well as in the PDF link below.

Activity Instructions (PDF)

4.5.5 Recovering Software Images

Restoring IOS Software Images

A router cannot function without its Cisco IOS software. Should the IOS be deleted or become corrupt, an administrator must then copy an image to the router for it to become operational again

One method to accomplish this would be to use the Cisco IOS image that was previously saved to the TFTP server. In the example in the figure, the IOS image on R1 was backed up to a TFTP server connected to R2. R1 is not able to reach that TFTP server in its current state.

When an IOS on a router is accidentally deleted from flash, the router is still operational because the IOS is running in RAM. However, it is crucial that the router is not rebooted at this time since it would not be able to find a valid IOS in flash.

In the figure, the IOS on router R1 has accidentally been deleted from flash. Unfortunately, the router has been rebooted and can no longer load an IOS. It is now loading the ROMmon prompt by default. While in this state, router R1 needs to retrieve the IOS which was previously copied to the TFTP server connected to R2. In this scenario, the TFTP will be directly connected to router R1. Having made preparations with the TFTP server, carry out the following procedure.

Step 1. Connect the devices.

- Connect the PC of the system administrator to the console port on the affected router.
- Connect the TFTP server to the first Ethernet port on the router. In the figure, R1 is a Cisco 1841, therefore the port is Fa0/0. Enable the TFTP server and configure it with a static IP address 192.168.1.1/24.

Step 2. Boot the router and set the ROMmon variables.

Because the router does not have a valid Cisco IOS image, the router boots automatically into ROMmon mode. There are very few commands available in ROMmon mode. You can view these commands by typing ? at the rommon> command prompt.

You must enter all of the variables listed in the figure. When you enter the ROMmon variables, be aware of the following:

- Variable names are case sensitive.
- Do not include any spaces before or after the = symbol.
- Where possible, use a text editor to cut and paste the variables into the terminal window. The full line must be typed accurately.
- Navigational keys are not operational.

Router R1 must now be configured with the appropriate values to connect to the TFTP server. The syntax of the ROMmon commands is very crucial. Although the IP addresses, subnet mask, and image name in the figure are only examples, it is vital that the syntax displayed be followed when configuring the router. Keep in mind that the actual variables will vary depending on your configuration.

When you have entered the variables, proceed to the next step.

Step 3. Enter the `tftpdnld` command at the ROMmon prompt.

The command displays the required environment variables and warns that all existing data in flash will be erased. Type **y** to proceed, and press **Enter**. The router attempts to connect to the TFTP server to initiate the download. When connected, the download begins as indicated by the exclamation mark (!) marks. Each ! indicates that one UDP segment has been received by the router.

You can use the `reset` command to reload the router with the new Cisco IOS image.

Using xmodem to Restore an IOS Image

Using the **tftpdnld** command is a very quick way of copying the image file. Another method for restoring a Cisco IOS image to a router is by using Xmodem. However, the file transfer is accomplished using the console cable and is therefore very slow when compared to the **tftpdnld** command.

If the Cisco IOS image is lost, the router goes into ROMmon mode when it boots up. ROMmon supports Xmodem. With that capability, the router can communicate with a *terminal emulation* application, such as HyperTerminal, on the PC of a system administrator. A system administrator who has a copy of the Cisco IOS image on a PC can restore it to the router by making a console connection between the PC and the router and running Xmodem from HyperTerminal.

The steps the administrator follows are shown in the figure.

Step 1. Connect the PC of the system administrator to the console port on the affected router. Open a terminal emulation session between the router R1 and the PC of the system administrator.

Step 2. Boot the router and issue the **xmodem** command at the ROMmon command prompt.

The command syntax is **xmodem** [**-cyr**] [*filename*]. The cyr option varies depending on the configuration. For instance, **-c** specifies CRC-16, **y** specifies the Ymodem protocol, and **r** copies the image to RAM. The filename is the name of the file to be transferred.

Accept all prompts when asked, as shown in the figure.

Step 3. The figure shows the process for sending a file using HyperTerminal. In this case, Select **Transfer > Send File**.

Step 4. Browse to the location of the Cisco IOS image you want to transfer and choose the Xmodem protocol. Click **Send**. A dialog box appears displaying the status of the download. It takes several seconds before the host and the router begin transferring the information.

As the download begins, the Packet and Elapsed fields increment. Take note of the estimated time remaining indicator. The download time could be dramatically improved if you change the connection speed of HyperTerminal and the router from 9600 b/s to 115000 b/s.

When the transfer is complete, the router automatically reloads with the new Cisco IOS.

4.5.6 Troubleshooting Cisco IOS Configurations

Cisco IOS Troubleshooting Commands

When you have a valid Cisco IOS image running on all the routers in the network, and all the configurations are backed up, you can manually tune configurations for individual devices to improve their performance in the network.

Two commands that are extensively used in day-to-day network administration are **show** and **debug**. The difference between the two is significant. A **show** command lists the configured parameters and their values. The **debug** command allows you to trace the execution of a process. Use the **show** command to verify configurations. Use the **debug** command to identify traffic flows through interfaces and router processes.

The figure summarizes the characteristics of the **show** and **debug** commands. The best time to learn about the output generated by these commands is when a network is fully operational. This way you will be able to recognize what is missing or incorrect when using the commands to troubleshoot a problem network.

Using the show Command

The **show** command displays static information. Use **show** commands when gathering facts for isolating problems in an internetwork, including problems with interfaces, nodes, media, servers, clients, or applications. You may also use it frequently to confirm that configuration changes have been implemented.

The example in the figure provides a sample output of the `show protocols` command. The Cisco IOS command guide lists 1,463 `show` commands. When you are at the command prompt, type `show ?` for a list of available `show` commands for the level and mode you are operating.

Using the `debug` Command

When you configure a router, the commands you enter initiate many more processes than you see in the simple line of code. Therefore, tracing your written configurations line-by-line does not reveal all the possibilities for error. Instead, you need some way of capturing data from the device as each step in a running process is initiated.

By default, the router sends the output from `debug` commands and system error messages to the console. Remember that you can redirect debug output to a syslog server.

Note: Debugging output is assigned high priority in the *CPU* process queue and can therefore interfere with normal production processes on a network. For this reason, use `debug` commands during quiet hours and only to troubleshoot specific problems.

The `debug` command displays dynamic data and events. Use `debug` to check the flow of protocol traffic for problems, protocol bugs, or misconfigurations. The `debug` command provides a flow of information about the traffic being seen (or not seen) on an interface, error messages generated by nodes on the network, protocol-specific diagnostic packets, and other useful troubleshooting data. Use `debug` commands when operations on the router or network must be viewed to determine if events or packets are working properly.

All `debug` commands are entered in privileged EXEC mode, and most `debug` commands take no arguments. To list and see a brief description of all the debugging command options, enter the `debug ?` command in privileged EXEC mode.

Caution: It is important to turn off debugging when you have finished your troubleshooting. The best way to ensure there are no lingering debugging operations running is to use the `no debug all` command.

Considerations when using the `debug` Command

It is one thing to use `debug` commands to troubleshoot a lab network that lacks end-user application traffic. It is another thing to use `debug` commands on a production network that users depend on for data flow. Without proper precautions, the impact of a broadly focused `debug` command could make matters worse.

With proper, selective, and temporary use of `debug` commands, you can obtain potentially useful information without needing a protocol analyzer or other third-party tool.

Other considerations for using `debug` commands are as follows:

- When the information you need from the `debug` command is interpreted and the debug (and any other related configuration setting, if any) is finished, the router can resume its faster switching. Problem-solving can be resumed, a better-targeted action plan created, and the network problem resolved.

- Be aware that the `debug` commands may generate too much data that is of little use for a specific problem. Normally, knowledge of the protocol or protocols being debugged is required to properly interpret the `debug` outputs.

- When using `debug` troubleshooting tools, be aware that output formats vary with each protocol. Some generate a single line of output per packet, others generate multiple lines of output per packet. Some **debug** commands generate large amounts of output; others generate only occasional output. Some generate lines of text, and others generate information in field format.

Commands Related to the debug Command

To effectively use debugging tools, you must consider the following:

- Impact that a troubleshooting tool has on router performance
- Most selective and focused use of the diagnostic tool
- How to minimize the impact of troubleshooting on other processes that compete for resources on the network device
- How to stop the troubleshooting tool when diagnosing is complete so that the router can resume its most efficient switching

To optimize your efficient use of the **debug** command, these commands can help you:

- The **service timestamps** command is used to add a time stamp to a debug or log message. This feature can provide valuable information about when debug elements occurred and the duration of time between events.
- The **show processes** command displays the CPU use for each process. This data can influence decisions about using a debug command if it indicates that the production system is already too heavily used for adding a debug command.
- The **no debug all** command disables all debug commands. This command can free up system resources after you finish debugging.
- The **terminal monitor** command displays debug output and system error messages for the current terminal and session. When you Telnet to a device and issue a **debug** command, you will not see output unless this commands is entered.

4.5.7 Recovering a Lost Router Password

About Password Recovery

Have you ever forgotten the password to a router? Maybe not, but sometime in your career, you can expect someone to forget, and you will need to recover it.

The first thing that you have to know about password recovery is that for security reasons, you need physical access to the router. You connect your PC to the router through a console cable.

The enable password and the enable secret password protect access to privileged EXEC and configuration modes. The enable password can be recovered, but the enable secret password is encrypted and must be replaced with a new password.

The *configuration register* is a concept that you will learn more about later in your studies. The configuration register is similar to your PC BIOS settings, which control the bootup process. Among other things, the BIOS tells the PC from which hard disk to boot. In a router, a configuration register, represented by a single hexadecimal value, tells the router what specific steps to take when powered on. Configuration registers have many uses, and password recovery is probably the most used.

Router Password Recovery Procedure

To recover a router password, do the following:

Prepare the Device

Step 1. Connect to the console port.

Step 2. If you have lost the enable password, you would still have access to user EXEC mode. Type `show version` at the prompt, and record the configuration register setting.

```
R>#show version
 <show command output omitted>
 Configuration register is 0x2102
 R1>
```

The configuration register is usually set to 0x2102 or 0x102. If you can no longer access the router (because of a lost login or TACACS password), you can safely assume that your configuration register is set to 0x2102.

Step 3. Use the power switch to turn off the router, and then turn the router back on.

Step 4. Issue a **Break** signal from the terminal within 60 seconds of power up to put the router into ROMmon. A Break signal is sent using a break key sequence appropriate for the terminal program and the operating system.

Click Bypass Startup in the figure.

Step 5. Type `confreg 0x2142` at the rommon 1> prompt. This causes the router to bypass the startup configuration where the forgotten enable password is stored.

Step 6. Type `reset` at the rommon 2> prompt. The router reboots, but ignores the saved configuration.

Step 7. Type `no` after each setup question, or press **Ctrl-C** to skip the initial setup procedure.

Step 8. Type `enable` at the Router> prompt. This puts you into enable mode, and you should be able to see the Router# prompt.

Click Access NVRAM in the figure.

Step 9. Type `copy startup-config running-config` to copy the NVRAM into memory. Be careful! Do not type `copy running-config startup-config` or you will erase your startup configuration.

Step 10. Type `show running-config`. In this configuration, the `shutdown` command appears under all interfaces because all the interfaces are currently shut down. Most importantly though, you can now see the passwords (enable password, enable secret, vty, console passwords) either in encrypted or unencrypted format. You can reuse unencrypted passwords. You must change encrypted passwords to a new password.

Click Reset Passwords in the figure.

Step 11. Type `configure terminal`. The R1(config)# prompt appears.

Step 12. Type `enable secret` *password* to change the enable secret password. For example:
```
R1(config)# enable secret cisco
```
Step 13. Issue the `no shutdown` command on every interface that you want to use. You can issue a `show ip interface brief` command to confirm that your interface configuration is correct. Every interface that you want to use should display up up.

Step 14. Type `config-register` *configuration_register_setting*. The *configuration_register_setting* is either the value you recorded in Step 2 or 0x2102 . For example:

```
R1(config)#config-register 0x2102
```
Step 15. Press **Ctrl-Z** or type `end` to leave configuration mode. The R1# prompt appears.

Step 16. Type `copy running-config startup-config` to commit the changes.

You have now completed password recovery. Entering the `show version` command will confirm that the router will use the configured config register setting on the next reboot.

4.6 Chapter Labs

4.6.1 Basic Security Configuration

In this lab, you will learn how to configure basic network security using the network shown in the topology diagram. You will learn how to configure router security three different ways: using the CLI, the auto-secure feature, and Cisco SDM. You will also learn how to manage Cisco IOS software.

4.6.2 Challenge Security Configuration

In this lab, you will configure security using the network shown in the topology diagram. If you need assistance, refer to the Basic Security lab. However, try to do as much on your own as possible. For this lab, do not use password protection or login on any console lines because they might cause accidental logout. However, you should still secure the console line using other means. Use **ciscoccna** for all passwords in this lab.

4.6.3 Troubleshooting Security Configuration

Your company just hired a new network engineer who has created some security issues in the network with misconfigurations and oversights. Your boss has asked you to correct the errors the new engineer has made configuring the routers. While correcting the problems, make sure that all the devices are secure but are still accessible by administrators, and that all networks are reachable. All routers must be accessible with SDM from PC1. Verify that a device is secure by using tools such as Telnet and ping. Unauthorized use of these tools should be blocked, but also ensure that authorized use is permitted. For this lab, do not use login or password protection on any console lines to prevent accidental lockout. Use **ciscoccna** for all passwords in this scenario.

Chapter Summary

The importance of network security cannot be under estimated. This chapter stressed the importance of developing an effective security policy and then adhering to what it requires you to do. You know the threats to your network, both from within and from without, and you know the basic steps you need to take to protect yourself from these threats. Moreover, you now understand the requirements to balance security against access.

Network attacks come from all directions and in many forms. Password attacks are easy to launch, but easily defended against. The tactics of social engineering require users to develop a degree of suspiciousness and care. Once an attacker gains network access, they can literally open all the locks. But attackers need not always gain access to wreak havoc. Denial of service attacks can be launched that can overload network resources to the point they can no longer function. Worms, viruses and Trojan horses can penetrate networks and continue spreading and infecting devices.

A key task in securing a network is to secure the routers. Routers are the gateway into the network and are obvious targets. Basic administrative talks including good physical security, maintaining updated IOS and backing up configuration files are a start. Cisco IOS software provides a wealth of security features to harden routers and close doors opened by used ports and services, most of which can be completed using the one-step lockdown feature of Cisco SDM.

This activity is a cumulative review of the chapter covering OSPF routing, authentication, and upgrading the Cisco IOS image.

Detailed instructions are provided within the activity as well as in the PDF link below.

Activity Instructions (PDF)

Chapter Quiz

Take the chapter quiz to test your knowledge.

Your Chapter Notes

CHAPTER 5

ACLs

Introduction

Network security is a huge subject, and much of it is far beyond the scope of this course. However, one of the most important skills a network administrator needs is mastery of access control lists (ACLs). Administrators use ACLs to stop traffic or permit only specified traffic while stopping all other traffic on their networks. This chapter includes an opportunity to develop your mastery of ACLs with a series of lessons, activities, and lab exercises.

Network designers use firewalls to protect networks from unauthorized use. Firewalls are hardware or software solutions that enforce network security policies. Consider a lock on a door to a room inside a building. The lock only allows authorized users with a key or access card to pass through the door. Similarly, a firewall filters unauthorized or potentially dangerous packets from entering the network. On a Cisco router, you can configure a simple firewall that provides basic traffic filtering capabilities using ACLs.

An ACL is a sequential list of permit or deny statements that apply to addresses or upper-layer protocols. ACLs provide a powerful way to control traffic into and out of your network. You can configure ACLs for all routed network protocols.

The most important reason to configure ACLs is to provide security for your network. This chapter explains how to use standard and extended ACLs as part of a security solution and teaches you how to configure them on a Cisco router. Included are tips, considerations, recommendations, and general guidelines on how to use ACLs.

5.1 Using ACLs to Secure Networks

5.1.1 A TCP Conversation

ACLs enable you to control traffic into and out of your network. This control can be as simple as permitting or denying network hosts or addresses. However, ACLs can also be configured to control network traffic based on the TCP port being used. To understand how an ACL works with TCP, let us look at the dialogue that occurs during a TCP conversation when you download a webpage to your computer.

When you request data from a web server, IP takes care of the communication between the PC and the server. TCP takes care of the communication between your web browser (application) and the network server software. When you send an e-mail, look at a webpage, or download a file, TCP is responsible for breaking data down into packets for IP before they are sent, and for assembling the data from the packets when they arrive. The TCP process is very much like a conversation in which two nodes on a network agree to pass data between one another.

Recall that TCP provides a connection-oriented, reliable, byte stream service. The term connection-oriented means that the two applications using TCP must establish a TCP connection with each other before they can exchange data. TCP is a full-duplex protocol, meaning that each TCP connection supports a pair of byte streams, each stream flowing in one direction. TCP includes a flow-control mechanism for each byte stream that allows the receiver to limit how much data the sender can transmit. TCP also implements a congestion-control mechanism.

Click the play button in the figure to view the animation.

The animation shows how a TCP/IP conversation takes place. TCP packets are marked with flags that denote their purpose: a SYN starts (synchronizes) the session; an ACK is an *acknowledgment* that an expected packet was received, and a FIN finishes the session. A SYN/ACK acknowledges that the transfer is synchronized. TCP data segments include the higher level protocol needed to direct the application data to the correct application.

Click the TCP/UDP Port Numbers button In the figure.

The TCP data segment also identifies the port matching the requested service. For example, HTTP is port 80, *SMTP* is port 25, and FTP is port 20 and port 21. The figure shows examples of UDP and TCP ports.

Click the buttons in the figure to explore TCP/UDP ports.

5.1.2 Packet Filtering

Refer to Figure in online course

Packet filtering, sometimes called static packet filtering, controls access to a network by analyzing the incoming and outgoing packets and passing or halting them based on stated criteria.

A router acts as a packet filter when it forwards or denies packets according to filtering rules. When a packet arrives at the packet-filtering router, the router extracts certain information from the packet header and makes decisions according to the filter rules as to whether the packet can pass through or be discarded. Packet filtering works at the Network layer of the Open Systems Interconnection (OSI) model, or the Internet layer of TCP/IP.

As a Layer 3 device, a packet-filtering router uses rules to determine whether to permit or deny traffic based on source and destination IP addresses, *source port* and *destination port*, and the protocol of the packet. These rules are defined using access control lists or ACLs.

Recall that an ACL is a sequential list of permit or deny statements that apply to IP addresses or upper-layer protocols. The ACL can extract the following information from the packet header, test it against its rules, and make "allow" or "deny" decisions based on:

- Source IP address
- Destination IP address
- ICMP message type

The ACL can also extract upper layer information and test it against its rules. Upper layer information includes:

- TCP/UDP source port
- TCP/UDP destination port

Click the buttons in the figure for an overview of how an ACL allows or denies a packet. Although the animations display packet filtering occurring at Layer 3, it should be noted that filtering could also occur at Layer 4.

Refer to Figure in online course

Packet Filtering Example

To understand the concept of how a router uses packet filtering, imagine that a guard has been posted at a locked door. The guard's instructions are to allow only people whose names appear on a list to pass through the door. The guard is filtering people based on the criterion of having their names on the authorized list.

For example, you could say, "Only permit web access to users from network A. Deny web access to users from network B, but permit them to have all other access." Refer to the figure to examine the decision path the packet filter uses to accomplish this task.

For this scenario, the packet filter looks at each packet as follows:

- If the packet is a TCP SYN from network A using port 80, it is allowed to pass. All other access is denied to those users.

- If the packet is a TCP SYN from network B using port 80, it is blocked. However, all other access is permitted.

This is just a simple example. You can configure multiple rules to further permit or deny services to specific users. You can also filter packets at the port level using an extended ACL, which is covered in Section 3.

5.1.3 What is an ACL?

An ACL is a router configuration script that controls whether a router permits or denies packets to pass based on criteria found in the packet header. ACLs are among the most commonly used objects in Cisco IOS software. ACLs are also used for selecting types of traffic to be analyzed, forwarded, or processed in other ways.

As each packet comes through an interface with an associated ACL, the ACL is checked from top to bottom, one line at a time, looking for a pattern matching the incoming packet. The ACL enforces one or more corporate security policies by applying a permit or deny rule to determine the fate of the packet. ACLs can be configured to control access to a network or subnet.

By default, a router does not have any ACLs configured and therefore does not filter traffic. Traffic that enters the router is routed according to the routing table. If you do not use ACLs on the router, all packets that can be routed through the router pass through the router to the next network segment.

Here are some guidelines for using ACLs:

- Use ACLs in firewall routers positioned between your internal network and an external network such as the Internet.

- Use ACLs on a router positioned between two parts of your network to control traffic entering or exiting a specific part of your internal network.

- Configure ACLs on border routers-routers situated at the edges of your networks. This provides a very basic buffer from the outside network, or between a less controlled area of your own network and a more sensitive area of your network.

- Configure ACLs for each network protocol configured on the border router interfaces. You can configure ACLs on an interface to filter inbound traffic, outbound traffic, or both.

Click the ACLs on a Router button in the figure.

The Three Ps

A general rule for applying ACLs on a router can be recalled by remembering the three Ps. You can configure one ACL per protocol, per direction, per interface:

- *One ACL per protocol-* To control traffic flow on an interface, an ACL must be defined for each protocol enabled on the interface.

- *One ACL per direction-* ACLs control traffic in one direction at a time on an interface. Two separate ACLs must be created to control inbound and outbound traffic.

- *One ACL per interface-* ACLs control traffic for an interface, for example, *Fast Ethernet* 0/0.

Writing ACLs can be a challenging and complex task. Every interface can have multiple protocols and directions defined. The router in the example has two interfaces configured for IP: AppleTalk and IPX. This router could possibly require 12 separate ACLs: one ACL for each protocol, times two for each direction, times two for the number of ports.

ACLs perform the following tasks:

- Limit network traffic to increase network performance. For example, if corporate policy does not allow video traffic on the network, ACLs that block video traffic could be configured and applied. This would greatly reduce the network load and increase network performance.

- Provide traffic flow control. ACLs can restrict the delivery of routing updates. If updates are not required because of network conditions, bandwidth is preserved.

- Provide a basic level of security for network access. ACLs can allow one host to access a part of the network and prevent another host from accessing the same area. For example, access to the Human Resources network can be restricted to select users.

- Decide which types of traffic to forward or block at the router interfaces. For example, an ACL can permit e-mail traffic, but block all Telnet traffic.

- Control which areas a client can access on a network.

- Screen hosts to permit or deny access to network services. ACLs can permit or deny a user to access file types, such as FTP or HTTP.

ACLs inspect network packets based on criteria, such as source address, destination address, protocols, and port numbers. In addition to either permitting or denying traffic, an ACL can classify traffic to enable priority processing down the line. This capability is similar to having a VIP pass at a concert or sporting event. The VIP pass gives selected guests privileges not offered to general admission ticket holders, such as being able to enter a restricted area and be escorted to their box seats.

5.1.4 ACL Operation

How ACLs Work

ACLs define the set of rules that give added control for packets that enter inbound interfaces, packets that relay through the router, and packets that exit outbound interfaces of the router. ACLs do not act on packets that originate from the router itself.

ACLs are configured either to apply to inbound traffic or to apply to outbound traffic.

- *Inbound ACLs-* Incoming packets are processed before they are routed to the outbound interface. An inbound ACL is efficient because it saves the overhead of routing lookups if the packet is discarded. If the packet is permitted by the tests, it is then processed for routing.

- *Outbound ACLs-* Incoming packets are routed to the outbound interface, and then they are processed through the outbound ACL.

ACL statements operate in sequential order. They evaluate packets against the ACL, from the top down, one statement at a time.

The figure shows the logic for an inbound ACL. If a packet header and an ACL statement match, the rest of the statements in the list are skipped, and the packet is permitted or denied as determined by the matched statement. If a packet header does not match an ACL statement, the packet is tested against the next statement in the list. This matching process continues until the end of the list is reached.

A final implied statement covers all packets for which conditions did not test true. This final test condition matches all other packets and results in a "deny" instruction. Instead of proceeding into or out of an interface, the router drops all of these remaining packets. This final statement is often referred to as the "implicit deny any statement" or the "deny all traffic" statement. Because of this statement, an ACL should have at least one permit statement in it; otherwise, the ACL blocks all traffic.

You can apply an ACL to multiple interfaces. However, there can be only one ACL per protocol, per direction, and per interface.

Click the Outbound ACLs button in the figure.

The figure shows the logic for an outbound ACL. Before a packet is forwarded to an outbound interface, the router checks the routing table to see if the packet is routable. If the packet is not routable, it is dropped. Next, the router checks to see whether the outbound interface is grouped to an ACL. Examples of outbound ACL operation are as follows:

- If the outbound interface is not grouped to an outbound ACL, the packet is sent directly to the outbound interface.

- If the outbound interface is grouped to an outbound ACL, the packet is not sent out on the outbound interface until it is tested by the combination of ACL statements that are associated with that interface. Based on the ACL tests, the packet is permitted or denied.

For outbound lists, "to permit" means to send the packet to the output buffer, and "to deny" means to discard the packet.

ACL and Routing and ACL Processes on a Router

The figure shows the logic of routing and ACL processes on a router. When a packet arrives at a router interface, the router process is the same, whether ACLs are used or not. As a frame enters an interface, the router checks to see whether the destination Layer 2 address matches its own or if the frame is a broadcast frame.

If the frame address is accepted, the frame information is stripped off and the router checks for an ACL on the inbound interface. If an ACL exists, the packet is now tested against the statements in the list.

If the packet matches a statement, the packet is either accepted or rejected. If the packet is accepted in the interface, it is then checked against routing table entries to determine the destination interface and switched to that interface.

Next, the router checks whether the destination interface has an ACL. If an ACL exists, the packet is tested against the statements in the list.

If the packet matches a statement, it is either accepted or rejected.

If there is no ACL or the packet is accepted, the packet is encapsulated in the new Layer 2 protocol and forwarded out the interface to the next device.

The Implied "Deny All Traffic" Criteria Statement

At the end of every access list is an implied "deny all traffic" criteria statement. It is also sometimes referred to as the "implicit deny any" statement. Therefore, if a packet does not match any of the ACL entries, it is automatically blocked. The implied "deny all traffic" is the default behavior of ACLs and cannot be changed.

There is a key caveat associated with this "deny all" behavior: For most protocols, if you define an inbound access list for traffic filtering, you should include explicit access list criteria statements to permit routing updates. If you do not, you might effectively lose communication from the interface when routing updates are blocked by the implicit "deny all traffic" statement at the end of the access list.

5.1.5 Types of Cisco ACLs

There are two types of Cisco ACLs, standard and extended.

Standard ACLs

Standard ACLs allow you to permit or deny traffic from source IP addresses. The destination of the packet and the ports involved do not matter. The example allows all traffic from network 192.168.30.0/24 network. Because of the implied "deny any" at the end, all other traffic is blocked with this ACL. Standard ACLs are created in global configuration mode.

Click the Extended ACL button in the figure.

Extended ACLs

Extended ACLs filter IP packets based on several attributes, for example, protocol type, source and destination IP address, destination IP address, source TCP or UDP ports, destination TCP or UDP ports, and optional protocol type information for finer granularity of control. In the figure, ACL 103 permits traffic originating from any address on the 192.168.30.0/24 network to any destination host port 80 (HTTP). Extended ACLs are created in global configuration mode.

The commands for ACLs are explained in the next few topics.

5.1.6 How a Standard ACL Works

A standard ACL is a sequential collection of permit and deny conditions that apply to IP addresses. The destination of the packet and the ports involved are not covered.

The decision process is mapped in the figure. Cisco IOS software tests addresses against the conditions one by one. The first match determines whether the software accepts or rejects the address. Because the software stops testing conditions after the first match, the order of the conditions is critical. If no conditions match, the address is rejected.

The two main tasks involved in using ACLs are as follows:

Step 1. Create an access list by specifying an access list number or name and access conditions.

Step 2. Apply the ACL to interfaces or terminal lines.

5.1.7 Numbering and Naming ACLs

Using numbered ACLs is an effective method for determining the ACL type on smaller networks with more homogeneously defined traffic. However, a number does not inform you of the purpose of the ACL. For this reason, starting with Cisco IOS Release 11.2, you can use a name to identify a Cisco ACL.

The figure summarizes the rule to designate numbered ACLs and named ACLs.

Regarding numbered ACLs, in case you are wondering why numbers 200 to 1299 are skipped, it is because those numbers are used by other protocols. This course focuses only on IP ACLs. For example, numbers 600 to 699 are used by AppleTalk, and numbers 800 to 899 are used by IPX.

5.1.8 Where to Place ACLs

> Refer to **Figure** in online course

The proper placement of an ACL to filter undesirable traffic makes the network operate more efficiently. ACLs can act as firewalls to filter packets and eliminate unwanted traffic. Where you place ACLs can reduce unnecessary traffic. For example, traffic that will be denied at a remote destination should not use network resources along the route to that destination.

Every ACL should be placed where it has the greatest impact on efficiency. The basic rules are:

- Locate extended ACLs as close as possible to the source of the traffic denied. This way, undesirable traffic is filtered without crossing the network infrastructure.

- Because standard ACLs do not specify destination addresses, place them as close to the destination as possible.

Let us consider an example of where to place ACLs in our network. The interface and network location is based on what you want the ACL to do.

In the figure, the administrator wants to prevent traffic originating in the 192.168.10.0/24 network from getting to the 192.168.30.0/24 network. An ACL on the outbound interface of R1 denies R1 the ability to send traffic to other places as well. The solution is to place a standard ACL on the inbound interface of R3 to stop all traffic from the source address 192.168.10.0/24. A standard ACL meets the needs because it is only concerned with source IP addresses.

Click the Extended ACL button in the figure.

Consider that administrators can only place ACLs on devices that they control. Therefore, placement must be determined in the context of where the control of the network administrator extends. In this figure, the administrator of the 192.168.10.0/24 and 192.168.11.0/24 networks (referred to as Ten and Eleven, respectively, in this example) wants to deny Telnet and FTP traffic from Eleven to the 192.168.30.0/24 network (Thirty, in this example). At the same time, other traffic must be permitted to leave Ten.

There are several ways to do this. An extended ACL on R3 blocking Telnet and FTP from Eleven would accomplish the task, but the administrator does not control R3. That solution also still allows unwanted traffic to cross the entire network, only to be blocked at the destination. This affects overall network efficiency.

One solution is to use an outbound extended ACL that specifies both source and destination addresses (Eleven and Thirty, respectively), and says, "Telnet and FTP traffic from Eleven is not allowed to go to Thirty." Place this extended ACL on the outbound S0/0/0 port of R1.

A disadvantage of this solution is that traffic from Ten would also be subject to some processing by the ACL, even though Telnet and FTP traffic is allowed.

The better solution is to move closer to the source and place an extended ACL on the inbound Fa0/2 interface of R1. This ensures that packets from Eleven do not enter R1, and subsequently cannot cross over into Ten, or even enter R2 or R3. Traffic with other destination addresses and ports is still permitted through R1.

5.1.9 General Guidelines for Creating ACLs

ACL Best Practices

Using ACLs requires attention to detail and great care. Mistakes can be costly in terms of downtime, troubleshooting efforts, and poor network service. Before starting to configure an ACL, basic planning is required. The figure presents guidelines that form the basis of an ACL best practices list.

Activity: Using ACLs to Secure Networks

5.2 Configuring Standard ACLs

5.2.1 Entering Criteria Statements

Before beginning to configure a standard ACL, we will review important ACL concepts covered in Section 1.

Recall that when traffic comes into the router, it is compared to ACL statements based on the order that the entries occur in the router. The router continues to process the ACL statements until it has a match. For this reason, you should have the most frequently used ACL entry at the top of the list. If no matches are found when the router reaches the end of the list, the traffic is denied because ACLs have an implied deny for all traffic not meeting any of the tested criteria. A single-entry ACL with only one deny entry has the effect of denying all traffic. You must have at least one permit statement in an ACL or all traffic is blocked.

For example, the two ACLs (101 and 102) in the figure have the same effect. Network 192.168.10.0 would be permitted to access network 192.168.30.0 while 192.168.11.0 would not be allowed.

5.2.2 Configuring a Standard ACL

Standard ACL Logic

In the figure, packets that come in Fa0/0 are checked for their source addresses:

```
access-list 2 deny host 192.168.10.1
 access-list 2 permit 192.168.10.0 0.0.0.255
 access-list 2 deny 192.168.0.0 0.0.255.255
 access-list 2 permit 192.0.0.0 0.255.255.255
```

If packets are permitted, they are routed through the router to an output interface. If packets are not permitted, they are dropped at the incoming interface.

Configuring Standard ACLs

To configure numbered standard ACLs on a Cisco router, you must first create the standard ACL and then activate the ACL on an interface.

The **access-list** global configuration command defines a standard ACL with a number in the range of 1 to 99. Cisco IOS Software Release 12.0.1 extended these numbers by allowing 1300 to 1999 to provide a maximum of 799 possible standard ACLs. These additional numbers are referred to as expanded IP ACLs.

The full syntax of the standard ACL command is as follows:

```
Router(config)#access-list access-list-number [deny | permit | remark] source
[source-wildcard] [log]
```

The full syntax of the standard ACL command to filter a specific host is as follows:

`Router(config)#access-list` *access-list-number* `[deny | permit]` *source* `[log]`

The figure provides a detailed explanation of the syntax for a standard ACL.

For example, to create a numbered ACL designated **10** that would permit network 192.168.10.0 /24, you would enter:

`R1(config)#access-list 10 permit 192.168.10.0 0.0.0.255`

Click the Remove ACL button in the figure.

The `no` form of this command removes a standard ACL. In the figure, the output of the `show access-list` command displays the current ACLs configured on router R1.

To remove the ACL, the global configuration `no access-list` command is used. Issuing the `show access-list` command confirms that access list 10 has been removed.

Click the Remark button in the figure.

Typically, administrators create ACLs and fully understand each the purpose of each statement within the ACL. However, when an ACL is revisited at a later time, it may no longer as obvious as it once was.

The `remark` keyword is used for documentation and makes access lists a great deal easier to understand. Each remark is limited to 100 characters. The ACL in the figure, although fairly simple, is used to provide an example. When reviewing the ACL in the configuration, the remark is also displayed.

The next topic explains how to use wildcard masking to identify specific networks and hosts.

5.2.3 ACL Wildcard Masking

Wildcard Masking

> Refer to
> **Figure**
> in online course

ACLs statements include masks, also called *wildcard masks*. A wildcard mask is a string of binary digits telling the router which parts of the subnet number to look at. Although wildcard masks have no functional relationship with subnet masks, they do provide a similar function. The mask determines how much of an IP source or destination address to apply to the address match. The numbers 1 and 0 in the mask identify how to treat the corresponding IP address bits. However, they are used for different purposes and follow different rules.

Wildcard masks and subnet masks are both 32 bits long and use binary 1s and 0s. Subnet masks use binary 1s and 0s to identify the network, subnet, and host portion of an IP address. Wildcard masks use binary 1s and 0s to filter individual or groups of IP addresses to permit or deny access to resources based on an IP address. By carefully setting wildcard masks, you can permit or deny a single or several IP addresses

Wildcard masks and subnet masks differ in the way they match binary 1s and 0s. Wildcard masks use the following rules to match binary 1s and 0s:

- Wildcard mask bit 0 - Match the corresponding bit value in the address
- Wildcard mask bit 1 - Ignore the corresponding bit value in the address

The figure explains how different wildcard masks filter IP addresses. As you look at the example, remember that binary 0 signifies a match, and that binary 1 signifies ignore.

Note: Wildcard masks are often referred to as an inverse mask. The reason is that, unlike a subnet mask in which binary 1 is equal to a match and binary 0 is not a match, the reverse is true.

Click the Wildcard Mask Example button in the figure.

Using a Wildcard Mask

The table in the figure shows the results of applying a 0.0.255.255 wildcard mask to a 32-bit IP address. Remember that a binary 0 indicates a value that is matched.

Wildcard Masks to Match IP Subnets

Calculating the wildcard mask can be a little confusing at first. The figure provides three examples of wildcard masks.

The first example the wildcard mask stipulates that every bit in the IP 192.168.1.1 must match exactly. The wildcard mask is equivalent to the subnet mask 255.255.255.255.

In the second example, the wildcard mask stipulates that anything will match. The wildcard mask is equivalent to the subnet mask 0.0.0.0.

In the third example, the wildcard mask stipulates that it will match any host within the 192.168.1.0 /24 network. The wildcard mask is equivalent to the subnet mask 255.255.255.0.

These examples were fairly simple and straightforward. However, the calculation of wildcard masks can get a little trickier.

Click the Wildcard Mask 2 button in the figure.

The two examples in the figure are more complicated than the last three you viewed. In example 1, the first two octets and first four bits of the third octet must match exactly. The last four bits in the third octet and the last octet can be any valid number. This results in a mask that checks for 192.168.16.0 to 192.168.31.0

Example 2 shows a wildcard mask that matches the first two octets, and the least significant bit in the third octet. The last octet and the first seven bits in the third octet can be any valid number. The result is a mask that would permit or deny all hosts from odd subnets within the 192.168.0.0 major network.

Calculating wildcard masks can be difficult, but you can do it easily by subtracting the subnet mask from 255.255.255.255.

Click the Example 1 button in the figure.

For example, assume you wanted to permit access to all users in the 192.168.3.0 network. Subtract the subnet mask which is 255.255.255.0 from 255.255.255.255 as indicated in the figure. The solution produces the wildcard mask 0.0.0.255.

Click the Example 2 button in the figure.

Now assume you wanted to permit network access for the 14 users in the subnet 192.168.3.32 /28. The subnet mask for the IP subnet is 255.255.255.240, therefore take the 255.255.255.255 and subtract from the subnet mask 255.255.255.240. The solution this time produces the wildcard mask 0.0.0.15.

Click the Example 3 button in the figure.

In this third example, assume you wanted to match only networks 192.168.10.0 and 192.168.11.0. Again, you take the 255.255.255.255 and subtract the regular subnet mask which in this case would be 255.255.254.0. The result is 0.0.1.255.

Although you could accomplish the same result with two statements such as:

```
R1(config)# access-list 10 permit 192.168.10.0 0.0.0.255
 R1(config)# access-list 10 permit 192.168.11.0 0.0.0.255
```

It is far more efficient to configure the wildcard mask such as:

R1(config)# `access-list 10 permit 192.168.10.0 0.0.1.255`

That may not seem more efficient, but when you consider if you wanted to match network 192.168.16.0 to 192.168.31.0 as follows:

```
R1(config)# access-list 10 permit 192.168.16.0 0.0.0.255
R1(config)# access-list 10 permit 192.168.17.0 0.0.0.255
R1(config)# access-list 10 permit 192.168.18.0 0.0.0.255
R1(config)# access-list 10 permit 192.168.19.0 0.0.0.255
R1(config)# access-list 10 permit 192.168.20.0 0.0.0.255
R1(config)# access-list 10 permit 192.168.21.0 0.0.0.255
R1(config)# access-list 10 permit 192.168.22.0 0.0.0.255
R1(config)# access-list 10 permit 192.168.23.0 0.0.0.255
R1(config)# access-list 10 permit 192.168.24.0 0.0.0.255
R1(config)# access-list 10 permit 192.168.25.0 0.0.0.255
R1(config)# access-list 10 permit 192.168.26.0 0.0.0.255
R1(config)# access-list 10 permit 192.168.27.0 0.0.0.255
R1(config)# access-list 10 permit 192.168.28.0 0.0.0.255
R1(config)# access-list 10 permit 192.168.29.0 0.0.0.255
R1(config)# access-list 10 permit 192.168.30.0 0.0.0.255
R1(config)# access-list 10 permit 192.168.31.0 0.0.0.255
```

You can see that configuring the following wildcard mask makes it far more efficient:

R1(config)# `access-list 10 permit 192.168.16.0 0.0.15.255`

Wildcard Bit Mask Keywords

> Refer to Figure in online course

Working with decimal representations of binary wildcard mask bits can be tedious. To simplify this task, the keywords **host** and **any** help identify the most common uses of wildcard masking. These keywords eliminate entering wildcard masks when identifying a specific host or network. They also make it easier to read an ACL by providing visual clues as to the source or destination of the criteria.

- The **host** option substitutes for the 0.0.0.0 mask. This mask states that all IP address bits must match or only one host is matched.

- The **any** option substitutes for the IP address and 255.255.255.255 mask. This mask says to ignore the entire IP address or to accept any addresses.

Example 1: Wildcard Masking Process with a Single IP Address

In the example, instead of entering `192.168.10.10 0.0.0.0`, you can use `host 192.168.10.10`.

Example 2: Wildcard Masking Process with a Match Any IP Address

In the example, instead of entering `0.0.0.0 255.255.255.255`, you can use the keyword **any** by itself.

The any and host Keywords

> Refer to Figure in online course

In this figure, we have two examples. Example 1 is displaying how to use the **any** option to substitute 0.0.0.0 for the IP address with a wildcard mask of 255.255.255.255.

Example 2 is displaying how to use the **host** option to substitute the wildcard mask.

5.2.4 Applying Standard ACLs to Interfaces

Standard ACL Configuration Procedures

After a standard ACL is configured, it is linked to an interface using the `ip access-group` command:

`Router(config-if)#ip access-group {access-list-number | access-list-name} {in | out}`

To remove an ACL from an interface, first enter the `no ip access-group` command on the interface, and then enter the global `no access-list` command to remove the entire ACL.

The figure lists the steps and syntax to configure and apply a numbered standard ACL on a router.

Click the Example 1 button in the figure for an example of an ACL to permit a single network.

This ACL allows only traffic from source network 192.168.10.0 to be forwarded out on S0/0/0. Traffic from networks other than 192.168.10.0 is blocked.

The first line identifies the ACL as access list 1. It permits traffic that matches the selected parameters. In this case, the IP address and wildcard mask identifying the source network is 192.168.10.0 0.0.0.255. Recall that there is an unseen implicit deny all statement that is equivalent to adding the line `access-list 1 deny 0.0.0.0 255.255.255.255`.

The `ip access-group 1 out` interface configuration command links and ties ACL 1 to the Serial 0/0/0 interface as an outbound filter.

Therefore, ACL 1 only permits hosts from the 192.168.10.0 /24 network to exit router R1. It denies any other network including the 192.168.11.0 network.

Click the Example 2 button in the figure for an example of an ACL that denies a specific host.

This ACL replaces the previous example, but also blocks traffic from a specific address. The first command deletes the previous version of ACL 1. The next ACL statement, denies the PC1 host located at 192.168.10.10. Every other host on the 192.168.10.0 /24 network is permitted. Again the implicit deny statement matches every other network.

The ACL is again reapplied to interface S0/0/0 in an outbound direction.

Click the Example 3 button in the figure for an example of an ACL that denies a specific host and permits a number of subnets.

This ACL replaces the previous example but still blocks traffic from the host PC1. It also permits all other LAN traffic to exit from router R1.

The first two commands are the same as the previous example. The first command deletes the previous version of ACL 1 and the next ACL statement denies the PC1 host located at 192.168.10.10.

The third line is new and permits all hosts from the 192.168.x.x /16 networks. This now means that all hosts from the 192.168.10.0 /24 network still match but now the hosts from the 192.168.11.0 network also match.

The ACL is again reapplied to interface S0/0/0 in an outbound direction. Therefore, both LANs attached to router R1 may exit the S0/0/0 interface with the exception of the PC1 host.

Using an ACL to Control VTY Access

Cisco recommends using SSH for administrative connections to routers and switches. If the Cisco IOS software image on your router does not support SSH, you can partially improve the security of administrative lines by restricting VTY access. Restricting VTY access is a technique that allows you to define which IP addresses are allowed Telnet access to the router EXEC process. You can control which administrative workstation or network manages your router with an ACL and an `access-class` statement to your VTY lines. You can also use this technique with SSH to further improve administrative access security.

The `access-class` command in line configuration mode restricts incoming and outgoing connections between a particular VTY (into a Cisco device) and the addresses in an access list.

Standard and extended access lists apply to packets that travel through a router. They are not designed to block packets that originate within the router. An outbound Telnet extended ACL does not prevent router-initiated Telnet sessions, by default.

Filtering Telnet traffic is typically considered an extended IP ACL function because it filters a higher level protocol. However, because you are using the `access-class` command to filter incoming or outgoing Telnet sessions by source address and apply filtering to VTY lines, you can use standard ACL statements to control VTY access.

The command syntax of the access-class command is:

`access-class` access-list-number {`in` [`vrf-also`] | `out`}

The parameter `in` restricts incoming connections between a particular Cisco device and the addresses in the access list, while the parameter `out` restricts outgoing connections between a particular Cisco device and the addresses in the access list.

An example allowing VTY 0 and 4 is shown in the figure. For example, the ACL in the figure is configured to permit networks 192.168.10.0 and 192.168.11.0 access to VTYs 0 - 4. All other networks are denied access to the VTYs.

The following should be considered when configuring access lists on VTYs:

- Identical restrictions should be set on all the VTYs, because a user can attempt to connect to any of them.

5.2.5 Editing Numbered ACLs

Editing Numbered ACLs

When configuring an ACL, the statements are added in the order that they are entered at the end of the ACL. However, there is no built-in editing feature that allows you to edit a change in an ACL. You cannot selectively insert or delete lines.

It is strongly recommended that any ACL be constructed in a text editor such as Microsoft Notepad. This allows you to create or edit the ACL and then paste it onto the router. For an existing ACL, you could use the `show running-config` command to display the ACL, copy and paste it into the text editor, make the necessary changes, and reload it.

For example, assume that the host IP address in the figure was incorrectly entered. Instead of the 192.168.10.100 host, it should have been the 192.168.10.11 host. Here are the steps to edit and correct ACL 20:

Step 1. Display the ACL using the `show running-config` command. The example in the figure uses the `include` keyword to display only the ACL statements.

Step 2. Highlight the ACL, copy it, and then paste it into Microsoft Notepad. Edit the list as required. Once the ACL is correctly displayed in Microsoft Notepad, highlight it and copy it.

Step 3. In global configuration mode, disable the access list using the `no access-list 20` command. Otherwise, the new statements would be appended to the existing ACL. Then paste the new ACL into the configuration of the router.

It should be mentioned that when using the `no access-list` command, no ACL is protecting your network. Also, be aware that if you make an error in the new list, you have to disable it and troubleshoot the problem. In that case, again, your network has no ACL during the correction process.

Commenting ACLs

You can use the **remark** keyword to include comments (remarks) about entries in any IP standard or extended ACL. The remarks make the ACL easier for you to understand and scan. Each remark line is limited to 100 characters.

The remark can go before or after a **permit** or **deny** statement. You should be consistent about where you put the remark so that it is clear which remark describes which **permit** or **deny** statement. For example, it would be confusing to have some remarks before the associated **permit** or **deny** statements and some remarks after.

To include a comment for IP numbered standard or extended ACLs, use the **access-list** *access-list number* **remark** *remark* global configuration command. To remove the remark, use the **no** form of this command.

In the first example, the standard ACL allows access to the workstation that belongs to Jones, and denies access to the workstation that belongs to Smith.

For an entry in a named ACL, use the **remark** configuration command. To remove the remark, use the **no** form of this command. The second example shows an extended named ACL. Recall from the earlier definition of extended ACLs that they are used to control specific port numbers or services. In the second example, the remark says that the workstation for Jones is not allowed to use outbound Telnet.

5.2.6 Creating Standard Named ACLs

Naming an ACL makes it easier to understand its function. For example, an ACL to deny FTP could be called NO_FTP. When you identify your ACL with a name instead of with a number, the configuration mode and command syntax are slightly different.

The figure shows the steps to create a standard named ACL.

Step 1. Starting from the global configuration mode, use the **ip access-list** command to create a named ACL. ACL names are alphanumeric, must be unique and must not begin with a number.

Step 2. From the named ACL configuration mode, use the **permit** or **deny** statements to specify one or more conditions for determining if a packet is forwarded or dropped.

Step 3. Return to privileged EXEC mode with the **end** command.

Click the Example button in the figure.

In the figure, the screen output shows the commands used to configure a standard named ACL on router R1, interface Fa0/0 that denies host 192.168.11.10 access to the 192.168.10.0 network.

Capitalizing ACL names is not required, but makes them stand out when viewing the running-config output.

5.2.7 Monitoring and Verifying ACLs

When you finish an ACL configuration, use Cisco IOS **show** commands to verify the configuration. In the figure the top example shows the Cisco IOS syntax to display the contents of all ACLs. The bottom example shows the result of issuing the **show access-lists** command on router R1. The capitalized ACL names, SALES and ENG stand out in the screen output.

Recall why you started configuring ACLs in the first place; you wanted to implement your organization's security policies. Now that you have verified that the ACLs are configured as you intended, the next step is to confirm that the ACLs work as planned.

The guidelines discussed earlier in this section, suggest that you configure ACLs on a test network and then implement the tested ACLs on the production network. Though a discussion on how to prepare an ACL test scenario is beyond the scope of this course, you need to know that confirming your ACLs work as planned can be a complex and time consuming process.

5.2.8 Editing Named ACLs

Named ACLs have a big advantage over numbered ACLs in that they are easier to edit. Starting with Cisco IOS Software Release 12.3, named IP ACLs allow you to delete individual entries in a specific ACL. You can use sequence numbers to insert statements anywhere in the named ACL. If you are using an earlier Cisco IOS software version, you can add statements only at the bottom of the named ACL. Because you can delete individual entries, you can modify your ACL without having to delete and then reconfigure the entire ACL.

The example in the figure shows an ACL applied to the S0/0/0 interface of R1. It restricted access to the web server. Looking at this example, you can see two things you have not yet seen in this course:

Click the Router Output button in the figure.

- In the first **show** command output, you can see that the ACL named WEBSERVER has three numbered lines indicating access rules for the webserver.

- To grant another workstation access in the list only requires inserting a numbered line. In the example, the workstation with the IP address 192.168.11.10 is being added.

- The final **show** command output verifies that the new workstation is now allowed access.

Standard ACLs are router configuration scripts that control whether a router permits or denies packets based on the source address. This activity focuses on defining filtering criteria, configuring standard ACLs, applying ACLs to router interfaces, and verifying and testing the ACL implementation.

Detailed instructions are provided within the activity as well as in the PDF link below.

Activity Instructions (PDF)

5.3 Configuring Extended ACLs

5.3.1 Extended ACLs

Testing Packets with Extended ACLs

For more precise traffic-filtering control, you can use extended ACLs numbered 100 to 199 and 2000 to 2699 providing a total of 800 possible extended ACLs. Extended ACLs can also be named.

Extended ACLs are used more often than standard ACLs because they provide a greater range of control and, therefore, add to your security solution. Like standard ACLs, extended ACLs check the source packet addresses, but they also check the destination address, protocols and port numbers (or services). This gives a greater range of criteria on which to base the ACL. For example, an extended ACL can simultaneously allow e-mail traffic from a network to a specific destination while denying file transfers and web browsing.

The figure shows the logical decision path used by an extended ACL built to filter on source and destination addresses, and protocol and port numbers. In this example, the ACL first filters on the source address, then on the port and protocol of the source. It then filters on the destination address, then on the port and protocol of the destination, and makes a final permit-deny decision.

Recall that entries in ACLs are processed one after the other, so a 'No' decision does not necessarily equal a 'Deny'. As you go through the logical decision path, note that a 'No' means go to the next entry until all the entries have been tested. Only when all the entries have been processed is the 'Permit' or 'Deny' decision finalized.

The next page provides an example of an extended ACL.

Testing for Ports and Services

The ability to filter on protocol and port number allows you to build very specific extended ACLs. Using the appropriate port number, you can specify an application by configuring either the port number or the name of a well-known port.

The figure shows some examples of how an administrator specifies a TCP or UDP port number by placing it at the end of the extended ACL statement. Logical operations can be used, such as equal (eq), not equal (neq), greater than (gt), and less than (lt).

Click the Ports button in the figure.

The figure shows how to generate a list of port numbers and keywords you can use while building an ACL using the `R1(config)#access-list 101 permit tcp any eq ?` command.

5.3.2 Configuring Extended ACLs

The procedural steps for configuring extended ACLs are the same as for standard ACLs, you first create the extended ACL and then activate it on an interface. However, the command syntax and parameters are more complex to support the additional features provided by extended ACLs.

The figure shows the common command syntax for extended ACLs. The scrolling field provides details for the keywords and parameters. As you work through this chapter, there are explanations and examples that will further your comprehension.

Click the Configuring Extended ACLs button in the figure.

The figure shows an example of how you might create an extended ACL specific to your network needs. In this example, the network administrator needs to restrict Internet access to allow only website browsing. ACL 103 applies to traffic leaving the 192.168.10.0 network, and ACL 104 to traffic coming into the network.

ACL 103 accomplishes the first part of the requirement. It allows traffic coming from any address on the 192.168.10.0 network to go to any destination, subject to the limitation that traffic goes to ports 80 (HTTP) and 443 (HTTPS) only.

The nature of HTTP requires that traffic flow back into the network, but the network administrator wants to restrict that traffic to HTTP exchanges from requested websites. The security solution must deny any other traffic coming into the network. ACL 104 does that by blocking all incoming traffic, except for the established connections. HTTP establishes connections starting with the original request and then through the exchange of ACK, FIN, and SYN messages.

Notice that the example uses the `established` parameter.

This parameter allows responses to traffic that originates from the 192.168.10.0 /24 network to return inbound on the s0/0/0. A match occurs if the TCP datagram has the ACK or reset (RST) bits set, which indicates that the packet belongs to an existing connection. With the `established` parameter, the router will allow only the established traffic to come back in and block all other traffic.

5.3.3 Applying Extended ACLs to Interfaces

Let us learn how to configure an extended access list by building on the previous example. Recall that we want to allow users to browse both insecure and secure websites. First consider whether the traffic you want to filter is going in or out. Trying to access websites on the Internet is traffic going out. Receiving e-mails from the Internet is traffic coming into the business. However, when considering how to apply an ACL to an interface, in and out take on different meanings depending on the point of view.

In the example in the figure, R1 has two interfaces. It has a serial port, S0/0/0, and a Fast Ethernet port, Fa0/0. The Internet traffic coming in is going in the S0/0/0 interface, but is going out the Fa0/0 interface to reach PC1. The example applies the ACL to the serial interface in both directions.

Click the Deny FTP button in the figure.

This is an example of denying FTP traffic from subnet 192.168.11.0 going to subnet 192.168.10.0, but permitting all other traffic. Note the use of wildcard masks. Remember that FTP requires ports 20 and 21, therefore you need to specify both `eq 20` and `eq 21` to deny FTP.

With extended ACLs, you can choose to use port numbers as in the example, or to call out a well-known port by name. In an earlier example of an extended ACL, the statements were written as follows:

```
access-list 114 permit tcp 192.168.20.0 0.0.0.255 any eq ftp
access-list 114 permit tcp 192.168.20.0 0.0.0.255 any eq ftp-data
```

Note that for FTP, both `ftp` and `ftp-data` need to be mentioned.

Click the Deny Telnet button in the figure.

This example denies Telnet traffic from 192.168.11.0, but allows all other IP traffic from any other source to any destination inbound on Fa0/1. Note the use of the `any` keywords, meaning from anywhere going to anywhere.

5.3.4 Creating Named Extended ACLs

You can create named extended ACLs in essentially the same way you created named standard ACLs. The commands to create a named ACL are different for standard and extended ACLs.

Beginning in privileged EXEC mode, follow these steps to create an extended ACL using names.

Step 1. Starting in the global configuration mode, use the `ip access-list extended` *name* command to define a named extended ACL.

Step 2. In named ACL configuration mode, specify the conditions you want to allow or deny.

Step 3. Return to privileged EXEC mode and verify your ACL with the `show access-lists` [*number* ¦ *name*] command.

Step 4. As an option and recommended step, save your entries in the configuration file with the `copy running-config startup-config` command.

To remove a named extended ACL, use the `no ip access-list extended` *name* global configuration command.

The figure shows the named version of the ACL you created earlier.

Extended ACLs are router configuration scripts that control whether a router permits or denies packets based on their source or destination address as well as protocols or ports. Extended ACLs provide more flexibility and granularity than standard ACLs. This activity focuses on defining filtering criteria, configuring extended ACLs, applying ACLs to router interfaces, and verifying and testing the ACL implementation.

Detailed instructions are provided within the activity as well as in the PDF link below.

Activity Instructions (PDF)

5.4 Configure Complex ACLs

5.4.1 What are Complex ACLs?

Types of Complex ACLs

Standard and extended ACLs can become the basis for complex ACLs that provide additional functionality. The table in the figure summarizes the three categories of complex ACLs.

5.4.2 Dynamic ACLs

What are Dynamic ACLs?

Lock-and-key is a traffic filtering security feature that uses dynamic ACLs, which are sometimes referred to as lock-and-key ACLs. Lock-and-key is available for IP traffic only. Dynamic ACLs are dependent on Telnet connectivity, authentication (local or remote), and extended ACLs.

Dynamic ACL configuration starts with the application of an extended ACL to block traffic through the router. Users who want to traverse the router are blocked by the extended ACL until they use Telnet to connect to the router and are authenticated. The Telnet connection is then dropped, and a single-entry dynamic ACL is added to the extended ACL that exists. This permits traffic for a particular period; idle and absolute timeouts are possible.

When to Use Dynamic ACLs

Some common reasons to use dynamic ACLs are as follows:

- When you want a specific remote user or group of remote users to access a host within your network, connecting from their remote hosts via the Internet. Lock-and-key authenticates the user and then permits limited access through your firewall router for a host or subnet for a finite period.

- When you want a subset of hosts on a local network to access a host on a remote network that is protected by a firewall. With lock-and-key, you can enable access to the remote host only for the desired set of local hosts. Lock-and-key requires the users to authenticate through a *AAA*, TACACS+ server, or other security server before it allows their hosts to access the remote hosts.

Benefits of Dynamic ACLs

Dynamic ACLs have the following security benefits over standard and static extended ACLs:

- Use of a challenge mechanism to authenticate individual users.
- Simplified management in large internetworks.
- In many cases, reduction of the amount of router processing that is required for ACLs.
- Reduction of the opportunity for network break-ins by network hackers.

- Creation of dynamic user access through a firewall, without compromising other configured security restrictions.

In the figure the user at PC1 is an administrator that requires a back door access to the 192.168.30.0 /24 network located on router R3. A dynamic ACL has been configured to allow FTP and HTTP on router R3 access but only for a limited time.

Dynamic ACL Examples

Consider a requirement for a network administrator on PC1 to gain periodic access to the network (192.168.30.0 /24) through router R3. To facilitate this requirement a dynamic ACL is configured on the serial interface S0/0/1 on router R3.

Although a detailed description of the configuration for a dynamic ACL is outside the scope of this course, it is useful to review the configuration steps.

Click the Config button in the figure to view an example of a dynamic ACL configuration.

Roll over each Step in the figure to review the dynamic ACL configuration steps.

5.4.3 Reflexive ACLs

What are Reflexive ACLs?

Reflexive ACLs force the reply traffic from the destination of a known recent outbound packet to go to the source of that outbound packet. This adds greater control to what traffic you allow into your network and increases the capabilities of extended access lists.

Network administrators use reflexive ACLs to allow IP traffic for sessions originating from their network while denying IP traffic for sessions originating outside the network. These ACLs allow the router to manage session traffic dynamically. The router examines the outbound traffic and when it sees a new connection, it adds an entry to a temporary ACL to allow replies back in. Reflexive ACLs contain only temporary entries. These entries are automatically created when a new IP session begins, for example, with an outbound packet, and the entries are automatically removed when the session ends.

Reflexive ACLs provide a truer form of session filtering than an extended ACL that uses the `established` parameter introduced earlier. Although similar in concept to the `established` parameter, reflexive ACLs also work for UDP and ICMP, which have no ACK or RST bits. The `established` option also does not work with applications that dynamically alter the source port for the session traffic. The `permit established` statement only checks ACK and RST bits, not source and destination address.

Reflexive ACLs are not applied directly to an interface but are "nested" within an extended named IP ACL that is applied to the interface.

Reflexive ACLs can be defined only with extended named IP ACLs. They cannot be defined with numbered or standard named ACLs or with other protocol ACLs. Reflexive ACLs can be used with other standard and static extended ACLs.

Benefits of Reflexive ACLs

Reflexive ACLs have the following benefits:

- Help secure your network against network hackers and can be included in a firewall defense.
- Provide a level of security against spoofing and certain DoS attacks. Reflexive ACLs are much harder to spoof because more filter criteria must match before a packet is permitted through.

For example, source and destination addresses and port numbers, not just ACK and RST bits, are checked.

- Simple to use and, compared to basic ACLs, provide greater control over which packets enter your network.

Reflexive ACL Example

The figure shows an example for which the administrator needs a reflexive ACL that permits ICMP outbound and inbound traffic, while it permits only TCP traffic that has been initiated from inside the network. Assume that all other traffic will be denied. The reflexive ACL is applied to the outbound interface of R2.

Click the Config button in the figure.

Although the complete configuration for reflexive ACLs is outside the scope of this course, the figure shows an example of the steps that are required to configure a reflexive ACL.

Roll over each Step in the figure to review the reflexive ACL configuration steps.

5.4.4 Time-based ACLs

What are Time-based ACLs?

Time-based ACLs are similar to extended ACLs in function, but they allow for access control based on time. To implement time-based ACLs, you create a time range that defines specific times of the day and week. You identify the time range with a name and then refer to it by a function. The time restrictions are imposed on the function itself.

Time-based ACLs have many benefits, such as:

- Offers the network administrator more control over permitting or denying access to resources.
- Allows network administrators to control logging messages. ACL entries can log traffic at certain times of the day, but not constantly. Therefore, administrators can simply deny access without analyzing the many logs that are generated during peak hours.

Time Based ACL Example

Although the complete configuration details for time-based ACLs are outside the scope of this course, the following example shows the steps that are required. In the example, a Telnet connection is permitted from the inside network to the outside network on Monday, Wednesday, and Friday during business hours.

Click the Config button in the figure.

Step 1. Define the time range to implement the ACL and give it a name-EVERYOTHERDAY, in this case.

Step 2. Apply the time range to the ACL.

Step 3. Apply the ACL to the interface.

The time range relies on the router system clock. The feature works best with Network Time Protocol (NTP) synchronization, but the router clock can be used.

5.4.5 Troubleshooting Common ACL Errors

Using the **show** commands described earlier reveals most of the more common ACL errors before they cause problems in your network. Hopefully, you are using a good test procedure to protect your network for errors during the development stage of your ACL implementation.

When you look at an ACL, check it against the rules you learned regarding how to build ACLs correctly. Most errors occur because these basic rules are ignored. In fact, the most common errors are entering ACL statements in the wrong order and not applying adequate criteria to your rules.

Let us look at a series of common problems and the solutions. Click each example as you read these explanations.

Click the Error # 1 button in the figure.

Host 192.168.10.10 has no connectivity with 192.168.30.12. Can you see the error in the output of the `show access-lists` command?

Solution - Look at the order of the ACL statements. Host 192.168.10.10 has no telnet connectivity with 192.168.30.12 because of the order of rule 10 in the access list. Because the router processes ACLs from the top down, statement 10 denies host 192.168.10.10, so statement 20 does not get processed. Statements 10 and 20 should be reversed. The last line allows all other non-TCP traffic that falls under IP (ICMP, UDP, and so on).

Click the Error # 2 button in the figure.

The 192.168.10.0 /24 network cannot use TFTP to connect to the 192.168.30.0 /24 network. Can you see the error in the output of the `show access-lists` command?

Solution - The 192.168.10.0 /24 network cannot use TFTP to connect to the 192.168.30.0 /24 network because TFTP uses the transport protocol UDP. Statement 30 in access list 120 allows all other TCP traffic. Because TFTP uses UDP, it is implicitly denied. Statement 30 should be `ip any any`.

This ACL works whether it is applied to Fa0/0 of R1 or S0/0/1of R3, or S0/0/0 or R2 in the incoming direction. However, based on the rule about placing extended ACLs closest to the source, the best option is on Fa0/0 of R1 because it allows undesirable traffic to be filtered without crossing the network infrastructure.

Click the Error # 3 button in the figure.

The 192.168.10.0 /24 network can use Telnet to connect to 192.168.30.0 /24, but this connection should not be allowed. Analyze the output from the `show access-lists` command and see whether you can find a solution. Where would you apply this ACL?

Solution - The 192.168.10.0 /24 network can use Telnet to connect to the 192.168.30.0 /24 network, because the Telnet port number in statement 10 of access list 130 is listed in the wrong position. Statement 10 currently denies any source with a port number that is equal to Telnet trying to establish a connection to any IP address. If you want to deny Telnet traffic inbound on S0/0/1, you should deny the destination port number that is equal to Telnet, for example, `deny tcp any any eq telnet`.

Click the Error # 4 button in the figure.

Host 192.168.10.10 can use Telnet to connect to 192.168.30.12, but this connection should not be allowed. Analyze the output from the `show access-lists` command.

Solution - Host 192.168.10.10 can use Telnet to connect to 192.168.30.12 because there are no rules that deny host 192.168.10.10 or its network as the source. Statement 10 of access list 140 denies the router interface from which traffic would be departing. However, as these packets depart the router, they have a source address of 192.168.10.10 and not the address of the router interface.

As in the solution for Error 2, this ACL should be applied to Fa0/0 of R1 in the incoming direction.

Click the Error # 5 button in the figure.

Host 192.168.30.12 can use Telnet to connect to 192.168.10.10, but this connection should not be allowed. Look at the output from the `show access-lists` command and find the error.

Solution - Host 192.168.30.12 can use Telnet to connect to 192.168.10.10 because the direction in which access list 150 is applied to an interface on R2 is incorrect. Statement 10 denies the source address of 192.168.30.12, but that address would only be the source if the traffic were outbound on S0/0/0, or inbound on S0/0/1.

Complex Flash Activity: Configure Complex ACLs

5.5 Chapter Labs

5.5.1 Basic Access Control Lists

An essential part of network security is being able to control what kind of traffic is being permitted to reach your network, and where that traffic is coming from. This lab will teach how to configure basic and extended access control lists to accomplish this goal.

This activity is a variation of Lab 5.5.1. Packet Tracer may not support all the tasks specified in the hands-on lab. This activity should not be considered equivalent to completing the hands-on lab. Packet Tracer is not a substitute for a hands-on lab experience with real equipment.

Detailed instructions are provided within the activity as well as in the PDF link below.

Activity Instructions (PDF)

5.5.2 Access Control Lists Challenge

In the Basic Access Control List lab you configured for the first time basic and extended access control lists as a network security measure. In this lab try to set up as much network security as possible without referring back to the Basic lab. This will allow you to gauge how much you learned in the Basic lab. Where necessary check your work using either the Basic lab or the answer key provided by your instructor.

This activity is a variation of Lab 5.5.2. Packet Tracer may not support all the tasks specified in the hands-on lab. This activity should not be considered equivalent to completing the hands-on lab. Packet Tracer is not a substitute for a hands-on lab experience with real equipment.

Detailed instructions are provided within the activity as well as in the PDF link below.

Activity Instructions (PDF)

5.5.3 Troubleshooting Access Control Lists

You work for a regional service provider that has recently experienced several security breaches. Your department has been asked to secure customer edge routers so that only the local management PCs are able to access VTY lines. To address this issue, you will configure ACLs on R2 so that networks directly connected to R3 cannot communicate to networks directly connected to R1, but still allow all other traffic.

Chapter Summary

An ACL is a router configuration script that uses packet filtering to control whether a router permits or denies packets to pass based on criteria found in the packet header. ACLs are also used for selecting types of traffic to be analyzed, forwarded, or processed in other ways. ACLs are among the most commonly used objects in Cisco IOS software.

There are different types of ACLs - standard, extended, named and numbered. In this chapter you learned the purpose of each of these ACL types and where they need to be placed in your network. You learned to configure ACLs on inbound and outbound interfaces. Special ACL types, dynamic, reflexive, and timed ACLs, were described. Guidelines and best practices for developing functional and effective ACLs were highlighted.

With the knowledge and skills you learned in this chapter you can now confidently, but with care, configure standard, extended, and complex ACLs, and verify and troubleshoot those configurations.

In this activity, you will demonstrate your ability to configure ACLs that enforce five security policies. In addition, you will configure PPP and OSPF routing. The devices are already configured with IP addressing.

Detailed instructions are provided within the activity as well as in the PDF link below.

Activity Instructions (PDF)

Chapter Quiz

Take the chapter quiz to test your knowledge.

Your Chapter Notes

CHAPTER 6

Teleworker Services

Chapter Introduction

Teleworking is working away from a traditional workplace, usually from a home office. The reasons for choosing teleworking are varied and include everything from personal convenience to allowing injured or shut-in employees opportunities to continue working during periods of convalescence.

Teleworking is a broad term referring to conducting work by connecting to a workplace from a remote location, with the assistance of telecommunications. Efficient teleworking is possible because of broadband Internet connections, virtual private networks (VPN), and more advanced technologies, including Voice over IP (VoIP) and videoconferencing. Teleworking can save money otherwise spent on travel, infrastructure, and facilities support.

Modern enterprises employ people who cannot commute to work every day or for whom working out of a home office is more practical. These people, called teleworkers, must connect to the company network so that they can work from their home offices.

This chapter explains how organizations can provide secure, fast, and reliable remote network connections for teleworkers.

6.1 Business Requirements for Teleworker Services

6.1.1 The Business Requirements for Teleworker Services

More and more companies are finding it beneficial to have teleworkers. With advances in broadband and wireless technologies, working away from the office no longer presents the challenges it did in the past. Workers can work remotely almost as if they were in the next cubicle or office. Organizations can cost-effectively distribute data, voice, video, and real-time applications extended over one common network connection, across their entire workforce no matter how remote and scattered they might be.

The benefits of telecommuting extend well beyond the ability for businesses to make profits. Telecommuting affects the social structure of societies, and can have positive effects on the environment.

For day-to-day business operations, it is beneficial to be able to maintain continuity in case weather, traffic congestion, natural disasters, or other unpredictable events affect workers from getting to the workplace. On a broader scale, the ability of businesses to provide increased service across time zones and international boundaries is greatly enhanced using teleworkers. Contracting and outsourcing solutions are easier to implement and manage.

From a social perspective, teleworking options increase the employment opportunities for various groups, including parents with small children, the handicapped, and people living in remote areas.

Teleworkers enjoy more quality family time, less travel-related stress, and in general provide their employers with increased productivity, satisfaction, and retention. In the age of climate change, teleworking is another way people can reduce their carbon footprint.

When designing network architectures that support a teleworking solution, designers must balance organizational requirements for security, infrastructure management, scalability, and affordability against the practical needs of teleworkers for ease of use, connection speeds, and reliability of service.

To allow businesses and teleworkers to function effectively, we must balance the selection of technologies and carefully design for telecommuting services.

6.1.2 The Teleworker Solution

Organizations need secure, reliable, and cost-effective networks to connect corporate headquarters, branch offices, and suppliers. With the growing number of teleworkers, enterprises have an increasing need for secure, reliable, and cost-effective ways to connect to people working in small offices and home offices (SOHOs), and other remote locations, with resources on corporate sites.

The figure illustrates the remote connection topologies that modern networks use to connect remote locations. In some cases, the remote locations only connect to the headquarters location, while in other cases, remote locations connect to multiple sites. The branch office in the figure connects to the headquarters and partner sites while the teleworker has a single connection to the headquarters.

Click the Options button in the figure.

The figure displays three remote connection technologies available to organizations for supporting teleworker services:

- Traditional private WAN Layer 2 technologies, including Frame Relay, ATM, and leased lines, provide many remote connection solutions. The security of these connections depends on the service provider.

- IPsec Virtual Private Networks (VPNs) offer flexible and scalable connectivity. Site-to-site connections can provide a secure, fast, and reliable remote connection to teleworkers. This is the most common option for teleworkers, combined with remote access over broadband, to establish a secure VPN over the public Internet. (A less reliable means of connectivity using the Internet is a dialup connection.)

- The term broadband refers to advanced communications systems capable of providing high-speed transmission of services, such as data, voice, and video, over the Internet and other networks. Transmission is provided by a wide range of technologies, including digital subscriber line (DSL) and *fiber-optic cable*, coaxial cable, wireless technology, and satellite. The broadband service data transmission speeds typically exceed 200 *kilobits per second* (kb/s), or 200,000 bits per second, in at least one direction: downstream (from the Internet to the user's computer) or upstream (from the user's computer to the Internet).

This chapter describes how each of these technologies operates, and introduces some of the steps needed to ensure that teleworker connections are secure.

To connect effectively to their organization's networks, teleworkers need two key sets of components: home office components and corporate components. The option of adding IP telephony components is becoming more common as providers extend broadband service to more areas.

Soon, voice over IP (VoIP) and videoconferencing components will become expected parts of the teleworkers toolkit.

As shown in the figure, telecommuting needs the following components:

- Home Office Components - The required home office components are a laptop or desktop computer, broadband access (cable or DSL), and a VPN router or VPN client software installed on the computer. Additional components might include a wireless *access point*. When traveling, teleworkers need an Internet connection and a VPN client to connect to the corporate network over any available dialup, network, or broadband connection.

- Corporate Components - Corporate components are VPN-capable routers, VPN concentrators, multifunction security appliances, authentication, and central management devices for resilient aggregation and termination of the VPN connections.

Typically, providing support for VoIP and videoconferencing requires upgrades to these components. Routers need Quality of Service (QoS) functionality. QoS refers to the capability of a network to provide better service to selected network traffic, as required by voice and video applications. An in-depth discussion of QoS is beyond the scope of this course.

The figure shows an encrypted VPN tunnel connecting the teleworker to the corporate network. This is the heart of secure and reliable teleworker connections. A VPN is a private data network that uses the public telecommunication infrastructure. VPN security maintains privacy using a *tunneling* protocol and security procedures.

This course presents the IPsec (IP Security) protocol as the favored approach to building secure VPN tunnels. Unlike earlier security approaches that apply security at the Application layer of the Open Systems Interconnection (OSI) model, IPsec works at the network or packet processing layer.

6.2 Broadband Services

6.2.1 Connecting Teleworkers to the WAN

[Refer to Figure in online course]

Teleworkers typically use diverse applications (for example, e-mail, web-based applications, mission-critical applications, real-time collaboration, voice, video, and videoconferencing) that require a high-bandwidth connection. The choice of access network technology and the need to ensure suitable bandwidth are the first considerations to address when connecting teleworkers.

Residential cable, DSL and broadband wireless are three options that provide high bandwidth to teleworkers. The low bandwidth provided by a dialup modem connection is usually not sufficient, although it is useful for mobile access while traveling. A modem dialup connection should only be considered when other options are unavailable.

Teleworkers require a connection to an ISP to access the Internet. ISPs offer various connection options. The main connection methods used by home and small business users are:

- *Dialup access* - An inexpensive option that uses any phone line and a modem. To connect to the ISP, a user calls the ISP access phone number. Dialup is the slowest connection option, and is typically used by mobile workers in areas where higher speed connection options are not available.

- *DSL* - Typically more expensive than dialup, but provides a faster connection. DSL also uses telephone lines, but unlike dialup access, DSL provides a continuous connection to the

Internet. DSL uses a special high-speed modem that separates the DSL signal from the telephone signal and provides an Ethernet connection to a host computer or LAN.

- *Cable modem* - Offered by cable television service providers. The Internet signal is carried on the same coaxial cable that delivers cable television. A special cable modem separates the Internet signal from the other signals carried on the cable and provides an Ethernet connection to a host computer or LAN.

- *Satellite* - Offered by satellite service providers. The computer connects through Ethernet to a satellite modem that transmits radio signals to the nearest point of presence (POP) within the satellite network.

In this section, you will learn how broadband services, such as DSL, cable, and broadband wireless, extend enterprise networks to enable teleworker access.

6.2.2 Cable

Accessing the Internet through a cable network is a popular option used by teleworkers to access their enterprise network. The cable system uses a coaxial cable that carries radio frequency (*RF*) signals across the network. Coaxial cable is the primary medium used to build cable TV systems.

Cable television first began in Pennsylvania in 1948. John Walson, the owner of an appliance store in a small mountain town, needed to solve poor over-the-air reception problems experienced by customers trying to receive TV signals from Philadelphia through the mountains. Walson erected an antenna on a utility pole on a local mountaintop that enabled him to demonstrate the televisions in his store with strong broadcasts coming from the three Philadelphia stations. He connected the antenna to his appliance store via a cable and modified signal boosters. He then connected several of his customers who were located along the cable path. This was the first community antenna television (*CATV*) system in the United States.

Walson's company grew over the years, and he is recognized as the founder of the cable television industry. He was also the first cable operator to use microwave to import distant television stations, the first to use coaxial cable to improve picture quality, and the first to distribute pay television programming.

Most cable operators use satellite dishes to gather TV signals. Early systems were one-way, with cascading amplifiers placed in series along the network to compensate for signal loss. These systems used taps to couple video signals from the main trunks to subscriber homes via *drop cables*.

Modern cable systems provide two-way communication between subscribers and the cable operator. Cable operators now offer customers advanced telecommunications services, including high-speed Internet access, digital cable television, and residential telephone service. Cable operators typically deploy hybrid fiber-coaxial (HFC) networks to enable high-speed transmission of data to cable modems located in a SOHO.

The figure illustrates the components of a typical modern cable system.

Roll over each component in the figure for a description of what it does.

The electromagnetic spectrum encompasses a broad range of frequencies.

Frequency is the rate at which current (or voltage) cycles occur, computed as the number of "waves" per second. Wavelength is the speed of propagation of the electromagnetic signal divided by its frequency in *cycles per second*.

Radio waves, generally called RF, constitute a portion of the electromagnetic spectrum between approximately 1 kilohertz (kHz) through 1 terahertz. When users tune a radio or TV set to find different radio stations or TV channels, they are tuning to different electromagnetic frequencies across that RF spectrum. The same principle applies to the cable system.

The cable TV industry uses a portion of the RF electromagnetic spectrum. Within the cable, different frequencies carry TV channels and data. At the subscriber end, equipment such as TVs, VCRs, and high-definition TV set-top boxes tune to certain frequencies that allow the user to view the channel or, using a cable modem, to receive high-speed Internet access.

A cable network is capable of transmitting signals on the cable in either direction at the same time. The following frequency scope is used:

- *Downstream* - The direction of an RF signal transmission (TV channels and data) from the source (headend) to the destination (subscribers). Transmission from source to destination is called the forward path. Downstream frequencies are in the range of 50 to 860 megahertz (MHz).

- *Upstream* - The direction of the RF signal transmission from subscribers to the headend, or the return or reverse path. Upstream frequencies are in the range of 5 to 42 MHz.

> Refer to **Figure** in online course

The Data-over-Cable Service Interface Specification (DOCSIS) is an international standard developed by CableLabs, a non-profit research and development consortium for cable-related technologies. CableLabs tests and certifies cable equipment vendor devices, such as cable modems and cable modem termination systems, and grants DOCSIS-certified or qualified status.

DOCSIS defines the communications and operation support interface requirements for a data-over-cable system, and permits the addition of high-speed data transfer to an existing CATV system. Cable operators employ DOCSIS to provide Internet access over their existing hybrid fiber-coaxial (HFC) infrastructure.

DOCSIS specifies the OSI Layer 1 and Layer 2 requirements:

- *Physical layer* - For data signals that the cable operator can use, DOCSIS specifies the channel widths (bandwidths of each channel) as 200 kHz, 400 kHz, 800 kHz, 1.6 MHz, 3.2 MHz, and 6.4 MHz. DOCSIS also specifies modulation techniques (the way to use the RF signal to convey digital data).

- *MAC* layer - Defines a deterministic *access method*, time-division multiple access (TDMA) or synchronous code division multiple access method (S-CDMA).

To understand the MAC layer requirements for DOCSIS, an explanation of how various communication technologies divide channel access is helpful. TDMA divides access by time. Frequency-division multiple access (FDMA) divides access by frequency. Code division multiple access (CDMA) employs spread-spectrum technology and a special coding scheme in which each transmitter is assigned a specific code.

An analogy that illustrates these concepts starts with a room representing a channel. The room is full of people needing to speak to one another-in other words, needing channel access. One solution is for the people to take turns speaking (time division). Another is for each person to speak at different pitches (frequency division). In CDMA, they would speak different languages. People speaking the same language can understand each other, but not other people. In radio CDMA used by many North American cell phone networks, each group of users has a shared code. Many codes occupy the same channel, but only users associated with a particular code can understand each other. S-CDMA is a proprietary version of CDMA developed by Terayon Corporation for data transmission across coaxial cable networks. S-CDMA scatters digital data up and down a wide frequency band and allows multiple subscribers connected to the network to transmit and receive concurrently. S-CDMA is secure and extremely resistant to noise.

Plans for frequency allocation bands differ between North American and European cable systems. Euro-DOCSIS is adapted for use in Europe. The main differences between DOCSIS and Euro-DOCSIS relate to channel bandwidths. TV technical standards vary across the world, which affects the way DOCSIS variants develop. International TV standards include NTSC in North American and parts of Japan; PAL in most of Europe, Asia, Africa, Australia, Brazil, and Argentina; and SECAM in France and some Eastern European countries.

More information is available at these websites:

- About DOCSIS: http://www.cablemodem.com/specifications
- About Euro-DOCSIS: http://www.eurocablelabs.com

Delivering services over a cable network requires different radio frequencies. Downstream frequencies are in the 50 to 860 MHz range, and the upstream frequencies are in the 5 to 42 MHz range.

Two types of equipment are required to send digital modem signals upstream and downstream on a cable system:

- Cable modem termination system (CMTS) at the headend of the cable operator
- Cable modem (CM) on the subscriber end

Roll over the components in the figure and observe the role each plays.

A headend CMTS communicates with CMs located in subscriber homes. The headend is actually a router with databases for providing Internet services to cable subscribers. The architecture is relatively simple, using a mixed optical-coaxial network in which *optical fiber* replaces the lower bandwidth coaxial.

A web of fiber trunk cables connects the headend to the nodes where optical-to-RF signal conversion takes place. The fiber carries the same broadband content for Internet connections, telephone service, and streaming video as the coaxial cable carries. Coaxial feeder cables originate from the node that carries RF signals to the subscribers.

In a modern HFC network, typically 500 to 2,000 active data subscribers are connected to a cable network segment, all sharing the upstream and downstream bandwidth. The actual bandwidth for Internet service over a CATV line can be up to 27 Mb/s on the download path to the subscriber and about 2.5 Mb/s of bandwidth on the upload path. Based on the cable network architecture, cable operator provisioning practices, and traffic load, an individual subscriber can typically get an access speed of between 256 kb/s and 6 Mb/s.

When high usage causes congestion, the cable operator can add additional bandwidth for data services by allocating an additional TV channel for high-speed data. This addition may effectively double the downstream bandwidth that is available to subscribers. Another option is to reduce the number of subscribers served by each network segment. To reduce the number of subscribers, the cable operator further subdivides the network by laying the fiber-optic connections closer and deeper into the neighborhoods.

6.2.3 DSL

DSL is a means of providing high-speed connections over installed copper wires. In this section, we look at DSL as one of the key teleworker solutions available.

Several years ago, Bell Labs identified that a typical voice conversation over a local loop only required bandwidth of 300 Hz to 3 kHz. For many years, the telephone networks did not use the bandwidth above 3 kHz. Advances in technology allowed DSL to use the additional bandwidth from 3 kHz up to 1 MHz to deliver high-speed data services over ordinary copper lines.

As an example, asymmetric DSL (ADSL) uses a frequency range from approximately 20 kHz to 1 MHz. Fortunately, only relatively small changes to existing telephone company infrastructure are required to deliver high-bandwidth data rates to subscribers. The figure shows a representation of bandwidth space allocation on a copper wire for ADSL. The blue area identifies the frequency range used by the voice-grade telephone service, which is often referred to as the plain old telephone service (*POTS*). The other colored spaces represent the frequency space used by the upstream and downstream DSL signals.

The two basic types of DSL technologies are asymmetric (ADSL) and symmetric (SDSL). All forms of DSL service are categorized as ADSL or SDSL, and there are several varieties of each type. ADSL provides higher downstream bandwidth to the user than upload bandwidth. SDSL provides the same capacity in both directions.

The different varieties of DSL provide different bandwidths, some with capabilities exceeding those of a T1 or E1 leased line. The transfer rates are dependent on the actual length of the local loop, and the type and condition of its cabling. For satisfactory service, the loop must be less than 5.5 kilometers (3.5 miles).

Refer to Figure in online course

Service providers deploy DSL connections in the last step of a local telephone network, called the local loop or last mile. The connection is set up between a pair of modems on either end of a copper wire that extends between the customer premises equipment (CPE) and the DSL access multiplexer (DSLAM). A DSLAM is the device located at the central office (CO) of the provider and concentrates connections from multiple DSL subscribers.

Click the DSL Connections button in the figure.

The figure shows the key equipment needed to provide a DSL connection to a SOHO. The two key components are the DSL transceiver and the DSLAM:

- *Transceiver* - Connects the computer of the teleworker to the DSL. Usually the transceiver is a DSL modem connected to the computer using a USB or Ethernet cable. Newer DSL transceivers can be built into small routers with multiple 10/100 switch ports suitable for home office use.

- *DSLAM* - Located at the CO of the carrier, the DSLAM combines individual DSL connections from users into one high-capacity link to an ISP, and thereby, to the Internet.

Click the DSL Router button and DSLAM in the figure.

The advantage that DSL has over cable technology is that DSL is not a shared medium. Each user has a separate direct connection to the DSLAM. Adding users does not impede performance, unless the DSLAM Internet connection to the ISP, or the Internet, becomes saturated.

Refer to Figure in online course

The major benefit of ADSL is the ability to provide data services along with POTS voice services.

When the service provider puts analog voice and ADSL on the same wire, the provider splits the POTS channel from the ADSL modem using filters or splitters. This setup guarantees uninterrupted regular phone service even if ADSL fails. When filters or splitters are in place, the user can use the phone line and the ADSL connection simultaneously without adverse effects on either service.

ADSL signals distort voice transmission and are split or filtered at the customer premises. There are two ways to separate ADSL from voice at the customer premises: using a microfilter or using a splitter.

A microfilter is a passive low-pass filter with two ends. One end connects to the telephone, and the other end connects to the telephone wall jack. This solution eliminates the need for a technician to visit the premises and allows the user to use any jack in the house for voice or ADSL service.

POTS splitters separate the DSL traffic from the POTS traffic. The POTS splitter is a passive device. In the event of a power failure, the voice traffic still travels to the voice switch in the CO of the carrier. Splitters are located at the CO and, in some deployments, at the customer premises. At the CO, the POTS splitter separates the voice traffic, destined for POTS connections, and the data traffic destined for the DSLAM.

The figure shows the local loop terminating on the customer premises at the demarcation point. The actual device is the *network interface* device (NID). This point is usually where the phone line enters the customer premises. At this point, a splitter can be attached to the phone line. The splitter forks the phone line; one branch provides the original house telephone wiring for telephones, and the other branch connects to the ADSL modem. The splitter acts as a low-pass filter, allowing only the 0 to 4 kHz frequencies to pass to or from the telephone. Installing the POTS splitter at the NID usually means that a technician must go to the customer site.

Because of this additional labor and technical support, most home installations today use microfilters, as shown in the figure. Using microfilters also has the advantage of providing wider connectivity through the residence. Since the POTS splitter separates the ADSL and voice signals at the NID, there is usually only one ADSL outlet available in the house.

Click the Microfilter button in the figure.

The figure shows a typical SOHO DSL layout using microfilters. In this solution, the user can install inline microfilters on each telephone, or install wall-mounted microfilters in place of regular telephone jacks. If you roll over the microfilters on the graphic, photos of Cisco products are shown.

Click the Splitter button in the figure.

If the service provider were to have installed a splitter, it would be placed between the NID and the inside telephone distribution system. One wire would go directly to the DSL modem, and the other would carry the voice signal to the telephones. If you roll over the splitter box on the graphic, a typical wiring scheme will be revealed.

6.2.4 Broadband Wireless

Broadband access by ADSL or cable provides teleworkers with faster connections than dialup, but until recently, SOHO PCs had to connect to a modem or a router over a Cat 5 (Ethernet) cable. Wireless networking, or Wi-Fi (wireless fidelity), has improved that situation, not only in the SOHO, but on enterprise campuses as well.

Using 802.11 networking standards, data travels from place to place on radio waves. What makes 802.11 networking relatively easy to deploy is that it uses the unlicensed radio spectrum to send and receive data. Most radio and TV transmissions are government regulated and require a license to use.

Beginning in 2007, computer manufacturers started building wireless network adapters into most laptop computers. As the price of chipsets for Wi-Fi continues to drop, it is becoming a very economical networking option for desktop computers as well.

The benefits of Wi-Fi extend beyond not having to use or install wired network connections. Wireless networking provides mobility. Wireless connections provide increased flexibility and productivity to the teleworker.

Until recently, a significant limitation of wireless access has been the need to be within the local transmission range (typically less than 100 feet) of a wireless router or wireless access point that has a wired connection to the Internet. Once a worker left the office or home, wireless access was not readily available.

However, with advances in technology, the reach of wireless connections has been extended. The concept of hotspots has increased access to wireless connections across the world. A hotspot is the area covered by one or more interconnected access points. Public gathering places, like coffee shops, parks, and libraries, have created Wi-Fi hotspots, hoping to increase business. By overlapping access points, hotspots can cover many square miles.

New developments in broadband wireless technology are increasing wireless availability. These include:

- Municipal Wi-Fi
- WiMAX
- Satellite Internet

Municipal governments have also joined the Wi-Fi revolution. Often working with service providers, cities are deploying municipal wireless networks. Some of these networks provide high-speed Internet access at no cost or for substantially less than the price of other broadband services. Other cities reserve their Wi-Fi networks for official use, providing police, fire fighters, and city workers remote access to the Internet and municipal networks.

Click the Single Router button in the figure.

The figure shows a typical home deployment using a single wireless router. This deployment uses the hub-and-spoke model. If the single wireless router fails, all connectivity is lost. Use your mouse to roll over the text box.

Click the Mesh button in the figure.

Most municipal wireless networks use a mesh topology rather than a hub-and-spoke model. A mesh is a series of access points (radio transmitters) as shown in the figure. Each access point is in range and can communicate with at least two other access points. The mesh blankets its area with radio signals. Signals travel from access point to access point through this cloud.

A meshed network has several advantages over single router hotspots. Installation is easier and can be less expensive because there are fewer wires. Deployment over a large urban area is faster. From an operational point of view, it is more reliable. If a node fails, others in the mesh compensate for it.

Click the WiMAX button in the figure.

WiMAX (Worldwide Interoperability for Microwave Access) is telecommunications technology aimed at providing wireless data over long distances in a variety of ways, from point-to-point links to full mobile cellular type access. WiMAX operates at higher speeds, over greater distances, and for a greater number of users than Wi-Fi. Because of its higher speed (bandwidth) and falling component prices, it is predicted that WiMAX will soon supplant municipal mesh networks for wireless deployments.

A WiMAX network consists of two main components:

- A tower that is similar in concept to a cellular telephone tower. A single WiMAX tower can provide coverage to an area as large as 3,000 square miles, or almost 7,500 square kilometers.
- A WiMAX receiver that is similar in size and shape to a PCMCIA card, or built into a laptop or other wireless device.

A WiMAX tower station connects directly to the Internet using a high-bandwidth connection (for example, a T3 line). A tower can also connect to other WiMAX towers using line-of-sight microwave links. WiMAX is thus able to provide coverage to rural areas out of reach of "last mile" cable and DSL technologies.

Click the Satellite button in the figure.

Satellite Internet services are used in locations where land-based Internet access is not available, or for temporary installations that are continually on the move. Internet access using satellites is available worldwide, including for vessels at sea, airplanes in flight, and vehicles moving on land.

There are three ways to connect to the Internet using satellites: one-way multicast, one-way terrestrial return, and two-way.

- One-way multicast satellite Internet systems are used for *IP multicast*-based data, audio, and video distribution. Even though most IP protocols require two-way communication, for Internet content, including web pages, one-way satellite-based Internet services can be "pushed" pages to local storage at end-user sites by satellite Internet. Full interactivity is not possible.

- One-way terrestrial return satellite Internet systems use traditional dialup access to send outbound data through a modem and receive downloads from the satellite.

- Two-way satellite Internet sends data from remote sites via satellite to a hub, which then sends the data to the Internet. The satellite dish at each location needs precise positioning to avoid interference with other satellites.

The figure illustrates a two-way satellite Internet system. Upload speeds are about one-tenth of the download speed, which is in the range of 500 kb/s.

The key installation requirement is for the antenna to have a clear view toward the equator, where most orbiting satellites are stationed. Trees and heavy rains can affect reception of the signals.

Two-way satellite Internet uses IP multicasting technology, which allows one satellite to serve up to 5,000 communication channels simultaneously. IP multicast sends data from one point to many points at the same time by sending data in a compressed format. Compression reduces the size of the data and the bandwidth.

Refer to Figure in online course

Wireless networking complies with a range of standards that routers and receivers use to communicate with each other. The most common standards are included in the *IEEE 802.11* wireless local area network (*WLAN*) standard, which addresses the 5 GHz and 2.4 GHz public (unlicensed) spectrum bands.

The terms 802.11 and Wi-Fi appear interchangeably, but this is incorrect. Wi-Fi is an industry-driven interoperability certification based on a subset of 802.11. The Wi-Fi specification came about because market demand led the *Wi-Fi Alliance* to begin certifying products before amendments to the 802.11 standard were complete. The 802.11 standard has since caught up with and passed Wi-Fi.

From the point of view of teleworkers, the most popular access approaches to connectivity are those defined by the *IEEE 802.11b* and *IEEE 802.11g* protocols. Security was originally intentionally weak in these protocols because of the restrictive export requirements of multiple governments. The latest standard, 802.11n, is a proposed amendment that builds on the previous 802.11 standards by adding multiple-input multiple-output (MIMO).

The 802.16 (or WiMAX) standard allows transmissions up to 70 Mb/s, and has a range of up to 30 miles (50 km). It can operate in licensed or unlicensed bands of the spectrum from 2 to 6 GHz.

In this activity, you will demonstrate your ability to add broadband devices and connections to Packet Tracer. Although you cannot configure DSL and cable modems, you can simulate end-to-end connectivity to teleworker devices.

Detailed instructions are provided within the activity as well as in the PDF link below.

Activity Instructions (PDF)

6.3 VPN Technology

6.3.1 VPNs and Their Benefits

The Internet is a worldwide, publicly accessible IP network. Because of its vast global proliferation, it has become an attractive way to interconnect remote sites. However, the fact that it is a public infrastructure poses security risks to enterprises and their internal networks. Fortunately, VPN technology enables organizations to create private networks over the public Internet infrastructure that maintain confidentiality and security.

Organizations use VPNs to provide a virtual WAN infrastructure that connects branch offices, home offices, business partner sites, and remote telecommuters to all or portions of their corporate network. To remain private, the traffic is encrypted. Instead of using a dedicated Layer 2 connection, such as a leased line, a VPN uses virtual connections that are routed through the Internet.

Earlier in this course, an analogy involving getting priority tickets for a stadium show was introduced. An extension to that analogy will help explain how a VPN works. Picture the stadium as a public place in the same way as the Internet is a public place. When the show is over, the public leaves through public aisles and doorways, jostling and bumping into each other along the way. Petty thefts are threats to be endured.

Consider how the performers leave. Their entourage all link arms and form cordons through the mobs and protect the celebrities from all the jostling and pushing. In effect, these cordons form tunnels. The celebrities are whisked through tunnels into limousines that carry them cocooned to their destinations. This section describes how VPNs work in much the same way, bundling data and safely moving it across the Internet through protective tunnels. An understanding of VPN technology is essential to be able to implement secure teleworker services on enterprise networks.

Analogy: Each LAN Is an IsLANd

We will use another analogy to illustrate the VPN concept from a different point of view. Imagine that you live on an island in a huge ocean. There are thousands of other islands all around you, some very close and others farther away. The normal way to travel is to take a ferry from your island to whichever island you wish to visit. Traveling on a ferry means that you have almost no privacy. Anything you do can be seen by someone else.

Assume that each island represents a private LAN, and the ocean is the Internet. When you travel by ferry, it is similar to when you connect to a web server or to another device through the Internet. You have no control over the wires and routers that make up the Internet, just like you have no control over the other people on the ferry. This leaves you susceptible to security issues if you try to connect between two private networks using a public resource.

Your island decides to build a bridge to another island so that there is an easier, more secure and direct way for people to travel between the two. It is expensive to build and maintain the bridge, even though the island you are connecting with is very close. But the need for a reliable, secure path is so great that you do it anyway. Your island would like to connect to a second island that is much farther away, but you decide that it is too expensive.

This situation is very much like having a leased line. The bridges (leased lines) are separate from the ocean (Internet), yet they are able to connect the islands (LANs). Many companies have chosen this route because of the need for security and reliability in connecting their remote offices. However, if the offices are very far apart, the cost can be prohibitively high-just like trying to build a bridge that spans a great distance.

So how does VPN fit into this analogy? We could give each inhabitant of the islands their own small submarine with these properties:

- Fast
- Easy to take with you wherever you go
- Able to hide you completely from any other boats or submarines
- Dependable
- Costs little to add additional submarines to your fleet once the first is purchased

Although they are traveling in the ocean along with other traffic, the inhabitants of our two islands could travel back and forth whenever they wanted to with privacy and security. That is essentially how a VPN works. Each remote member of your network can communicate in a secure and reliable manner using the Internet as the medium to connect to the private LAN. A VPN can grow to accommodate more users and different locations much easier than a leased line. In fact, scalability is a major advantage that VPNs have over typical leased lines. Unlike leased lines, where the cost increases in proportion to the distances involved, the geographic locations of each office matter little in the creation of a VPN.

Refer to Figure in online course

Organizations using VPNs benefit from increased flexibility and productivity. Remote sites and teleworkers can connect securely to the corporate network from almost any place. Data on a VPN is encrypted and undecipherable to anyone not entitled to have it. VPNs bring remote hosts inside the firewall, giving them close to the same levels of access to network devices as if they were in a corporate office.

The figure shows leased lines in red. The blue lines represent VPN-based connections. Consider these benefits when using VPNs:

- *Cost savings* - Organizations can use cost-effective, third-party Internet transport to connect remote offices and users to the main corporate site. This eliminates expensive dedicated WAN links and modem banks. By using broadband, VPNs reduce connectivity costs while increasing remote connection bandwidth.
- *Security* - Advanced encryption and authentication protocols protect data from unauthorized access.
- *Scalability* - VPNs use the Internet infrastructure within ISPs and carriers, making it easy for organizations to add new users. Organizations, big and small, are able to add large amounts of capacity without adding significant infrastructure.

6.3.2 Types of VPNs

Refer to Figure in online course

Organizations use site-to-site VPNs to connect dispersed locations in the same way as a leased line or Frame Relay connection is used. Because most organizations now have Internet access, it makes sense to take advantage of the benefits of site-to-site VPNs. As illustrated in the figure, site-to-site VPNs also support company intranets and business partner extranets.

In effect, a site-to-site VPN is an extension of classic WAN networking. Site-to-site VPNs connect entire networks to each other. For example, they can connect a branch office network to a company headquarters network.

In a site-to-site VPN, hosts send and receive TCP/IP traffic through a VPN *gateway*, which could be a router, PIX firewall appliance, or an Adaptive Security Appliance (ASA). The VPN gateway is responsible for encapsulating and encrypting outbound traffic for all of the traffic from a particular site and sending it through a VPN tunnel over the Internet to a peer VPN gateway at the target site. On receipt, the peer VPN gateway strips the headers, decrypts the content, and relays the packet toward the target host inside its private network.

Mobile users and telecommuters use remote access VPNs extensively. In the past, corporations supported remote users using dialup networks. This usually involved a toll call and incurring long distance charges to access the corporation.

Most teleworkers now have access to the Internet from their homes and can establish remote VPNs using broadband connections. Similarly, a mobile worker can make a local call to a local ISP to access the corporation through the Internet. In effect, this marks an evolutionary advance in dialup networks. Remote access VPNs can support the needs of telecommuters, mobile users, as well as extranet consumer-to-business.

In a remote-access VPN, each host typically has VPN client software. Whenever the host tries to send any traffic, the VPN client software encapsulates and encrypts that traffic before sending it over the Internet to the VPN gateway at the edge of the target network. On receipt, the VPN gateway handles the data in the same way as it would handle data from a site-to-site VPN.

6.3.3 VPN Components

A VPN creates a private network over a public network infrastructure while maintaining confidentiality and security. VPNs use cryptographic tunneling protocols to provide protection against packet sniffing, sender authentication, and message integrity.

The figure illustrates a typical VPN topology. Components required to establish this VPN include:

- An existing network with servers and workstations
- A connection to the Internet
- VPN gateways, such as routers, firewalls, VPN concentrators, and ASAs, that act as endpoints to establish, manage, and control VPN connections
- Appropriate software to create and manage VPN tunnels

The key to VPN effectiveness is security. VPNs secure data by encapsulating or encrypting the data. Most VPNs can do both.

- Encapsulation is also referred to as tunneling, because encapsulation transmits data transparently from network to network through a shared network infrastructure.
- Encryption codes data into a different format using a secret key. Decryption decodes encrypted data into the original unencrypted format.

Encapsulation and encryption are discussed in more detail later in this course.

6.3.4 Characteristics of Secure VPNs

VPNs use advanced encryption techniques and tunneling to permit organizations to establish secure, end-to-end, private network connections over the Internet.

The foundation of a secure VPN is data confidentiality, data integrity, and authentication:

- *Data confidentiality* - A common security concern is protecting data from eavesdroppers. As a design feature, data confidentiality aims at protecting the contents of messages from interception by unauthenticated or unauthorized sources. VPNs achieve confidentiality using mechanisms of encapsulation and encryption.

- *Data integrity* - Receivers have no control over the path the data has traveled and therefore do not know if the data has been seen or handled while it journeyed across the Internet. There is always the possibility that the data has been modified. Data integrity guarantees that no tampering or alterations occur to data while it travels between the source and destination. VPNs typically use hashes to ensure data integrity. A hash is like a checksum or a seal that guarantees that no one has read the content, but it is more robust. Hashes are explained in the next topic.

- *Authentication* - Authentication ensures that a message comes from an authentic source and goes to an authentic destination. User identification gives a user confidence that the party with whom the user establishes communications is who the user thinks the party is. VPNs can use passwords, digital certificates, smart cards, and biometrics to establish the identity of parties at the other end of a network.

6.3.5 VPN Tunneling

Incorporating appropriate data confidentiality capabilities into a VPN ensures that only the intended sources and destinations are capable of interpreting the original message contents.

Tunneling allows the use of public networks like the Internet to carry data for users as though the users had access to a private network. Tunneling encapsulates an entire packet within another packet and sends the new, composite packet over a network. This figure lists the three classes of protocols that tunneling uses.

To illustrate the concept of tunneling and the classes of tunneling protocols, consider an example of sending a holiday card through traditional mail. The holiday card has a message inside. The card is the passenger protocol. The sender puts the card inside an envelope (encapsulating protocol) with proper addressing applied. The sender then drops the envelope into a mailbox for delivery. The postal system (carrier protocol) picks up and delivers the envelope to the mailbox of the recipient. The two endpoints in the carrier system are the "tunnel interfaces." The recipient removes the holiday card (extracts the passenger protocol) and reads the message.

Click the Encapsulation button in the figure to view an illustration of the encapsulation process.

This figure illustrates an e-mail message traveling through the Internet over a VPN connection. PPP carries the message to the VPN device, where the message is encapsulated within a Generic Route Encapsulation (*GRE*) packet. GRE is a tunneling protocol developed by Cisco Systems that can encapsulate a wide variety of protocol packet types inside IP tunnels, creating a virtual point-to-point link to Cisco routers at remote points over an IP internetwork. In the figure, the outer packet source and destination addressing is assigned to "tunnel interfaces" and is made routable across the network. Once a composite packet reaches the destination tunnel interface, the inside packet is extracted.

6.3.6 VPN Data Integrity

If plain text data is transported over the public Internet, it can be intercepted and read. To keep the data private, it needs to be encrypted. VPN encryption encrypts the data and renders it unreadable to unauthorized receivers.

For encryption to work, both the sender and the receiver must know the rules used to transform the original message into its coded form. VPN encryption rules include an algorithm and a key. An algorithm is a mathematical function that combines a message, text, digits, or all three with a key. The output is an unreadable cipher string. Decryption is extremely difficult or impossible without the correct key.

In the example, Gail wants to send a financial document to Jeremy across the Internet. Gail and Jeremy have previously agreed on a secret shared key. At Gail's end, the VPN client software combines the document with the secret shared key and passes it through an encryption algorithm. The output is undecipherable cipher text. The cipher text is then sent through a VPN tunnel over the Internet. At the other end, the message is recombined with the same shared secret key and processed by the same encryption algorithm. The output is the original financial document, which is now readable to Jeremy.

> Refer to **Figure** in online course

The degree of security provided by any encryption algorithm depends on the length of the key. For any given key length, the time that it takes to process all of the possibilities to decrypt cipher text is a function of the computing power of the computer. Therefore, the shorter the key, the easier it is to break, but at the same time, the easier it is to pass the message.

Some of the more common encryption algorithms and the length of keys they use are as follows:

- *Data Encryption Standard (DES)* algorithm - Developed by IBM, DES uses a 56-bit key, ensuring high-performance encryption. DES is a symmetric key cryptosystem. Symmetric and asymmetric keys are explained below.

- *Triple DES (3DES) algorithm* - A newer variant of DES that encrypts with one key, decrypts with another different key, and then encrypts one final time with another key. 3DES provides significantly more strength to the encryption process.

- *Advanced Encryption Standard (AES)* - The National Institute of Standards and Technology (NIST) adopted AES to replace the existing DES encryption in cryptographic devices. AES provides stronger security than DES and is computationally more efficient than 3DES. AES offers three different key lengths: 128, 192, and 256-bit keys.

- *Rivest, Shamir, and Adleman (RSA)* - An asymmetrical key cryptosystem. The keys use a bit length of 512, 768, 1024, or larger.

Symmetric Encryption

Encryption algorithms such as DES and 3DES require a shared secret key to perform encryption and decryption. Each of the two computers must know the key to decode the information. With symmetric key encryption, also called secret key encryption, each computer encrypts the information before sending it over the network to the other computer. Symmetric key encryption requires knowledge of which computers will be talking to each other so that the same key can be configured on each computer.

For example, a sender creates a coded message where each letter is substituted with the letter that is two letters down in the alphabet; "A" becomes "C," and "B" becomes "D", and so on. In this case, the word SECRET becomes UGETGV. The sender has already told the recipient that the secret key is "shift by 2." When the recipient receives the message UGETGV, the recipient computer decodes the message by shifting back two letters and calculating SECRET. Anyone else who sees the message sees only the encrypted message, which looks like nonsense unless the person knows the secret key.

The question is, how do the encrypting and decrypting devices both have the shared secret key? You could use e-mail, courier, or overnight express to send the shared secret keys to the administrators of the devices. Another easier and more secure method is asymmetric encryption.

Asymmetric Encryption

Asymmetric encryption uses different keys for encryption and decryption. Knowing one of the keys does not allow a hacker to deduce the second key and decode the information. One key encrypts the message, while a second key decrypts the message. It is not possible to encrypt and decrypt with the same key.

Public key encryption is a variant of asymmetric encryption that uses a combination of a private key and a public key. The recipient gives a public key to any sender with whom the recipient wants to communicate. The sender uses a private key combined with the recipient's public key to encrypt the message. Also, the sender must share their public key with the recipient. To decrypt a message, the recipient will use the public key of the sender with their own private key.

Hashes contribute to data integrity and authentication by ensuring that unauthorized persons do not tamper with transmitted messages. A hash, also called a message digest, is a number generated from a string of text. The hash is smaller than the text itself. It is generated using a formula in such a way that it is extremely unlikely that some other text will produce the same hash value.

The original sender generates a hash of the message and sends it with the message itself. The recipient decrypts the message and the hash, produces another hash from the received message, and compares the two hashes. If they are the same, the recipient can be reasonably sure the integrity of the message has not been affected.

In the figure, someone is trying to send Jeremy a check for US$100. At the remote end, Alex Jones (likely a criminal) is trying to cash the check for $1,000. As the check progressed through the Internet, it was altered. Both the recipient and dollar amounts were changed. In this case, if a data integrity algorithm was used, the hashes would not match, and the transaction would no longer be valid.

VPN data is transported over the public Internet. As shown, there is potential for this data to be intercepted and modified. To guard against this threat, hosts can add a hash to the message. If the transmitted hash matches the received hash, the integrity of the message has been preserved. However, if there is no match, the message was altered.

VPNs use a message authentication code to verify the integrity and the authenticity of a message, without using any additional mechanisms. A keyed hashed message authentication code (HMAC) is a data integrity algorithm that guarantees the integrity of the message.

A HMAC has two parameters: a message input and a secret key known only to the message originator and intended receivers. The message sender uses a HMAC function to produce a value (the message authentication code), formed by condensing the secret key and the message input. The message authentication code is sent along with the message. The receiver computes the message authentication code on the received message using the same key and HMAC function as the sender used, and compares the result computed with the received message authentication code. If the two values match, the message has been correctly received and the receiver is assured that the sender is a member of the community of users that share the key. The cryptographic strength of the HMAC depends upon the cryptographic strength of the underlying hash function, on the size and quality of the key, and the size of the hash output length in bits.

There are two common HMAC algorithms:

- *Message Digest 5 (MD5)* - Uses a 128-bit shared secret key. The variable length message and 128-bit shared secret key are combined and run through the HMAC-MD5 hash algorithm. The output is a 128-bit hash. The hash is appended to the original message and forwarded to the remote end.

- *Secure Hash Algorithm 1 (SHA-1)* - Uses a 160-bit secret key. The variable length message and the 160-bit shared secret key are combined and run through the HMAC-SHA-1 hash algorithm. The output is a 160-bit hash. The hash is appended to the original message and forwarded to the remote end.

Click the VPN Authentication button in the figure.

When conducting business long distance, it is necessary to know who is at the other end of the phone, e-mail, or fax. The same is true of VPN networks. The device on the other end of the VPN tunnel must be authenticated before the communication path is considered secure. There are two peer authentication methods:

- *Pre-shared key (PSK)* - A secret key that is shared between the two parties using a secure channel before it needs to be used. PSKs use symmetric key cryptographic algorithms. A PSK is entered into each peer manually and is used to authenticate the peer. At each end, the PSK is combined with other information to form the authentication key.

- *RSA signature* - Uses the exchange of digital certificates to authenticate the peers. The local device derives a hash and encrypts it with its private key. The encrypted hash (digital signature) is attached to the message and forwarded to the remote end. At the remote end, the encrypted hash is decrypted using the public key of the local end. If the decrypted hash matches the recomputed hash, the signature is genuine.

Take a look at an *RSA demonstration* for an example of RSA encryption.

6.3.7 IPsec Security Protocols

IPsec is protocol suite for securing IP communications which provides encryption, integrity, and authentication. IPsec spells out the messaging necessary to secure VPN communications, but relies on existing algorithms.

There are two main IPsec framework protocols.

- *Authentication Header (AH)* - Use when confidentiality is not required or permitted. AH provides data authentication and integrity for IP packets passed between two systems. It verifies that any message passed from R1 to R2 has not been modified during transit. It also verifies that the origin of the data was either R1 or R2. AH does not provide data confidentiality (encryption) of packets. Used alone, the AH protocol provides weak protection. Consequently, it is used with the ESP protocol to provide data encryption and tamper-aware security features.

- *Encapsulating Security Payload (ESP)* - Provides confidentiality and authentication by encrypting the IP packet. IP packet encryption conceals the data and the identities of the source and destination. ESP authenticates the inner IP packet and ESP header. Authentication provides data origin authentication and data integrity. Although both encryption and authentication are optional in ESP, at a minimum, one of them must be selected.

Click the IPsec Framework button in the figure.

IPsec relies on existing algorithms to implement encryption, authentication, and key exchange. Some of the standard algorithms that IPsec uses are as follows:

- DES - Encrypts and decrypts packet data.
- 3DES - Provides significant encryption strength over 56-bit DES.
- AES - Provides stronger encryption, depending on the key length used, and faster throughput.

- MD5 - Authenticates packet data, using a 128-bit shared secret key.
- SHA-1 - Authenticates packet data, using a 160-bit shared secret key.
- DH - Allows two parties to establish a shared secret key used by encryption and hash algorithms, for example, DES and MD5, over an insecure communications channel.

The figure shows how IPsec is configured. IPsec provides the framework, and the administrator chooses the algorithms used to implement the security services within that framework. There are four IPsec framework squares to be filled.

- When configuring an IPsec gateway to provide security services, first choose an IPsec protocol. The choices are ESP or ESP with AH.
- The second square is an encryption algorithm if IPsec is implemented with ESP. Choose the encryption algorithm that is appropriate for the desired level of security: DES, 3DES, or AES.
- The third square is authentication. Choose an authentication algorithm to provide data integrity: MD5 or SHA.
- The last square is the Diffie-Hellman (DH) algorithm group. Which establishes the sharing of key information between peers. Choose which group to use, DH1 or DH2.

Activity: VPN Technology

actvity

Chapter Summary

> Refer to **Figure** in online course

In this chapter, you learned of the growing importance of teleworkers. You can describe an organization's requirements for providing teleworker services in terms of what the teleworker needs and what the organization needs to provide: reliable, cost-effective connectivity. Among the favored ways to connect teleworkers, you can describe how to use broadband services including DSL, cable, and wireless. Further, you know how VPN technology can be used to provide secure teleworker services in organizations, including the importance, benefits, role, and impact of VPN technology, and the types of access, components, tunneling, and encryption.

> Refer to **Figure** in online course
>
> Refer to **Packet Tracer Activity** for this chapter

This activity requires you to configure a `default route` as well as `dynamic routing` using RIP version 2. You will also add broadband devices to the network. Finally, you will set up ACLs on two routers to control network traffic.

Detailed instructions are provided within the activity as well as in the PDF link below.

Activity Instructions (PDF)

> Go to the online course to take the quiz.

Chapter Quiz

Take the chapter quiz to test your knowledge.

Your Chapter Notes

CHAPTER 7

IP Addressing Services

Chapter Introduction

> Refer to Figure in online course

The Internet and IP-related technologies have experienced rapid growth. One reason for the growth has been due in part to the flexibility of the original design. However, that design did not anticipate the Internet's popularity and the resulting demand for IP addresses. For example, every host and device on the Internet requires a unique IP version 4 (*IPv4*) address. Because of the dramatic growth, the number of available IP addresses is quickly running out.

To cope with the depletion of IP addresses, several short-term solutions were developed. Two short-term solutions are private addresses and Network Address Translation (NAT).

An inside host typically receives its IP address, subnet mask, default gateway IP address, DNS server IP address, and other information from a Dynamic Host Configuration Protocol (DHCP) server. Instead of providing inside hosts with valid Internet IP addresses, the DHCP server usually provides IP addresses from a private pool of addresses. The problem is that these hosts may still require valid IP addresses to access Internet resources. This is where NAT comes in.

NAT enables inside network hosts to borrow a legitimate Internet IP address while accessing Internet resources. When the requested traffic returns, the legitimate IP address is repurposed and available for the next Internet request by an inside host. Using NAT, network administrators only need one or a few IP addresses for the router to provide to the hosts, instead of one unique IP address for every client joining the network. Although it sounds inefficient, the process is actually very efficient, because host traffic occurs very quickly.

Although private addresses with DHCP and NAT have helped reduce the need for IP addresses, it is estimated that we will run out of unique IPv4 addresses by 2010. For this reason, in the mid-1990s, the IETF requested proposals for a new IP addressing scheme. The IP Next Generation (*IPng*) working group responded. By 1996, the IETF started releasing a number of RFCs defining *IPv6*.

The main feature of IPv6 that is driving adoption today is the larger address space: addresses in IPv6 are 128 bits long versus 32 bits in IPv4.

This chapter describes how to implement DHCP, NAT, and IPv6 on enterprise networks.

7.1 DHCP

7.1.1 Introducing DHCP

> Refer to Figure in online course

What is DHCP?

Every device that connects to a network needs an IP address. Network administrators assign static IP addresses to routers, servers, and other network devices whose locations (physical and logical) are not likely to change. Administrators enter static IP addresses manually when they configure devices to join the network. Static addresses also enable administrators to manage those devices remotely.

However, computers in an organization often change locations, physically and logically. Administrators are unable to keep up with having to assign new IP addresses every time an employee moves to a different office or cubicle. Desktop clients do not require a static address. Instead, a workstation can use any address within a range of addresses. This range is typically within an IP subnet. A workstation within a specific subnet can be assigned any address within a specified range. Other items such as the subnet mask, default gateway, and Domain Name System (DNS) server are assigned a value which is common either to that subnet or entire administrated network. For example, all hosts within the same subnet will receive different host IP addresses, but will receive the same subnet mask and default gateway IP address."

Recall from CCNA Exploration: Network Fundamentals that DHCP makes the process of assigning new IP addresses almost transparent. DHCP assigns IP addresses and other important network configuration information dynamically. Because desktop clients typically make up the bulk of network nodes, DHCP is an extremely useful and timesaving tool for network administrators. RFC 2131 describes DHCP.

Administrators typically prefer a network server to offer DHCP services, because these solutions are scalable and relatively easy to manage. However, in a small branch or SOHO location, a Cisco router can be configured to provide DHCP services without the need for an expensive dedicated server. A Cisco IOS feature set called Easy IP offers an optional, full-featured DHCP server.

7.1.2 DHCP Operation

DHCP Operation

Providing IP addresses to clients is the most fundamental task performed by a DHCP server. DHCP includes three different address allocation mechanisms to provide flexibility when assigning IP addresses:

- *Manual Allocation:* The administrator assigns a pre-allocated IP address to the client and DHCP only communicates the IP address to the device.

- *Automatic Allocation:* DHCP automatically assigns a static IP address permanently to a device, selecting it from a pool of available addresses. There is no lease and the address is permanently assigned to a device.

- *Dynamic Allocation:* DHCP automatically dynamically assigns, or leases, an IP address from a pool of addresses for a limited period of time chosen by the server, or until the client tells the DHCP server that it no longer needs the address.

This section focuses on dynamic allocation.

DHCP works in a client/server mode and operates like any other client/server relationship. When a PC connects to a DHCP server, the server assigns or leases an IP address to that PC. The PC connects to the network with that leased IP address until the lease expires. The host must contact the DHCP server periodically to extend the lease. This lease mechanism ensures that hosts that move or power off do not hold onto addresses that they do not need. The DHCP server returns these addresses to the address pool and reallocates them as necessary.

Click the Discover button in the figure.

When the client boots or otherwise wants to join a network, it completes four steps in obtaining a lease. In the first step, the client broadcasts a DHCPDISCOVER message. The DHCPDISCOVER message finds DHCP servers on the network. Because the host has no valid IP information at bootup, it uses L2 and L3 broadcast addresses to communicate with the server.

Click the Offer button in the figure.

When the DHCP server receives a DHCDISCOVER message, it finds an available IP address to lease, creates an ARP entry consisting of the MAC address of the requesting host and the leased IP address, and transmits a binding offer with a DHCPOFFER message. The DHCPOFFER message is sent as a unicast, using the L2 MAC address of the server as the source address and the L2 address of the client as the destination.

Note: Under certain circumstances, the DHCP message exchange from the server may be broadcasted and not unicasted.

Click the Request button in the figure.

When the client receives the DHCPOFFER from the server, it sends back a DHCPREQUEST message. This message has two purposes: lease origination and lease renewal and verification. When used for lease origination, the DHCPREQUEST of the client is requesting that the IP information be verified just after it has been assigned. The message provides error checking to ensure that the assignment is still valid. The DHCPREQUEST also serves as a binding acceptance notice to the selected server and an implicit decline to any other servers that may have provided the host a binding offer.

Many enterprise networks use multiple DHCP servers. The DHCPREQUEST message is sent in the form of a broadcast to inform this DHCP server and any other DHCP servers about the accepted offer.

Click the Acknowledge button in the figure.

On receiving the DHCPREQUEST message, the server verifies the lease information, creates a new ARP entry for the client lease, and replies with a unicast DHCPACK message. The DHCPACK message is a duplicate of the DHCPOFFER, except for a change in the message type field. When the client receives the DHCPACK message, it logs the configuration information and performs an ARP lookup for the assigned address. If it does not receive a reply, it knows that the IP address is valid and starts using it as its own.

Clients lease the information from the server for an administratively defined period. Administrators configure DHCP servers to set the leases to time out at different intervals. Most ISPs and large networks use default lease durations of up to three days. When the lease expires, the client must ask for another address, although the client is typically reassigned the same address.

The DHCPREQUEST message also addresses the dynamic DHCP process. The IP information sent in the DHCPOFFER might have been offered to another client during the dynamic allocation. Each DHCP server creates pools of IP addresses and associated parameters. Pools are dedicated to individual, logical IP subnets. The pools allow multiple DHCP servers to respond and IP clients to be mobile. If multiple servers respond, a client can choose only one of the offers.

7.1.3 BOOTP and DHCP

BOOTP and DHCP

The Bootstrap Protocol (*BOOTP*), defined in RFC 951, is the predecessor of DHCP and shares some operational characteristics. BOOTP is a way to download address and boot configurations for diskless workstations. A diskless workstation does not have a hard drive or an operating system. For example, many automated cash register systems at your local super market are examples of diskless workstations. Both DHCP and BOOTP are client/server based and use UDP ports 67 and 68. Those ports are still known as BOOTP ports.

DHCP and BOOTP have two components, as shown in the figure. The server is a host with a static IP address that allocates, distributes, and manages IP and configuration data assignments. Each allocation (IP and configuration data) is stored on the server in a data set called a binding. The client is any device using DHCP as a method for obtaining IP addressing or supporting configuration information.

To understand the functional differences between BOOTP and DHCP, consider the four basic IP parameters needed to join a network:

- IP address
- Gateway address
- Subnet mask
- DNS server address

There are three primary differences between DHCP and BOOTP:

- The main difference is that BOOTP was designed for manual pre-configuration of the host information in a server database, while DHCP allows for dynamic allocation of network addresses and configurations to newly attached hosts. When a BOOTP client requests an IP address, the BOOTP server searches a predefined table for an entry that matches the MAC address for the client. If an entry exists, the corresponding IP address for that entry is returned to the client. This means that the binding between the MAC address and the IP address must have already been configured in the BOOTP server.

- DHCP allows for recovery and reallocation of network addresses through a leasing mechanism. Specifically, DHCP defines mechanisms through which clients can be assigned an IP address for a finite lease period. This lease period allows for reassignment of the IP address to another client later, or for the client to get another assignment if the client moves to another subnet. Clients may also renew leases and keep the same IP address. BOOTP does not use leases. Its clients have reserved IP address which cannot be assigned to any other host.

- BOOTP provides a limited amount of information to a host. DHCP provides additional IP configuration parameters, such as WINS and domain name.

DHCP Message Format

The developers of DHCP needed to maintain compatibility with BOOTP and consequently used the same BOOTP message format. However, because DHCP has more functionality than BOOTP, the DHCP options field was added. When communicating with older BOOTP clients, the DHCP options field is ignored.

The figure shows the format of a DHCP message. The fields are as follows:

- *Operation Code (OP)* - Specifies the general type of message. A value of 1 indicates a request message; a value of 2 is a reply message.

- *Hardware Type* - Identifies the type of hardware used in the network. For example, 1 is Ethernet, 15 is Frame Relay, and 20 is a serial line. These are the same codes used in ARP messages.

- *Hardware Address* length - 8 bits to specify the length of the address.

- *Hops* - Set to 0 by a client before transmitting a request and used by relay agents to control the forwarding of DHCP messages.

- *Transaction Identifier* - 32-bit identification generated by the client to allow it to match up the request with replies received from DHCP servers.

- *Seconds -* Number of seconds elapsed since a client began attempting to acquire or renew a lease. Busy DHCP servers use this number to prioritize replies when multiple client requests are outstanding.

- *Flags -* Only one of the 16 bits is used, which is the broadcast flag. A client that does not know its IP address when it sends a request, sets the flag to 1. This value tells the DHCP server or relay agent receiving the request that it should send the reply back as a broadcast.

- *Client IP Address -* The client puts its own IP address in this field if and only if it has a valid IP address while in the bound state; otherwise, it sets the field to 0. The client can only use this field when its address is actually valid and usable, not during the process of acquiring an address.

- *Your IP Address -* IP address that the server assigns to the client.

- *Server IP Address -* Address of the server that the client should use for the next step in the bootstrap process, which may or may not be the server sending this reply. The sending server always includes its own IP address in a special field called the Server Identifier DHCP option.

- *Gateway IP Address -* Routes DHCP messages when DHCP relay agents are involved. The gateway address facilitates communications of DHCP requests and replies between the client and a server that are on different subnets or networks.

- *Client Hardware Address -* Specifies the Physical layer of the client.

- *Server Name -* The server sending a DHCPOFFER or DHCPACK message may optionally put its name in this field. This can be a simple text nickname or a DNS domain name, such as dhcpserver.netacad.net.

- *Boot Filename -* Optionally used by a client to request a particular type of boot file in a DHCPDISCOVER message. Used by a server in a DHCPOFFER to fully specify a boot file directory and filename.

- *Options -* Holds DHCP options, including several parameters required for basic DHCP operation. This field is variable in length. Both client and server may use this field.

Refer to
Figure
in online course

DHCP Discovery and Offer Methods

These figures provide some detail of the packet content of the DHCP discover and offer messages.

When a client wants to join the network, it requests addressing values from the network DHCP server. If a client is configured to receive its IP settings dynamically, it transmits a DHCPDISCOVER message on its local physical subnet when it boots or senses an active network connection. Because the client has no way of knowing the subnet to which it belongs, the DHCPDISCOVER is an IP broadcast (destination IP address of 255.255.255.255). The client does not have a configured IP address, so the source IP address of 0.0.0.0 is used. As you see in the figure, the client IP address (CIADDR), default gateway address (GIADDR), and subnetwork mask are all marked with question marks.

Click the DHCP Offer button in the figure.

The DHCP server manages the allocation of the IP addresses and answers configuration requests from clients.

When the DHCP server receives the DHCPDISCOVER message, it responds with a DHCPOFFER message. This message contains initial configuration information for the client, including the MAC address of the client, followed by the IP address that the server is offering, the subnet mask, the lease duration, and the IP address of the DHCP server making the offer. The subnet mask and default gateway are specified in the options field, subnet mask, and router options, respectively.

The DHCPOFFER message can be configured to include other information, such as the lease renewal time, domain name server, and *NetBIOS* Name Service (Microsoft Windows Internet Name Service [Microsoft WINS]).

The server determines the configuration, based on the hardware address of the client as specified in the CHADDR field.

As shown in the diagram, the DHCP server has responded to the DHCPDISCOVER by assigning values to the CIADDR and subnetwork mask.

Administrators set up DHCP servers to assign addresses from predefined pools. Most DHCP servers also allow the administrator to define specifically which client MAC addresses can be serviced and automatically assign them the same IP address each time.

DHCP uses User Datagram Protocol (UDP) as its transport protocol. The client sends messages to the server on port 67. The server sends messages to the client on port 68.

The client and server acknowledge messages, and the process is complete. The client sets the CIADDR only when a host is in a bound state, which means that the client has confirmed and is using the IP address.

For more information on DHCP, see "Cisco IOS DHCP Server" at: http://www.cisco.com/en/US/docs/ios/12_0t/12_ot1/feature/guide/Easyip2.html.

7.1.4 Configuring a DHCP Server

Configuring a DHCP Server

Cisco routers running Cisco IOS software provide full support for a router to act as a DHCP server. The Cisco IOS DHCP server assigns and manages IP addresses from specified address pools within the router to DHCP clients.

The steps to configure a router as a DHCP server are as follows:

Step 1. Define a range of addresses that DHCP is not to allocate. These are usually static addresses reserved for the router interface, switch management IP address, servers, and local network printers.

Step 2. Create the DHCP pool using the `ip dhcp pool` command.

Step 3. Configure the specifics of the pool.

You should specify the IP addresses that the DHCP server should not assign to clients. Typically, some IP addresses belong to static network devices, such as servers or printers. DHCP should not assign these IP addresses to other devices. A best practice is to configure excluded addresses in global configuration mode before creating the DHCP pool. This ensures that DHCP does not assign reserved addresses accidentally. To exclude specific addresses, use the `ip dhcp excluded-address` command.

Click the DHCP Pool button in the figure.

Configuring a DHCP server involves defining a pool of addresses to assign. The `ip dhcp pool` command creates a pool with the specified name and puts the router in DHCP configuration mode, which is identified by the `Router(dhcp-config)#` prompt.

Click the DHCP Tasks button in the figure.

This figure lists the tasks to complete the DHCP pool configuration. Some of these are optional, while others must be configured.

You must configure the available addresses and specify the subnet network number and mask of the DHCP address pool. Use the `network` statement to define the range of available addresses.

You should also define the default gateway or router for the clients to use with the **default-router** command. Typically, the gateway is the LAN interface of the router. One address is required, but you can list up to eight addresses.

The next DHCP pool commands are considered optional. For example, you can configure the IP address of the DNS server that is available to a DHCP client using the **dns-server** command. When configured, one address is required, but up to eight addresses can be listed.

Other parameters include configuring the duration of the DHCP lease. The default setting is one day, but you can change this by using the **lease** command. You can also configure a NetBIOS WINS server that is available to a Microsoft DHCP client. Usually, this would be configured in an environment that supports pre-Windows 2000 clients. Because most installations now have clients with newer Windows operating system, this parameter is usually not required.

Click the DHCP Example button in the figure.

This figure displays a sample configuration with basic DHCP parameters configured on router R1.

Disabling DHCP

The DHCP service is enabled by default on versions of Cisco IOS software that support it. To disable the service, use the **no service dhcp** command. Use the **service dhcp** global configuration command to re-enable the DHCP server process. Enabling the service has no effect if the parameters are not configured.

Verifying DHCP

To illustrate how a Cisco router can be configured to provide DHCP services, refer to the figure. PC1 has not been powered up and therefore does not have an IP address.

Router R1 has been configured with the following commands:

```
ip dhcp excluded-address 192.168.10.1 192.168.10.9
ip dhcp excluded-address 192.168.10.254
ip dhcp pool LAN-POOL-1
 network 192.168.10.0 255.255.255.0
 default-router 192.168.10.1
 domain-name span.com
```

To verify the operation of DHCP, use the **show ip dhcp binding** command. This command displays a list of all IP address to MAC address bindings that have been provided by the DHCP service.

To verify that messages are being received or sent by the router, use the **show ip dhcp server statistics** command. This command displays count information regarding the number of DHCP messages that have been sent and received.

Click the DHCP-1 button in the figure.

As you can see in the figure, currently there are no bindings or statistics being displayed.

Now, assume that PC1 has been powered and completed its booting process.

Click the DHCP-2 button on the figure.

Notice that the binding information now displays that the IP address of 192.168.10.10 has been bound to a MAC address. The statistics are also displaying DHCPDISCOVER, DHCPREQUEST, DHCPOFFER, and DHCPACK activity.

Click the DHCP Client button in the figure.

The **ipconfig /all** command displays the TCP/IP configured parameters on PC1. Because PC1 was connected to the network segment 192.168.10.0 /24, it automatically received an IP address, DNS suffix, and default gateway from that pool. There is no DHCP interface configuration required. If a PC is connected to a network segment that has a DHCP pool available, it can obtain an IP address automatically.

So how does PC2 receive an IP address? Router R1 would have to be configured to provide a 192.168.11.0 /24 DHCP pool as follows:

```
ip dhcp excluded-address 192.168.11.1 192.168.11.9
 ip dhcp excluded-address 192.168.11.254
 ip dhcp pool LAN-POOL-2
 network 192.168.11.0 255.255.255.0
  default-router 192.168.11.1
 domain-name span.com
```

When PC2 has completed its booting process, it is provided with an IP address for the network segment to which it is connected.

Click the Verifying DHCP-3 button in the figure.

Notice that the DHCP bindings now indicate that two hosts have been provided with IP addresses. The DHCP statistics are also reflecting the exchange of DHCP messages.

Another useful command to view multiple pools is the `show ip dhcp pool` command.

Click the DHCP Pools button in the figure.

This command summarizes the DHCP pool information.

7.1.5 Configuring a DHCP Client

Configuring a DHCP Client

Typically, small broadband routers for home use, such as Linksys routers, can be configured to connect to an ISP using a DSL or cable modem. In most cases, small home routers are set to acquire an IP address automatically from their ISPs. For example, the figure shows the default WAN setup page for a Linksys WRVS4400N router. Notice that the Internet connection type is set to Automatic Configuration - DHCP. This means that when the router is connected to a cable modem, for example, it is a DHCP client and requests an IP address from the ISP.

Sometimes, Cisco routers in SOHO and branch sites have to be configured in a similar manner. The method used depends on the ISP. However, in its simplest configuration, the Ethernet interface is used to connect to a cable modem. To configure an Ethernet interface as a DHCP client, the `ip address dhcp` command must be configured.

Click the DHCP Client button in the figure.

In the figure, assume that an ISP has been configured to provide select customers with IP addresses from the 209.165.201.0 / 27 range. The output confirms the assigned address.

7.1.6 DHCP Relay

What is DHCP Relay?

In a complex hierarchical network, enterprise servers are usually contained in a server farm. These servers may provide DHCP, DNS, TFTP, and FTP services for the clients. The problem is that the network clients typically are not on the same subnet as those servers. Therefore, the clients must locate the servers to receive services and often these services are located using broadcast messages.

In the figure, PC1 is attempting to acquire an IP address from the DHCP server located at 192.168.11.5. In this scenario router R1 is not configured as a DHCP server.

Click the Host Problem button in the figure.

In the figure, PC1 is attempting to renew its IP address. To do so, the **ipconfig /release** command is issued. Notice that the IP address is released and the current address is now 0.0.0.0. Next, the **ipconfig /renew** command is issued. This initiates the host to broadcast a DHCPDISCOVER message. However, PC1 is unable to locate the DHCP server. What happens when the server and the client are separated by a router and therefore are not on the same network segment? Remember, routers do not forward broadcasts.

Note: Certain Windows clients have a feature called Automatic Private IP Addressing (APIPA). With this feature, a Windows computer can automatically assign itself an IP address in the 169.254.x.x range in the event that a DHCP server is not available or does not exist on the network.

To make matters worse, DHCP is not the only critical service that uses broadcasts. For example, Cisco routers and other devices may use broadcasts to locate TFTP servers or to locate an authentication server such as a TACACS server.

As a solution to this problem, an administrator could add DHCP servers on all the subnets. However, running these services on several computers creates both cost and administrative overhead.

A simpler solution is to configure the Cisco IOS *helper address* feature on intervening routers and switches. This solution enables routers to forward DHCP broadcasts to the DHCP servers. When a router forwards address assignment/parameter requests, it is acting as a DHCP relay agent.

For example, PC1 would broadcast a request to locate a DHCP server. If router R1 were configured as a DHCP relay agent, it would intercept this request and forward it to the DHCP server located on subnet 192.168.11.0.

To configure router R1 as a DHCP relay agent, you need to configure the nearest interface to the client with the `ip helper-address` interface configuration command. This command relays broadcast requests for key services to a configured address. Configure the IP helper address on the interface receiving the broadcast.

Click the Relay Config button in the figure.

Router R1 is now configured as a DHCP relay agent. It accepts broadcast requests for the DHCP service and then forwards them as a unicast to the IP address 192.168.11.5.

Click the Host Renew button in the figure.

As you can see, PC1 is now able to acquire an IP address from the DHCP server.

DHCP is not the only service that the router can be configured to relay. By default, the `ip helper-address` command forwards the following eight UDP services:

- Port 37: Time
- Port 49: TACACS
- Port 53: DNS
- Port 67: DHCP/BOOTP server
- Port 68: DHCP/BOOTP client
- Port 69: TFTP
- Port 137: NetBIOS name service
- Port 138: NetBIOS datagram service

To specify additional ports, use the `ip forward-protocol` command to specify exactly which types of broadcast packets to forward.

7.1.7 Configuring a DHCP Server Using SDM

Configuring a DHCP Server Using SDM

Cisco routers can also be configured as a DHCP server using SDM. In this example, router R1 will be configured as the DHCP server on the Fa0/0 and Fa0/1interfaces.

Click the DHCP Tasks button in the figure.

The DHCP server function is enabled under Additional Tasks in the Configure tab. From the list of tasks, click on the DHCP folder and then select **DHCP Pools** to add a new pool. Click **Add** to create the new DHCP pool.

Click the Add Pool button in the figure.

The Add DHCP Pool window contains the options you need to configure the DHCP IP address pool. The IP addresses that the DHCP server assigns are drawn from a common pool. To configure the pool, specify the starting and ending IP addresses of the range.

Cisco SDM configures the router to automatically exclude the LAN interface IP address in the pool. You must not use the network or subnetwork IP address or broadcast address on the network in the range of addresses that you specify.

If you need to exclude other IP addresses in the range, you can do so by adjusting the starting and ending IP addresses. For instance, if you needed to exclude IP addresses 192.168.10.1 through 192.168.10.9, you would set the Starting IP address to 192.168.10.10. This allows the router to begin address assignment with 192.168.10.10.

The other options that are available are:

- *DNS Server1 and DNS Server2* - The DNS server is typically a server that maps a known device name with its IP address. If you have a DNS server configured for your network, enter the IP address for the server here. If there is an additional DNS server on the network, you can enter the IP address for that server in this field.

- *WINS Server1 and WINS Server2* - Recall that WINS configuration is typically in environments that support pre-Windows 2000 clients.

- *Import All DHCP Options into the DHCP Server Database* - Allows the DHCP options to be imported from a higher level server, and is typically used in conjunction with an Internet DHCP server. This option allows you to pull higher level information without having to configure it in for this pool.

Click the DHCP Pools button in the figure.

This screen provides you with a summary of the pools configured on your router. In this example, there have been two pools configured, one for each of the Fast Ethernet interfaces on the R1 router.

7.1.8 Troubleshooting DHCP

Troubleshooting DHCP Configuration

DHCP problems can arise for a multitude of reasons, such as software defects in operating systems, NIC drivers, or DHCP/BOOTP relay agents, but the most common are configuration issues.

Because of the number of potentially problematic areas, a systematic approach to troubleshooting is required.

Troubleshooting Task 1: Resolve IP Address Conflicts

An IP address lease can expire on a client still connected to a network. If the client does not renew the lease, the DHCP server can reassign that IP address to another client. When the client reboots, it requests an IP address. If the DHCP server does not respond quickly, the client uses the last IP address. The situation then arises that two clients are using the same IP address, creating a conflict.

The `show ip dhcp conflict` command displays all address conflicts recorded by the DHCP server. The server uses the `ping` command to detect conflicts. The client uses Address Resolution Protocol (ARP) to detect clients. If an address conflict is detected, the address is removed from the pool and not assigned until an administrator resolves the conflict.

This example displays the detection method and detection time for all IP addresses that the DHCP server has offered that have conflicts with other devices.

```
R2# show ip dhcp conflict
 IP address    Detection Method  Detection time
 192.168.1.32  Ping              Feb 16 2007 12:28 PM
 192.168.1.64  Gratuitous ARP    Feb 23 2007 08:12 AM
```

Troubleshooting Task 2: Verify Physical Connectivity

First, use the `show interface` *interface* command to confirm that the router interface acting as the default gateway for the client is operational. If the state of the interface is anything other than up, the port does not pass traffic, including DHCP client requests.

Troubleshooting Task 3: Test Network Connectivity by Configuring a Client Workstation with a Static IP Address

When troubleshooting any DHCP issue, verify network connectivity by configuring a static IP address on a client workstation. If the workstation is unable to reach network resources with a statically configured IP address, the root cause of the problem is not DHCP. At this point, network connectivity troubleshooting is required.

Troubleshooting Task 4: Verify Switch Port Configuration (STP Portfast and Other Commands)

If the DHCP client is unable to obtain an IP address from the DHCP server on startup, attempt to obtain an IP address from the DHCP server by manually forcing the client to send a DHCP request.

If there is a switch between the client and the DHCP server, verify that the port has STP PortFast enabled and trunking/channeling disabled. The default configuration is PortFast disabled and trunking/channeling auto, if applicable. These configuration changes resolve the most common DHCP client issues that occur with an initial installation of a Catalyst switch. A review of CCNA Exploration: LAN Switching and Wireless assists in solving this issue.

Troubleshooting Task 5: Distinguishing Whether DHCP Clients Obtain IP Address on the Same Subnet or VLAN as DHCP Server

It is important to distinguish whether DHCP is functioning correctly when the client is on the same subnet or VLAN as the DHCP server. If the DHCP is working correctly, the problem may be the DHCP/BOOTP relay agent. If the problem persists even with testing DHCP on the same subnet or VLAN as the DHCP server, the problem may actually be with the DHCP server.

Refer to Figure in online course

Verify Router DHCP/BOOTP Relay Configuration

When the DHCP server is located on a separate LAN from the client, the router interface facing the client must be configured to relay DHCP requests. This is accomplished by configuring the IP helper address. If the IP helper address is not configured properly, client DHCP requests are not forwarded to the DHCP server.

Follow these steps to verify the router configuration:

Step 1. Verify that the `ip helper-address` command is configured on the correct interface. It must be present on the inbound interface of the LAN containing the DHCP client workstations and must be directed to the correct DHCP server. In the figure, the output of the `show running-config` command verifies that the DHCP relay IP address is referencing the DHCP server address at 192.168.11.5.

Step 2. Verify that the global configuration command `no service dhcp` has not been configured. This command disables all DHCP server and relay functionality on the router. The command `service dhcp` does not appear in the configuration, because it is the default configuration.

Verify that the Router Is Receiving DHCP Requests Using `debug` Commands.

On routers configured as DHCP servers, the DHCP process fails if the router is not receiving requests from the client. As a troubleshooting task, verify that the router is receiving the DHCP request from the client. This troubleshooting step involves configuring an access control list for debugging output. The debug access control list is not intrusive to the router.

In global configuration mode, create the following access control list:

`access-list 100 permit ip host 0.0.0.0 host 255.255.255.255`

Start debugging by using ACL 100 as the defining parameter. In exec mode, enter the following `debug` command:

`debug ip packet detail 100`

The output in the figure shows that the router is receiving the DHCP requests from the client. The source IP address is 0.0.0.0 because the client does not yet have an IP address. The destination is 255.255.255.255 because the DHCP discovery message from the client is a broadcast. The UDP source and destination ports, 68 and 67, are the typical ports used for DHCP.

This output only shows a summary of the packet and not the packet itself. Therefore, it is not possible to determine if the packet is correct. Nevertheless, the router did receive a broadcast packet with the source and destination IP and UDP ports that are correct for DHCP.

Verify that the Router Is Receiving and Forwarding DHCP Request Using `debug ip dhcp server packet` Command

A useful command for troubleshooting DHCP operation is the `debug ip dhcp server events` command. This command reports server events, like address assignments and database updates. It is also used for decoding DHCP receptions and transmissions.

DHCP assigns IP addresses and other important network configuration information dynamically. Cisco routers can use the Cisco IOS feature set, Easy IP, as an optional, full-featured DHCP server. Easy IP leases configurations for 24 hours by default. In this activity, you will configure DHCP services on two routers and test your configuration.

Detailed instructions are provided within the activity as well as in the PDF link below.

Activity Instructions (PDF)

7.2 Scaling Networks with NAT

7.2.1 Private and Public IP Addressing

All public *Internet addresses* must be registered with a Regional Internet Registry (RIR). Organizations can lease public addresses from an ISP. Only the registered holder of a public Internet address can assign that address to a network device.

You may have noticed that all the examples in this course use a somewhat restricted number of IP addresses. You may also have noticed the similarity between these numbers and numbers you have used in a small network to view the setup web pages of many brands of printers, DSL and cable routers, and other peripherals. These are reserved private Internet addresses drawn from the three blocks shown in the figure. These addresses are for private, internal network use only. RFC 1918 specifies that private addresses are not to be routed over the Internet. This sometimes sees private addresses described as ""non-routable"". However, packets with private addresses can be routed within private internetworks.

Unlike public IP addresses, private IP addresses are a reserved block of numbers that can be used by anyone. That means two networks, or two million networks, can each use the same private addresses. To protect the public Internet address structure, ISPs typically configure the border routers to prevent privately addressed traffic from being forwarded over the Internet.

By providing more address space than most organizations could obtain through a RIR, private addressing gives enterprises considerable flexibility in network design. This enables operationally and administratively convenient addressing schemes as well as easier growth.

However, because you cannot route private addresses over the Internet, and there are not enough public addresses to allow organizations to provide one to every one of their hosts, networks need a mechanism to translate private addresses to public addresses at the edge of their network that works in both directions. Without a translation system, private hosts behind a router in the network of one organization cannot connect with private hosts behind a router in other organizations over the Internet.

Network Address Translation (NAT) provides this mechanism. Before NAT, a host with a private address could not access the Internet. Using NAT, individual companies can address some or all of their hosts with private addresses and use NAT to provide access to the Internet.

For a more in-depth look at the development of the RIR system, see the Cisco Internet Protocol Journal article at http://www.cisco.com/web/about/ac123/ac147/archived_issues/ipj_4-4/regional_internet_registries.html.

7.2.2 What is NAT?

What is NAT?

NAT is like the receptionist in a large office. Assume you have left instructions with the receptionist not to forward any calls to you unless you request it. Later on, you call a potential client and leave a message for them to call you back. You tell the receptionist that you are expecting a call from this client, and you ask the receptionist to put them through to your telephone.

The client calls the main number to your office, which is the only number the client knows. When the client tells the receptionist who they are looking for, the receptionist checks a lookup table that matches your name to your extension. The receptionist knows that you requested this call; therefore, the receptionist forwards the caller to your extension.

So while the DHCP server assigns IP dynamic addresses to devices inside the network, NAT-enabled routers retain one or many valid Internet IP addresses outside of the network. When the client sends packets out of the network, NAT translates the internal IP address of the client to an external address. To outside users, all traffic coming to and going from the network has the same IP address or is from the same pool of addresses.

NAT has many uses, but its key use is to save IP addresses by allowing networks to use private IP addresses. NAT translates private, internal addresses into public, external addresses. NAT has an added benefit of adding a degree of privacy and security to a network because it hides internal IP addresses from outside networks.

A NAT-enabled device typically operates at the border of a *stub network*. In our example, R2 is the border router. A stub network is a network that has a single connection to its neighbor network. As seen from the ISP, R2 forms a stub network.

When a host inside the stub network, say PC1, PC2, or PC 3, wants to transmit to a host on the outside, the packet is forwarded to R2, the *border gateway* router. R2 performs the NAT process, translating the internal private address of the host to a public, outside, routable address.

In NAT terminology, the inside network is the set of networks that are subject to translation. The outside network refers to all other addresses. IP addresses have different designations based on whether they are on the private network or on the public network (Internet) and whether the traffic is incoming or outgoing.

Click the Terminology button in the figure.

The figure shows how to refer to the interfaces when configuring NAT. Assume that router R2 has been configured to provide NAT features. It has a pool of publicly available addresses to lend to inside hosts. This section uses the following terms when discussing NAT:

- *Inside local address* - Usually not an IP address assigned by a RIR or service provider and is most likely an RFC 1918 private address. In the figure, the IP address 192.168.10.10 is assigned to the host PC1 on the inside network.

- *Inside global address* - Valid public address that the inside host is given when it exits the NAT router. When traffic from PC1 is destined for the web server at 209.165.201.1, router R2 must translate the address. In this case, IP address 209.165.200.226 is used as the inside global address for PC1.

- *Outside global address* - Valid public IP address assigned to a host on the Internet. For example, the web server is reachable at IP address 209.165.201.1.

- *Outside local address* - The local IP address assigned to a host on the outside network. In most situations, this address will be identical to the outside global address of that outside device.

Note: In this course, we will be referencing the inside local address, inside global address, and the outside global address. The use of the outside local address is outside the scope of this course.

The "inside" of a NAT configuration is not synonymous with private addresses as defined by RFC 1918. Although "inside" addresses are usually private addresses, NAT can translate between "outside" and "inside" public addresses.

How Does NAT Work?

Refer to Figure in online course

In this example, an inside host (192.168.10.10) wants to communicate with an outside web server (209.165.201.1). It sends a packet to R2, the NAT-configured border gateway for the network.

Use the controls on the figure to start the animation.

R2 reads the source IP address of the packet and checks if the packet matches the criteria specified for translation. R2 has an ACL that identifies the inside network as valid hosts for translation.

Therefore, it translates an inside local IP address to an inside global IP address, which in this case is 209.165.200.226. It stores this mapping of the local to global address in the NAT table.

The router then sends the packet to its destination. When the web server responds, the packet comes back to the global address of R2 (209.165.200.226).

R2 refers to its NAT table and sees that this was a previously translated IP address. Therefore, it translates the inside global address to the inside local address, and the packet is forwarded to PC1 at IP address 192.168.10.10. If it does not find a mapping, the packet is dropped.

Dynamic Mapping and Static Mapping

There are two types of NAT translation: dynamic and static.

Dynamic NAT uses a pool of public addresses and assigns them on a first-come, first-served basis. When a host with a private IP address requests access to the Internet, dynamic NAT chooses an IP address from the pool that is not already in use by another host. This is the mapping described so far.

Static NAT uses a one-to-one mapping of local and global addresses, and these mappings remain constant. Static NAT is particularly useful for web servers or hosts that must have a consistent address that is accessible from the Internet. These internal hosts may be enterprise servers or networking devices.

Both static and dynamic NAT require that enough public addresses are available to satisfy the total number of simultaneous user sessions.

For another look at how dynamic NAT works, go to http://www.cisco.com/warp/public/556/nat.swf.

NAT Overload

NAT overloading (sometimes called Port Address Translation or PAT) maps multiple private IP addresses to a single public IP address or a few addresses. This is what most home routers do. Your ISP assigns one address to your router, yet several members of your family can simultaneously surf the Internet.

With NAT overloading, multiple addresses can be mapped to one or to a few addresses because each private address is also tracked by a port number. When a client opens a TCP/IP session, the NAT router assigns a port number to its source address. NAT overload ensures that clients use a different TCP port number for each client session with a server on the Internet. When a response comes back from the server, the source port number, which becomes the destination port number on the return trip, determines to which client the router routes the packets. It also validates that the incoming packets were requested, thus adding a degree of security to the session.

Click the controls to start and pause the animation.

The animation illustrates the process. NAT overload uses unique source port numbers on the inside global IP address to distinguish between translations. As NAT processes each packet, it uses a port number (1331 and 1555 in this example) to identify the client from which the packet originated. The source address (SA) is the inside local IP address with the TCP/IP assigned port number attached. The destination address (DA) is the outside local IP address with the service port number attached, in this case port 80: HTTP.

At the border gateway router (R2), NAT overload changes the SA to the inside global IP address of the client, again with the port number attached. The DA is the same address, but is now referred to as the outside global IP address. When the web server replies, the same path is followed but in reverse.

Port numbers are encoded in 16 bits. The total number of internal addresses that can be translated to one external address could theoretically be as high as 65,536 per IP address. However, realistically, the number of internal addresses that can be assigned a single IP address is around 4,000.

Click the Next Available Port button in the figure.

In the previous example, the client port numbers in the two SAs, 1331 and 1555, do not change at the border gateway. This is not a very likely scenario because there is a good chance that these numbers may have already been attached to other ongoing sessions.

NAT overload attempts to preserve the original source port. However, if this source port is already used, NAT overload assigns the first available port number starting from the beginning of the appropriate port group 0-511, 512-1023, or 1024-65535. When there are no more ports available and there is more than one external IP address configured, NAT overload moves to the next IP address to try to allocate the original source port again. This process continues until it runs out of available ports and external IP addresses.

In the figure, both hosts have somehow chosen the same port number 1444. This is acceptable for the inside address, because they both have unique private IP addresses. However, at the border gateway, the port numbers need to be changed-otherwise, two packets from two hosts would leave R2 with the same source address. NAT overload has given the second address the first available port number, which in this case happens to be 1445.

Differences Between NAT and NAT Overload

Summarizing the differences between NAT and NAT overload will help your understanding. NAT generally only translates IP addresses on a 1:1 correspondence between publicly exposed IP addresses and privately held IP addresses. NAT overload modifies both the private IP address and port number of the sender. NAT overload chooses the port numbers seen by hosts on the public network.

NAT routes incoming packets to their inside destination by referring to the incoming source IP address given by the host on the public network. With NAT overload, there is generally only one or a very few publicly exposed IP addresses. Incoming packets from the public network are routed to their destinations on the private network by referring to a table in the NAT overload device that tracks public and private port pairs. This is called connection tracking.

7.2.3 Benefits and Drawbacks of Using NAT

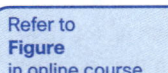

Benefits and Drawbacks of Using NAT

NAT provides many benefits and advantages. However, there are some drawbacks to using NAT, including the lack of support for some types of traffic.

The benefits of using NAT include the following:

- NAT conserves the legally registered addressing scheme by allowing the privatization of intranets. NAT conserves addresses through application port-level multiplexing. With NAT overload, internal hosts can share a single public IP address for all external communications. In this type of configuration, very few external addresses are required to support many internal hosts.

- NAT increases the flexibility of connections to the public network. Multiple pools, backup pools, and load-balancing pools can be implemented to ensure reliable public network connections.

- NAT provides consistency for internal network addressing schemes. On a network without private IP addresses and NAT, changing public IP addresses requires the renumbering of all hosts on the existing network. The costs of renumbering hosts can be significant. NAT allows the existing scheme to remain while supporting a new public addressing scheme. This means an organization could change ISPs and not need to change any of its inside clients.

- NAT provides network security. Because private networks do not advertise their addresses or internal topology, they remain reasonably secure when used in conjunction with NAT to gain controlled external access. However, NAT does not replace firewalls.

However, NAT does have some drawbacks. The fact that hosts on the Internet appear to communicate directly with the NAT device, rather than with the actual host inside the private network, creates a number of issues. In theory, a single globally unique IP address can represent many privately addressed hosts. This has advantages from a privacy and security point of view, but in practice, there are drawbacks.

The first disadvantage affects performance. NAT increases switching delays because the translation of each IP address within the packet headers takes time. The first packet is process-switched, meaning it always goes through the slower path. The router must look at every packet to decide whether it needs translation. The router needs to alter the IP header, and possibly alter the TCP or UDP header. Remaining packets go through the fast-switched path if a cache entry exists; otherwise, they too are delayed.

Many Internet protocols and applications depend on end-to-end functionality, with unmodified packets forwarded from the source to the destination. By changing end-to-end addresses, NAT prevents some applications that use IP addressing. For example, some security applications, such as digital signatures, fail because the source IP address changes. Applications that use physical addresses instead of a qualified domain name do not reach destinations that are translated across the NAT router. Sometimes, this problem can be avoided by implementing static NAT mappings.

End-to-end IP traceability is also lost. It becomes much more difficult to trace packets that undergo numerous packet address changes over multiple NAT hops, making troubleshooting challenging. On the other hand, hackers who want to determine the source of a packet find it difficult to trace or obtain the original source or destination address.

Using NAT also complicates tunneling protocols, such as IPsec, because NAT modifies values in the headers that interfere with the integrity checks done by IPsec and other tunneling protocols.

Services that require the initiation of TCP connections from the outside network, or stateless protocols such as those using UDP, can be disrupted. Unless the NAT router makes a specific effort to support such protocols, incoming packets cannot reach their destination. Some protocols can accommodate one instance of NAT between participating hosts (passive mode FTP, for example), but fail when both systems are separated from the Internet by NAT.

7.2.4 Configuring Static NAT

Refer to Figure in online course

Static NAT

Remember that static NAT is a one-to-one mapping between an inside address and an outside address. Static NAT allows connections initiated by external devices to inside devices. For instance, you may want to map an inside global address to a specific inside local address that is assigned to your web server.

Configuring static NAT translations is a simple task. You need to define the addresses to translate and then configure NAT on the appropriate interfaces. Packets arriving on an inside interface from the identified IP address are subject to translation. Packets arriving on an outside interface addressed to the identified IP address are subject to translation.

The figure explains the commands for the steps. You enter static translations directly into the configuration. Unlike dynamic translations, these translations are always in the NAT table.

Click the Example button in the figure.

The figure is a simple static NAT configuration applied to both interfaces. The router always translates packets from the host inside the network with the private address of 192.168.10.254 into an outside address of 209.165.200.254. The host on the Internet directs web requests to the public IP address 209.165.200.254, and router R2 always forwards that traffic to the server at 192.168.10.254.

7.2.5 Configuring Dynamic NAT

Configuring Dynamic NAT

While static NAT provides a permanent mapping between an internal address and a specific public address, dynamic NAT maps private IP addresses to public addresses. These public IP addresses come from a NAT pool. Dynamic NAT configuration differs from static NAT, but it also has some similarities. Like static NAT, it requires the configuration to identify each interface as an inside or outside interface. However, rather than creating a static map to a single IP address, a pool of inside global addresses is used.

Click the Commands button in the figure for the steps to configure dynamic NAT.

To configure dynamic NAT, you need an ACL to permit only those addresses that are to be translated. When developing your ACL, remember there is an implicit "deny all" at the end of each ACL. An ACL that is too permissive can lead to unpredictable results. Cisco advises against configuring access contol lists referenced by NAT commands with the `permit any` command. Using `permit any` can result in NAT consuming too many router resources, which can cause network problems.

Click the Example button in the figure.

This configuration allows translation for all hosts on the 192.168.10.0 and 192.168.11.0 networks when they generate traffic that enters S0/0/0 and exits S0/1/0. These hosts are translated to an available address in the 209.165.200.226 - 209.165.200.240 range.

7.2.6 Configuring NAT Overload

Configuring NAT Overload for a Single Public IP Address

There are two possible ways to configure overloading, depending on how the ISP allocates public IP addresses. In the first instance, the ISP allocates one public IP address to the organization, and in the other, it allocates more than one public IP address.

The figure shows the steps to follow to configure NAT overload with a single IP address. With only one public IP address, the overload configuration typically assigns that public address to the outside interface that connects to the ISP. All inside addresses are translated to the single IP address when leaving the outside interface.

Click the Commands button in the figure for the steps to configure NAT overload.

The configuration is similar to dynamic NAT, except that instead of a pool of addresses, the `interface` keyword is used to identify the outside IP address. Therefore, no NAT pool is defined. The `overload` keyword enables the addition of the port number to the translation.

Click the Example button in the figure.

This example shows how NAT overload is configured. In the example, all hosts from network 192.168.0.0 /16 (matching ACL 1) sending traffic through router R2 to the Internet are translated to IP address 209.165.200.225 (interface S0/1/0 IP address). The traffic flows are identified by port numbers, because the **overload** keyword was used.

Configuring NAT Overload for a Pool of Public IP Addresses

In the scenario where the ISP has provided more than one public IP address, NAT overload is configured to use a pool. The primary difference between this configuration and the configuration for dynamic, one-to-one NAT is that the **overload** keyword is used. Remember that the **overload** keyword enables port address translation.

Click the Commands button in the figure for the stpes to configure NAT overload using a pool of addresses.

Click the Example button in the figure.

In this example, the configuration establishes overload translation for NAT pool NAT-POOL2. The NAT pool contains addresses 209.165.200.226 - 209.165.200.240 and is translated using PAT. Hosts in the 192.168.0.0 /16 network are subject to translation. Finally, the inside and outside interfaces are identified.

7.2.7 Configuring Port Forwarding

Port Forwarding

Port forwarding (sometimes referred to as tunneling) is the act of forwarding a network port from one network node to another. This technique can allow an external user to reach a port on a private IP address (inside a LAN) from the outside through a NAT-enabled router.

Typically, peer-to-peer file-sharing programs and key operations, such as web serving and outgoing FTP, require that router ports be forwarded or opened to allow these applications to work. Because NAT hides internal addresses, peer-to-peer only works from the inside out where NAT can map register outgoing requests against incoming replies.

The problem is that NAT does not allow requests initiated from the outside. This situation can be resolved with manual intervention. Port forwarding allows you to identify specific ports that can be forwarded to inside hosts.

Recall that Internet software applications interact with user ports that need to be open or available to those applications. Different applications use different ports. For example, Telnet uses port 23, FTP uses ports 20 and 21, HTTP port 80, and SMTP uses port 25. This makes it predictable for applications and routers to identify network services. For example, HTTP operates through the well-known port 80. When you enter the address http://cisco.com, the browser displays the Cisco Systems, Inc. website. Notice that we do not have to specify the HTTP port number for the page requests because the application assumes port 80.

Configuring Port Forwarding

Port forwarding allows users on the Internet to access internal servers by using the WAN port address and the matched external port number. When users send these types of requests to your WAN port IP address via the Internet, the router forwards those requests to the appropriate servers on your LAN. For security reasons, broadband routers do not by default permit any external network request to be forwarded to an inside host.

For instance, the figure is displaying the Single Port Forwarding window of a Linksys WRVS4400N business-class SOHO router. Currently, port forwarding is not configured.

Click the Port Forwarding Example button in the figure.

You can enable port forwarding for applications and specify the inside local address to forward the request to. For example, in the figure, HTTP service requests coming into this Linksys is now forwarded to the web server with the inside local address of 192.168.1.254. If the external WAN IP address of the SOHO router is 209.165.200.158, the external user could enter http://209.165.200.158 and the Linksys router would redirect the HTTP request to the internal web server at IP address 192.168.1.254, using the default port number 80.

We could specify a port different from the default port 80. However, the external user would have to know the specific port number to use.

The approach you take to configure port forwarding depends on the brand and model of the broadband router in the network. However, there are some generic steps to follow. If the instructions supplied by your ISP or that came with the router do not provide adequate guidance, the website www.portforward.com provides guides for several broadband routers. You can follow the instructions to add or delete ports as required to meet the needs of any applications you want to allow or deny.

7.2.8 Verifying and Troubleshooting NAT Configurations

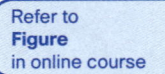

Verifying NAT and NAT Overload

It is important to verify NAT operation. There are several useful router commands to view and clear NAT translations. This topic explains how to verify NAT operation using tools available on Cisco routers.

One of the most useful commands when verifying NAT operation is the `show ip nat translations` command. Before using the `show` commands to verify NAT, you must clear any dynamic translation entries that might still be present, because by default, dynamic address translations time out from the NAT translation table after a period of non-use.

In the figure, router R2 has been configured to provide NAT overload to the 192.168.0.0 /16 clients. When the internal hosts exit router R2 to the Internet, they are translated to the IP address of the serial interface with a unique source port number.

Assume that the two hosts in the internal network have been accessing web services from the Internet.

Click on the NAT Translations button in the figure.

Notice that the output of the `show ip nat translations` command displays the details of the two NAT assignments. Adding `verbose` to the command displays additional information about each translation, including how long ago the entry was created and used.

The command displays all static translations that have been configured as well as any dynamic translations that have been created by traffic. Each translation is identified by protocol as well as inside and outside local and global addresses.

Click on the NAT Statistics button in the figure.

The `show ip nat statistics` command displays information about the total number of active translations, NAT configuration parameters, how many addresses are in the pool, and how many have been allocated.

In the figure, the hosts have initiated web traffic as well as ICMP traffic.

Alternatively, use the `show run` command and look for NAT, access command list, interface, or pool commands with the required values. Examine these carefully and correct any errors you discover.

By default, translation entries time out after 24 hours, unless the timers have been reconfigured with the `ip nat translation timeout` *timeout_ seconds* command in global configuration mode.

Click the Cleared NAT button in the figure.

It is sometimes useful to clear the dynamic entries sooner than the default. This is especially true when testing the NAT configuration. To clear dynamic entries before the timeout has expired, use the `clear ip nat translation` global command.

The table in the figure is displaying the various ways to clear the NAT translations. You can be very specific about which translation to clear, or you can clear all translations from the table using the `clear ip nat translation *` global command, as shown in the example.

Only the dynamic translations are cleared from the table. Static translations cannot be cleared from the translation table.

Troubleshooting NAT and NAT Overload Configuration

When you have IP connectivity problems in a NAT environment, it is often difficult to determine the cause of the problem. The first step in solving your problem is to rule out NAT as the cause. Follow these steps to verify that NAT is operating as expected:

Step 1. Based on the configuration, clearly define what NAT is supposed to achieve. This may reveal a problem with the configuration.

Step 2. Verify that correct translations exist in the translation table using the `show ip nat translations` command.

Step 3. Use the `clear` and `debug` commands to verify that NAT is operating as expected. Check to see if dynamic entries are recreated after they are cleared.

Step 4. Review in detail what is happening to the packet, and verify that routers have the correct routing information to move the packet.

Use the `debug ip nat` command to verify the operation of the NAT feature by displaying information about every packet that is translated by the router. The `debug ip nat detailed` command generates a description of each packet considered for translation. This command also outputs information about certain errors or exception conditions, such as the failure to allocate a global address.

The figure shows a sample `debug ip nat` output. In the output you can see that inside host 192.168.10.10 initiated traffic to outside host 209.165.200.254 and has been translated to address 209.165.200.225.

When decoding the debug output, note what the following symbols and values indicate:

- *- The asterisk next to NAT indicates that the translation is occurring in the fast-switched path. The first packet in a conversation is always process-switched, which is slower. The remaining packets go through the fast-switched path if a cache entry exists.

- s=- Refers to the source IP address.

- a.b.c.d—->w.x.y.z - Indicates that source address a.b.c.d is translated to w.x.y.z.

- d=- Refers to the destination IP address.

- [xxxx]- The value in brackets is the IP identification number. This information may be useful for debugging in that it enables correlation with other packet traces from protocol analyzers.

You can view the following demonstrations about verifying and troubleshooting NAT at these sites:

Flash Animation Case Study: Can Ping Host, but Cannot Telnet: This is a seven-minute Flash animation on why a device can ping the host, but cannot telnet: http://www.cisco.com/warp/public/556/index.swf.

Flash Animation Case Study: Cannot Ping Beyond NAT: This is a ten-minute Flash animation on why a device cannot ping beyond NAT: http://www.cisco.com/warp/public/556/TS_NATcase2/index.swf.

Refer to **Packet Tracer Activity** for this chapter

NAT translates non-routable private, internal addresses into routable, public addresses. NAT has an added benefit of providing a degree of privacy and security to a network because it hides internal IP addresses from outside networks. In this activity, you will configure dynamic and static NAT.

Detailed instructions are provided within the activity as well as in the PDF link below.

Activity Instructions (PDF)

7.3 IPv6

7.3.1 Reasons for Using IPv6

Refer to **Figure** in online course

Why We Need More Address Space

To comprehend the IP addressing issues facing network administrators today, consider that the IPv4 address space provides approximately 4,294,967,296 unique addresses. Of these, only 3.7 billion addresses are assignable because the IPv4 addressing system separates the addresses into classes and reserves addresses for multicasting, testing, and other specific uses.

Based on figures as recent as January 2007, about 2.4 billion of the available IPv4 addresses are already assigned to end users or ISPs. That leaves roughly 1.3 billion addresses still available from the IPv4 address space. Despite this seemingly large number, IPv4 address space is running out.

Click the Play button in the figure to see just how fast this has happened over the past 14 years.

Over the past decade, the Internet community has analyzed IPv4 address exhaustion and published mountains of reports. Some reports predict IPv4 address exhaustion by 2010, and others say it will not happen until 2013.

Click the Shrinking button in the figure to see how the available address space is shrinking.

The growth of the Internet, matched by increasing computing power, has extended the reach of IP-based applications.

Click the Why IPv6 button in the figure and consider what is forcing a change to IPv6.

The pool of numbers is shrinking for the following reasons:

- *Population growth* - The Internet population is growing. In November 2005, Cisco estimated that there were approximately 973 million users. This number has doubled since then. In addition, users stay on longer, reserving IP addresses for longer periods and are contacting more and more peers daily.

- *Mobile users* - Industry has delivered more than one billion mobile phones. More than 20 million IP-enabled mobile devices, including personal digital assistants (*PDAs*), pen tablets, notepads, and barcode readers, have been delivered. More and more IP-enabled mobile devices are coming online every day. Old mobile phones did not need IP addresses, but new ones do.

- *Transportation* - There will be more than one billion automobiles by 2008. Newer models are IP-enabled to allow remote monitoring to provide timely maintenance and support. Lufthansa already provides Internet connectivity on their flights. More carriers, including ships at sea, will provide similar services.

- *Consumer electronics* - The newest home appliances allow remote monitoring using IP technology. Digital Video Recorders (DVRs) that download and update program guides from the Internet are an example. Home networking can connect these appliances.

Reasons for Using IPv6

Movement to change from IPv4 to IPv6 has already begun, particularly in Europe, Japan, and the Asia-Pacific region. These areas are exhausting their allotted IPv4 addresses, which makes IPv6 all the more attractive and necessary. Japan officially started the move in 2000 when the Japanese government mandated the incorporation of IPv6 and set a deadline of 2005 to upgrade existing systems in every business and public sector. Korea, China, and Malaysia have launched similar initiatives.

In 2002, the European Community IPv6 Task Force forged a strategic alliance to foster IPv6 adoption worldwide. The North American IPv6 Task Force has set out to engage the North American markets to adopt IPv6. The first significant North American advances are coming from the U.S. Department of Defense (*DoD*). Looking into the future and knowing the advantages of IP-enabled devices, DoD mandated, as early as 2003, that all new equipment purchased not only be IP-enabled, but also be IPv6-capable. In fact, all U.S. government agencies must start using IPv6 across their core networks by 2008, and the agencies are working to meet that deadline.

The ability to scale networks for future demands requires a limitless supply of IP addresses and improved mobility that DHCP and NAT alone cannot meet. IPv6 satisfies the increasingly complex requirements of hierarchical addressing that IPv4 does not provide.

Given the huge installed base of IPv4 in the world, it is not difficult to appreciate that transitioning to IPv6 from IPv4 deployments is a challenge. There are, however, a variety of techniques, including an auto-configuration option, to make the transition easier. The transition mechanism you use depends on the needs of your network.

The figure compares the binary and alphanumeric representations of IPv4 and IPv6 addresses. An IPv6 address is a 128-bit binary value, which can be displayed as 32 hexadecimal digits. IPv6 should provide sufficient addresses for future Internet growth needs for many years to come. There are enough IPv6 addresses to allocate more than the entire IPv4 Internet address space to everyone on the planet.

Click the Perspective button in the figure.

So what happened to IPv5? IPv5 was used to define an experimental real-time streaming protocol. To avoid any confusion, it was decided to not use IPv5 and name the new IP protocol IPv6.

IPv6 would not exist were it not for the recognized depletion of available IPv4 addresses. However, beyond the increased IP address space, the development of IPv6 has presented opportunities to apply lessons learned from the limitations of IPv4 to create a protocol with new and improved features.

A simplified header architecture and protocol operation translates into reduced operational expenses. Built-in security features mean easier security practices that are sorely lacking in many current networks. However, perhaps the most significant improvement offered by IPv6 is the address autoconfiguration features it has.

The Internet is rapidly evolving from a collection of stationary devices to a fluid network of mobile devices. IPv6 allows mobile devices to quickly acquire and transition between addresses as they move among foreign networks, with no need for a foreign agent. (A foreign agent is a router that can function as the point of attachment for a mobile device when it roams from its home network to a foreign network.)

Address autoconfiguration also means more robust plug-and-play network connectivity. Autoconfiguration supports consumers who can have any combination of computers, printers, digital cameras, digital radios, IP phones, Internet-enabled household appliances, and robotic toys connected to their home networks. Many manufacturers already integrate IPv6 into their products.

Many of the enhancements that IPv6 offers are explained in this section, including:

- Enhanced IP addressing
- Simplified header
- Mobility and security
- Transition richness

Enhanced IP Addressing

A larger address space offers several enhancements, including:

- Improved global reachability and flexibility.
- Better aggregation of IP prefixes announced in routing tables.
- *Multihomed hosts*. Multihoming is a technique to increase the reliability of the Internet connection of an IP network. With IPv6, a host can have multiple IP addresses over one physical upstream link. For example, a host can connect to several ISPs.
- Autoconfiguration that can include Data Link layer addresses in the address space.
- More plug-and-play options for more devices.
- Public-to-private, end-to-end readdressing without address translation. This makes peer-to-peer (P2P) networking more functional and easier to deploy.
- Simplified mechanisms for address renumbering and modification.

Click the Simple Header button in the figure.

The figure compares the simplified IPv6 header structure to the IPv4 header. The IPv4 header has 20 octets and 12 basic header fields, followed by an options field and a data portion (usually the *Transport layer* segment). The IPv6 header has 40 octets, three IPv4 basic header fields, and five additional header fields.

The IPv6 simplified header offers several advantages over IPv4:

- Better routing efficiency for performance and forwarding-rate scalability
- No broadcasts and thus no potential threat of broadcast storms
- No requirement for processing checksums
- Simplified and more efficient extension header mechanisms
- Flow labels for per-flow processing with no need to open the transport inner packet to identify the various traffic flows

Enhanced Mobility and Security

Mobility and security help ensure compliance with *mobile IP* and IP Security (IPsec) standards functionality. Mobility enables people with mobile network devices, many with wireless connectivity, to move around in networks.

- The IETF Mobile IP standard is available for both IPv4 and IPv6. The standard enables mobile devices to move without breaks in established network connections. Mobile devices use a home address and a care-of address to achieve this mobility. With IPv4, these addresses are manually configured. With IPv6, the configurations are dynamic, giving Ipv6-enabled devices built-in mobility.

- IPsec is available for both IPv4 and IPv6. Although the functionalities are essentially identical in both environments, IPsec is mandatory in IPv6, making the IPv6 Internet more secure.

Transition Richness

IPv4 will not disappear overnight. Rather, it will coexist with and then gradually be replaced by IPv6. For this reason, IPv6 was delivered with migration techniques to cover every conceivable IPv4 upgrade case. However, many were ultimately rejected by the technology community.

Currently, there are three main approaches:

- *Dual stack*
- *6to4* tunneling
- NAT-PT, *ISATAP* tunneling, and *Teredo* tunneling (last resort methods)

Some of these approaches are discussed in more detail later in the chapter.

The current advice for transitioning to IPv6 is "Dual stack where you can, tunnel where you must!"

7.3.2 IPv6 Addressing

IPv6 Address Representation

You know the 32-bit IPv4 address as a series of four 8-bit fields, separated by dots. However, larger 128-bit IPv6 addresses need a different representation because of their size. IPv6 addresses use colons to separate entries in a series of 16-bit hexadecimal.

Click the Representation button in the figure.

The figure shows the address **2031:0000:130F:0000:0000:09C0:876A:130B**. IPv6 does not require explicit address string notation. The figure shows how to shorten the address by applying the following guidelines:

- Leading zeros in a field are optional. For example, the field 09C0 equals 9C0, and the field 0000 equals 0. So 2031:**0000**:130F:0000:0000:**09C0**:876A:130B can be written as 2031:**0**:130F:0000:0000:**9C0**:876A:130B.

- Successive fields of zeros can be represented as two colons "::". However, this shorthand method can only be used once in an address. For example 2031:0:130F:**0000:0000**:9C0:876A:130B can be written as 2031:0:130F::9C0:876A:130B.

- An unspecified address is written as "::" because it contains only zeros.

Using the "::" notation greatly reduces the size of most addresses as shown. An address parser identifies the number of missing zeros by separating any two parts of an address and entering 0s until the 128 bits are complete.

Click the Examples button in the figure for some additional examples.

IPv6 Global Unicast Address

IPv6 has an address format that enables aggregation upward eventually to the ISP. *Global unicast addresses* typically consists of a 48-bit global routing prefix and a 16-bit subnet ID. Individual organizations can use a 16-bit subnet field to create their own local addressing hierarchy. This field allows an organization to use up to 65,535 individual subnets.

At the top of the figure, it can be seen how additional hierarchy is added to the 48-bit global routing prefix with the registry prefix, ISP Prefix, and site prefix.

The current global unicast address that is assigned by the *IANA* uses the range of addresses that start with binary value 001 (2000::/3), which is 1/8 of the total IPv6 address space and is the largest block of assigned addresses. The IANA is allocating the IPv6 address space in the ranges of 2001::/16 to the five RIR registries (ARIN, RIPE NCC, APNIC, LACNIC, and AfriNIC).

For more information, refer to RFC 3587, IPv6 Global Unicast Address Format, which replaces RFC 2374.

Reserved Addresses

The IETF reserves a portion of the IPv6 address space for various uses, both present and future. Reserved addresses represent 1/256th of the total IPv6 address space. Some of the other types of IPv6 addresses come from this block.

Private Addresses

A block of IPv6 addresses is set aside for private addresses, just as is done in IPv4. These private addresses are local only to a particular link or site, and are therefore never routed outside of a particular company network. Private addresses have a first octet value of "FE" in hexadecimal notation, with the next hexadecimal digit being a value from 8 to F.

These addresses are further divided into two types, based upon their scope.

- **Site-local addresses**, are addresses similar to the RFC 1918 Address Allocation for Private Internets in IPv4 today. The scope of these addresses is an entire site or organization. However, the use of site-local addresses is problematic and is being deprecated as of 2003 by RFC 3879. In hexadecimal, site-local addresses begin with "FE" and then "C" to "F" for the third hexadecimal digit.

- ***Link-local addresses*, are new to the concept of addressing with IP in the Network layer. These addresses have a smaller scope than site-local addresses; they refer only to a particular physical link (physical network). Routers do not forward datagrams using link-local addresses at all, not even within the organization; they are only for local communication on a particular physical network segment. They are used for link communications such as automatic address configuration, neighbor discovery, and router discovery. Many IPv6 routing protocols also use link-local addresses. Link-local addresses begin with "FE" and then have a value from "8" to "B" for the third hexadecimal digit.**

Loopback Address

Just as in IPv4, a provision has been made for a special loopback IPv6 address for testing; datagrams sent to this address "loop back" to the sending device. However, in IPv6 there is just one address, not a whole block, for this function. The loopback address is 0:0:0:0:0:0:0:1, which is normally expressed using zero compression as "::1".

Unspecified Address

In IPv4, an IP address of all zeroes has a special meaning; it refers to the host itself, and is used when a device does not know its own address. In IPv6, this concept has been formalized, and the all-zeroes address (0:0:0:0:0:0:0:0) is named the "unspecified" address. It is typically used in the source field of a datagram that is sent by a device that seeks to have its IP address configured. You can apply address compression to this address; because the address is all zeroes, the address becomes just "::".

IPv6 Address Management

IPv6 addresses use interface identifiers to identify interfaces on a link. Think of them as the host portion of an IPv6 address. Interface identifiers are required to be unique on a specific link. Interface identifiers are always 64 bits and can be dynamically derived from a Layer 2 address (MAC).

You can assign an IPv6 address ID statically or dynamically:

- Static assignment using a manual interface ID
- Static assignment using an EUI-64 interface ID
- *Stateless autoconfiguration*
- DHCP for IPv6 (DHCPv6)

Manual Interface ID Assignment

One way to statically assign an IPv6 address to a device is to manually assign both the prefix (network) and interface ID (host) portion of the IPv6 address. To configure an IPv6 address on a Cisco router interface, use the **ipv6 address** *ipv6-address/prefix-length* command in interface configuration mode. The following example shows the assignment of an IPv6 address to the interface of a Cisco router:

```
RouterX(config-if)#ipv6 address 2001:DB8:2222:7272::72/64
```

EUI-64 Interface ID Assignment

Another way to assign an IPv6 address is to configure the prefix (network) portion of the IPv6 address and derive the interface ID (host) portion from the Layer 2 MAC address of the device, which is known as the *EUI-64* interface ID.

Click the EUI-64 button in the figure.

The EUI-64 standard explains how to stretch IEEE 802 MAC addresses from 48 to 64 bits by inserting the 16-bit 0xFFFE in the middle at the 24th bit of the MAC address to create a 64-bit, unique interface identifier.

To configure an IPv6 address on a Cisco router interface and enable IPv6 processing using EUI-64 on that interface, use the **ipv6 address** *ipv6-prefix/prefix-length* **eui-64** command in interface configuration mode. The following example shows the assignment of an EUI-64 address to the interface of a Cisco router:

```
RouterX(config-if)#ipv6 address 2001:DB8:2222:7272::/64 eui-64
```

Stateless Autoconfiguration

Autoconfiguration automatically configures the IPv6 address. In IPv6, it is assumed that non-PC devices, as well as computer terminals, will be connected to the network. The autoconfiguration mechanism was introduced to enable plug-and-play networking of these devices to help reduce administration overhead.

DHCPv6 (Stateful)

DHCPv6 enables DHCP servers to pass configuration parameters, such as IPv6 network addresses, to IPv6 nodes. It offers the capability of automatic allocation of reusable network addresses and additional configuration flexibility. This protocol is a stateful counterpart to IPv6 stateless address autoconfiguration (RFC 2462), and can be used separately or concurrently with IPv6 stateless address autoconfiguration to obtain configuration parameters.

For more information on IPv6 address assignment visit the following: http://www.netbsd.org/docs/network/ipv6/.

7.3.3 IPv6 Transition Strategies

IPv6 Transition Strategies

The transition from IPv4 does not require upgrades on all nodes at the same time. Many transition mechanisms enable smooth integration of IPv4 and IPv6. Other mechanisms that allow IPv4 nodes to communicate with IPv6 nodes are available. Different situations demand different strategies. The figure illustrates the richness of available transition strategies.

Recall the advice: "Dual stack where you can, tunnel where you must." These two methods are the most common techniques to transition from IPv4 to IPv6.

Dual Stacking

Dual stacking is an integration method in which a node has implementation and connectivity to both an IPv4 and IPv6 network. This is the recommended option and involves running IPv4 and IPv6 at the same time. Router and switches are configured to support both protocols, with IPv6 being the preferred protocol.

Tunneling

The second major transition technique is tunneling. There are several tunneling techniques available, including:

- Manual IPv6-over-IPv4 tunneling - An IPv6 packet is encapsulated within the IPv4 protocol. This method requires dual-stack routers.

- Dynamic 6to4 tunneling - Automatically establishes the connection of IPv6 islands through an IPv4 network, typically the Internet. It dynamically applies a valid, unique IPv6 prefix to each IPv6 island, which enables the fast deployment of IPv6 in a corporate network without address retrieval from the ISPs or registries.

Other less popular tunneling techniques that are beyond the scope of this course include:

- Intra-Site Automatic Tunnel Addressing Protocol (ISATAP) tunneling - Automatic overlay tunneling mechanism that uses the underlying IPv4 network as a link layer for IPv6. ISATAP tunnels allow individual IPv4 or IPv6 dual-stack hosts within a site to communicate with other such hosts on a virtual link, creating an IPv6 network using the IPv4 infrastructure.

- Teredo tunneling - An IPv6 transition technology that provides host-to-host automatic tunneling instead of gateway tunneling. This approach passes unicast IPv6 traffic when dual-stacked hosts (hosts that are running both IPv6 and IPv4) are located behind one or multiple IPv4 NATs.

NAT-Protocol Translation (NAT-PT)

Cisco IOS Release 12.3(2)T and later (with the appropriate feature set) also include NAT-PT between IPv6 and IPv4. This translation allows direct communication between hosts that use different versions of the IP protocol. These translations are more complex than IPv4 NAT. At this time, this translation technique is the least favorable option and should be used as a last resort.

7.3.4 Cisco IOS Dual Stack

Cisco IOS Dual Stack

Dual stacking is an integration method that allows a node to have connectivity to an IPv4 and IPv6 network simultaneously. Each node has two protocol stacks with the configuration on the same interface or on multiple interfaces.

The dual-stack approach to IPv6 integration, in which nodes have both IPv4 and IPv6 stacks, will be one of the most commonly used integration methods. A dual-stack node chooses which stack to use based on the destination address of the packet. A dual-stack node should prefer IPv6 when it is available. Old IPv4-only applications continue to work as before. New and modified applications take advantage of both IP layers.

A new application programming interface (*API*) has been defined to support IPv4 and IPv6 addresses and DNS requests. An API facilitates the exchange of messages or data between two or more different software applications. An example of an API is the virtual interface between two software functions, such as a word processor and a spreadsheet. The API is built into software applications to translate IPv4 into IPv6, and vice versa using the IP conversion mechanism. New applications can use both IPv4 and IPv6.

Experience in porting IPv4 applications to IPv6 suggests that for most applications, there is a minimal change in some localized places inside the source code. This technique is well known and has been applied in the past for other protocol transitions. It enables gradual application upgrades, one by one, to IPv6.

Click the Configuring IPv6 Interface button in the figure.

Cisco IOS Release 12.2(2)T and later (with the appropriate feature set) are IPv6-ready. As soon as you configure basic IPv4 and IPv6 on the interface, the interface is dual-stacked and forwards IPv4 and IPv6 traffic on that interface. Note that an IPv4 and an IPv6 address have been configured.

Using IPv6 on a Cisco IOS router requires that you use the global configuration command `ipv6 unicast-routing`. This command enables the forwarding of IPv6 datagrams.

You must configure all interfaces that forward IPv6 traffic with an IPv6 address using the `ipv6 address` *IPv6-address* [*/prefix length*] interface command.

7.3.5 IPv6 Tunneling

IPv6 Tunneling

Tunneling is an integration method where an IPv6 packet is encapsulated within another protocol, such as IPv4. This method enables the connection of IPv6 islands without needing to convert the intermediary networks to IPv6. When IPv4 is used to encapsulate the IPv6 packet, a protocol type of 41 is specified in the IPv4 header, and the packet includes a 20-byte IPv4 header with no options and an IPv6 header and payload. It also requires dual-stack routers.

Tunneling presents these two issues. The maximum transmission unit (*MTU*) is effectively decreased by 20 octets if the IPv4 header does not contain any optional fields. In addition, a tunneled network is often difficult to troubleshoot.

Tunneling is an intermediate integration and transition technique and should not be considered as a final solution. A native IPv6 architecture should be the ultimate goal.

Manually Configured IPv6 Tunnel

A manually configured tunnel is equivalent to a permanent link between two IPv6 domains over an IPv4 backbone. The primary use is for stable connections that require regular secure communication between two edge routers or between an end system and an edge router, or for connection to remote IPv6 networks. The end routers must be dual stacked, and the configuration cannot change dynamically as network and routing needs change.

Administrators manually configure a static IPv6 address on a tunnel interface, and assign manually configured static IPv4 addresses to the tunnel source and the tunnel destination. The host or router at each end of a configured tunnel must support both the IPv4 and IPv6 protocol stacks. Manually configured tunnels can be configured between border routers or between a border router and a host.

7.3.6 Routing Considerations with IPv6

Routing Configurations with IPv6

Refer to Figure in online course

Like IPv4 classless interdomain routing (*CIDR*), IPv6 uses longest prefix match routing. IPv6 uses modified versions of most of the common routing protocols to handle longer IPv6 addresses and different header structures.

Larger address spaces make room for large address allocations to ISPs and organizations. An ISP aggregates all of the prefixes of its customers into a single prefix and announces the single prefix to the IPv6 Internet. The increased address space is sufficient to allow organizations to define a single prefix for their entire network.

But how does this affect router performance? A brief review of how a router functions in a network helps illustrate how IPv6 affects routing. Conceptually, a router has three functional areas:

- The control plane handles the interaction of the router with the other network elements, providing the information needed to make decisions and control the overall router operation. This plane runs processes such as routing protocols and network management. These functions are generally complex.

- The data plane handles packet forwarding from one physical or logical interface to another. It involves different switching mechanisms such as process switching and Cisco Express Forwarding (CEF) on Cisco IOS software routers.

- Enhanced services include advanced features applied when forwarding data, such as packet filtering, quality of service (QoS), encryption, translation, and accounting.

IPv6 presents each of these functions with specific new challenges.

IPv6 Control Plane

Enabling IPv6 on a router starts its control plane operating processes specifically for IPv6. Protocol characteristics shape the performance of these processes and the amount of resources necessary to operate them:

- *IPv6 address size -* Address size affects the information-processing functions of a router. Systems using a 64-bit CPU, bus, or memory structure can pass both the IPv4 source and destination address in a single processing cycle. For IPv6, the source and destination addresses require two cycles each-four cycles to process source and destination address information. As a result, routers relying exclusively on software processing are likely to perform slower than when in an IPv4 environment.

- *Multiple IPv6 node addresses -* Because IPv6 nodes can use several IPv6 unicast addresses, memory consumption of the Neighbor Discovery cache may be affected.

- *IPv6 routing protocols -* IPv6 routing protocols are similar to their IPv4 counterparts, but since an IPv6 prefix is four times larger than an IPv4 prefix, routing updates have to carry more information.

- *Routing table Size -* Increased IPv6 address space leads to larger networks and a much larger Internet. This implies larger routing tables and higher memory requirements to support them.

IPv6 Data Plane

The data plane forwards IP packets based on the decisions made by the control plane. The forwarding engine parses the relevant IP packet information and does a lookup to match the parsed information against the forwarding policies defined by the control plane. IPv6 affects the performance of parsing and lookup functions:

- *Parsing IPv6 extension headers -* Applications, including mobile IPv6, often use IPv6 address information in extension headers, thus increasing their size. These additional fields require additional processing. For example, a router using ACLs to filter Layer 4 information needs to apply the ACLs to packets with extension headers as well as those without. If the length of the extension header exceeds the fixed length of the hardware register of the router, hardware switching fails, and packets may be punted to software switching or dropped. This severely affects the forwarding performance of the router.

- *IPv6 address lookup -* IPv6 performs a lookup on packets entering the router to find the correct output interface. In IPv4, the forwarding decision process parses a 32-bit destination address. In IPv6, the forwarding decision could conceivably require parsing a 128-bit address. Most routers today perform lookups using an application-specific integrated circuit (ASIC) with a fixed configuration that performs the functions for which it was originally designed - IPv4. Again, this could result in punting packets into slower software processing, or dropping them all together.

RIPng Routing Protocol

IPv6 routes use the same protocols and techniques as IPv4. Although the addresses are longer, the protocols used in routing IPv6 are simply logical extensions of the protocols used in IPv4.

RFC 2080 defines Routing Information Protocol next generation (*RIPng*) as a simple routing protocol based on RIP. RIPng is no more or less powerful than RIP, however, it provides a simple way to bring up an IPv6 network without having to build a new routing protocol.

RIPng is a distance vector routing protocol with a limit of 15 hops that uses split horizon and *poison reverse updates* to prevent routing loops. Its simplicity comes from the fact that it does not require any global knowledge of the network. Only neighboring routers exchange local messages.

RIPng includes the following features:

- Based on IPv4 RIP version 2 (RIPv2) and is similar to RIPv2
- Uses IPv6 for transport
- Includes the IPv6 prefix and next-hop IPv6 address
- Uses the *multicast group FF02::9* as the destination address for RIP updates (this is similar to the broadcast function performed by RIP in IPv4)
- Sends updates on UDP port 521
- Is supported by Cisco IOS Release 12.2(2)T and later

In dual-stacked deployments, both RIP and RIPng are required.

7.3.7 Configuring IPv6 Addresses

Enabling IPv6 on Cisco Routers

There are two basic steps to activate IPv6 on a router. First, you must activate IPv6 traffic-forwarding on the router, and then you must configure each interface that requires IPv6.

By default, IPv6 traffic-forwarding is disabled on a Cisco router. To activate it between interfaces, you must configure the global command **ipv6 unicast-routing**.

The **ipv6 address** command can configure a global IPv6 address. The link-local address is automatically configured when an address is assigned to the interface. You must specify the entire 128-bit IPv6 address or specify to use the 64-bit prefix by using the **eui-64** option.

IPv6 Address Configuration Example

You can completely specify the IPv6 address or compute the host identifier (rightmost 64 bits) from the EUI-64 identifier of the interface. In the example, the IPv6 address of the interface is configured using the EUI-64 format.

Alternatively, you can completely specify the entire IPv6 address to assign a router interface an address using the **ipv6 address** *ipv6-address*/*prefix-length* command in interface configuration mode.

Configuring an IPv6 address on an interface automatically configures the link-local address for that interface.

Cisco IOS IPv6 Name Resolution

There are two ways to perform name resolution from the Cisco IOS software process:

- Define a static name for an IPv6 address using the **ipv6 host name** [*port*] *ipv6-address1* [*ipv6-address2...ipv6-address4*] command. You can define up to four IPv6 addresses for one hostname. The port option refers to the Telnet port to be used for the associated host.

- Specify the DNS server used by the router with the **ip name-server** *address* command. The address can be an IPv4 or IPv6 address. You can specify up to six DNS servers with this command.

7.3.8 Configuring RIPng with IPv6

Configure RIPng with IPv6

When configuring supported routing protocols in IPv6, you must create the routing process, enable the routing process on interfaces, and customize the routing protocol for your particular network.

Before configuring the router to run IPv6 RIP, globally enable IPv6 using the **ipv6 unicast-routing** global configuration command, and enable IPv6 on any interfaces on which IPv6 RIP is to be enabled.

To enable RIPng routing on the router, use the **ipv6 router rip** *name* global configuration command. The *name* parameter identifies the RIP process. This process name is used later when configuring RIPng on participating interfaces.

For RIPng, instead of using the **network** command to identify which interfaces should run RIPng, you use the command **ipv6 rip** *name* **enable** in interface configuration mode to enable RIPng on an interface. The *name* parameter must match the name parameter in the **ipv6 router rip** command.

Enabling RIP on an interface dynamically creates a "router rip" process if necessary.

Example: RIPng for IPv6 Configuration

The example shows a network of two routers. Router R1 is connected to the default network. On both router R2 and router R1, the name RT0 identifies the RIPng process. RIPng is enabled on the first Ethernet interface of router R1 using the **ipv6 rip RT0 enable** command. Router R2 shows that RIPng is enabled on both Ethernet interfaces using the **ipv6 rip RT0 enable** command.

Chapter 7: IP Addressing Services   203

This configuration allows Ethernet 1 on router R2 and the Ethernet 0 interfaces of both routers to exchange RIPng routing information.

7.3.9 Verifying and Troubleshooting RIPng

Verifying and Troubleshooting RIPng for IPv6

After configuring RIPng, verification is required. The figure lists the various show commands you can use.

Click the Troubleshooting button in the figure.

If you discover during verification that RIPng is not working properly, you need to troubleshoot.

The figure lists the commands used to troubleshoot RIPng problems.

Flash Activity

7.4 Chapter Labs

7.4.1 Basic DHCP and NAT Configuration

In this lab, you will configure the DHCP and NAT IP services. One router is the DHCP server. The other router forwards DHCP requests to the server. You will also configure both static and dynamic NAT configurations, including NAT overload. When you have completed the configurations, verify the connectivity between the inside and outside addresses.

This activity is a variation of Lab 7.4.1. Packet Tracer may not support all the tasks specified in the hands-on lab. This activity should not be considered equivalent to completing the hands-on lab. Packet Tracer is not a substitute for a hands-on lab experience with real equipment.

Detailed instructions are provided within the activity as well as in the PDF link below.

Activity Instructions (PDF)

7.4.2 Challenge DHCP and NAT Configuration

In this lab, configure the IP address services using the network shown in the topology diagram. If you need assistance, refer back to the basic DHCP and NAT configuration lab. However, try to do as much on your own as possible.

This activity is a variation of Lab 7.4.2. Packet Tracer may not support all the tasks specified in the hands-on lab. This activity should not be considered equivalent to completing the hands-on lab. Packet Tracer is not a substitute for a hands-on lab experience with real equipment.

Detailed instructions are provided within the activity as well as in the PDF link below.

Activity Instructions (PDF)

7.4.3 Troubleshooting DHCP and NAT

The routers at your company were configured by an inexperienced network engineer. Several errors in the configuration have resulted in connectivity issues. Your boss has asked you to troubleshoot and correct the configuration errors and document your work. Using your knowledge of

DHCP, NAT, and standard testing methods, find and correct the errors. Make sure all clients have full connectivity.

> **Refer to Packet Tracer Activity for this chapter**

This activity is a variation of Lab 7.4.3. Packet Tracer may not support all the tasks specified in the hands-on lab. This activity should not be considered equivalent to completing the hands-on lab. Packet Tracer is not a substitute for a hands-on lab experience with real equipment.

Detailed instructions are provided within the activity as well as in the PDF link below.

Activity Instructions (PDF)

Chapter Summary

This chapter has dealt with the key solutions to the problem of diminishing Internet address space. You have learned how to use DHCP to assign private IP addresses inside your network. This conserves public address space and saves considerable administrative overhead in managing adds, moves and changes. You learned how to implement NAT and NAT overload to conserve public address space and build private secure intranets without affecting your ISP connection. However, NAT has drawbacks in terms of its negative affects on device performance, security, mobility and end-to-end connectivity.

Overall, the ability to scale networks for future demands requires a limitless supply of IP addresses and improved mobility that DHCP and NAT alone cannot meet. IPv6 satisfies the increasingly complex requirements of hierarchical addressing that IPv4 does not provide. The emergence of IPv6 not only deals with the depletion of IPv4 addresses and shortcomings of NAT, it provides new and improved features. In the brief introduction to IPv6 in this lesson, you learned how IPv6 addresses are structured, how they will enhance network security and mobility, and how the IPv4 world will transition to IPv6.

Check Your Understanding

In this culminating activity, you will configure PPP, OSPF, DHCP, NAT and default routing to ISP. You will then verify your configuration.

Detailed instructions are provided within the activity as well as in the PDF link below.

Activity Instructions (PDF)

Chapter Quiz

Take the chapter quiz to test your knowledge.

Your Chapter Notes

CHAPTER 8

Network Troubleshooting

Chapter Introduction

Once a network is operational, administrators have to monitor its performance for the sake of the organization's productivity. From time-to-time network outages can occur. Sometimes they are planned and their impact on the organization easily managed. Sometimes they are not planned and their impact on the organization can be severe. In the event of an unexpected network outage administrators must be able to troubleshoot and bring the network back into full production. In this chapter you will learn a systematic process for troubleshooting network outages.

8.1 Establishing the Network Performance Baseline

8.1.1 Documenting Your Network

Documenting Your Network

To efficiently diagnose and correct network problems, a network engineer needs to know how a network has been designed and what the expected performance for this network should be under normal operating conditions. This information is called the network baseline and is captured in documentation such as configuration tables and topology diagrams.

Network configuration documentation provides a logical diagram of the network and detailed information about each component. This information should be kept in a single location, either as hard copy or on the network on a protected website. Network documentation should include these components:

- Network configuration table
- End-system configuration table
- Network topology diagram

Network Configuration Table

Contains accurate, up-to-date records of the hardware and software used in a network. The network configuration table should provide the network engineer with all the information necessary to identify and correct the network fault.

Click the Router and Switch Documentation button in the figure.

The table in the figure illustrates the data set that should be included for all components:

- Type of device, model designation
- IOS image name
- Device network hostname

- Location of the device (building, floor, room, rack, panel)
- If it is a modular device, include all module types and in which module slot they are located
- Data Link layer addresses
- Network layer addresses
- Any additional important information about physical aspects of the device

Click the End-System Documentation button in the figure.

End-system Configuration Table

Contains baseline records of the hardware and software used in end-system devices such as servers, network management consoles, and desktop workstations. An incorrectly configured end system can have a negative impact on the overall performance of a network.

For troubleshooting purposes, the following information should be documented:

- Device name (purpose)
- Operating system and version
- IP address
- Subnet mask
- Default gateway, DNS server, and WINS server addresses
- Any high-bandwidth network applications that the end-system runs

Click the Network Topology Diagram button in the figure.

Network Topology Diagram

Graphical representation of a network, which illustrates how each device in a network is connected and its logical architecture. A topology diagram shares many of the same components as the network configuration table. Each network device should be represented on the diagram with consistent notation or a graphical symbol. Also, each logical and physical connection should be represented using a simple line or other appropriate symbol. Routing protocols can also be shown.

At a minimum, the topology diagram should include:

- Symbols for all devices and how they are connected
- Interface types and numbers
- IP addresses
- Subnet masks

8.1.2 Documenting Your Network

Network Documentation Process

Refer to Figure in online course

The figure shows the network documentation process.

Roll over each stage in the figure to learn more about the process.

When you document your network, you may have to gather information directly from routers and switches. Commands that are useful to the network documentation process include:

- The `ping` command is used to test connectivity with neighboring devices before logging in to them. Pinging to other PCs in the network also initiates the MAC address auto-discovery process.

- The `telnet` command is used to log in remotely to a device for accessing configuration information.

- The `show ip interface brief` command is used to display the up or down status and IP address of all interfaces on a device.

- The `show ip route` command is used to display the routing table in a router to learn the directly connected neighbors, more remote devices (through learned routes), and the routing protocols that have been configured.

- The `show cdp neighbor detail` command is used to obtain detailed information about directly connected Cisco neighbor devices.

Refer to **Packet Tracer Activity** for this chapter

This activity covers the steps to take to discover a network using primarily the `telnet`, `show cdp neighbors detail`, and `show ip route` commands. This is Part I of a two-part activity.

The topology you see when you open the Packet Tracer activity does not reveal all of the details of the network. The details have been hidden using the cluster function of Packet Tracer. The network infrastructure has been collapsed, and the topology in the file shows only the end devices. Your task is to use your knowledge of networking and discovery commands to learn about the full network topology and document it.

Detailed instructions are provided within the activity as well as in the PDF link below.

Activity Instructions (PDF)

8.1.3 Why is Establishing a Network Baseline Important?

Refer to **Figure** in online course

Establishing a network performance baseline requires collecting key performance data from the ports and devices that are essential to network operation. This information helps to determine the "personality" of the network and provides answers to the following questions:

- How does the network perform during a normal or average day?
- Where are the underutilized and over-utilized areas?
- Where are the most errors occurring?
- What thresholds should be set for the devices that need to be monitored?
- Can the network deliver the identified policies?

Measuring the initial performance and availability of critical network devices and links allows a network administrator to determine the difference between abnormal behavior and proper network performance as the network grows or traffic patterns change. The baseline also provides insight into whether the current network design can deliver the required policies. Without a baseline, no standard exists to measure the optimum nature of network traffic and congestion levels.

In addition, analysis after an initial baseline tends to reveal hidden problems. The collected data reveals the true nature of congestion or potential congestion in a network. It may also reveal areas in the network that are underutilized and quite often can lead to network redesign efforts based on quality and capacity observations.

8.1.4 Steps for Establishing a Network Baseline

Planning for the First Baseline

> Refer to Figure in online course

Because the initial network performance baseline sets the stage for measuring the effects of network changes and subsequent troubleshooting efforts, it is important to plan for it carefully. Here are the recommended steps for planning the first baseline:

Step 1. Determine what types of data to collect

When conducting the initial baseline, start by selecting a few variables that represent the defined policies. If too many data points are selected, the amount of data can be overwhelming, making analysis of the collected data difficult. Start out simply and fine-tune along the way. Generally, some good starting measures are interface utilization and CPU utilization. The figure shows some screenshots of interface and CPU utilization data, as displayed by a *network management system* called WhatsUp Gold.

Click the Devices and Ports of Interest button in the figure.

Step 2. Identify devices and ports of interest

The next step is to identify those key devices and ports for which performance data should be measured. Devices and ports of interest include:

- Network device ports that connect to other network devices
- Servers
- Key users
- Anything else considered critical to operations

In topology shown in the figure, the network administrator has highlighted the devices and ports of interest to monitor during the baseline test. The devices of interest include routers R1, R2, and R3, PC1 (the Admin terminal), and SRV1 (the Web/TFTP server). The ports of interest include those ports on R1, R2, and R3 that connect to the other routers or to switches, and on router R2, the port that connects to SRV1 (Fa0/0).

By narrowing the ports polled, the results are concise, and network management load is minimized. Remember that an interface on a router or switch can be a virtual interface, such as a switch virtual interface (SVI).

This step is easier if you have configured the device port description fields to indicate what connects to the port. For example, for a router port that connects to the distribution switch in the Engineering workgroup, you might configure the description, "Engineering LAN distribution switch."

Click the Determine Baseline Duration button in the figure.

Step 3. Determine the baseline duration

It is important that the length of time and the baseline information being gathered are sufficient to establish a typical picture of the network. This period should be at least seven days to capture any daily or weekly trends. Weekly trends are just as important as daily or hourly trends.

The figure shows examples of several screenshots of CPU utilization trends captured over a daily, weekly, monthly, and yearly period. The work week trends are too short to accurately reveal the recurring nature of the utilization surge that occurs every weekend on Saturday evening when a major database backup operation consumes network bandwidth. This recurring pattern is revealed in the monthly trend. The yearly trend shown in the example is too long a duration to provide meaningful baseline performance details. A baseline needs to last no more than six weeks, unless specific long-term trends need to be measured. Generally, a two-to-four-week baseline is adequate.

You should not perform a baseline measurement during times of unique traffic patterns because the data would provide an inaccurate picture of normal network operations. You would get an inaccurate measure of network performance if you performed a baseline measurement on a holiday or during a month when most of the company is on vacation.

Baseline analysis of the network should be conducted on a regular basis. Perform an annual analysis of the entire network or baseline different sections of the network on a rotating basis. Analysis must be conducted regularly to understand how the network is affected by growth and other changes.

Measuring Network Performance Data

Sophisticated network management software is often used to baseline large and complex networks. For example, the Fluke Network SuperAgent module enables administrators to automatically create and review reports using its Intelligent Baselines feature. This feature compares current performance levels with historical observations and can automatically identify performance problems and applications that do not provide expected levels of service.

Click the Manual Commands button in the figure.

In simpler networks, the baseline tasks may require a combination of manual data collection and simple network protocol inspectors. Establishing an initial baseline or conducting a performance-monitoring analysis may require many hours or days to accurately reflect network performance. Network management software or protocol inspectors and sniffers may run continuously over the course of the data collection process. Hand collection using **show** commands on individual network devices is extremely time consuming and should be limited to mission-critical network devices.

8.2 Troubleshooting Methodologies and Tools

8.2.1 A General Approach to Troubleshooting

Network engineers, administrators, and support personnel realize that troubleshooting is a process that takes the greatest percentage their time. Using efficient troubleshooting techniques shortens overall troubleshooting time when working in a production environment.

Two extreme approaches to troubleshooting almost always result in disappointment, delay, or failure. At one extreme is the theorist, or rocket scientist, approach. At the other extreme is the impractical, or caveman, approach.

The rocket scientist analyzes and reanalyzes the situation until the exact cause at the root of the problem has been identified and corrected with surgical precision. While this process is fairly reliable, few companies can afford to have their networks down for the hours or days that it can take for this exhaustive analysis.

The caveman's first instinct is to start swapping cards, cables, hardware, and software until miraculously the network begins operating again. This does not mean that the network is working properly, just that it is operating. While this approach may achieve a change in symptoms faster, it is not very reliable, and the root cause of the problem may still be present.

Since both of these approaches are extremes, the better approach is somewhere in the middle using elements of both. It is important to analyze the network as a whole rather than in a piecemeal fashion. A systematic approach minimizes confusion and cuts down on time otherwise wasted with trial and error.

8.2.2 Using Layered Models for Troubleshooting

Refer to Figure in online course

OSI Versus TCP/IP Layered Models

Logical networking models, such as the OSI and TCP/IP models, separate network functionality into modular layers. When troubleshooting, these layered models can be applied to the physical network to isolate network problems. For example, if the symptoms suggest a physical connection problem, the network technician can focus on troubleshooting the circuit that operates at the Physical layer. If that circuit functions properly, the technician looks at areas in another layer that could be causing the problem.

OSI Reference Model

The OSI model provides a common language for network engineers and is commonly used in troubleshooting networks. Problems are typically described in terms of a given OSI model layer.

The OSI reference model describes how information from a software application in one computer moves through a network medium to a software application in another computer.

The upper layers (5-7) of the OSI model deal with application issues and generally are implemented only in software. The Application layer is closest to the end user. Both users and Application layer processes interact with software applications that contain a communications component.

The lower layers (1-4) of the OSI model handle data-transport issues. Layers 3 and 4 are generally implemented only in software. The Physical layer (Layer 1) and Data Link layer (Layer 2) are implemented in hardware and software. The Physical layer is closest to the physical network medium, such as the network cabling, and is responsible for actually placing information on the medium.

TCP/IP Model

Similar to the OSI networking model, the TCP/IP networking model also divides networking architecture into modular layers. The figure shows how the TCP/IP networking model maps to the layers of the OSI networking model. It is this close mapping that allows the TCP/IP suite of protocols to successfully communicate with so many networking technologies.

The Application layer in the TCP/IP suite actually combines the functions of the three OSI model layers: Session, Presentation, and Application. The Application layer provides communication between applications such as FTP, HTTP, and SMTP on separate hosts.

The Transport layers of TCP/IP and OSI directly correspond in function. The Transport layer is responsible for exchanging segments between devices on a TCP/IP network.

The TCP/IP Internet layer relates to the OSI Network layer. The Internet layer is responsible for placing messages in a fixed format that allows devices to handle them.

The TCP/IP network access layer corresponds to the OSI physical and Data Link layers. The network access layer communicates directly with the network media and provides an interface between the architecture of the network and the Internet layer.

Click the Devices at the OSI layers button in the figure.

Roll over each device to show which OSI Layers you commonly need to troubleshoot for that type of device.

8.2.3 General Troubleshooting Procedures

The stages of the general troubleshooting process are:

- *Stage 1 Gather symptoms -* Troubleshooting begins with the process of gathering and documenting symptoms from the network, end systems, and users. In addition, the network administrator determines which network components have been affected and how the functionality of the network has changed compared to the baseline. Symptoms may appear in many different forms, including alerts from the network management system, console messages, and user complaints. While gathering symptoms, questions should be used as a method of localizing the problem to a smaller range of possibilities.

- *Stage 2 Isolate the problem -* The problem is not truly isolated until a single problem, or a set of related problems, is identified. To do this, the network administrator examines the characteristics of the problems at the logical layers of the network so that the most likely cause can be selected. At this stage, the network administrator may gather and document more symptoms depending on the problem characteristics that are identified.

- *Stage 3 Correct the problem -* Having isolated and identified the cause of the problem, the network administrator works to correct the problem by implementing, testing, and documenting a solution. If the network administrator determines that the corrective action has created another problem, the attempted solution is documented, the changes are removed, and the network administrator returns to gathering symptoms and isolating the problem.

These stages are not mutually exclusive. At any point in the process, it may be necessary to return to previous stages. For instance, it may be required to gather more symptoms while isolating a problem. Additionally, when attempting to correct a problem, another unidentified problem could be created. As a result, it would be necessary to gather the symptoms, isolate, and correct the new problem.

A troubleshooting policy should be established for each stage. A policy provides a consistent manner in which to perform each stage. Part of the policy should include documenting every important piece of information.

8.2.4 Troubleshooting Methods

Troubleshooting Methods

There are three main methods for troubleshooting networks:

- Bottom up
- Top down
- Divide and conquer

Each approach has its advantages and disadvantages. This topic describes the three methods and provides guidelines for choosing the best method for a specific situation.

Bottom-Up Troubleshooting Method

In bottom-up troubleshooting you start with the physical components of the network and move up through the layers of the OSI model until the cause of the problem is identified. Bottom-up troubleshooting is a good approach to use when the problem is suspected to be a physical one. Most networking problems reside at the lower levels, so implementing the bottom-up approach often results in effective results. The figure shows the bottom-up approach to troubleshooting.

The disadvantage with the bottom-up troubleshooting approach is it requires that you check every device and interface on the network until the possible cause of the problem is found. Remember that each conclusion and possibility must be documented so there can be a lot of paper work associated with this approach. A further challenge is to determine which devices to start examining first.

Click the Top-Down Method button in the figure.

Top-Down Troubleshooting Method

In top-down troubleshooting your start with the end-user applications and move down through the layers of the OSI model until the cause of the problem has been identified. End-user applications of an end system are tested before tackling the more specific networking pieces. Use this approach for simpler problems or when you think the problem is with a piece of software.

The disadvantage with the top-down approach is it requires checking every network application until the possible cause of the problem is found. Each conclusion and possibility must be documented. and the challenge is to determine which application to start examining first.

Click the Divide-and-Conquer Method button in the figure.

Divide-and-Conquer Troubleshooting Method

When you apply the divide-and-conquer approach toward troubleshooting a networking problem, you select a layer and test in both directions from the starting layer.

In divide-and-conquer troubleshooting you start by collecting user experience of the problem, document the symptoms and then, using that information, make an informed guess as to which OSI layer to start your investigation. Once you verify that a layer is functioning properly, assume that the layers below it are functioning and work up the OSI layers. If an OSI layer is not functioning properly, work your way down the OSI layer model.

For example, if users can't access the web server and you can ping the server, then you know that the problem is above Layer 3. If you can't ping the server, then you know the problem is likely at a lower OSI layer.

Guidelines for Selecting a Troubleshooting Method

To quickly resolve network problems, take the time to select the most effective network troubleshooting method. Examine the figure. Use the process shown in the figure to help you select the most efficient troubleshooting method.

Here is an example of how you would choose a troubleshooting method for a specific problem. Two IP routers are not exchanging routing information. The last time this type of problem occurred it was a protocol issue. So you choose the divide-and-conquer troubleshooting method. Your analysis reveals that there is connectivity between the routers so you start your troubleshooting efforts at the physical or Data Link layer, confirm connectivity and begin testing the TCP/IP-related functions at next layer up in the OSI model, the Network layer.

8.2.5 Gathering Symptoms

Gathering Symptoms

To determine the scope of the problem gather (document) the symptoms. The figure shows the a flow chart of this process. Each step in this process is briefly described here:

Step 1. Analyze existing symptoms - Analyze symptoms gathered from the trouble ticket, users, or end systems affected by the problem to form a definition of the problem.

Step 2. Determine ownership - If the problem is within your system, you can move onto the next stage. If the problem is outside the boundary of your control, for example, lost Internet connectivity outside of the *autonomous system*, you need to contact an administrator for the external system before gathering additional network symptoms.

Step 3. Narrow the scope - Determine if the problem is at the core, distribution, or access layer of the network. At the identified layer, analyze the existing symptoms and use your knowledge of the network topology to determine which pieces of equipment are the most likely cause.

Step 4. Gather symptoms from suspect devices - Using a layered troubleshooting approach, gather hardware and software symptoms from the suspect devices. Start with the most likely possibility, and use knowledge and experience to determine if the problem is more likely a hardware or software configuration problem.

Step 5. Document symptoms - Sometimes the problem can be solved using the documented symptoms. If not, begin the isolating phase of the general troubleshooting process.

Click the Commands button in the figure.

Use the Cisco IOS commands to gather symptoms about the network. The table in the figure describes the common Cisco IOS commands you can use to help you gather the systems of a network problem.

Although the **debug** command is an important tool for gathering symptoms it generates a large amount of console message traffic and the performance of a network device can be noticeably affected. Make sure you warn network users that a troubleshooting effort is underway and that network performance may be affected. Remember to disable debugging when you are done.

Questioning End Users

When you question end users about a network problem they may be experiencing, use effective questioning techniques. This way you will get the information you need to effectively document the symptoms of a problem. The table in the figure provides some guidelines and end-user example questions.

8.2.6 Troubleshooting Tools

Software Troubleshooting Tools

A wide variety of software and hardware tools are available to make troubleshooting easier. These tools may be used to gather and analyze symptoms of network problems and often provide monitoring and reporting functions that can be used to establish the network baseline.

NMS Tools

Network management system (*NMS*) tools include device-level monitoring, configuration, and fault management tools. The figure shows an example display from the What's Up Gold NMS software. These tools can be used to investigate and correct network problems. Network monitoring software graphically displays a physical view of network devices, allowing network managers to monitor remote devices without actually physically checking them. Device management software provides dynamic status, statistics, and configuration information for switched products. Examples of commonly used network management tools are *CiscoView*, HP Openview, Solar Winds, and What's Up Gold.

Click the Knowledge Base button in the figure to see an example of a knowledge base website.

Knowledge Bases

On-line network device vendor knowledge bases have become indispensable sources of information. When vendor-based knowledge bases are combined with Internet search engines like Google, a network administrator has access to a vast pool of experience-based information.

The figure shows the Cisco **Tools & Resources** page found at http://www.cisco.com. This is a free tool providing information on Cisco-related hardware and software. It contains troubleshooting procedures, implementation guides, and original white papers on most aspects of networking technology.

Click the Baselining Tools button in the figure to see some examples of baselining tools.

Baselining Tools

Many tools for automating the network documentation and baselining process are available. These tools are available for Windows, Linux, AUX operating systems. The figure shows a screen capture of the SolarWinds LAN surveyor and CyberGauge software. Baselining tools help you with common baseling documentation tasks. For example they can help you draw network diagrams, help you to keep network software and hardware documentation up-to-date and help you to cost-effectively measure baseline network bandwidth use.

Click the Protocol Analyzer button in the figure to see an example of a typical protocol analyzer application.

Protocol Analyzers

A protocol analyzer decodes the various protocol layers in a recorded frame and presents this information in a relatively easy to use format. The figure shows a screen capture of the Wireshark protocol analyzer. The information displayed by a protocol analyzer includes, the physical, data link, protocol and descriptions for each frame. Most protocol analyzers can filter traffic that meets certain criteria so that, for example, all traffic to and from a particular device can be captured.

Hardware Troubleshooting Tools

Click the buttons in the figure to see examples of various hardware troubleshooting tools.

Network Analysis Module

A network analysis module (NAM) can be installed in Cisco Catalyst 6500 series switches and Cisco 7600 series routers to provide a graphical representation of traffic from local and remote switches and routers. The NAM is a embedded browser-based interface that generates reports on the traffic that consumes critical network resources. In addition, the NAM can capture and decode packets and track response times to pinpoint an application problem to the network or the server.

Digital Multimeters

Digital multimeters (DMMs) are test instruments that are used to directly measure electrical values of voltage, current, and resistance. In network troubleshooting, most of the multimedia tests involve checking power-supply voltage levels and verifying that network devices are receiving power.

Cable Testers

Cable testers are specialized, handheld devices designed for testing the various types of data communication cabling. Cabling testers can be used to detect broken wires, crossed-over wiring, shorted connections, and improperly paired connections. These devices can be inexpensive continuity testers, moderately priced data cabling testers, or expensive time-domain reflectometers (*TDRs*).

TDRs are used to pinpoint the distance to a break in a cable. These devices send signals along the cable and wait for them to be reflected. The time between sending the signal and receiving it back is converted into a distance measurement. The TDR function is normally packaged with data cabling testers. TDRs used to test fiber optic cables are known as optical time-domain reflectometers (OTDRs).

Cable Analyzers

Cable analyzers are multifunctional handheld devices that are used to test and certify copper and fiber cables for different services and standards. The more sophisticated tools include advanced troubleshooting diagnostics that measure distance to performance defect (NEXT, RL), identify corrective actions, and graphically display crosstalk and impedance behavior. Cable analyzers also typically include PC-based software. Once field data is collected the handheld device can upload its data and up-to-date and accurate reports can be created.

Portable *Network Analyzers*

Portable devices that are used for troubleshooting switched networks and VLANs. By plugging the network analyzer in anywhere on the network, a network engineer can see the switch port to which the device is connected and the average and peak utilization. The analyzer can also be used to discover VLAN configuration, identify top network talkers, analyze network traffic, and view interface details. The device can typically output to a PC that has network monitoring software installed for further analysis and troubleshooting.

Research Activity

The following are links to various troubleshooting tools.

Software Tools

Network Management Systems:

> http://www.ipswitch.com/products/whatsup/index.asp?t=demo
>
> http://www.solarwinds.com/products/network_tools.aspx

Baselining Tools:

> http://www.networkuptime.com/tools/enterprise/

Knowledge Bases:

> http://www.cisco.com

Protocol Analyzers:

> http://www.flukenetworks.com/fnet/en-us/products/OptiView+Protocol+Expert/

Hardware Tools

Cisco Network Analyzer Module (NAM):

> http://www.cisco.com/en/US/docs/net_mgmt/network_analysis_module_software/3.5/user/guide/user.html

Cable Testers:

> http://www.flukenetworks.com/fnet/en-us/products/CableIQ+Qualification+Tester/Demo.htm

Cable Analyzers:

> http://www.flukenetworks.com/fnet/en-us/products/DTX+CableAnalyzer+Series/Demo.htm

Network Analyzers:

> http://www.flukenetworks.com/fnet/en-us/products/OptiView+Series+III+Integrated+Network+Analyzer/Demos.htm

8.3 Common WAN Implementation Issues

8.3.1 WAN Communications

A communications provider or a *common carrier* normally owns the data links that make up a WAN. The links are made available to subscribers for a fee and are used to interconnect LANs or connect to remote networks. WAN data transfer speed (bandwidth) is considerably slower than the common LAN bandwidth. The charges for link provision are the major cost element, therefore the WAN implementation must aim to provide maximum bandwidth at acceptable cost. With user pressure to provide more service access at higher speeds and management pressure to contain cost, determining the optimal WAN configuration is not an easy task.

WANs carry a variety of traffic types, such as data, voice, and video. The design selected must provide adequate capacity and transit times to meet the requirements of the enterprise. Among other specifications, the design must consider the topology of the connections between the various sites, the nature of those connections, and bandwidth capacity.

Older WANs often consisted of data links directly connecting remote mainframe computers. Today's WANs connect geographically separated LANs. WAN technologies function at the lower three layers of the OSI reference model. End-user stations, servers, and routers communicate across LANs, and the WAN data links terminate at local routers.

Routers determine the most appropriate path to the destination of the data from the Network layer headers and transfer the packets to the appropriate data link connection for delivery on the physical connection. Routers can also provide quality of service (QoS) management, which allots priorities to the different traffic streams.

8.3.2 Steps in WAN Design

Businesses install WAN connectivity to meet the strategic business requirement of moving data between external branches. Because WAN connectivity is important to the business and expensive, you need to design the WAN in a systematic manner. This figure shows the WAN design steps.

Each time a modification to an existing WAN is considered, these steps should be followed. However, because many WANs have evolved over time, some of the guidelines discussed here may not have been considered. WAN modifications may arise from expanding the enterprise WAN servers or accommodating new work practices and business methods.

These are the steps for designing or modifying a WAN:

Step 1. Locate LANs - Establish the source and destination endpoints that will connect through the WAN.

Step 2. Analyze traffic - Know what data traffic must be carried, its origin, and its destination. WANs carry a variety of traffic types with varying requirements for bandwidth, latency, and jitter. For each pair of endpoints and for each traffic type, information is needed on the various traffic characteristics.

Step 3. Plan the topology - The topology is influenced by geographic considerations but also by requirements such as availability. A high requirement for availability requires extra links that provide alternative data paths for redundancy and load balancing.

Step 4. Estimate the required bandwidth - Traffic on the links may have varying requirements for latency and jitter.

Step 5. Choose the WAN technology - Suitable link technologies must be selected.

Step 6. Evaluate costs - When all the requirements are established, installation and operational costs for the WAN can be determined and compared with the business need driving the WAN implementation.

As shown in the figure, the design steps describe here are not a linear process. Several iterations of these steps may be necessary before a design is finalized. To maintain optimal performance of the WAN, continued monitoring and re-evaluation is required.

8.3.3 WAN Traffic Considerations

The table in the figure shows the wide variety of traffic types and their varying requirements of bandwidth, latency, and jitter that WAN links are required to carry.

To determine traffic flow conditions and timing of a WAN link, you need to analyze the traffic characteristics specific to each LAN that is connected to the WAN. Determining traffic characteristics may involve consulting the network users and evaluating their needs.

8.3.4 WAN Topology Considerations

After establishing LAN endpoints and traffic characteristics, the next step in implementing a WAN is to design a suitable topology. Designing a WAN topology essentially consists of the following:

Selecting an interconnection pattern or layout for the links between the various locations

Selecting the technologies for those links to meet the enterprise requirements at an acceptable cost

Click the buttons in the figure to view an example of each type of WAN topology.

Many WANs use a star topology. As the enterprise grows and new branches are added, the branches are connected back to the head office, producing a traditional star topology. Star endpoints are sometimes cross-connected, creating a mesh or partial mesh topology. This provides for many possible combinations for interconnections. When designing, re-evaluating, or modifying a WAN, a topology that meets the design requirements must be selected.

In selecting a layout, there are several factors to consider. More links increase the cost of the network services, but having multiple paths between destinations increases reliability. Adding more network devices to the data path increase latency and decreases reliability. Generally, each packet must be completely received at one node before it can be passed to the next.

Click the Hierarchical button in the figure.

When many locations must be joined, a hierarchical solution is recommended. For example, imagine an enterprise that is operational in every country of the European Union and has a branch in every town with a population over 10,000. Each branch has a LAN, and it has been decided to interconnect the branches. A mesh network is clearly not feasible because there would be hundreds of thousands of links.

The answer is to implement a hierarchical topology. Group the LANs in each area and interconnected them to form a region, interconnect the regions to form the core of the WAN. The area could be based on the number of locations to be connected with an upper limit of between 30 and 50. The area would have a star topology, with the hubs of the stars linked to form the region. Regions could be geographic, connecting between three and 10 areas, and the hub of each region could be linked point-to-point.

A three-layer hierarchy is often useful when the network traffic mirrors the enterprise branch structure and is divided into regions, areas, and branches. It is also useful when there is a central service to which all branches must have access but traffic levels are insufficient to justify direct connection of a branch to the service.

The LAN at the center of the area may have servers providing area-based as well as local service. Depending on the traffic volumes and types, the access connections may be dialup, leased, or frame relay. Frame Relay facilitates some meshing for redundancy without requiring additional physical connections. Distribution links could be Frame Relay or ATM, and the network core could be ATM or leased line.

When planning simpler networks, a hierarchical topology should still be considered because it may provide for better network scalability. The hub at the center of a two-layer model is also a core, but with no other core routers connected to it. Likewise, in a single-layer solution, the area hub serves as the regional hub and the core hub. This allows easy and rapid future growth because the basic design can be replicated to add new service areas.

WAN Connection Technologies

A typical private WAN uses a combination of technologies that are usually chosen based on traffic type and volume. ISDN, DSL, Frame Relay, or leased lines are used to connect individual branches into an area. Frame Relay, ATM, or leased lines are used to connect external areas back to the backbone. ATM or leased lines form the WAN backbone. Technologies that require the establishment of a connection before data can be transmitted, such as basic telephone, ISDN, or X.25, are not suitable for WANs that require rapid response time or low latency.

Different parts of an enterprise may be directly connected with leased lines, or they may be connected with an access link to the nearest point-of-presence (POP) of a shared network. Frame Relay and ATM are examples of shared networks. Leased lines are typically more expensive than access links but are available at virtually any bandwidth and provide very low latency and jitter.

ATM and Frame Relay networks carry traffic from several customers over the same internal links. The enterprise has no control over the number of links or hops that data must traverse in the shared network. It cannot control the time data must wait at each node before moving to the next link. This uncertainty in latency and jitter makes these technologies unsuitable for some types of network traffic. However, the disadvantages of a shared network may often be outweighed by the reduced cost. Because several customers are sharing the link, the cost to each is generally less than the cost of a direct link of the same capacity.

Although ATM is a shared network, it has been designed to produce minimal latency and jitter through high-speed internal links sending easily manageable units of data, called cells. ATM cells have a fixed length of 53 bytes, 48 bytes for data and 5 bytes for the header. ATM is widely used for carrying delay-sensitive traffic.

Frame Relay may also be used for delay-sensitive traffic, often using QoS mechanisms to give priority to the more sensitive data.

Many enterprise WANs have connections to the Internet. Although the Internet may pose a security problem it does provides an alternative for inter-branch traffic. Part of the traffic that must be considered during design is going to or coming from the Internet. Common implementations are to have each network in the company connect to a different ISP, or to have all company networks connect to a single ISP from a core layer connection.

8.3.5 WAN Bandwidth Considerations

Recall that a network supports the business needs of a company. Many companies rely on the high-speed transfer of data between remote locations. Consequently, higher bandwidth is crucial because it allows more data to be transmitted in a given time. When bandwidth is inadequate, competition between various types of traffic causes response times to increase, which reduces employee productivity and slows down critical web-based business processes.

The figure shows how WAN links are typically classified either high or low speed.

8.3.6 Common WAN Implementation Issues

The figure summarizes the common WAN implement issues and the questions you need to answer before you can effectively implement a WAN.

8.3.7 Case Study: WAN Troubleshooting from an ISP's Perspective

The graphic illustrates the typical questions that the technical support desk of an ISP should ask a customer that is calling for support.

A significant proportion of the support calls received by an ISP refer to slowness of the Network. To troubleshoot this effectively, you have to isolate the individual components and test each one as follows:

Individual PC host - A large number of user applications open on the PC at the same time may be responsible for the slowness that is being attributed to the Network. Tools like the Task Manager in a Windows PC can help determine CPU utilization.

LAN - If the customer has network monitoring software on their LAN, the network manager should be able to tell them whether the bandwidth on the LAN is frequently reaching 100 percent utilization. This is a problem that the customer company would need to solve internally. This is why a network baseline and an ongoing monitoring is so important.

Link from the edge of the user network to the edge of the ISP - Test the link from the customer edge router to the edge router of the ISP by asking the customer to log in to their router and send a hundred 1500 byte pings (stress pings) to the IP address of the ISP edge router. This problem is not something the customer can fix it is the ISP's responsibility to engage the link provider to fix this.

Backbone of the ISP - The ISP customer service representative can run stress pings from the ISP edge router to the edge router of the customer. They can also run stress pings across each link that customer traffic traverses. By isolating and testing each link, the ISP can determine which link is causing the problem.

Server being accessed - In some cases the slowness, being attributed to the network, may be caused by server congestion. This problem is the hardest to diagnose and it should be the last option pursued after all other options have been eliminated.

In this activity, you and another student will build the network displayed in the topology diagram. You will configure NAT, DHCP, and OSPF, and then verify connectivity. When the network is fully operational, one student will introduce several errors. Then the other student will use troubleshooting skills to isolate and solve the problem. Then the students will reverse roles and repeat the process. This activity can be done on real equipment or with Packet Tracer.

8.4 Network Troubleshooting

8.4.1 Interpreting Network Diagrams to Identify Problems

It is nearly impossible to troubleshoot any type of network connectivity issue without a network diagram that depicts IP addresses, IP routes, devices such as firewalls and switches, and so on. Generally, both logical and physical topologies aid in troubleshooting.

Physical Network Diagram

A physical network diagram shows the physical layout of the devices connected to the network. Knowing how devices are physically connected is necessary for troubleshooting problems at the Physical layer, such as cabling or hardware problems. Information recorded on the diagram typically includes:

- Device type
- Model and manufacturer
- Operating system version
- Cable type and identifier
- Cable specification
- Connector type
- Cabling endpoints

The figure shows an example of a physical network diagram that provides information about the physical location of the network devices, the types of cabling between them, and the cable identification numbers. This information would be primarily used for troubleshooting physical problems with devices or cabling. In addition to the physical network diagram, some administrators also include actual photographs of their wiring closets as part of their network documentation.

Logical Network Diagram

A logical network diagram shows how data is transferred on the network. Symbols are used to represent network elements such as routers, servers, hubs, hosts, VPN concentrators, and security devices. Information recorded on a logical network diagram may include:

- Device identifiers
- IP address and subnet
- Interface identifiers
- Connection type
- DLCI for virtual circuits
- Site-to-site VPNs
- Routing protocols
- Static routes
- Data-link protocols
- WAN technologies used

Click the Logical button in the figure to see an example of a logical network diagram.

The figure shows the same network but this time provides logical information such as specific device IP addresses, network numbers, port numbers, signal types, and DCE assignments for serial links. This information could be used for troubleshooting problems at all OSI layers.

8.4.2 Physical Layer Troubleshooting

Symptoms of Physical Layer Problems

> Refer to Figure in online course

The Physical layer transmits bits from one computer to another and regulates the transmission of a stream of bits over the physical medium. The Physical layer is the only layer with physically tangible properties, such as wires, cards, and antennas.

Failures and suboptimal conditions at the Physical layer not only inconvenience users but could impact the productivity of the entire company. Networks that experience these kinds of conditions usually come to a grinding halt. Because the upper layers of the OSI model depend on the Physical layer to function, a network technician must have the ability to effectively isolate and correct problems at this layer.

A Physical layer problem occurs when the physical properties of the connection are substandard, causing data to be transferred at a rate that is consistently less than the rate of data flow established in the baseline. If there is a problem with suboptimal operation at the Physical layer, the network may be operational, but performance is consistently or intermittently lower than the level specified in the baseline.

Common symptoms of network problems at the Physical layer include:

- *Performance lower than baseline* - If performance is unsatisfactory all the time, the problem is probably related to a poor configuration, inadequate capacity somewhere, or some other systemic problem. If performance varies and is not always unsatisfactory, the problem is probably related to an error condition or is being affected by traffic from other sources. The most common reasons for slow or poor performance include overloaded or underpowered servers, unsuitable switch or router configurations, traffic congestion on a low-capacity link, and chronic frame loss.

- *Loss of connectivity* - If a cable or device fails, the most obvious symptom is a loss of connectivity between the devices that communicate over that link or with the failed device or interface, as indicated by a simple ping test. Intermittent loss of connectivity could indicate a loose or oxidized connection.

- *High collision* counts - *Collision domain* problems affect the local medium and disrupt communications to Layer 2 or Layer 3 infrastructure devices, local servers, or services. Collisions are normally a more significant problem on shared media than on switch ports. Average collision counts on shared media should generally be below 5 percent, although that number is conservative. Be sure that judgments are based on the average and not a peak or spike in collisions. Collision-based problems may often be traced back to a single source. It may be a bad cable to a single station, a bad uplink cable on a hub or port on a hub, or a link that is exposed to external electrical noise. A noise source near a cable or hub can cause collisions even when there is no apparent traffic to cause them. If collisions get worse in direct proportion to the level of traffic, if the amount of collisions approaches 100 percent, or if there is no good traffic at all, the cable system may have failed.

- *Network bottlenecks or congestion* - If a router, interface, or cable fails, routing protocols may redirect traffic to other routes that are not designed to carry the extra capacity. This can result in congestion or bottlenecks in those parts of the network.

- *High CPU utilization rates* - High CPU utilization rates are a symptom that a device, such as a router, switch, or server, is operating at or exceeding its design limits. If not addressed quickly, CPU overloading can cause a device to shut down or fail.

- *Console error messages* - Error messages reported on the device console indicate a Physical layer problem.

Causes of Physical Layer Problems

Issues that commonly cause network problems at the Physical layer include:

Power-related

Power-related issues are the most fundamental reason for network failure. The main AC power flows into either an external or internal AC to DC transformer module within a device. The transformer provides correctly modulated DC current, which acts to power device circuits, connectors, ports, and the fans used for device cooling. If a power-related issue is suspected, a physical inspection of the power module is often carried out. Check the operation of the fans, and ensure that the chassis intake and exhaust vents are clear. If other nearby units have also powered down, suspect a power failure at the main power supply.

Hardware faults

Faulty network interface cards (*NICs*) can be the cause of network transmission errors due to late collisions, short frames, and *jabber*. Jabber is often defined as the condition in which a network device continually transmits random, meaningless data onto the network. Other likely causes of jabber are faulty or corrupt NIC driver files, bad cabling, or grounding problems.

Cabling faults

Many problems can be corrected by simply reseating cables that have become partially disconnected. When performing a physical inspection, look for damaged cables, improper cable types, and poorly crimped RJ-45s. Suspect cables should be tested or exchanged with a known functioning cable.

Check for connections between devices which incorrectly use crossover cables, or hub and switch ports that are incorrectly cabled using crossover cables. Split-pair cables either operate poorly or not at all, depending on the Ethernet speed used, the length of the split segment, and how far it is located from either end.

Problems with fiber-optic cables may be caused by dirty connectors, excessively tight bends, and swapped RX/TX connections when polarized.

Problems with coaxial cable often occur at the connectors. When the center conductor on the coaxial cable end is not straight and of the correct length, a good connection is not achieved.

Attenuation

An attenuated data bitstream is when the *amplitude* of the bits is reduced while traveling across a cable. If attenuation is severe, the receiving device cannot always successfully distinguish the component bits of the stream from each other. This ends in a garbled transmission and results in a request from the receiving device for retransmission of the missed traffic by the sender. Attenuation can be caused if a cable length exceeds the design limit for the media (for example, an Ethernet cable is limited to 100 meters (328 feet) for good performance), or when there is a poor connection resulting from a loose cable or dirty or oxidized contacts.

Noise

Local electromagnetic interference (*EMI*) is commonly known as noise. There are four types of noise that are most significant to data networks:

- Impulse noise that is caused by voltage fluctuations or current spikes induced on the cabling.

- Random (white) noise that is generated by many sources, such as *FM* radio stations, police radio, building security, and avionics for automated landing.

- Alien crosstalk, which is noise induced by other cables in the same pathway.

- Near end crosstalk (NEXT), which is noise originating from crosstalk from other adjacent cables or noise from nearby electric cables, devices with large electric motors, or anything that includes a transmitter more powerful than a cell phone.

Interface configuration errors

Many things can be misconfigured on an interface to cause it to go down, causing a loss of connectivity with attached network segments. Examples of configuration errors that affect the Physical layer include:

- Serial links reconfigured as asynchronous instead of synchronous
- Incorrect clock rate
- Incorrect clock source
- Interface not turned on

Exceeding design limits

A component may be operating suboptimally at the Physical layer because it is being utilized at a higher *average rate* than it is configured to operate. When troubleshooting this type of problem, it becomes evident that resources for the device are operating at or near the maximum capacity and there is an increase in the number of interface errors.

CPU overload

Symptoms include processes with high CPU utilization percentages, input queue drops, slow performance, router services such as Telnet and ping are slow or fail to respond, or there are no routing updates. One of the causes of CPU overload in a router is high traffic. If some interfaces are regularly overloaded with traffic, consider redesigning the traffic flow in the network or upgrading the hardware.

> Refer to Figure in online course

To isolate problems at the Physical layers do the following:

Check for bad cables or connections

Verify that the cable from the source interface is properly connected and is in good condition. Your cable tester might reveal an open wire. For example, in the figure, the Fluke CableIQ tester has revealed that wires 7 and 8 are displaying a fault. When doubting the integrity of a cable, swap suspect cables with a known working cable. If in doubt that the connection is good, remove the cable, do a physical inspection of both the cable and the interface, and then reseat the cable. Use a cable tester with suspect wall jacks to ensure that the jack is properly wired.

Check that the correct cabling standard is adhered to throughout the network

Verify that the proper cable is being used. A crossover cable may be required for direct connections between some devices. Ensure that the cable is correctly wired. For example, in the figure, the Fluke CableIQ meter has detected that although a cable was good for Fast Ethernet, it is not qualified to support 1000BASE-T because wires 7 and 8 were not correctly connected. These wires are not required for Fast Ethernet, but are required in *Gigabit* Ethernet.

Check that devices are cabled correctly

Check to make sure that all cables are connected to their correct ports or interfaces. Make sure that any cross-connects are properly patched to the correct location. This is where having a neat and organized wiring closet saves you a great deal of time.

Verify proper interface configurations

Check that all switch ports are set in the correct VLAN and that spanning-tree, speed, and duplex settings are correctly configured. Confirm that any active ports or interfaces are not shut down.

Check operational statistics and data error rates

Use Cisco `show` commands to check for statistics such as collisions and input and output errors. The characteristics of these statistics vary depending on the protocols used on the network.

8.4.3 Data Link Layer Troubleshooting

Symptoms of Data Link Layer Problems

Troubleshooting Layer 2 problems can be a challenging process. The configuration and operation of these protocols are critical to creating a functional, well-tuned network.

Data Link layer problems cause common symptoms that assist in identifying Layer 2 issues. Recognizing these symptoms helps narrow down the number of possible causes. Common symptoms of network problems at the Data Link layer include:

No functionality or connectivity at the Network layer or above

Some Layer 2 problems can stop the exchange of frames across a link, while others only cause network performance to degrade.

Network is operating below baseline performance levels

There are two distinct types of suboptimal Layer 2 operation that can occur in a network:

- Frames take an illogical path to their destination but do arrive. An example of a problem which could cause frames to take a suboptimal path is a poorly designed Layer 2 spanning-tree topology. In this case, the network might experience high-bandwidth usage on links that should not have that level of traffic.

- Some frames are dropped. These problems can be identified through error counter statistics and console error messages that appear on the switch or router. In an Ethernet environment, an extended or continuous ping also reveals if frames are being dropped.

Excessive broadcasts

Modern operating systems use broadcasts extensively to discover network services and other hosts. Where excessive broadcasts are observed, it is important to identify the source of the broadcasts. Generally, excessive broadcasts result from one of the following situations:

- Poorly programmed or configured applications
- Large Layer 2 *broadcast domains*
- Underlying network problems, such as STP loops or route *flapping*.

Console messages

In some instances, a router recognizes that a Layer 2 problem has occurred and sends alert messages to the console. Typically, a router does this when it detects a problem with interpreting incoming frames (encapsulation or framing problems) or when keepalives are expected but do not arrive. The most common console message that indicates a Layer 2 problem is a line protocol down message.

Causes of Data Link Layer Problems

Issues at the Data Link layer that commonly result in network connectivity or performance problems include:

Encapsulation errors

An encapsulation error occurs because the bits placed in a particular field by the sender are not what the receiver expects to see. This condition occurs when the encapsulation at one end of a WAN link is configured differently from the encapsulation used at the other end.

Address mapping errors

In topologies such as point-to-multipoint, Frame Relay, or broadcast Ethernet, it is essential that an appropriate Layer 2 destination address be given to the frame. This ensures its arrival at the correct destination. To achieve this, the network device must match a destination Layer 3 address with the correct Layer 2 address using either static or dynamic maps.

When using static maps in Frame Relay, an incorrect map is a common mistake. Simple configuration errors can result in a mismatch of Layer 2 and Layer 3 addressing information.

In a dynamic environment, the mapping of Layer 2 and Layer 3 information can fail for the following reasons:

- Devices may have been specifically configured not to respond to ARP or Inverse-ARP requests.
- The Layer 2 or Layer 3 information that is cached may have physically changed.
- Invalid ARP replies are received because of a misconfiguration or a security attack.

Framing errors

Frames usually work in groups of 8 bit bytes. A framing error occurs when a frame does not end on an 8-bit byte boundary. When this happens, the receiver may have problems determining where one frame ends and another frame starts. Depending on the severity of the framing problem, the interface may be able to interpret some of the frames. Too many invalid frames may prevent valid keepalives from being exchanged.

Framing errors can be caused by a noisy serial line, an improperly designed cable (too long or not properly shielded), or an incorrectly configured channel service unit (CSU) line clock.

STP failures or loops

The purpose of Spanning Tree Protocol (STP) is to resolve a redundant physical topology into a tree-like topology by blocking redundant ports. Most STP problems revolve around these issues:

- Forwarding loops that occur when no port in a redundant topology is blocked and traffic is forwarded in circles indefinitely. When the forwarding loop starts, it usually congests the lowest bandwidth links along its path. If all the links are of the same bandwidth, all links are congested. This congestion causes packet loss and leads to a downed network in the affected L2 domain.

- Excessive flooding because of a high rate of STP topology changes. The role of the topology change mechanism is to correct Layer 2 forwarding tables after the forwarding topology has changed. This is necessary to avoid a connectivity outage because, after a topology change, some MAC addresses previously accessible through particular ports might become accessible through different ports. A topology change should be a rare event in a well-configured network. When a link on a switch port goes up or down, there is eventually a topology change when the STP state of the port is changing to or from forwarding. However, when a port is flapping (oscillating between up and down states), this causes repetitive topology changes and flooding.

- Slow STP convergence or reconvergence, which can be caused by a mismatch between the real and documented topology, a configuration error, such as an inconsistent configuration of STP timers, an overloaded switch CPU during convergence, or a software defect.

Troubleshooting Layer 2 - PPP

The difficulty in troubleshooting Layer 2 technologies, such as PPP and Frame Relay, is the unavailability of common Layer 3 troubleshooting tools, such as ping, to assist with anything but the identification that the network is down. It is only through a thorough understanding of the protocols and their operation that a network technician is able to choose the appropriate troubleshooting methodology and Cisco IOS commands to solve the problem in an efficient manner.

Most of the problems that occur with PPP involve link negotiation. The steps for troubleshooting PPP are as follows:

Step 1. Check that the appropriate encapsulation is in use at both ends, using the `show interfaces serial` command. In the figure for Step 1, the command output reveals that R2 has been incorrectly configured to use HDLC encapsulation.

Step 2. Confirm that the Link Control Protocol (LCP) negotiations have succeeded by checking the output for the LCP Open message.

Click the Step 2 button in the figure.

In the figure, the encapsulation on R2 has been changed to PPP. The output of the `show interfaces serial` command shows the LCP Open message, which indicates that the LCP negotiations have succeeded.

Step 3. Verify authentication on both sides of the link using the `debug ppp authentication` command.

Click the Step 3 button in the figure.

In the figure, the output of the `debug ppp authentication` command shows that R1 is unable to authenticate R2 using CHAP, because the username and password for R2 have not been configured on R1.

Refer to Chapter 2, "PPP" for further details on troubleshooting PPP implementations.

Troubleshooting Layer 2 - Frame Relay

Troubleshooting Frame Relay network issues can be broken down into four steps:

Step 1. Verify the physical connection between the CSU/data service unit (DSU) and the router. In the figure, the physical connections between the routers R2 and R3 and their corresponding CSU/DSU can be verified using a cable tester and by verifying that all status LEDs on the CSU/DSU unit are green. In the figure, some of the status lights for the CSU/DSU at R3 are red, indicating a potential connectivity problem between the CSU/DSU and router R3.

Step 2. Verify that the router and Frame Relay provider are properly exchanging LMI information by using the `show frame-relay lmi` command.

Click the Step 2 button in the figure.

In the figure, the output of the `show frame-relay lmi` command at R2 shows no errors or lost messages. This indicates that R2 and the Frame Relay provider switch are properly exchanging LMI information.

Step 3. Verify that the PVC status is active by using the `show frame-relay pvc` command.

Click the Step 3 button in the figure.

In the figure, the output of the `show frame-relay pvc` command at R2 verifies that the PVC status is active.

Step 4. Verify that the Frame Relay encapsulation matches on both routers with the `show interfaces serial` command.

Click the Step 4 button in the figure.

In the figure, the output of the `show interfaces serial` command at routers R2 and R3 shows that there is an encapsulation mismatch between them. R3 has been incorrectly configured to use HDLC encapsulation instead of Frame Relay.

For further details on troubleshooting Frame Relay implementations, see Chapter 3, "Frame Relay".

Troubleshooting Layer 2 - STP Loops

If you suspect that an STP loop is causing a Layer 2 problem, verify if the Spanning Tree Protocol is running on each of the switches. A switch should only have STP disabled if it is not part of a physically looped topology. To verify STP operation, use the `show spanning-tree` command on each switch. If you discover that STP is not operating, you can enable it using the `spanning-tree vlan ID` command.

Use these steps to troubleshoot forwarding loops:

Step 1. Identify that an STP loop is occurring.

When a forwarding loop has developed in the network, these are the usual symptoms:

- Loss of connectivity to, from, and through the affected network regions
- High CPU utilization on routers connected to affected segments or VLANs
- High link utilization (often 100 percent)
- High switch *backplane* utilization (compared to the baseline utilization)
- Syslog messages that indicate packet looping in the network (for example, *Hot Standby Router Protocol* duplicate IP address messages)
- Syslog messages that indicate constant address relearning or MAC address flapping messages
- Increasing number of output drops on many interfaces

Step 2. Discover the topology (scope) of the loop.

The highest priority is to stop the loop and restore network operation. To stop the loop, you must know which ports are involved. Look at the ports with the highest link utilization (packets per second). The `show interface` command displays the utilization for each interface. Make sure that you record this information before proceeding to the next step. Otherwise, it could be difficult later on to determine the cause of the loop.

Step 3. Break the loop.

Shut down or disconnect the involved ports one at a time. After you disable or disconnect each port, check whether the switch backplane utilization is back to a normal level. Document your findings. Keep in mind that some ports may not be sustaining the loop but rather are flooding the traffic arriving with the loop. When you shut down such flooding ports, you only reduce backplane utilization a small amount, but you do not stop the loop.

Step 4. Find and fix the cause of the loop.

Determining why the loop began is often the most difficult part of the process, because the reasons can vary. It is also difficult to formalize an exact procedure that works in every case. First, investigate the topology diagram to find a redundant path.

For every switch on the redundant path, check for these issues:

- Does the switch know the correct STP root?
- Is the root port identified correctly?
- Are Bridge Protocol Data Units (*BPDUs*) received regularly on the root port and on ports that are supposed to be blocking?
- Are BPDUs sent regularly on non-root, designated ports?

Step 5. Restore the redundancy.

After the device or link that is causing the loop has been found and the problem has been resolved, restore the redundant links that were disconnected.

We have only touched lightly on the subject of troubleshooting STP loops. Troubleshooting loops and other STP problems is complex, and a detailed discussion is beyond the scope of this course. However, if you want to learn more about troubleshooting STP problems, an excellent techinical note is available at: http://cisco.com/en/US/tech/tk389/tk621/technologies_tech_note09186a0080136673.shtml#troubleshoot.

8.4.4 Network Layer Troubleshooting

Symptoms of Network Layer Problems

Network layer problems include any problem that involves a Layer 3 protocol, both routed protocols and routing protocols. This topic focuses primarily on IP routing protocols.

Problems at the Network layer can cause network failure or suboptimal performance. Network failure is when the network is nearly or completely nonfunctional, affecting all users and applications using the network. These failures are usually noticed quickly by users and network administrators, and are obviously critical to the productivity of a company. Network optimization problems usually involve a subset of users, applications, destinations, or a particular type of traffic. Optimization issues in general can be more difficult to detect and even harder to isolate and diagnose because they usually involve multiple layers or even the host computer itself. Determining that the problem is a Network layer problem can take time.

Troubleshooting Layer 3 Problems

In most networks, static routes are used in combination with dynamic routing protocols. Improper configuration of static routes can lead to less than optimal routing and, in some cases, create routing loops or parts of the network to become unreachable.

Troubleshooting dynamic routing protocols requires a thorough understanding of how the specific routing protocol functions. Some problems are common to all routing protocols, while other problems are particular to the individual routing protocol.

There is no single template for solving Layer 3 problems. Routing problems are solved with a methodical process, using a series of commands to isolate and diagnose the problem.

Here are some areas to explore when diagnosing a possible problem involving routing protocols:

General network issues

Often a change in the topology, such as a down link, may have other affects on other areas of the network that might not be obvious at the time. This may include the installation of new routes, static or dynamic, removal of other routes, and so on.

Some of the things to consider include:

- Has anything in the network changed recently?
- Is there anyone currently working on the network infrastructure?

Connectivity issues

Check for any equipment and connectivity problems, including power problems such as outages and environmental problems such as overheating. Also check for Layer 1 problems, such as cabling problems, bad ports, and ISP problems.

Neighbor issues

If the routing protocol establishes an adjacency with a neighbor, check to see if there are any problems with the routers forming neighbor relationships.

Topology database

If the routing protocol uses a topology table or database, check the table for anything unexpected, such as missing entries or unexpected entries.

Routing table

Check the routing table for anything unexpected, such as missing routes or unexpected routes. Use **debug** commands to view routing updates and routing table maintenance.

8.4.5 Transport Layer Troubleshooting

Common Access List Issues

Network problems can arise from Transport layer problems on the router, particularly at the edge of the network where security technologies are examining and modifying the traffic. This topic discusses two of the most commonly implemented Transport layer security technologies. They are access control lists (ACLs) and Network Address Translation (NAT).

Click the Access List Issues button in the figure.

The most common issues with ACLs are caused by improper configuration. There are eight areas where misconfigurations commonly occur:

Selection of traffic flow

The most common router misconfiguration is applying the ACL to incorrect traffic. Traffic is defined by both the router interface through which the traffic is traveling and the direction in which this traffic is traveling. An ACL must be applied to the correct interface, and the correct traffic direction must be selected to function properly. If the router is running both ACLs and NAT, the order in which each of these technologies is applied to a traffic flow is important:

- Inbound traffic is processed by the inbound ACL before being processed by outside-to-inside NAT.
- Outbound traffic is processed by the outbound ACL after being processed by inside-to-outside NAT.

Order of access control elements

The elements in an ACL should be from specific to general. Although, an ACL may have an element to specifically permit a particular traffic flow, packets will never match that element if they are being denied by another element earlier in the list.

Implicit deny all

In a situation where high security is not required on the ACL, forgetting about this implicit access control element may be the cause of an ACL misconfiguration.

Addresses and wildcard masks

Complex wildcard masks provide significant improvements in efficiency, but are more subject to configuration errors. An example of a complex wildcard mask is using the address 10.0.32.0 and wildcard mask 0.0.32.15 to select the first 15 *host addresses* in either the 10.0.0.0 network or the 10.0.32.0 network.

Selection of Transport layer protocol

When configuring ACLs, it is important that only the correct Transport layer protocols be specified. Many network engineers, when unsure if a particular traffic flow uses a TCP port or a UDP port, configure both. Specifying both opens a hole through the firewall, possibly giving intruders an avenue into the network. It also introduces an extra element into the ACL, so the ACL takes longer to process, introducing more latency into network communications.

Source and destination ports

Properly controlling the traffic between two hosts requires symmetric access control elements for inbound and outbound ACLs. Address and port information for traffic generated by a replying host is the mirror image of address and port information for traffic generated by the initiating host.

Use of the `established` keyword

The `established` keyword increases the security provided by an ACL. However, if the keyword is applied to an outbound ACL, unexpected results may occur.

Uncommon protocols

Misconfigured ACLs often cause problems for less common protocols than TCP and UDP. Uncommon protocols that are gaining popularity are VPN and encryption protocols.

Troubleshooting Access Control Lists

A useful command for viewing ACL operation is the `log` keyword on ACL entries. This keyword instructs the router to place an entry in the system log whenever that entry condition is matched. The logged event includes details of the packet that matched the ACL element.

The `log` keyword is especially useful for troubleshooting and also provides information on intrusion attempts being blocked by the ACL.

Refer to Figure in online course

Common NAT Issues

The biggest problem with all NAT technologies is interoperability with other network technologies, especially those that contain or derive information from host network addressing in the packet. Some of these technologies include:

- *BOOTP and DHCP -* Both protocols manage the automatic assignment of IP addresses to clients. Recall that the first packet that a new client sends is a DHCP-Request broadcast IP packet. The DHCP-Request packet has a source IP address of 0.0.0.0. Because NAT requires both a valid destination and source IP address, BOOTP and DHCP can have difficulty operating over a router running either static or dynamic NAT. Configuring the IP helper feature can help solve this problem.

- *DNS and WINS* - Because a router running dynamic NAT is changing the relationship between inside and outside addresses regularly as table entries expire and are recreated, a DNS or WINS server outside the NAT router does not have an accurate representation of the network inside the router. Configuring the IP helper feature can help solve this problem.

- *SNMP* - Similar to DNS packets, NAT is not able to alter the addressing information stored in the data payload of the packet. Because of this, an SNMP management station on one side of a NAT router may not be able to contact SNMP agents on the other side of the NAT router. Configuring the IP helper feature can help solve this problem.

- *Tunneling and encryption protocols* - Encryption and tunneling protocols often require that traffic be sourced from a specific UDP or TCP port, or use a protocol at the Transport layer that cannot be processed by NAT. For example, IPsec tunneling protocols and generic routing encapsulation protocols used by VPN implementations cannot be processed by NAT. If encryption or tunneling protocols must be run through a NAT router, the network administrator can create a static NAT entry for the required port for a single IP address on the inside of the NAT router.

If encryption or tunneling protocols must be run through a NAT router, the network administrator can create a static NAT entry for the required port for a single IP address on the inside of the NAT router.

One of the more common NAT configuration errors is forgetting that NAT affects both inbound and outbound traffic. An inexperienced network administrator might configure a static NAT entry to redirect inbound traffic to a specific inside backup host. This static NAT statement also changes the source address of traffic from that host, possibly resulting in undesirable and unexpected behaviors or in suboptimal operation.

Improperly configured timers can also result in unexpected network behavior and suboptimal operation of dynamic NAT. If NAT timers are too short, entries in the NAT table may expire before replies are received, so packets are discarded. The loss of packets generates retransmissions, consuming more bandwidth. If timers are too long, entries may stay in the NAT table longer than necessary, consuming the available connection pool. In busy networks, this may lead to memory problems on the router, and hosts may be unable to establish connections if the dynamic NAT table is full.

Refer to Chapter 7, "IP Addressing Services" for further details on troubleshooting NAT configuration.

8.4.6 Application Layer Troubleshooting

Application Layer Overview

> Refer to Figure in online course

Most of the Application layer protocols provide user services. Application layer protocols are typically used for network management, file transfer, distributed file services, terminal emulation, and e-mail. However, new user services are often added, such as VPNs, VoIP, and so on.

The most widely known and implemented TCP/IP Application layer protocols include:

- *Telnet* - Enables users to establish terminal session connections with remote hosts.

- *HTTP* - Supports the exchanging of text, graphic images, sound, video, and other multimedia files on the web.

- *FTP* - Performs interactive file transfers between hosts.

- *TFTP* - Performs basic interactive file transfers typically between hosts and networking devices.
- *SMTP* - Supports basic message delivery services.
- *POP* - Connects to mail servers and downloads e-mail.
- *Simple Network Management Protocol (SNMP)* - Collects management information from network devices.
- *DNS* - Maps IP addresses to the names assigned to network devices.
- *Network File System (NFS)* - Enables computers to mount drives on remote hosts and operate them as if they were local drives. Originally developed by Sun Microsystems, it combines with two other Application layer protocols, external data representation (XDR) and remote-procedure call (*RPC*), to allow transparent access to remote network resources.

Click the Application Protocols and Ports button in the figure to view a list of application protocols and their associated ports.

Symptoms of Application Layer Problems

Application layer problems prevent services from being provided to application programs. A problem at the Application layer can result in unreachable or unusable resources when the Physical, Data Link, Network, and Transport layers are functional. It is possible to have full network connectivity, but the application simply cannot provide data.

Another type of problem at the Application layer occurs when the Physical, Data Link, Network, and Transport layers are functional, but the data transfer and requests for network services from a single network service or application do not meet the normal expectations of a user.

A problem at the Application layer may cause users to complain that the network or the particular application that they are working with is sluggish or slower than usual when transferring data or requesting network services.

The figure shows some of the possible symptoms of Application layer problems.

Troubleshooting Application Layer Problems

The same general troubleshooting process that is used to isolate problems at the lower layers can also be used to isolate problems at the Application layer. The concepts are the same, but the technological focus has shifted to involve things such as refused or timed out connections, access lists, and DNS issues.

The steps for troubleshooting Application layer problems are as follows:

Step 1. Ping the default gateway.

If successful, Layer 1 and Layer 2 services are functioning properly.

Step 2. Verify end-to-end connectivity.

Use an extended ping if attempting the ping from a Cisco router. If successful, Layer 3 is operating correctly. If Layers 1-3 are functioning properly, the issue must exist at a higher layer.

Step 3. Verify access list and NAT operation.

To troubleshoot access control lists, use the following steps:

- Use the **show access-list** command. Are there any ACLs that could be stopping traffic? Notice which access lists have matches.

- Clear the access-list counters with the `clear access-list counters` command and try to establish a connection again.
- Verify the access-list counters. Have any increased? Should they increase?

To troubleshoot NAT, use the following steps:

- Use the `show ip nat translations` command. Are there any translations? Are the translations as expected?
- Clear the NAT translations with the `clear ip nat translation *` command and try to access the external resource again.
- Use the `debug ip nat` command and examine the output.
- Look at the running configuration file. Are the `ip nat inside` and `ip nat outside` commands located on the right interfaces? Is the NAT pool correctly configured? Is the ACL correctly identifying the hosts?

If the ACLs and NAT are functioning as expected, the problem must lie in a higher layer.

Step 4. Troubleshoot upper layer protocol connectivity.

Even though there may be IP connectivity between a source and a destination, problems may still exist for a specific upper layer protocol, such as FTP, HTTP, or Telnet. These protocols ride on top of the basic IP transport but are subject to protocol-specific problems relating to packet filters and firewalls. It is possible that everything except mail works between a given source and destination.

Troubleshooting an upper layer protocol connectivity problem requires understanding the process of the protocol. This information is usually found in the latest RFC for the protocol or on the developer web page.

Correcting Application Layer Problems

The steps for correcting Application layer problems are as follows:

Step 1: Make a backup. Before proceeding, ensure that a valid configuration has been saved for any device on which the configuration may be modified. This provides for recovery to a known initial state.

Step 2: Make an initial hardware or software configuration change. If the correction requires more than one change, make only one change at a time.

Step 3: Evaluate and document each change and its results. If the results of any problem-solving steps are unsuccessful, immediately undo the changes. If the problem is intermittent, wait to see if the problem occurs again before evaluating the effect of any change.

Step 4: Determine if the change solves the problem. Verify that the change actually resolves the problem without introducing any new problems. The network should be returned to the baseline operation, and no new or old symptoms should be present. If the problem is not solved, undo all the changes. If new or additional problems are discovered, modify the correction plan.

Step 5: Stop when the problem is solved. Stop making changes when the original problem appears to be solved.

Step 6: If necessary, get assistance from outside resources. This may be a co-worker, a consultant, or Cisco Technical Assistance Center (*TAC*). On rare occasions, a core dump may be necessary, which creates output that a specialist at Cisco Systems can analyze.

Step 7: Document. Once the problem is resolved, document the solution.

Refer to Packet Tracer Activity for this chapter

To successfully complete this activity, you need your final documentation for the PT Activity 8.1.2: Network Discovery and Documentation you completed previously in this chapter. This documentation should have an accurate topology diagram and addressing table. If you do not have this documentation, then ask your Instructor for accurate versions.

Detailed instructions are provided within the activity as well as in the PDF link below.

Activity Instructions (PDF)

8.5 Chapter Labs

8.5.1 Troubleshooting Enterprise Networks 1

Refer to Lab Activity for this chapter

You have been asked to correct configuration errors in the company network. For this lab, do not use login or password protection on any console lines to prevent accidental lockout. Use **ciscoccna** for all passwords in this scenario.

Note: Because this lab is cumulative, you will be using all the knowledge and troubleshooting techniques that you have acquired from the previous material to successfully complete this lab.

Refer to Packet Tracer Activity for this chapter

This activity is a variation of Lab 8.5.1. Packet Tracer may not support all the tasks specified in the hands-on lab. This activity should not be considered equivalent to completing the hands-on lab. Packet Tracer is not a substitute for a hands-on lab experience with real equipment.

Detailed instructions are provided within the activity as well as in the PDF link below.

Activity Instructions (PDF)

8.5.2 Troubleshooting Enterprise Networks 2

Refer to Lab Activity for this chapter

For this lab, do not use login or password protection on any console lines to prevent accidental lockout. Use **ciscoccna** for all passwords in this lab.

Note: Because this lab is cumulative, you will be using all the knowledge and troubleshooting techniques that you have acquired from the previous material to successfully complete this lab.

Refer to Packet Tracer Activity for this chapter

This activity is a variation of Lab 8.5.2. Packet Tracer may not support all the tasks specified in the hands-on lab. This activity should not be considered equivalent to completing the hands-on lab. Packet Tracer is not a substitute for a hands-on lab experience with real equipment.

Detailed instructions are provided within the activity as well as in the PDF link below.

Activity Instructions (PDF)

8.5.3 Troubleshooting Enterprise Networks 3

Refer to Lab Activity for this chapter

For this lab do not use login or password protection on any console lines to prevent accidental lockout. Use ciscoccna for all passwords in this scenario.

Note: Because this lab is cumulative, you will be using all the knowledge and troubleshooting techniques that you have acquired from the previous material to successfully complete this lab.

Refer to Packet Tracer Activity for this chapter

This activity is a variation of Lab 8.5.3. Packet Tracer may not support all the tasks specified in the hands-on lab. This activity should not be considered equivalent to completing the hands-on lab. Packet Tracer is not a substitute for a hands-on lab experience with real equipment.

Detailed instructions are provided within the activity as well as in the PDF link below.

Activity Instructions (PDF)

Chapter Summary

In this chapter, you learned that a network baseline is required for effective troubleshooting. Creating a baseline begins with ensuring that network documentation is up to date and accurate. Proper network documentation includes a network configuration table for all devices and a topology diagram that reflects the current state of the network. When the network has been fully documented, a baseline measurement of network performance should be carried out over a period of several weeks to a month to establish the personality of the network. The first baseline is created during a time of stable and normal operation.

The most effective way to troubleshoot is with a systematic approach using a layered model, such as the OSI model or the TCP/IP model. Three methods commonly used to troubleshoot include bottom up, top down, and divide and conquer. Each method has its advantages and disadvantages, and you learned the guidelines for choosing which method to apply. You also learned about the various software and hardware tools that are used by network professionals to gather symptoms and troubleshoot network problems.

Although they operate primarily at the first three OSI layers, WANs have implementation issues that can affect the operation of the rest of the network. You learned about some of the considerations for implementing WANs and common problems that WANs introduce into networks, such as security threats, bandwidth problems, latency, and QoS issues.

Finally, you explored the symptoms and causes of common problems at each of the OSI layers and the steps for troubleshooting them.

CYU

In this comprehensive CCNA skills activity, the XYZ Corporation uses a combination of Frame Relay and PPP for WAN connections. The HQ router provides access to the server farm and the Internet through NAT. HQ also uses a basic firewall ACL to filter inbound traffic. Each Branch router is configured for inter-VLAN routing and DHCP. Routing is achieved through EIGRP as well as static and default routes. The VLANs, VTP, and STP are configured on each of the switched networks. Port security is enabled and wireless access is provided. Your job is to successfully implement all of these technologies, leveraging what you have learned over the four Exploration courses leading up to this culminating activity.

Detailed instructions are provided within the activity as well as in the PDF link below.

Activity Instructions (PDF)

Chapter Quiz

Take the chapter quiz to test your knowledge.

Your Chapter Notes

Glossary

10 Mbps
10 million bits per second
A unit of information transfer rate. Ethernet carries 10 Mbps.

100BASE-FX
100-Mbps baseband Fast Ethernet specification using two strands of multimode fiber-optic cable per link. To guarantee proper signal timing, a 100BASE-FX link cannot exceed 1310 feet (400 m) in length. Based on the IEEE 802.3 standard.

100BASE-T
100-Mbps baseband Fast Ethernet specification using UTP wiring. Like the 10BASE-T technology on which it is based, 100BASE-T sends link pulses over the network segment when no traffic is present. However, these link pulses contain more information than those used in 10BASE-T. Based on the IEEE 802.3 standard.

100BASE-T4
100-Mbps baseband Fast Ethernet specification using four pairs of Category 3, 4, or 5 UTP wiring. To guarantee proper signal timing, a 100BASE-T4 segment cannot exceed 325 feet (100 m) in length. Based on the IEEE 802.3 standard.

100BASE-TX
100-Mbps baseband Fast Ethernet specification using two pairs of either UTP or STP wiring. The first pair of wires is used to receive data; the second is used to transmit. To guarantee proper signal timing, a 100BASE-TX segment cannot exceed 325 feet (100 m) in length. Based on the IEEE 802.3 standard.

100BASE-X
100-Mbps baseband Fast Ethernet specification that refers to the 100BASE-FX and 100BASE-TX standards for Fast Ethernet over fiber-optic cabling. Based on the IEEE 802.3 standard.

100VG-AnyLAN
100-Mbps Fast Ethernet and Token Ring media technology using four pairs of Category 3, 4, or 5 UTP cabling. This high-speed transport technology, developed by Hewlett-Packard, can be made to operate on existing 10BASE-T Ethernet networks. Based on the IEEE 802.12 standard.

10BASE2
10-Mbps baseband Ethernet specification using 50-ohm thin coaxial cable. 10BASE2, which is part of the IEEE 802.3 specification, has a distance limit of 600 feet (185 m) per segment.

10BASE5
10-Mbps baseband Ethernet specification using standard (thick) 50-ohm baseband coaxial cable. 10BASE5, which is part of the IEEE 802.3 baseband physical layer specification, has a distance limit of 1640 feet (500 m) per segment.

10BASE-F
10-Mbps baseband Ethernet specification that refers to the 10BASE-FB, 10BASE-FL, and 10BASE-FP standards for Ethernet over fiber-optic cabling.

10BASE-FB
10-Mbps baseband Ethernet specification using fiber-optic cabling. 10BASE-FB is part of the IEEE 10BASE-F specification. It is not used to connect user stations, but instead provides a synchronous signaling backbone that allows additional segments and repeaters to be connected to the network. 10BASE-FB segments can be up to 6560 feet (2000 m) long.

10BASE-FL
10-Mbps baseband Ethernet specification using fiber-optic cabling. 10BASE-FL is part of the IEEE 10BASE-F specification and, while able to interoperate with FOIRL, is designed to replace the FOIRL specification. 10BASE-FL segments can be up to 3280 feet (1000 m) long if used with FOIRL, and up to 6560 feet (2000 m) if 10BASE-FL is used exclusively.

10BASE-FP
10-Mbps fiber-passive baseband Ethernet specification using fiber-optic cabling. 10BASE-FP is part of the IEEE 10BASE-F specification. It organizes a number of computers into a star topology without the use of repeaters. 10BASE-FP segments can be up to 1640 feet (500 m) long.

10BASE-T
10-Mbps baseband Ethernet specification using two pairs of twisted-pair cabling (Category 3, 4, or 5): one pair for transmitting data and the other for receiving data. 10BASE-T, which is part of the IEEE 802.3 specification, has a distance limit of approximately 328 feet (100 m) per segment.

10Broad36
10-Mbps broadband Ethernet specification using broadband coaxial cable. 10Broad36, which is part of the IEEE 802.3 specification, has a distance limit of 11810 feet (3600 m) per segment.

370 block mux channel
See block multiplexer channel.

4B/5B local fiber
4-byte/5-byte local fiber
Fiber channel physical media used for FDDI and ATM. Supports speeds of up to 100 Mbps over multimode fiber.

4-byte/5-byte local fiber
See 4B/5B local fiber.

500-CS
500 series communication server
Cisco multiprotocol communication server that combines the capabilities of a terminal server, a telecommuting server, a protocol translator, and an asynchronous router in one unit.

6to4
Common transition mechanism to enable a smooth integration of IPv4 to IPv6. This mechanism uses the reserved prefix 2002::/16 to allow an IPv4 Internet-connected site to create and use a /48 IPv6 prefix based on a single globally routable or reachable IPv4 address. 6to4 is also known as 6to4 tunneling.

8B/10B local fiber
8-byte/10-byte local fiber
Fiber channel physical media that supports speeds up to 149.76 Mbps over multimode fiber.

8-byte/10-byte local fiber
See 8B/10B local fiber.

AAA
Authentication, Authorization, and Accounting
AAA is a protocol, specified in RFC 2903 and several other RFCs, for specifying who can access a system or network, how they can access it, and what they did while they were connected.

ABR
1) available bit rate. QOS class defined by the ATM Forum for ATM networks. ABR is used for connections that do not require timing relationships between source and destination. ABR provides no guarantees in terms of cell loss or delay, providing only best-effort service. Traffic sources adjust their transmission rate in response to information they receive describing the status of the network and its capability to successfully deliver data. Compare with CBR, UBR, and VBR.
2) area border router. Router located on the border of one or more OSPF areas that connects those areas to the backbone network. ABRs are considered members of both the OSPF backbone and the attached areas. They therefore maintain routing tables describing both the backbone topology and the topology of the other areas.

absorption
Absorption is the physical phenomenon that occurs when radio frequency waves are absorbed by objects such as walls.

Abstract Syntax Notation One
See ASN1.

AC
alternating current
Electrical current that reverses its direction regularly and continually. It is the form of electrical power found in residential and commercial buildings.

access card

I/O card in the LightStream 2020 ATM switch. Together with their associated line cards, access cards provide data transfer services for a switch using physical interfaces such as OC-3c. A LightStream 2020 switch can have up to 10 access cards.

Access card is also known as a paddle card.

access control list

List kept by Cisco routers to control access to or from the router for a number of services (for example, to prevent packets with a certain IP address from leaving a particular interface on the router).

access gateway

A gateway that supports both bearer traffic and signaling traffic. For example, a gateway that terminates ISDN is an access gateway.

access method

1) Generally, the way in which network devices access the network medium.
2) Software within an SNA processor that controls the flow of information through a network.

access point

See AP.

access server

Communications processor that connects asynchronous devices to a LAN or WAN through network and terminal emulation software. Performs both synchronous and asynchronous routing of supported protocols. Sometimes called a network access server. Compare with communication server.

accounting management

One of five categories of network management defined by ISO for management of OSI networks. Accounting management subsystems are responsible for collecting network data relating to resource usage.

ACK

acknowledgment
Notification sent from one network device to another to acknowledge that some event (for example, receipt of a message) has occurred. Compare to NAK.

acknowledgment

See ACK.

acknowledgment number

Next expected TCP octet.

ACL

Access Control List
List kept by Cisco routers to control access to or from the router for a number of services (for example, to prevent packets with a certain IP address from leaving a particular interface on the router).

ACR

allowed cell rate
Parameter defined by the ATM Forum for ATM traffic management. ACR varies between the MCR and the PCR, and is dynamically controlled using congestion control mechanisms.

ACSE

association control service element
An OSI convention used to establish, maintain, or terminate a connection between two applications.

active hub

Multiported device that amplifies LAN transmission signals.

ad hoc

Ad hoc describes a WLAN topology, also called independent basic service set, where mobile clients connect directly without an intermediate access point.

adapter

See NIC (network interface card).

adaptive routing

See dynamic routing.

address

Data structure or logical convention used to identify a unique entity, such as a particular process or network device.

address mapping

Technique that allows different protocols to interoperate by translating addresses from one format to another. For example, when routing IP over X.25, the IP addresses must be mapped to the X.25 addresses so that the IP packets can be transmitted by the X.25 network.

address mask
Bit combination used to describe which portion of an address refers to the network or subnet and which part refers to the host.
An address mask is also known as a mask.

address resolution
Generally, a method for resolving differences between computer addressing schemes. Address resolution usually specifies a method for mapping network layer (Layer 3) addresses to data link layer (Layer 2) addresses.

Address Resolution Protocol
See ARP.

adjacency
Relationship formed between selected neighboring routers and end nodes for the purpose of exchanging routing information. Adjacency is based upon the use of a common media segment.

administrative distance
A rating of the trustworthiness of a routing information source. In Cisco routers, administrative distance is expressed as a numerical value between 0 and 255. The higher the value, the lower the trustworthiness rating.

admission control
See traffic policing.

ADSU
ATM data service unit
Terminal adapter used to access an ATM network via an HSSI-compatible device.

ADU
Aironet Desktop Utility
ADU is a utility used by Cisco Aironet 802.11a/b/g network cards for wireless configuration.

Advanced Program-to-Program Communication
See APPC.

Advanced Research Projects Agency
See ARPA.

Advanced Research Projects Agency Network
See ARPANET.

advertising
Router process in which routing or service updates are sent at specified intervals so that other routers on the network can maintain lists of usable routes.

AES
Advanced Encryption Standard
AES replaced WEP as the most secure method of encrypting data. AES is an option for WPA2.

AFI
1) Authority and Format ID. One byte of the NSAP address, actually a binary value between 0 and 99, used to specify the IDI format and DSP syntax of the address and the authority that assigned the address. See NSAP address.
2) Address Family Identifier. A 2 byte field in a RIP message. It identifies the routed protocol and is normally set to two for IP. The only exception is a request for a router's (or host's) full routing table, in which case it will be set to zero. AFI is set to all 1s if authentication is enabled in RIPv2.

agent
1) Generally, software that processes queries and returns replies on behalf of an application.
2) In NMSs, process that resides in all managed devices and reports the values of specified variables to management stations.
3) In Cisco hardware architecture, an individual processor card that provides one or more media interfaces.

AGS+
Multiprotocol, high-end Cisco router optimized for large corporate internetworks. The AGS+ runs the Cisco IOS software and features a modular approach that provides for easy and efficient scalability.

AIS
alarm indication signal
In a T1 transmission, an all-ones signal transmitted in lieu of the normal signal to maintain transmission continuity and to indicate to the receiving terminal that there is a transmission fault that is located either at, or upstream from, the transmitting terminal.

alarm
Message notifying an operator or administrator of a network problem.

alarm indication signal
See AIS.

a-law
The ITU-T companding standard used in the conversion between analog and digital signals in PCM systems. A-law is used primarily in European telephone networks and is similar to the North American mu-law standard.

algorithm
Well-defined rule or process for arriving at a solution to a problem. In networking, algorithms are commonly used to determine the best route for traffic from a particular source to a particular destination.

alias
See entity.

allowed cell rate
See ACR.

alternate mark inversion
See AMI.

AM
amplitude modulation
Modulation technique whereby information is conveyed through the amplitude of the carrier signal. Compare with FM and PAM.

American National Standards Institute
See ANSI.

American Standard Code for Information Interchange
See ASCII.

AMI
alternate mark inversion
Line-code type used on T1 and E1 circuits. In AMI, zeros are represented by 01 during each bit cell, and ones are represented by 11 or 00, alternately, during each bit cell. AMI requires that the sending device maintain ones density. Ones density is not maintained independent of the data stream. Compare with B8ZS. AMI is also know as binary coded alternate mark inversion.

amplitude
Maximum value of an analog or a digital waveform.

amplitude modulation
See AM.

analog transmission
Signal transmission over wires or through the air in which information is conveyed through variation of some combination of signal amplitude, frequency, and phase.

ANSI
American National Standards Institute
Voluntary organization comprised of corporate, government, and other members that coordinates standards-related activities, approves U.S. national standards, and develops positions for the United States in international standards organizations. ANSI helps develop international and U.S. standards relating to, among other things, communications and networking. ANSI is a member of the IEC and the ISO.

ANSI X3T9.5
See X3T9.5.

anycast
A type of IPv6 network addressing and routing scheme whereby data is routed to the "nearest" or "best" destination as viewed by the routing topology. A packet sent to an anycast address is delivered to the closest interface, as defined by the routing protocols in use, identified by the anycast address. It shares the same address format as an IPv6 global unicast address.

AON
Application-Oriented Networking
Technology that changes how applications are deployed, integrated, and managed. It does so by delivering common application infrastructure functions as network-based services. Cisco AON helps to dramatically lower the cost and complexity of deploying applications and maintaining application infrastructure by relocating these repeatable functions, such as application security, messaging, logging, and event capture, into the network and onto routers and switches.

AP

access point

Device that connects wireless communication devices together to form a wireless network, analogous to a hub connecting wired devices to form a LAN. The AP usually connects to a wired network, and can relay data between wireless devices and wired devices. Several APs can link together to form a larger network that allows roaming.

APaRT

automated packet recognition/translation
Technology that allows a server to be attached to CDDI or FDDI without requiring the reconfiguration of applications or network protocols. APaRT recognizes specific data link layer encapsulation packet types and, when these packet types are transferred from one medium to another, translates them into the native format of the destination device.

API

application programming interface
Specification of function-call conventions that defines an interface to a service.

Apollo Domain

Proprietary network protocol suite developed by Apollo Computer for communication on proprietary Apollo networks.

APPC

Advanced Program-to-Program Communication
IBM SNA system software that allows high-speed communication between programs on different computers in a distributed computing environment. APPC establishes and tears down connections between communicating programs, and consists of two interfaces, a programming interface and a data-exchange interface. The former replies to requests from programs requiring communication; the latter establishes sessions between programs. APPC runs on LU 6.2 devices.

AppleTalk

Series of communications protocols designed by Apple Computer. Two phases currently exist. Phase 1, the earlier version, supports a single physical network that can have only one network number and be in one zone. Phase 2, the more recent version, supports multiple logical networks on a single physical network and allows networks to be in more than one zone.

application

Program that performs a function directly for a user. FTP and Telnet clients are examples of network applications.

Application layer

Layer 7 of the OSI reference model. This layer provides services to application processes (such as electronic mail, file transfer, and terminal emulation) that are outside of the OSI model. The application layer identifies and establishes the availability of intended communication partners (and the resources required to connect with them), synchronizes cooperating applications, and establishes agreement on procedures for error recovery and control of data integrity. Corresponds roughly with the transaction services layer in the SNA model.

application programming interface

See API.

Application-Oriented Networking

See AON.

ARCnet

Attached Resource Computer Network
A 2.5-Mbps token-bus LAN developed in the late 1970s and early 1980s by Datapoint Corporation.

area

Logical set of network segments (either CLNS-, DECnet-, or OSPF-based) and their attached devices. Areas are usually connected to other areas via routers, making up a single autonomous system.

area border router

See ABR.

ARM

asynchronous response mode
HDLC communication mode involving one primary station and at least one secondary station, where either the primary or one of the secondary stations can initiate transmissions.

ARP

address resolution protocol.
Internet protocol used to map an IP address to a MAC address. Defined in RFC 826. Compare with RARP.

ARPA

Advanced Research Projects Agency
Research and development organization that is part of DoD. ARPA is responsible for numerous technological advances in communications and networking. ARPA evolved into DARPA, and then back into ARPA again in 1994.

ARPANET

Advanced Research Projects Agency Network
Landmark packet-switching network established in 1969. ARPANET was developed in the 1970s by BBN and funded by ARPA (and later DARPA). It eventually evolved into the Internet. The term ARPANET was officially retired in 1990.

ARQ

1) automatic repeat request. Communication technique in which the receiving device detects errors and requests retransmissions.
2) admission request. In VoIP, ARQ is used with the H.323 protocol.

AS

Collection of networks under a common administration sharing a common routing strategy. Autonomous systems are subdivided by areas. An autonomous system must be assigned a unique 16-bit number by the IANA.

ASBR

autonomous system boundary router
ABR located between an OSPF autonomous system and a non-OSPF network. ASBRs run both OSPF and another routing protocol, such as RIP. ASBRs must reside in a nonstub OSPF area.

ASCII

American Standard Code for Information Interchange
8-bit code for character representation (7 bits plus parity).

ASM-CS

Cisco multiprotocol communication server designed to connect asynchronous devices to any LAN or WAN using TCP/IP, LAT, or SLIP. It can be configured to interface with Ethernet or Token Ring LANs or synchronous serial networks.

ASN.1

Abstract Syntax Notation One
OSI language for describing data types independent of particular computer structures and representation techniques. Described by ISO International Standard 8824.

associated

A station is configured properly to allow it to wirelessly communicate with an access point.

association control service element

See ACSE.

associative memory

Memory that is accessed based on its contents, not on its memory address.
Associative memory is also known as content addressable memory (CAM).

AST

automatic spanning tree.
Function that supports the automatic resolution of spanning trees in SRB networks, providing a single path for spanning explorer frames to traverse from a given node in the network to another. AST is based on the IEEE 802.1 standard.

asynchronous response mode

See ARM.

asynchronous time-division multiplexing

See ATDM.

Asynchronous Transfer Mode

See ATM.

asynchronous transmission

Term describing digital signals that are transmitted without precise clocking. Such signals generally have different frequencies and phase relationships. Asynchronous transmissions usually encapsulate individual characters in control bits (called start and stop bits) that designate the beginning and end of each character. Compare with isochronous transmission, plesiochronous transmission, and synchronous transmission.

ATDM
asynchronous time-division multiplexing
Method of sending information that resembles normal TDM, except that time slots are allocated as needed rather than preassigned to specific transmitters. Compare with FDM, statistical multiplexing, and TDM.

ATM
Asynchronous Transfer Mode
International standard for cell relay in which multiple service types (such as voice, video, or data) are conveyed in fixed-length (53-byte) cells. Fixed-length cells allow cell processing to occur in hardware, thereby reducing transit delays. ATM is designed to take advantage of high-speed transmission media such as E3, SONET, and T3.

ATM data service unit
See ADSU.

ATM Forum
International organization jointly founded in 1991 by Cisco Systems, NET/ADAPTIVE, Northern Telecom, and Sprint that develops and promotes standards-based implementation agreements for ATM technology. The ATM Forum expands on official standards developed by ANSI and ITU-T, and develops implementation agreements in advance of official standards.

ATM management
See ATMM.

ATM UNI
See UNI.

ATMM
ATM management
Process that runs on an ATM switch that controls VCI translation and rate enforcement.

Attached Resource Computer Network
See ARCnet.

attachment unit interface
See AUI.

attenuation
Loss of communication signal energy.

attribute
Configuration data that defines the characteristics of database objects such as the chassis, cards, ports, or virtual circuits of a particular device. Attributes might be preset or user-configurable. On a LightStream 2020 ATM switch, attributes are set using the configuration program or CLI commands.

AUI
attachment unit interface
IEEE 802.3 interface between an MAU and a network interface card (NIC). The term AUI can also refer to the rear panel port to which an AUI cable might attach, such as those found on a Cisco LightStream Ethernet access card. AUI is also known as transceiver cable.

authentication
In security, the verification of the identity of a person or process.

authority zone
Associated with DNS, an authority zone is a section of the domain-name tree for which one name server is the authority.

Automated Packet Recognition/Translation
See APaRT.

automatic call reconnect
Feature permitting automatic call rerouting away from a failed trunk line.

automatic repeat request
See ARQ.

automatic spanning tree
See AST.

autonomous access point
An autonomous access point is the type used in a distributed WLAN solution. Each autonomous access point is configured individually and does not rely on a wireless controller.

autonomous system
See AS.

autonomous system boundary router
See ASBR.

AutoQoS
Cisco AutoQoS is a feature that automates consistent deployment of QoS features across Cisco routers and switches to ensure high-quality application performance. Once enabled, it automatically configures the device with QoS features and variables which are based on Cisco best-practice recommendations. Users can subsequently tune parameters that are generated by Cisco AutoQoS to suit their particular application needs, as desired.

autoreconfiguration
Process performed by nodes within the failure domain of a Token Ring network. Nodes automatically perform diagnostics in an attempt to reconfigure the network around the failed areas.

available bit rate
See ABR.

average rate
The average rate, in kilobits per second (kbps), at which a given virtual circuit will transmit.

B channel
bearer channel
In ISDN, a full-duplex, 64-kbps channel used to send user data. Compare to D channel, E channel, and H channel.

B8ZS
binary 8-zero substitution
Line-code type, used on T1 and E1 circuits, in which a special code is substituted whenever 8 consecutive zeros are sent through the link. This code is then interpreted at the remote end of the connection. This technique guarantees ones density independent of the data stream. Sometimes called bipolar 8-zero substitution. Compare with AMI.

back end
Node or software program that provides services to a front end.

backbone
The part of a network that acts as the primary path for traffic that is most often sourced from, and destined for, other networks.

backbone cabling
Cabling that provides interconnections between wiring closets, wiring closets and the POP, and between buildings that are part of the same LAN.
Backbone cabling is also known as vertical cabling.

backoff
The retransmission delay enforced when a collision occurs.

backplane
Physical connection between an interface processor or card and the data buses and power distribution buses inside a Cisco chassis.

backward explicit congestion notification
See BECN.

balanced configuration
In HDLC, a point-to-point network configuration with two combined stations.

bandwidth
The difference between the highest and lowest frequencies available for network signals. Bandwidth is also used to describe the rated throughput capacity of a given network medium or protocol.

bandwidth allocation
See bandwidth reservation.

bandwidth reservation
Process of assigning bandwidth to users and applications served by a network. Involves signing priority to different flows of traffic based on how critical and delay-sensitive they are. This makes the best use of available bandwidth, and if the network becomes congested, lower-priority traffic can be dropped.
Bandwidth reservation is also known as bandwidth allocation.

Banyan VINES
See VINES.

BARRNet
Bay Area Regional Research Network
Regional network serving the San Francisco Bay Area. The BARRNet backbone is composed of four University of California cam-

puses (Berkeley, Davis, Santa Cruz, and San Francisco), Stanford University, Lawrence Livermore National Laboratory, and NASA Ames Research Center. BARRNet is now part of BBN Planet.

baseband

Characteristic of a network technology where only one carrier frequency is used. Ethernet is an example of a baseband network. Contrast with broadband.
Baseband is also known as narrowband.

bash

Bourne-again shell
Interactive UNIX shell based on the traditional Bourne shell, but with increased functionality. The LynxOS bash shell is presented when you log in to a LightStream 2020 ATM switch as root (bash#) or fldsup (bash$).

basic configuration

The minimal configuration information entered when a new router, switch, or other configurable network device is installed on a network. The basic configuration for a LightStream 2020 ATM switch, for example, includes IP addresses, the date, and parameters for at least one trunk line. The basic configuration enables the device to receive a full configuration from the NMS.

basic encoding rules

See BER.

Basic Rate Interface

See BRI.

basic service area

See BSA.

basic service set

See BSS.

baud

Unit of signaling speed equal to the number of discrete signal elements transmitted per second. Baud is synonymous with bits per second (bps), if each signal element represents exactly 1 bit.

Bay Area Regional Research Network

See BARRNet.

BBN

Bolt, Beranek, and Newman, Inc.
High-technology company located in Massachusetts that developed and maintained the ARPANET (and later, the Internet) core gateway system.

BBN Planet

Subsidiary company of BBN that operates a nationwide Internet access network composed in part by the former regional networks BARRNET, NEARNET, and SURAnet.

Bc

committed burst
Negotiated tariff metric in Frame Relay internetworks. The maximum amount of data (in bits) that a Frame Relay internetwork is committed to accept and transmit at the CIR.

BE

excess burst
Negotiated tariff metric in Frame Relay internetworks. The number of bits that a Frame Relay internetwork will attempt to transmit after Bc is accommodated. Be data is, in general, delivered with a lower probability than Bc data because Be data can be marked as DE by the network.

beacon

1) Frame from a Token Ring or FDDI device indicating a serious problem with the ring, such as a broken cable. A beacon frame contains the address of the station assumed to be down. See failure domain.
2) In wireless technology, a beacon is a wireless LAN packet that signals the availability and presence of the wireless device. Beacon packets are sent by access points and base stations; however, client radio cards send beacons when operating in computer to computer (Ad Hoc) mode.

bearer channel

See B channel.

Because It's Time Network
See BITNET.

BECN
Backward Explicit Congestion Notification
Bit set by a Frame Relay network in frames traveling in the opposite direction of frames encountering a congested path. DTE receiving frames with the BECN bit set can request that higher-level protocols take flow control action as appropriate. Compare with FECN.

Bell Communications Research
See Bellcore.

Bell operating company
See BOC.

Bellcore
Bell Communications Research
Organization that performs research and development on behalf of the RBOCs.

Bellman-Ford routing algorithm
See distance vector routing algorithm.

BER
1) bit error rate. The ratio of received bits that contain errors.
2) basic encoding rules. Rules for encoding data units described in the ISO ASN.1 standard.

Berkeley Standard Distribution
See BSD.

BERT
Bit error rate tester
Device that determines the BER on a given communications channel.

best-effort delivery
Describes a network system that does not use a sophisticated acknowledgment system to guarantee reliable delivery of information.

BGP
Border Gateway Protocol
Interdomain routing protocol that replaces EGP. BGP exchanges reachability information with other BGP systems. BGP is defined by RFC 1163.

BGP4
BGP Version 4
Version 4 of the predominant interdomain routing protocol used on the Internet. BGP4 supports CIDR and uses route aggregation mechanisms to reduce the size of routing tables.

big-endian
Method of storing or transmitting data in which the most significant bit or byte is presented first. Compare with little-endian.

binary
A numbering system characterized by ones and zeros (1 = on, 0 = off).

binary 8-zero substitution
See B8ZS.

binary coded alternate mark inversion
See AMI.

binary synchronous communication
See BSC.

biphase coding
Bipolar coding scheme originally developed for use in Ethernet. Clocking information is embedded into and recovered from the synchronous data stream without the need for separate clocking leads. The biphase signal contains no direct current energy.

bipolar 8-zero substitution
See B8ZS.

BISDN
Broadband ISDN. ITU-T communication standards designed to handle high-bandwidth applications such as video. BISDN currently uses ATM technology over SONET-based transmission circuits to provide data rates from 155 to 622 Mbps and beyond. Contrast with N-ISDN.

bit
Binary digit used in the binary numbering system. A bit can be 0 or 1.

bit error rate
See BER.

bit error rate tester
See BERT.

bit rate
Speed at which bits are transmitted, usually expressed in bits per second (bps).

BITNET
Because It's Time Network
Low-cost, low-speed academic network consisting primarily of IBM mainframes and 9600-bps leased lines. BITNET is now part of CREN.

BITNET III
Dial-up service providing connectivity for members of CREN.

bit-oriented protocol
Class of data link layer communication protocols that can transmit frames regardless of frame content. Compared with byte-oriented protocols, bit-oriented protocols provide full-duplex operation and are more efficient and reliable. Compare with byte-oriented protocol.

bits per second
Abbreviated bps.

black hole
Routing term for an area of the internetwork where packets enter, but do not emerge, due to adverse conditions or poor system configuration within a portion of the network.

block multiplexer channel
IBM-style channel that implements the FIPS-60 channel, a U.S. channel standard. This channel is also referred to as OEMI channel and 370 block mux channel.

blocking
In a switching system, a condition in which no paths are available to complete a circuit. Blocking is also used to describe a situation in which one activity cannot begin until another has been completed.

blower
Internal cooling fan used in larger router and switch chassis such as the Cisco AGS+, the Cisco 7000, and the LightStream 2020.

BNC connector
Standard connector used to connect IEEE 802.3 10BASE2 coaxial cable to an MAU.

BNN
boundary network node
In SNA terminology, a subarea node that provides boundary function support for adjacent peripheral nodes. This support includes sequencing, pacing, and address translation. BNN is also known as a boundary node.

BOC
Abbreviation for Bell Operating Company.

Bolt, Beranek, and Newman, Inc.
See BBN.

boot programmable read-only memory
See boot PROM.

boot PROM
boot programmable read-only memory
Chip mounted on a printed circuit board used to provide executable boot instructions to a computer device.

BOOTP
Bootstrap Protocol
Protocol used by a network node to determine the IP address of its Ethernet interfaces, in order to affect network booting.

Bootstrap Protocol
See BOOTP.

border gateway
Router that communicates with routers in other autonomous systems.

Border Gateway Protocol
See BGP.

bot
Application that runs automated tasks.

boundary network node
See BNN.

boundary node
See BNN.

BPDU
bridge protocol data unit
Spanning-Tree Protocol hello packet that is sent out at configurable intervals to exchange information among bridges in the network.

BRI

Basic Rate Interface

ISDN interface composed of two B channels and one D channel for circuit-switched communication of voice, video, and data. Compare with PRI.

bridge

Device that connects and passes packets between two network segments that use the same communications protocol. Bridges operate at the data link layer (layer 2) of the OSI reference model. In general, a bridge will filter, forward, or flood an incoming frame based on the MAC address of that frame.

bridge forwarding

Process that uses entries in a filtering database to determine whether frames with a given MAC destination address can be forwarded to a given port or ports. Described in the IEEE 802.1 standard.

bridge group

Cisco bridging feature that assigns network interfaces to a particular spanning-tree group. Bridge groups can be compatible with the IEEE 802.1 or the DEC specification.

bridge number

Number that identifies each bridge in an SRB LAN. Parallel bridges must have different bridge numbers.

bridge protocol data unit

See BPDU.

bridge static filtering

Process in which a bridge maintains a filtering database consisting of static entries. Each static entry equates a MAC destination address with a port that can receive frames with this MAC destination address and a set of ports on which the frames can be transmitted. Defined in the IEEE 802.1 standard.

Bridge-Group Virtual Interface

See BVI.

broadband

Transmission system that multiplexes multiple independent signals onto one cable. In telecommunications terminology, any channel having a bandwidth greater than a voice-grade channel (4 kHz). In LAN terminology, a coaxial cable on which analog signaling is used. Also called wideband. Contrast with baseband.

Broadband ISDN

See BISDN.

broadcast

Data packet that will be sent to all nodes on a network. Broadcasts are identified by a broadcast address. Compare with multicast and unicast.

broadcast address

Special address reserved for sending a message to all stations. Generally, a broadcast address is a MAC destination address of all ones. Compare with multicast address and unicast address.

broadcast domain

The set of all devices that will receive broadcast frames originating from any device within the set. Broadcast domains are typically bounded by routers because routers do not forward broadcast frames.

broadcast search

Propagation of a search request to all network nodes if the location of a resource is unknown to the requester.

broadcast storm

Undesirable network event in which many broadcasts are sent simultaneously across all network segments. A broadcast storm uses substantial network bandwidth and, typically, causes network time-outs.

browser

See WWW browser.

BSA

basic service area

Area of radio frequency coverage provided by an access point. To extend the BSA, or to simply add wireless devices and extend the range of an existing wired system, you can add an access point. A BSA is also known as a microcell.

BSD
Berkeley Standard Distribution
Term used to describe any of a variety of UNIX-type operating systems based on the UC Berkeley BSD operating system.

BSS
basic service set
WLAN infrastructure mode whereby mobile clients use a single access point for connectivity to each other or to wired network resources.

BT
burst tolerance
Parameter defined by the ATM Forum for ATM traffic management. For VBR connections, BT determines the size of the maximum burst of contiguous cells that can be transmitted.

buffer
Storage area used for handling data in transit. Buffers are used in internetworking to compensate for differences in processing speed between network devices. Bursts of data can be stored in buffers until they can be handled by slower processing devices.
A buffer is also known as a packet buffer.

buffering
Storing data until it can be handled by other devices or processes. Buffering is typically used when there is a difference between the rate at which data is received and the rate at which it can be processed.

burst tolerance
See BT.

bus
1) Common physical signal path composed of wires or other media across which signals can be sent from one part of a computer to another. Bus is also known as highway.
2) See bus topology.

bus and tag channel
IBM channel, developed in the 1960s, incorporating copper multiwire technology. Replaced by the ESCON channel.

bus topology
Linear LAN architecture in which transmissions from network stations propagate the length of the medium and are received by all other stations. Compare with ring topology, star topology, and tree topology.

bypass mode
Operating mode on FDDI and Token Ring networks in which an interface has been removed from the ring.

bypass relay
Allows a particular Token Ring interface to be shut down and thus effectively removed from the ring.

byte
Term used to refer to a series of consecutive binary digits that are operated upon as a unit (for example, an 8-bit byte).

byte reversal
Process of storing numeric data with the least-significant byte first. Used for integers and addresses on devices with Intel microprocessors.

byte-oriented protocol
Class of data-link communications protocols that use a specific character from the user character set to delimit frames. These protocols have largely been replaced by bit-oriented protocols. Compare with bit-oriented protocol.

CA
congestion avoidance
The mechanism by which a LightStream-based ATM network controls traffic entering the network to minimize delays. In order to use resources most efficiently, lower-priority traffic is discarded at the edge of the network if conditions indicate that it cannot be delivered.

cable
Transmission medium of copper wire or optical fiber wrapped in a protective cover.

cable television
See CATV.

caching
Form of replication in which information learned during a previous transaction is used to process later transactions.

call admission control
Traffic management mechanism used in ATM networks that determines whether the network can offer a path with sufficient bandwidth for a requested VCC.

call priority
Priority assigned to each origination port in circuit-switched systems. This priority defines the order in which calls are reconnected. Call priority also defines which calls can or cannot be placed during a bandwidth reservation.

call setup time
The time required to establish a switched call between DTE devices.

CAM
Content-addressable memory. See associative memory.

carrier
Electromagnetic wave or alternating current of a single frequency, suitable for modulation by another, data-bearing signal.

carrier detect
See CD.

carrier sense multiple access/collision detect
See CSMA/CD.

CAS
channel-associated signaling
The transmission of signaling information within the voice channel. CAS signaling often is referred to as robbed-bit signaling because user bandwidth is being robbed by the network for other purposes.

Catalyst 1600 Token Ring Switch
Cisco Token Ring switch that offers full-duplex dedicated LAN segments to individual servers and other workstations that require high-speed switching access. The Catalyst 1600 provides up to 12 switched Token Ring interfaces and low latency switching between servers and clients across a backbone.

Catalyst 5000
Cisco modular switching system that allows connection to Ethernet, CDDI, FDDI, and ATM LANs and backbones. The Catalyst 5000 switch performs store-and-forward packet switching and allows the user to dedicate 10- or 100-Mbps connections to existing LAN segments or high-performance end stations.

Catalyst Workgroup Switch
Series of Cisco workgroup switches that enhance the network performance of Ethernet client/server workgroups. The Catalyst Workgroup Switch integrates software enhancements for network management and provides a 100-Mbps interface to servers and dedicated Ethernet-to-desktop workstations.

catchment areas
Zone that falls within an area that can be served by an internetworking device such as a hub.

Category 1 cabling
One of five grades of UTP cabling described in the EIA/TIA-568B standard. Category 1 cabling is used for telephone communications and is not suitable for transmitting data. Compare with Category 2 cabling, Category 3 cabling, Category 4 cabling, and Category 5 cabling.

Category 2 cabling
One of five grades of UTP cabling described in the EIA/TIA-568B standard. Category 2 cabling is capable of transmitting data at speeds up to 4 Mbps. Compare with Category 1 cabling, Category 3 cabling, Category 4 cabling, and Category 5 cabling.

Category 3 cabling
One of five grades of UTP cabling described in the EIA/TIA-568B standard. Category 3 cabling is used in 10BASE-T networks and can transmit data at speeds up to 10 Mbps. Compare with Category 1 cabling, Category 2 cabling, Category 4 cabling, and Category 5 cabling.

Category 4 cabling
One of five grades of UTP cabling described in the EIA/TIA-568B standard. Category 4 cabling is used in Token Ring networks and can transmit data at speeds up to 16 Mbps. Com-

pare with Category 1 cabling, Category 2 cabling, Category 3 cabling, and Category 5 cabling.

Category 5 cabling
One of five grades of UTP cabling described in the EIA/TIA-568B standard. Category 5 cabling is used for running CDDI and can transmit data at speeds up to 100 Mbps. Compare with Category 1 cabling, Category 2 cabling, Category 3 cabling, and Category 4 cabling.

catenet
Network in which hosts are connected to diverse networks, which themselves are connected with routers. The Internet is a prominent example of a catenet.

CATV
cable television
Communication system where multiple channels of programming material are transmitted to homes using broadband coaxial cable. Formerly called Community Antenna Television.

CBDS
Connectionless Broadband Data Service. European high-speed, packet-switched, datagram-based WAN networking technology. Similar to SMDS.

CBR
constant bit rate
QOS class defined by the ATM Forum for ATM networks. CBR is used for connections that depend on precise clocking to ensure undistorted delivery. Compare with ABR, UBR, and VBR.

CBWFQ
class-based weighted fair queueing
Extends the standard WFQ functionality to provide support for user-defined traffic classes. For CBWFQ, you define traffic classes based on match criteria including protocols, access control lists (ACLs), and input interfaces.

CCITT
Consultative Committee for International Telegraph and Telephone
International organization responsible for the development of communications standards. CCITT is now known as the ITU-T.

CCK
complementary code keying
CCK is a modulation technique used in IEEE 802.11b-compliant wireless LANs for transmission at 5.5 and 11 Mbps.

CCS
common channel signaling
Signaling system used in telephone networks that separates signaling information from user data. A specified channel is exclusively designated to carry signaling information for all other channels in the system.

CCX
Cisco Compatible Extensions
The CCX program for WLAN devices is an evolving set of specification for interoperabililty, which facilitates testing of vendor clients and provides tested compatibility with licensed Cisco infrastructure innovations.

CD
carrier detect
Signal that indicates whether an interface is active. Also, a signal generated by a modem indicating that a call has been connected.

CDDI
Copper Distributed Data Interface
Implementation of FDDI protocols over STP and UTP cabling. CDDI transmits over relatively short distances, about 325 feet (100 m), providing data rates of 100 Mbps using a dual-ring architecture to provide redundancy. Based on the ANSI Twisted-Pair Physical Medium Dependent (TPPMD) standard. Compare with FDDI.

CDDI/FDDI workgroup concentrator
See Cisco Workgroup Concentrator.

CDP
Cisco Discovery Protocol
Media- and protocol-independent device-discovery protocol that runs on all Cisco-manufactured equipment including routers, access servers, bridges, and switches. Using CDP, a device can advertise its existence to other devices and receive information about other devices on the same LAN or on the remote side of a WAN. Runs on all media that support SNAP,

including LANs, Frame Relay, and ATM media.

CDPD
Cellular Digital Packet Data
Open standard for two-way wireless data communication over high-frequency cellular telephone channels. Allows data transmissions between a remote cellular link and a NAP. Operates at 19.2 Kbps.

CDVT
cell delay variation tolerance
Parameter defined by the ATM Forum for ATM traffic management. In CBR transmissions, determines the level of jitter that is tolerable for the data samples taken by the PCR.

cell
1) The basic unit for ATM switching and multiplexing. Cells contain identifiers that specify the data stream to which they belong. Each cell consists of a 5-byte header and 48 bytes of payload. See also cell relay.
2) In wireless technology, a cell is the area of radio range or coverage in which the wireless devices can communicate with the base station. The size of the cell depends upon the speed of the transmission, the type of antenna used, and the physical environment, as well as other factors.

cell delay variation tolerance
See CDVT.

cell line card
See CLC.

cell loss priority
See CLP.

cell payload scrambling
Technique used on the LightStream 2020 ATM switch to maintain framing on some medium-speed edge and trunk interfaces.

cell relay
Network technology based on the use of small, fixed-size packets, or cells. Because cells are fixed-length, they can be processed and switched in hardware at high speeds. Cell relay is the basis for many high-speed network protocols including ATM, IEEE 802.6, and SMDS.

cells per second
See cps.

Cellular Digital Packet Data
See CDPD.

cellular radio
Technology that uses radio transmissions to access telephonecompany networks. Service is provided in a particular area by a low-power transmitter.

CEMAC
circuit emulation access card
T1 or E1 circuit emulation card in the LightStream 2020 ATM switch.

central office
See CO.

Centrex
AT and T PBX that provides direct inward dialing and automatic number identification of the calling PBX.

CFRAD
See Cisco FRAD.

CGMP
Cisco Group Management Protocol
A Cisco-developed protocol that runs between Cisco routers and Catalyst switches to leverage IGMP information on Cisco routers to make Layer 2 forwarding decisions on Catalyst switch ports that are attached to interested receivers.

CGS
Compact Gateway Server
Cisco midrange multiprotocol router designed for medium to small regional and district environments. The CGS is a 2-slot router that supports up to four interfaces (all of the same type).

Challenge Handshake Authentication Protocol
See CHAP.

channel
1) A communication path. Multiple channels can be multiplexed over a single cable in certain environments.

2) In IBM, the specific path between large computers (such as mainframes) and attached peripheral devices.

Channel Interface Processor
See CIP.

channel service unit
See CSU.

channel-attached
Pertaining to attachment of devices directly by data channels (input/output channels) to a computer.

channelized E1
Access link operating at 2.048 Mbps that is subdivided into 30 B-channels and 1 D-channel. Supports DDR, Frame Relay, and X.25. Compare with channelized T1.

channelized T1
Access link operating at 1.544 Mbps that is subdivided into 24 channels (23 B-channels and 1 D-channel) of 64 Kbps each. The individual channels or groups of channels connect to different destinations. Supports DDR, Frame Relay, and X.25. Compare with channelized E1.
Channelized T1 is also known as fractional T1.

CHAP
Challenge Handshake Authentication Protocol
Security feature supported on lines using PPP encapsulation that prevents unauthorized access. CHAP does not itself prevent unauthorized access, it merely identifies the remote end. The router or access server then determines whether that user is allowed access. Compare to PAP.

chat script
String of text that defines the login "conversation" that occurs between two systems. Consists of expect-send pairs that define the string that the local system expects to receive from the remote system and what the local system should send as a reply.

Cheapernet
Industry term used to refer to the IEEE 802.3 10BASE2 standard or the cable specified in that standard. Compare with Thinnet.

checksum
1) Method for checking the integrity of transmitted data. A checksum is an integer value computed from a sequence of octets taken through a series of arithmetic operations. The value is recomputed at the receiving end and compared for verification.
2) Calculated checksum of the header and data fields.

choke packet
Packet sent to a transmitter to tell it that congestion exists and that it should reduce its sending rate.

CIA
Specification for running IP over ATM in a manner that takes full advantage of the features of ATM. Defined in RFC 1577.

CICNet
Regional network that connects academic, research, nonprofit, and commercial organizations in the Midwestern United States. Founded in 1988, CICNet was a part of the NSFNET and was funded by the NSF until the NSFNET dissolved in 1995.

CIDR
classless interdomain routing
Technique supported by BGP4 and based on route aggregation. CIDR allows routers to group routes together in order to cut down on the quantity of routing information carried by the core routers. With CIDR, several IP networks appear to networks outside the group as a single, larger entity.

CIO
Cisco Information Online
Online service available to Cisco customers that provides electronic services and online information relating to Cisco products. CIO services include product information, software updates, release notes, technical tips, configuration notes, brochures, and download offerings.

CIP
Channel Interface Processor
Channel attachment interface for Cisco 7000 series routers. The CIP is used to connect a host mainframe to a control unit, eliminating the need for an FEP for channel attachment.

CIR

committed information rate
The rate at which a Frame Relay network agrees to transfer information under normal conditions, averaged over a minimum increment of time. CIR, measured in bits per second, is one of the key negotiated tariff metrics.

circuit

Communications path between two or more points.

circuit emulation access card

See CEMAC.

circuit group

Grouping of associated serial lines that link two bridges. If one of the serial links in a circuit group is in the spanning tree for a network, any of the serial links in the circuit group can be used for load balancing. This load-balancing strategy avoids data ordering problems by assigning each destination address to a particular serial link.

circuit switching

Switching system in which a dedicated physical circuit path must exist between sender and receiver for the duration of the "call." Used heavily in the telephone company network. Circuit switching can be contrasted with contention and token passing as a channel-access method, and with message switching and packet switching as a switching technique.

Cisco 1000

Any of the Cisco 1000 series LAN Extenders and routers. The Cisco 1000 series are easy-to-install, inexpensive, multiprotocol access products designed for small offices and other remote sites. The Cisco 1000 series includes an ISDN router, an asynchronous router, and LAN extenders.

Cisco 2500

Any of the Cisco 2500 series routers and access servers, including single LAN routers; mission-specific, low-end routers; router/hub combinations; access servers; and dual LAN routers. The Cisco 2500 is designed for small offices and other remote sites and runs the Cisco IOS software.

The Cisco 2500 series is also known as Cisco Access Server 2500 series.

Cisco 4000

Any of the Cisco 4000 series routers designed for a wide variety of network computing environments. The Cisco 4000 series routers run the Cisco IOS software and can be optimized for particular environments with custom configurations.

Cisco 5100

Cisco data communications platform that combines the functions of a Cisco access server with analog and digital modems, CSUs, and T1 channel banks. The Cisco 5100 is optimized for high-speed modem access and is well-suited for dial-up applications, including host access, electronic mail, file transfer, and dial-in access to a LAN.
Cisco 5100 is also kknown as Cisco Access Server 5100.

Cisco 7000

Any of the Cisco 7000 series of routers (the Cisco 7000 or the Cisco 7010), a high-end router platform that supports a wide range of network interfaces and media types and is designed for use in enterprise networks. Cisco 7000 series routers run the Cisco IOS software and support online software reconfiguration, OIR, fast boot, environmental monitoring, self-diagnostics, redundant power supplies, and Flash memory.

Cisco 7500

Any of the Cisco 7500 series of routers, a high-end multiprotocol router platform designed for use in enterprise networks. Cisco 7500 series routers run the Cisco IOS software and implement a distributed multiprocessor architecture consisting of the CyBus, the RSP, and the VIP.

Cisco Access Server 2500

See Cisco 2500.

Cisco Access Server 5100

See Cisco 5100.

Cisco Discovery Protocol

See CDP.

Cisco Extended Bus
See CxBus.

Cisco FRAD
Cisco Frame Relay access device
Cisco product that supports Cisco IOS Frame Relay SNA services and can be upgraded to be a full-function multiprotocol router. The Cisco FRAD connects SDLC devices to Frame Relay without requiring an existing LAN. However, the Cisco FRAD does support attached LANs and can perform conversion from SDLC to Ethernet and Token Ring.

Cisco Frame Relay access device
See Cisco FRAD.

Cisco Information Online
See CIO.

Cisco Internetwork Operating System software
See Cisco IOS software.

Cisco IOS software
Cisco Internetwork Operating System software Cisco system software that provides common functionality, scalability, and security for all products under the CiscoFusion architecture. The Cisco IOS software allows centralized, integrated, and automated installation and management of internetworks, while ensuring support for a wide variety of protocols, media, services, and platforms.

Cisco LightStream 100
Cisco LightStream 100 ATM switch
A fully nonblocking ATM switch operating at up to 2.4 Gbps and supporting multiple ATM lines of 155-Mbps data speed as well as a variety of LAN and WAN interfaces. The LightStream 100 switch can serve as part of an ATM workgroup or small campus backbone connecting a number of ATM routers, multilayer LAN switches, and high-performance servers and clients.

Cisco LightStream 2020
Cisco LightStream 2020 Enterprise ATM switch
For campus and wide-area applications. The LightStream 2020 ATM switch supports trunks operating at T1/E1 data rates and provides a migration path through T3/E3 into a SONET/SDH OC-3 trunk. The LightStream 2020 intelligent edge modules support a variety of services including frame forwarding, Frame Relay, ATM UNI, and LAN internetworking.

Cisco Workgroup Adapter
Series of Cisco workgroup adapters that allow workstations to connect to CDDI or FDDI interfaces operating at 100 Mbps.

Cisco Workgroup Concentrator
Series of Cisco workgroup concentrators that combines the compact form factor of workgroup concentrators with the versatility of modular hubs. Supports from 4 to 32 combinations of CDDI or FDDI ports.

ciscoBus controller
See SP.

CiscoFusion
Cisco internetworking architecture that "fuses" together the scalability, stability, and security advantages of the latest routing technologies with the performance benefits of ATM and LAN switching, and the management benefits of VLANs.

CiscoView
GUI-based device-management software application that provides dynamic status, statistics, and comprehensive configuration information for Cisco internetworking devices. In addition to displaying a physical view of Cisco device chassis, CiscoView also provides device monitoring functions and basic troubleshooting capabilities, and can be integrated with several leading SNMP-based network management platforms.

CiscoWorks
Series of SNMP-based internetwork management software applications. CiscoWorks includes applications for monitoring router and access server status, managing configuration files, and troubleshooting network problems. CiscoWorks applications are integrated on several SNMP-based network management platforms, including SunNet Manager, HP OpenView, and IBM NetView.

CKIP
Cisco Key Integrity Protocol
CKIP is the Cisco implementation of PPK.

Class A station
See DAS.

Class B station
See SAS.

class of service
See COS.

Class-based weighted fair queueing
See CBWFQ.

classfull network
Network that uses traditional IP network addresses of class A, class B, and class C.

classical IP over ATM
See CIA.

classless interdomain routing
See CIDR.

classless network
Network that does not use the traditional IP network addressing (class A, class B, and class C), but defines the network boundary using a prefix value that indicates the number of bits used for the network portion.

CLAW
Common Link Access for Workstations
Data link layer protocol used by channel-attached RISC System/6000 series systems and by IBM 3172 devices running TCP/IP off-load. CLAW improves efficiency of channel use and allows the CIP to provide the functionality of a 3172 in TCP/IP environments and support direct channel attachment. The output from TCP/IP mainframe processing is a series of IP datagrams that the router can switch without modifications.

CLC
cell line card
Card on the LightStream 2020 ATM switch that, in conjunction with an access card, supports up to two OC-3c edge ports or one OC-3c trunk port. A CLC can be configured as an edge card or a trunk card.

Clear To Send
See CTS.

CLEC
Competitive Local Exchange Carrier
A company that builds and operates communication networks in metropolitan areas and provides its customers with an alternative to the local telephone company.

CLI
command-line interface
The command-line interface on the LightStream 2020 that runs on NPs and Sun SPARCstations and is used to monitor and control an ATM network.

client
1) Node or software program (front-end device) that requests services from a server. See also back end, front end, and server.
2) In wireless technology, a client is a radio device that uses the services of an Access Point to communicate wirelessly with other devices on a local area network.

client-server computing
Term used to describe distributed computing (processing) network systems in which transaction responsibilities are divided into two parts: client (front end) and server (back end). Both terms (client and server) can be applied to software programs or actual computing devices. Compare with peer-to-peer computing. Client-server computing is also known as distributed computing.

client-server model
Common way to describe network services and the model user processes (programs) of those services. Examples include the nameserver/nameresolver paradigm of the DNS and fileserver/file-client relationships such as NFS and diskless hosts.

CLNP
Connectionless Network Protocol
Protocol stack developed originally as a replacement for TCP/IP with the anticipation that this OSI suite would take over being based upon the standard OSI 7-layer model. This has not happened, however one protocol within

CLNP called IS-IS has become very popular within the Internet community due to its scalability as the Internet grows.

CLNS

Connectionless Network Service
The OSI network layer service similar to bare IP service. A CLNS entity communicates over Connectionless Network Protocol (CLNP) with its peer CLNS entity. CLNP is the OSI equivalent of IP. CLNP provides the interface between CLNS and upper layers. CLNS does not perform connection setup or termination because paths are determined independently for each packet that is transmitted through a network. In addition, CLNS provides best-effort delivery, which means that no guarantee exists that data will not be lost, corrupted, miss-ordered, or duplicated. CLNS relies on transport layer protocols to perform error detection and correction.

CLP

cell loss priority
Field in the ATM cell header that determines the probability of a cell being dropped if the network becomes congested. Cells with CLP = 0 are insured traffic, which is unlikely to be dropped. Cells with CLP = 1 are best-effort traffic, which might be dropped in congested conditions in order to free up resources to handle insured traffic.

cluster controller

1) Generally, an intelligent device that provides the connections for a cluster of terminals to a data link.
2) In SNA, a programmable device that controls the input/output operations of attached devices. Typically, an IBM 3174 or 3274 device.

CMI

coded mark inversion
ITU-T line coding technique specified for STS-3c transmissions. Also used in DS-1 systems.

CMIC

Cisco Message Integrity Check
The Cisco implementation of MIC.

CMIP

Common Management Information Protocol
OSI network management protocol created and standardized by ISO for the monitoring and control of heterogeneous networks.

CMIS

Common Management Information Services
OSI network management service interface created and standardized by ISO for the monitoring and control of heterogeneous networks.

CMNS

Connection-Mode Network Service
Extends local X.25 switching to a variety of media (Ethernet, FDDI, Token Ring).

CMT

connection management
FDDI process that handles the transition of the ring through its various states (off, active, connect, and so on), as defined by the ANSI X3T9.5 specification.

CO

central office
Local telephone company office to which all local loops in a given area connect and in which circuit switching of subscriber lines occurs.

coaxial cable

Cable consisting of a hollow outer cylindrical conductor that surrounds a single inner wire conductor. Two types of coaxial cable are currently used in LANs: 50-ohm cable, which is used for digital signaling, and 75-ohm cable, which is used for analog signal and high-speed digital signaling.

code bits

Control functions, such as setup and termination of a session.

CODEC

coder-decoder
Device that typically uses PCM to transform analog signals into a digital bit stream, and digital signals back into analog.

coded mark inversion

See CMI.

coder-decoder
See CODEC.

coding
Electrical techniques used to convey binary signals.

collapsed backbone
Nondistributed backbone in which all network segments are interconnected by way of an internetworking device. A collapsed backbone might be a virtual network segment existing in a device such as a hub, a router, or a switch.

collision
In Ethernet, the result of two nodes transmitting simultaneously. The frames from each device impact and are damaged when they meet on the physical media.

collision detection
See CSMA/CD.

collision domain
In Ethernet, the network area within which frames that have collided are propagated. Repeaters and hubs propagate collisions; LAN switches, bridges and routers do not.

command-line interface
command-line interface
The command-line interface on the LightStream 2020 that runs on NPs and Sun SPARCstations and is used to monitor and control an ATM network.

Committed Burst
See Bc.

committed information rate
See CIR.

common carrier
Licensed, private utility company that supplies communication services to the public at regulated prices.

common channel signaling
See CCS.

Common Link Access for Workstations
See CLAW.

Common Management Information Protocol
See CMIP.

Common Management Information Services
See CMIS.

common mode
Term used to describe problems involving either the hot or neutral wires and the safety ground wire on a power line.

Common Programming Interface for Communications
See CPI-C.

communication
Transmission of information.

communication controller
In SNA, a subarea node (such as an IBM 3745 device) that contains an NCP.

communication server
Communications processor that connects asynchronous devices to a LAN or WAN through network and terminal emulation software. Performs only asynchronous routing of IP and IPX. Compare with access server.

communications line
The physical link (such as wire or a telephone circuit) that connects one or more devices to one or more other devices.

community
In SNMP, a logical group of managed devices and NMSs in the same administrative domain.

Community Antenna Television
Now known as CATV. See CATV.

community string
Text string that acts as a password and is used to authenticate messages sent between a management station and a router containing an SNMP agent. The community string is sent in every packet between the manager and the agent.

Compact Gateway Server
See CGS.

companding

Contraction derived from the opposite processes of compression and expansion. Part of the PCM process whereby analog signal values are logically rounded to discrete scale-step values on a nonlinear scale. The decimal step number is then coded in its binary equivalent prior to transmission. The process is reversed at the receiving terminal using the same nonlinear scale. Compare with compression and expansion.

Compressed Serial Link Internet Protocol

See CSLIP.

compression

The running of a data set through an algorithm that reduces the space required to store or the bandwidth required to transmit the data set. Compare with companding and expansion.

Computer Science Network

See CSNET.

concentrator

See hub.

conductor

Any material with a low resistance to electrical current. Any material capable of carrying an electrical current.

configuration management

One of five categories of network management defined by ISO for management of OSI networks. Configuration management subsystems are responsible for detecting and determining the state of a network.

configuration register

In Cisco routers, a 16-bit, user-configurable value that determines how the router functions during initialization. The configuration register can be stored in hardware or software. In hardware, the bit position is set using a jumper. In software, the bit position is set by specifying a hexadecimal value using configuration commands.

congestion

Traffic in excess of network capacity.

congestion avoidance

See CA.

connection management

See CMT.

connectionless

Term used to describe data transfer without the existence of a virtual circuit. Compare with connection-oriented.

Connectionless Broadband Data Service

See CBDS.

Connectionless Network Protocol

See CLNP.

Connectionless Network Service

See CLNS.

Connection-Mode Network Service

See CMNS.

connection-oriented

Term used to describe data transfer that requires the establishment of a virtual circuit.

Connection-Oriented Network Protocol

See CONP.

CONP

Connection-Oriented Network Protocol OSI protocol providing connection-oriented operation to upper-layer protocols.

console

DTE through which commands are entered into a host.

constant bit rate

See CBR.

Consultative Committee for International Telegraph

See CCITT.

content-addressable memory

See associative memory.

contention

Access method in which network devices compete for permission to access the physical medium. Contrast with circuit switching and token passing.

ControlStream traffic management
Traffic management scheme used by the LightStream 2020 ATM switch. Includes congestion avoidance, traffic shaping, and traffic policing, and allows links to operate at high levels of utilization by scaling back lower-priority, delay-tolerant traffic at the edge of the network when congestion begins to occur.

convergence
The speed and ability of a group of internetworking devices running a specific routing protocol to agree on the topology of an internetwork after a change in that topology.

conversation
In SNA, an LU 6.2 session between two transaction programs.

Copper Distributed Data Interface
See CDDI.

core gateway
The primary routers in the Internet.

core router
In a packet-switched star topology, a router that is part of the backbone and that serves as the single pipe through which all traffic from peripheral networks must pass on its way to other peripheral networks.

Corporation for Open Systems
See COS.

Corporation for Research and Educational Networking
See CREN.

COS
1) class of service. Indication of how an upper-layer protocol requires that a lower-layer protocol treat its messages. In SNA subarea routing, COS definitions are used by subarea nodes to determine the optimal route to establish a given session. A COS definition comprises a virtual route number and a transmission priority field. Also known as type of service (TOS).
2) Corporation for Open Systems. Organization that promulgates the use of OSI protocols through conformance testing, certification, and related activities.

cost
Arbitrary value, typically based on hop count, media bandwidth, or other measures, that is assigned by a network administrator and used to compare various paths through an internetwork environment. Cost values are used by routing protocols to determine the most favorable path to a particular destination: the lower the cost, the better the path.
Cost is also known as path cost.

count to infinity
Problem that can occur in routing algorithms that are slow to converge, in which routers continuously increment the hop count to particular networks. Typically, some arbitrary hop-count limit is imposed to prevent this problem.

CPE
customer premises equipment
Terminating equipment, such as terminals, telephones, and modems, supplied by the telephone company, installed at customer sites, and connected to the telephone company network.

CPI-C
Common Programming Interface for Communications
Platform-independent API developed by IBM and used to provide portability in APPC applications.

cps
cells per second

CPU
central processing unit
The part of a computer that controls all the other parts. It fetches instructions from memory and decodes them. This may cause it to transfer data to or from memory or to activate peripherals to perform input or output.

CQ
custom queuing
Queuing method that is used to guarantee bandwidth for traffic by assigning queue space to each protocol.

CRC
cyclic redundancy check
Error-checking technique in which the frame recipient calculates a remainder by dividing frame contents by a prime binary divisor and compares the calculated remainder to a value stored in the frame by the sending node.

CREN
Corporation for Research and Educational Networking
The result of a merger of BITNET and CSNET. CREN is devoted to providing Internet connectivity to its members, which include the alumni, students, faculty, and other affiliates of participating educational and research institutions, via BITNET III.

cross talk
Interfering energy transferred from one circuit to another.

CSLIP
Compressed Serial Link Internet Protocol
Extension of SLIP that, when appropriate, allows just header information to be sent across a SLIP connection, reducing overhead and increasing packet throughput on SLIP lines.

CSMA/CD
carrier sense multiple access/collision detect
Media-access mechanism wherein devices ready to transmit data first check the channel for a carrier. If no carrier is sensed for a specific period of time, a device can transmit. If two devices transmit at once, a collision occurs and is detected by all colliding devices. This collision subsequently delays retransmissions from those devices for some random length of time. CSMA/CD access is used by Ethernet and IEEE 802.3.

CSNET
Computer Science Network
Large internetwork consisting primarily of universities, research institutions, and commercial concerns. CSNET merged with BITNET to form CREN.

CSU
channel service unit
Digital interface device that connects end-user equipment to the local digital telephone loop. Often referred to together with DSU, as CSU/DSU.

csumon
Tool available on the LightStream 2020 ATM switch, accessible from the bash shell. Csumon allows connection to an external CSU/DSU on a low-speed line for monitoring and control purposes, and can display statistics on the internal CSU/DSU of a medium-speed line.

CTS
Clear To Send. Circuit in the EIA/TIA-232 specification that is activated when DCE is ready to accept data from DTE.

custom queuing
See CQ.

customer premises equipment
See CPE.

cut sheet
A rough diagram indicating where cable runs are located and the numbers of rooms they lead to.

cut-through packet switching
Packet switching approach that streams data through a switch so that the leading edge of a packet exits the switch at the output port before the packet finishes entering the input port. A device using cut-through packet switching reads, processes, and forwards packets as soon as the destination address is looked up, and the outgoing port determined. Contrast with store and forward packet switching.
Cut-through packet switching is also known as on-the-fly packet switching.

CxBus
Cisco Extended Bus
Data bus for interface processors on Cisco 7000 series routers that operates at 533 Mbps.

CyBus
1.067-Gbps data bus for interface processors. Used in the Cisco 7500 series routers.

cycles per second
See hertz.

cyclic redundancy check
See CRC.

D channel
data channel
1) Full-duplex, 16-kbps (BRI) or 64-kbps (PRI) ISDN channel. Compare to B channel, E channel, and H channel.
2) In SNA, a device that connects a processor and main storage with peripherals.

D4 framing
See SF.

DARPA
Defense Advanced Research Projects Agency U.S. government agency that funded research for and experimentation with the Internet. Evolved from ARPA, and then, in 1994, back to ARPA.

DARPA Internet
Obsolete term referring to the Internet. See Internet.

data
Upper-layer protocol data.

data bus connector
See DB connector.

data channel
See D channel.

data circuit-terminating equipment
See DCE.

data communications equipment
See DCE.

Data Encryption Standard
See DES.

data flow control layer
Layer 5 of the SNA architectural model. This layer determines and manages interactions between session partners, particularly data flow. Corresponds to the session layer of the OSI model.

data link control layer
Layer 2 in the SNA architectural model. Responsible for the transmission of data over a particular physical link. Corresponds roughly to the data link layer of the OSI model.

data link layer
Layer 2 of the OSI reference model. This layer provides reliable transit of data across a physical link. The data link layer is concerned with physical addressing, network topology, line discipline, error notification, ordered delivery of frames, and flow control. The IEEE has divided this layer into two sublayers: the MAC sublayer and the LLC sublayer. Sometimes simply called link layer. Roughly corresponds to the data link control layer of the SNA model.

Data Movement Processor
See DMP.

data service unit
See DSU.

data set ready
See DSR.

data sink
Network equipment that accepts data transmissions.

data stream
All data transmitted through a communications line in a single read or write operation.

data terminal equipment
See DTE.

data terminal ready
See DTR.

datagram
Logical grouping of information sent as a network layer unit over a transmission medium without prior establishment of a virtual circuit. IP datagrams are the primary information units in the Internet. The terms frame, message, packet, and segment are also used to describe logical information groupings at various layers of the OSI reference model and in various technology circles.

data-link connection identifier
See DLCI.

data-link switching
See DLSw.

dB
decibel
The ratio between two signal levels. It is a unitless physical measurement of signal strength.

DB connector
data bus connector
Type of connector used to connect serial and parallel cables to a data bus. DB connector names are of the format DB-x, where x represents the number of (wires) within the connector. Each line is connected to a pin on the connector, but in many cases, not all pins are assigned a function. DB connectors are defined by various EIA/TIA standards.

dBi
A ratio of decibels to an isotropic antenna that is commonly used to measure antenna gain. The greater the dBi value, the higher the gain, and the more acute the angle of coverage.

DC
direct current
Electrical current that travels in only one direction. Direct current is generally used in electronic circuits.

DCA
Defense Communications Agency
U.S. government organization responsible for DDN networks such as MILNET. DCA is now known as DISA.

DCE
data communications equipment
Data communications equipment (EIA expansion) or data circuit-terminating equipment (ITU-T expansion). The devices and connections of a communications network that comprise the network end of the user-to-network interface. The DCE provides a physical connection to the network, forwards traffic, and provides a clocking signal used to synchronize data transmission between DCE and DTE devices. Modems and interface cards are examples of DCE.

dCEF
Cisco Express Forwarding
Advanced Layer 3 IP forwarding technology designed to optimize network performance and scalability.

DDM
Distributed Data Management
Software in an IBM SNA environment that provides peer-to-peer communication and file sharing. One of three SNA transaction services.

DDN
Defense Data Network
U.S. military network composed of an unclassified network (MILNET) and various secret and top-secret networks. DDN is operated and maintained by DISA.

DDR
dial-on-demand routing
Technique whereby a Cisco router can automatically initiate and close a circuit-switched session as transmitting stations demand. The router spoofs keepalives so that end stations treat the session as active. DDR permits routing over ISDN or telephone lines using an external ISDN terminal adaptor or modem.

DE
discard eligible. See tagged traffic.

de facto standard
Standard that exists by nature of its widespread use. Compare with de jure standard.

de jure standard
Standard that exists because of its approval by an official standards body. Compare with de facto standard.

decibels
See dB.

DECnet
Digital Equipment Corporation Network
Group of communications products (including a protocol suite) developed and supported by Digital Equipment Corporation. DECnet/OSI (also called DECnet Phase V) is the most recent iteration and supports both OSI protocols and proprietary Digital protocols. Phase IV Prime supports inherent MAC addresses that allow

DECnet nodes to coexist with systems running other protocols that have MAC address restrictions.

DECnet routing
Digital Equipment Corporation Network routing

Proprietary routing scheme introduced by Digital Equipment Corporation in DECnet Phase III. In DECnet Phase V, DECnet completed its transition to OSI routing protocols (ES-IS and IS-IS).

decorative raceway
Type of wall-mounted channel with removable cover used to support horizontal cabling. Decorative raceway is big enough to hold two cables.

decryption
The reverse application of an encryption algorithm to encrypted data, thereby restoring that data to its original, unencrypted state.

dedicated LAN
Network segment allocated to a single device. Used in LAN switched network topologies.

dedicated line
Communications line that is indefinitely reserved for transmissions, rather than switched as transmission is required.

default route
Routing table entry that is used to direct frames for which a next hop is not explicitly listed in the routing table.

Defense Advanced Research Projects Agency
See DARPA.

Defense Communications Agency
See DCA.

Defense Data Network
See DDN.

Defense Information Systems Agency
See DISA.

Defense Intelligence Agency
See DIA.

delay
1) The time between the initiation of a transaction by a sender and the first response received by the sender.
2) The time required to move a packet from source to destination over a given path.

demand priority
Media access method used in 100VG-AnyLAN that uses a hub that can handle multiple transmission requests and can process traffic according to priority, making it useful for servicing time-sensitive traffic such as multimedia and video. Demand priority eliminates the overhead of packet collisions, collision recovery, and broadcast traffic typical in Ethernet networks.

demarc
Demarcation point between carrier equipment and CPE.

demodulation
Process of returning a modulated signal to its original form. Modems perform demodulation by taking an analog signal and returning it to its original (digital) form.

demultiplexing
The separating of multiple input streams that have been multiplexed into a common physical signal back into multiple output streams.

dense mode PIM
See PIM dense mode.

Department of Defense
See DoD.

Department of Defense Intelligence Information Systems
See DNSIX.

Dependent LU
See DLU.

DES
Data Encryption Standard
Standard cryptographic algorithm developed by the U.S. NBS.

designated bridge
The bridge that incurs the lowest path cost when forwarding a frame from a segment to the route bridge.

Designated Intermediate System
See DIS.

designated router
OSPF router that generates LSAs for a multiaccess network and has other special responsibilities in running OSPF. Each multiaccess OSPF network that has at least two attached routers has a designated router that is elected by the OSPF Hello protocol. The designated router enables a reduction in the number of adjacencies required on a multiaccess network, which in turn reduces the amount of routing protocol traffic and the size of the topological database.

destination address
Address of a network device that is receiving data.

destination MAC
See DMAC.

destination port
Number of the called port.

destination service access point
See DSAP.

deterministic load distribution
Technique for distributing traffic between two bridges across a circuit group. Guarantees packet ordering between source-destination pairs and always forwards traffic for a source-destination pair on the same segment in a circuit group for a given circuit-group configuration.

Deutsche Industrie Norm
See DIN.

Deutsche Industrie Norm connector
See DIN connector.

device
See node.

DFS
Dynamic Frequency Selection
DFS dynamically instructs a transmitter to switch to another channel whenever a particular condition (such as the presence of a radar signal) is met. Prior to transmitting, the DFS mechanism of a device monitors its available operating spectrum, listening for a radar signal. If a signal is detected, the channel associated with the radar signal is vacated or flagged as unavailable for use by the transmitter.

DIA
Document Interchange Architecture
Defines the protocols and data formats needed for the transparent interchange of documents in an SNA network. One of three SNA transaction services.

dial backup
Feature supported by Cisco routers that provides protection against WAN downtime by allowing the network administrator to configure a backup serial line through a circuit-switched connection.

dial-on-demand routing
See DDR.

dial-up line
Communications circuit that is established by a switched-circuit connection using the telephone company network.

differential encoding
Digital encoding technique whereby a binary value is denoted by a signal change rather than a particular signal level.

differential Manchester encoding
Digital coding scheme where a mid-bit-time transition is used for clocking, and a transition at the beginning of each bit time denotes a zero. The coding scheme used by IEEE 802.5 and Token Ring networks.

Diffusing Update Algorithm
See DUAL.

Digital Network Architecture
See DNA.

digital signal
Language of computers comprising only two states, on and off which are indicated by a series of voltage pulses.

digital signal level 0
See DS-0.

digital signal level 1
See DS-1.

digital signal level 3
See DS-3.

Dijkstra's algorithm
See SPF.

DIN
Deutsche Industrie Norm
German national standards organization.

DIN connector
Deutsche Industrie Norm connector
Multipin connector used in some Macintosh and IBM PC-compatible computers, and on some network processor panels.

dipole
A type of low-gain (2.2-dBi) antenna consisting of two (often internal) elements. Compare with isotropic.

direct memory access
See DMA.

directed search
Search request sent to a specific node known to contain a resource. A directed search is used to determine the continued existence of the resource and to obtain routing information specific to the node. See also broadcast search.

directionality
The coverage around the antenna. An omnidirectional WLAN antenna transmits and receives signals in all horizontal directions equally. A directional antenna focuses the signal from the access point into a smaller coverage area resulting in a stronger signal in this direction.

directory services
Services that help network devices locate service providers.

DIS
Designated Intermediate System
Elected and will conduct the flooding over the media. The DIS is analogous to the designated router in Open Shortest Path First (OSPF) Protocol, even though the details including election process and adjacencies within a multi-access media differ significantly. The DIS is elected by priority. The highest priority becomes the DIS. This is configurable on an interface basis. In the case of a tie, the router with the highest SNPA (MAC) address will become the DIS.

DISA
Defense Information Systems Agency
U.S. military organization responsible for implementing and operating military information systems, including the DDN.

discard eligible
See DE.

disk assembly
The combination of a hard disk drive, a floppy disk drive, and a disk power supply on a LightStream 2020 ATM switch. Each NP card in a LightStream 2020 chassis has its own disk assembly.

Distance Vector Multicast Routing Protocol
See DVMRP.

distance vector routing algorithm
Class of routing algorithms that iterate on the number of hops in a route to find a shortest-path spanning tree. Distance vector routing algorithms call for each router to send its entire routing table in each update, but only to its neighbors. Distance vector routing algorithms can be prone to routing loops, but are computationally simpler than link state routing algorithms.
Distance vector routing algorithm is also known as Bellman-Ford routing algorithm.

distortion delay
Problem with a communication signal resulting from nonuniform transmission speeds of the components of a signal through a transmission medium. Also called group delay.

distributed computing (processing)
See client-server computing.

Distributed Data Management
See DDM.

Distributed Queue Dual Bus
See DQDB.

Distributed Weighted Fair Queuing
See dWFQ.

DLCI
data-link connection identifier
Value that specifies a PVC or SVC in a Frame Relay network. In the basic Frame Relay specification, DLCIs are locally significant (connected devices might use different values to specify the same connection). In the LMI extended specification, DLCIs are globally significant (DLCIs specify individual end devices).

DLSw
Data-Link Switching
Interoperability standard, described in RFC 1434, that provides a method for forwarding SNA and NetBIOS traffic over TCP/IP networks using data link layer switching and encapsulation. DLSw uses Switch-to-Switch Protocol (SSP) instead of SRB, eliminating the major limitations of SRB, including hop-count limits, broadcast and unnecessary traffic, timeouts, lack of flow control, and lack of prioritization schemes.

DLSw+
Data Link Switching Plus
Cisco implementation of the DLSw standard for SNA and NetBIOS traffic forwarding. DLSw+ goes beyond the standard to include the advanced features of the current Cisco RSRB implementation, and provides additional functionality to increase the overall scalability of data-link switching.

DLU
dependent logical unit
An LU that depends on the SSCP to provide services for establishing sessions with other LUs.

DMA
direct memory access
The transfer of data from a peripheral device, such as a hard disk drive, into memory without that data passing through the microprocessor. DMA transfers data into memory at high speeds with no processor overhead.

DMAC
Destination MAC
The MAC address specified in the Destination Address field of a packet. Compare with SMAC.

DMP
Data Movement Processor
Processor on the Catalyst 5000 that, along with the multiport packet buffer memory interface, performs the frame-switching function for the switch. The DMP also handles translational bridging between the Ethernet and FDDI interfaces, IP segmentation, and intelligent bridging with protocol-based filtering.

DNA
Digital Network Architecture
Network architecture developed by Digital Equipment Corporation. The products that embody DNA (including communications protocols) are collectively referred to as DECnet.

DNIS
Dialed Number Identification Service
DNIS is also known as called number.

DNS
Domain Naming System
System used in the Internet for translating names of network nodes into addresses.

DNS ALG
Domain Naming System Application Level Gateway
Protocol that can be used in NAT-PT translations to map network addresses dynamically based on DNS queries. Compare with NAT-PT and SIIT.

DNSIX
Department of Defense Intelligence Information System Network Security for Information Exchange
Collection of security requirements for networking defined by the U.S. Defense Intelligence Agency.

Document Interchange Architecture
See DIA.

DoD
Department of Defense
U.S. government organization that is responsible for national defense. The DoD has frequently funded communication protocol development.

domain
1) In the Internet, a portion of the naming hierarchy tree that refers to general groupings of networks based on organization-type or geography.
2) In SNA, an SSCP and the resources it controls.
3) In IS-IS, a logical set of networks.
4) Networking system developed by Apollo Computer (now part of Hewlett-Packard) for use in its engineering workstations.

Domain Naming System
See DNS.

domain specific part
See DSP.

dot address
Refers to the common notation for IP addresses in the form <a.b.c.d> where each number a represents, in decimal, 1 byte of the 4-byte IP address.
Dot address is also known as dotted notation or four-part dotted notation.

dotted notation
See dot address.

downlink station
See ground station.

downstream physical unit
See DSPU.

DQDB
Distributed Queue Dual Bus
Data link layer communication protocol, specified in the IEEE 802.6 standard, designed for use in MANs. DQDB, which permits multiple systems to interconnect using two unidirectional logical buses, is an open standard that is designed for compatibility with carrier transmission standards, and is aligned with emerging standards for BISDN. SMDS Interface Protocol (SIP) is based on DQDB.

DRAM
Dynamic random-access memory
RAM that stores information in capacitors that must be periodically refreshed. Delays can occur because DRAMs are inaccessible to the processor when refreshing their contents. However, DRAMs are less complex and have greater capacity than SRAMs.

drop
Point on a multipoint channel where a connection to a networked device is made.

drop cable
Generally, a cable that connects a network device (such as a computer) to a physical medium. A type of AUI.

DS-0 or DS0
digital signal level 0
Framing specification used in transmitting digital signals over a single channel at 64-kbps on a T1 facility. Compare with DS-1 and DS-3.

DS-1
digital signal level 1
Framing specification used in transmitting digital signals at 1.544-Mbps on a T1 facility (in the United States) or at 2.108-Mbps on an E1 facility (in Europe). Compare with DS-0 and DS-3.

DS-1 domestic trunk interface
See DS-1/DTI.

DS-1/DTI
digital signal level 1/domestic trunk interface
Interface circuit used for DS-1 applications with 24 trunks.

DS-3
Digital signal level 3
Framing specification used for transmitting digital signals at 44.736-Mbps on a T3 facility. Compare with DS-0 and DS-1.

DSAP
destination service access point
The SAP of the network node designated in the Destination field of a packet. Compare to SSAP.

DSP
domain specific part
The part of a CLNS address that contains an area identifier, a station identifier, and a selector byte.

DSPU
downstream physical unit
1) In SNA, a PU that is located downstream from the host.
2) Cisco IOS software feature that enables a router to function as a PU concentrator for SNA PU 2 nodes. PU concentration at the router simplifies the task of PU definition at the upstream host while providing additional flexibility and mobility for downstream PU devices. This feature is sometimes referred to as DSPU concentration. See also PU and SNA.

DSPU concentration
See DSPU and PU.

DSR
data set ready
EIA/TIA-232 interface circuit that is activated when DCE is powered up and ready for use.

DSSS
Direct Sequence Spread Spectrum
DSSS is one of the modulation techniques provided for by the IEEE 802.11 and the one chosen by the 802.11 Working Group for the widely used IEEE 802.11b devices.

DSU
data service unit
Device used in digital transmission that adapts the physical interface on a DTE device to a transmission facility such as T1 or E1. The DSU is also responsible for such functions as signal timing. Often referred to together with CSU, as CSU/DSU.

DSX-1
Cross-connection point for DS-1 signals.

DTE
data terminal equipment
Device at the user end of a user-network interface that serves as a data source, destination, or both. DTE connects to a data network through a DCE device (for example, a modem) and typically uses clocking signals generated by the DCE. DTE includes such devices as computers, protocol translators, and multiplexers. Compare with DCE.

DTMF
dual tone multifrequency
Use of two simultaneous voice-band tones for dialing (such as touch tone).

DTR
data terminal ready
EIA/TIA-232 circuit that is activated to let the DCE know when the DTE is ready to send and receive data.

DUAL
Diffusing Update Algorithm
Convergence algorithm used in Enhanced IGRP that provides loop-free operation at every instant throughout a route computation. Allows routers involved in a topology change to synchronize at the same time, while not involving routers that are unaffected by the change.

dual counter-rotating rings
Network topology in which two signal paths, whose directions are opposite one another, exist in a token-passing network. FDDI and CDDI are based on this concept.

dual homing
Network topology in which a device is connected to the network by way of two independent access points (points of attachment). One access point is the primary connection, and the other is a standby connection that is activated in the event of a failure of the primary connection.

Dual IS-IS
See Integrated IS-IS.

dual stack
A common transition mechanism to enable a smooth integration of IPv4 to IPv6. Compare with IPv6-over-IPv4 tunnels.

dual tone multifrequency
See DTMF.

dual-homed station
Device attached to multiple FDDI rings to provide redundancy.

DVMRP

Distance Vector Multicast Routing Protocol
Internetwork gateway protocol, largely based on RIP, that implements a typical dense mode IP multicast scheme. DVMRP uses IGMP to exchange routing datagrams with its neighbors.

dWFQ

Distributed Weighted Fair Queuing
Special high-speed version of WFQ that provides bandwidth allocations and delay bounds to specified IP traffic sources by segregating the traffic into flows or classes and then providing non-first-in, first-out (FIFO) service to the various queues according to their assigned weights. In order to use dWFQ, dCEF switching must be enabled on the interface.

dynamic address resolution

Use of an address resolution protocol to determine and store address information on demand.

dynamic random-access memory

See DRAM.

dynamic routing

Routing that adjusts automatically to network topology or traffic changes.
Dynamic routing is also known as adaptive routing.

E channel

echo channel
64-kbps ISDN circuit-switching control channel. The E channel was defined in the 1984 ITU-T ISDN specification, but was dropped in the 1988 specification. Compare with B channel, D channel, and H channel.

E.164

ITU-T recommendation for international telecommunication numbering, especially in ISDN, BISDN, and SMDS. An evolution of standard telephone numbers.

E1

Wide-area digital transmission scheme used predominantly in Europe that carries data at a rate of 2.048 Mbps. E1 lines can be leased for private use from common carriers. Compare with T1.

E3

Wide-area digital transmission scheme used predominantly in Europe that carries data at a rate of 34.368 Mbps. E3 lines can be leased for private use from common carriers. Compare with T3.

EAP

Extensible Authentication Protocol
Universal authentication framework frequently used in wireless networks defined by RFC 3748. Although the EAP protocol is not limited to WLANs and can be used for wired LAN authentication, it is most often used in WLANs. The WPA and WPA2 standards have adopted five EAP types as their official authentication mechanisms.

early token release

Technique used in Token Ring networks that allows a station to release a new token onto the ring immediately after transmitting, instead of waiting for the first frame to return. This feature can increase the total bandwidth on the ring.

EBCDIC

extended binary coded decimal interchange code
Any of a number of coded character sets developed by IBM consisting of 8-bit coded characters. This character code is used by older IBM systems and telex machines. Compare with ASCII.

ECC

edge card control
Process on the NP of a LightStream 2020 ATM switch that performs per-card processing for an edge card. Such processing includes protocol management (ATM connection management) and media-specific (Ethernet and FDDI) management tasks, internetworking operations such as packet forwarding and filtering, and network management tasks.

echo channel

See E channel.

ECMA
European Computer Manufacturers Association
Group of European computer vendors who have done substantial OSI standardization work.

ECNM
Enterprise Composite Network Model
Framework used by network professionals to describe and analyze any modern enterprise network. It takes a complex enterprise network design and breaks it down into three functional areas including the Enterprise Campus, Enterprise Edge, and the Service Provider Edge.

edge card
Line card on the LightStream 2020 ATM switch that is configured to communicate with devices outside the ATM network. Edge cards offer Ethernet, FDDI, frame forwarding, Frame Relay, OC-3c, and UNI interfaces.

edge card control
See ECC.

edge device
Network entity such as a LAN segment, host, or router that connects to a LightStream 2020 ATM switch via an edge card. Edge devices send and receive the data that passes through the ATM network.

EDI
electronic data interchange
The electronic communication of operational data such as orders and invoices between organizations.

EDIFACT
Electronic Data Interchange for Administration, Commerce, and Transport
Data exchange standard administered by the United Nations to be a multi-industry EDI standard.

EEPROM
electrically erasable programmable read-only memory
EPROM that can be erased using electrical signals applied to specific pins.

EIA
Electronic Industries Association
Group that specifies electrical transmission standards. The EIA and TIA have developed numerous well-known communications standards, including EIA/TIA-232 and EIA/TIA-449.

EIA/TIA-232
Electronic Industries Association/Telecommunications Industry Association 232
Common physical layer interface standard, developed by EIA and TIA, that supports unbalanced circuits at signal speeds of up to 64 kbps. Closely resembles the V.24 specification. EIA/TIA-232 was formerly known as RS-232.

EIA/TIA-449
Electronic Industries Association/Telecommunications Industry Association 449
Popular physical layer interface developed by EIA and TIA. Essentially, a faster (up to 2 Mbps) version of EIA/TIA-232 capable of longer cable runs.
EIA/TIA-449 was formerly known as RS-449.

EIA/TIA-568
Electronic Industries Association/Telecommunications Industry Association 568
Standard that describes the characteristics and applications for various grades of UTP cabling.

EIA/TIA-606
Electronic Industries Association/Telecommunications Industry Association 606
Administration standard for the telecommunications infrastructure of commercial buildings. It includes the following administration areas: terminations, media, pathways, spaces, and bounding and grounding.

EIA-530
Electronic Industries Association 530
REFers to two electrical implementations of EIA/TIA-449: RS-422 (for balanced transmission) and RS-423 (for unbalanced transmission).

EIGRP
Enhanced Interior Gateway Routing Protocol
Advanced version of IGRP developed by Cisco. Provides superior convergence properties and

operating efficiency, and combines the advantages of link state protocols with those of distance vector protocols.

EIP
Ethernet Interface Processor
Interface processor card on the Cisco 7000 series routers. The EIP provides high-speed (10-Mbps) AUI ports that support Ethernet Version 1 and Ethernet Version 2 or IEEE 802.3 interfaces, and a high-speed data path to other interface processors.

EIRP
Effective Isotropic Radiated Power
EIRP is the effective power in front of the antenna. The EIRP of a transmitter is the power that the transmitter appears to have if the transmitter were an isotropic radiator (if the antenna radiated equally in all directions). By virtue of the gain of a radio antenna (or dish), a beam is formed that preferentially transmits the energy in one direction. The EIRP is estimated by adding the gain (of the antenna) and the transmitter power (of the radio).

EISA
Extended Industry-Standard Architecture
32-bit bus interface used in PCs, PC-based servers, and some UNIX workstations and servers.

ELAN
emulated local area network
ATM network in which an Ethernet or Token Ring LAN is emulated using a client-server model. ELANs are composed of an LEC, an LES, a BUS, and an LECS. Multiple ELANs can exist simultaneously on a single ATM network. ELANs are defined by the LANE specification.

electrically erasable programmable read-only memory
See EEPROM.

electromagnetic interference
See EMI.

electromagnetic pulse
See EMP.

electronic data interchange
See EDI.

Electronic Data Interchange for Administration, Co
See EDIFACT.

Electronic Industries Association
See EIA.

electronic mail
See e-mail.

Electronic Messaging Association
See EMA.

electrostatic discharge
See ESD.

EMA
1) Enterprise Management Architecture. Digital Equipment Corporation network management architecture, based on the OSI network management model.
2) Electronic Messaging Association. Forum devoted to standards and policy work, education, and development of electronic messaging systems such as electronic mail, voice mail, and facsimile.

e-mail
electronic mail
Widely used network application in which mail messages are transmitted electronically between end users over various types of networks using various network protocols.

EMI
electromagnetic interference
Interference by electromagnetic signals that can cause reduced data integrity and increased error rates on transmission channels.

EMIF
ESCON Multiple Image Facility
Mainframe I/O software function that allows one ESCON channel to be shared among multiple logical partitions on the same mainframe.

EMP
electromagnetic pulse
Caused by lightning and other high-energy phenomena. Capable of coupling enough energy into unshielded conductors to destroy electronic devices.

emulated LAN
See ELAN.

emulation mode
Function of an NCP that enables it to perform activities equivalent to those performed by a transmission control unit. For example, with CiscoWorks, the NetView PU 2 emulates the IBM 3274.

encapsulation
The wrapping of data in a particular protocol header. For example, Ethernet data is wrapped in a specific Ethernet header before network transit. Also, when bridging dissimilar networks, the entire frame from one network is simply placed in the header used by the data link layer protocol of the other network.

encapsulation bridging
Carries Ethernet frames from one router to another across disparate media, such as serial and FDDI lines. Contrast with translational bridging.

encoder
Device that modifies information into the required transmission format.

encoding
Process by which bits are represented by voltages.

encryption
The application of a specific algorithm to data so as to alter the appearance of the data making it incomprehensible to those who are not authorized to see the information.

end of transmission
See EOT.

end point
Device at which a virtual circuit or virtual path begins or ends.

end system
See ES.

End System Hello
See ESH.

End System-to-Intermediate System
See ES-IS.

Energy Sciences Network
See ESnet.

Enhanced IGRP
See EIGRP.

Enhanced Interior Gateway Routing Protocol
See EIGRP.

Enhanced Monitoring Services
Set of analysis tools on the Catalyst 5000 switch, consisting of an integrated RMON agent and the SPAN. These tools provide traffic monitoring, and network segment analysis and management.

Enterprise Composite Network Model
See ECNM.

Enterprise Management Architecture
See EMA.

enterprise network
Large and diverse network connecting most major points in a company or other organization. Differs from a WAN in that it is privately owned and maintained.

Enterprise Network Model
Also known as Enterprise Composite Network Model. See ECNM.

Enterprise System Connection
See ESCON.

Enterprise System Connection channel
See ESCON channel.

entity
Generally, an individual, manageable network device.
An entity is also known as an alias.

EOT
end of transmission
Generally, a character that signifies the end of a logical group of characters or bits.

EPROM
erasable programmable read-only memory
Nonvolatile memory chips that are programmed after they are manufactured, and, if necessary, can be erased by some means and reprogrammed. Compare with EEPROM and PROM.

equalization
Technique used to compensate for communications channel distortions.

erasable programmable read-only memory
See EPROM.

error control
Technique for detecting and correcting errors in data transmissions.

error-correcting code
Code having sufficient intelligence and incorporating sufficient signaling information to enable the detection and correction of many errors at the receiver.

error-detecting code
Code that can detect transmission errors through analysis of received data based on the adherence of the data to appropriate structural guidelines.

ES
end system
Any non-routing host or node. ES lives in a particular area.

ESCON
Enterprise System Connection
IBM channel architecture that specifies a pair of fiber-optic cables, with either LEDs or lasers as transmitters and a signaling rate of 200 Mbps.

ESCON channel
IBM channel for attaching mainframes to peripherals such as storage devices, backup units, and network interfaces. This channel incorporates fiber channel technology. The ESCON channel replaces the bus and tag channel. Compare with parallel channel.

ESCON Multiple Image Facility
See EMIF.

ESD
electrostatic discharge
A flow or spark of electricity that originates from a static source such as a carpet and arcs across a gap to another object.

ESF
Extended Superframe Format
Framing type used on T1 circuits that consists of 24 frames of 192 bits each, with the 193rd bit providing timing and other functions. ESF is an enhanced version of SF.

ESH
End System Hello
An IS-IS hello packet type. It is part of the ES-IS spec 9542; similar to IRDP in TCP/IP; used for routers (ISs) and End Systems (ESs) to detect each other and form adjacencies.

ES-IS
End System-to-Intermediate System
ES-IS discovery protocols used for routing between end systems and intermediate systems. ES-IS is an analogous to ARP in IP. Although not technically a routing protocol, ES-IS is commonly used with routing protocols to provide end-to-end data movement through an internetwork. Routing between end systems and intermediate systems is sometimes referred to as Level 0 routing.

ESnet
Energy Sciences Network
Data communications network managed and funded by the U.S. Department of Energy Office of Energy Research (DOE/OER). Interconnects the DOE to educational institutions and other research facilities.

ESS
extended service set
WLAN infrastruce mode whereby two or more basic service sets are connected by a common distribution system. An ESS generally includes a common SSID to allow roaming from access

point to access point without requiring client configuration.

Ethernet
Baseband LAN specification invented by Xerox Corporation and developed jointly by Xerox, Intel, and Digital Equipment Corporation. Ethernet networks use CSMA/CD and run over a variety of cable types at 10 Mbps. Ethernet is similar to the IEEE 802.3 series of standards.

Ethernet Interface Processor
See EIP.

ETSI
European Telecommunication Standards Institute
Organization created by the European PTTs and the European Community (EC) to propose telecommunications standards for Europe.

EUI-64
Extended Universal Identifier (EUI)-64 address
This is an IPv6 address format created by taking an interface's MAC address (which is 48 bits in length) and inserting another 16-bit hexadecimal string (FFFE) between the OUI (first 24 bits) and unique serial number (last 24 bits) of the MAC address. To ensure that the chosen address is from a unique Ethernet MAC address, the seventh bit in the high-order byte is set to 1 (equivalent to the IEEE G/L bit) to indicate the uniqueness of the 48-bit address.

EUnet
European Internet
European commercial Internet service provider. EUnet is designed to provide electronic mail, news, and other Internet services to European markets.

European Academic Research Network
See EARN.

European Computer Manufacturers Association
See ECMA.

European Internet
See EUnet.

European Telecommunication Standards Institute
See ETSI.

event
Network message indicating operational irregularities in physical elements of a network or a response to the occurrence of a significant task, typically the completion of a request for information.

Excess Burst
See Be.

excess rate
Traffic in excess of the insured rate for a given connection. Specifically, the excess rate equals the maximum rate minus the insured rate. Excess traffic is delivered only if network resources are available and can be discarded during periods of congestion. Compare with insured rate and maximum rate.

exchange identification
See XID.

EXEC
The interactive command processor of the Cisco IOS software.

expansion
The process of running a compressed data set through an algorithm that restores the data set to its original size. Compare with companding and compression.

expectational acknowledgment
Type of acknowledgment scheme in which the acknowledgment number refers to the octet expected next.

expedited delivery
Option set by a specific protocol layer telling other protocol layers (or the same protocol layer in another network device) to handle specific data more rapidly.

explicit route
In SNA, a route from a source subarea to a destination subarea, as specified by a list of subarea nodes and transmission groups that connect the two.

explorer frame
Frame sent out by a networked device in a SRB environment to determine the optimal route to another networked device.

Extended Binary Coded Decimal Interchange Code
See EBCDIC.

Extended Industry-Standard Architecture
See EISA.

extended service set
See ESS.

Extended Superframe Format
See ESF.

Extended Universal Identifier (EUI)-64
See EUI-64.

Extensible Authentication Protocol
See EAP.

exterior gateway protocol
Any internetwork protocol used to exchange routing information between autonomous systems.

failure domain
Area in which a failure has occurred in a Token Ring, defined by the information contained in a beacon. When a station detects a serious problem with the network (such as a cable break), it sends a beacon frame that includes the station reporting the failure, its NAUN, and everything in between. Beaconing in turn initiates a process called autoreconfiguration.

fan-out unit
Device that allows multiple devices on a network to communicate using a single network attachment.

Fast Ethernet
Any of a number of 100-Mbps Ethernet specifications. Fast Ethernet offers a speed increase ten times that of the 10BASE-T Ethernet specification, while preserving such qualities as frame format, MAC mechanisms, and MTU. Such similarities allow the use of existing 10BASE-T applications and network management tools on Fast Ethernet networks. Based on an extension to the IEEE 802.3 specification. Compare with Ethernet.

Fast Ethernet Interface Processor
See FEIP.

Fast Sequenced Transport
See FST.

Fast Serial Interface Processor
See FSIP.

fast switching
Cisco feature whereby a route cache is used to expedite packet switching through a router. Contrast with slow switching.

fault management
One of five categories of network management defined by ISO for management of OSI networks. Fault management attempts to ensure that network faults are detected and controlled.

FCC
Federal Communications Commission
U.S. government agency that supervises, licenses, and controls electronic and electromagnetic transmission standards.

fcload
function card load
Low-level software module in the LightStream 2020 ATM switch that is invoked by higher-level modules to load software from the NP to a function card.

FCS
frame check sequence
Refers to the extra characters added to a frame for error control purposes. Used in HDLC, Frame Relay, and other data link layer protocols.

FDDI
Fiber Distributed Data Interface
LAN standard, defined by ANSI X3T9.5, specifying a 100-Mbps token-passing network using fiber-optic cable, with transmission distances of up to 2 km. FDDI uses a dual-ring architecture to provide redundancy. Compare with CDDI and FDDI II.

FDDI II
Fiber Distributed Data Interface II
ANSI standard that enhances FDDI. FDDI II provides isochronous transmission for connectionless data circuits and connection-oriented voice and video circuits. Compare with FDDI.

FDDI Interface Processor
See FIP.

FDM
frequency-division multiplexing
Technique whereby information from multiple channels can be allocated bandwidth on a single wire based on frequency. Compare with ATDM, statistical multiplexing, and TDM.

FECN
Forward Explicit Congestion Notification
Bit set by a Frame Relay network to inform DTE receiving the frame that congestion was experienced in the path from source to destination. DTE receiving frames with the FECN bit set can request that higher-level protocols take flow-control action as appropriate. Compare with BECN.

Federal Communications Commission
See FCC.

Federal Networking Council
See FNC.

FEIP
Fast Ethernet Interface Processor
Interface processor on the Cisco 7000 series routers. The FEIP supports up to two 100-Mbps 100BASE-T ports.

FEP
front-end processor
Device or board that provides network interface capabilities for a networked device. In SNA, typically an IBM 3745 device.

FF
frame forwarding
Interface on the LightStream 2020 ATM switch that allows any traffic based on HDLC or SDLC frames to traverse the ATM network. Frame forwarding circuits are port-to-port, and only one PVC is allowed between a pair of ports. Frame forwarding is supported by the low-speed interface module, which offers V.35, EIA/TIA-449, or X.21 physical interfaces.

FF02::1
IPv6 multicast address identifying all nodes on a link.

FF02::2
IPv6 multicast address identifying all routers on a link.

FF02::5
IPv6 multicast address identifying all OSPF routers on the link-local scope. It is equivalent to the multicast address 224.0.0.5 in OSPFv2.

FF02::6
IPv6 multicast address identifying all OSPF designated routers on the link-local scope. It is equivalent to the multicast address 224.0.0.6 in OSPFv2.

FF02::9
IPv6 multicast address identifying all IPv6 RIPng routers on link.

FF05::1:FFXX:XXXX
IPv6 multicast address used to create neighbor solicitation messages which are sent on a local link when a node wants to determine the link-layer address of another node on the same local link. Similar to ARP in IPv4.

FF05::101
IPv6 multicast address identifying all NTP servers in the site (site-local scope).

Fiber Distributed Data Interface
See FDDI.

Fiber Distributed Data Interface II
See FDDI II.

fiber-optic cable
Physical medium capable of conducting modulated light transmission. Compared with other transmission media, fiber-optic cable is more expensive, but is not susceptible to electromagnetic interference, and is capable of higher data rates.
Fiber-optic cable is also known as optical fiber.

fiber-optic interrepeater link
See FOIRL.

FID0
format indicator 0
One of several formats that an SNA TH can use. An FID0 TH is used for communication between an SNA node and a non-SNA node.

FID1
format indicator 1
One of several formats that an SNA TH can use. An FID1 TH encapsulates messages between two subarea nodes that do not support virtual and explicit routes.

FID2
format indicator 2
One of several formats that an SNA TH can use. An FID2 TH is used for transferring messages between a subarea node and a PU 2, using local addresses.

FID3
format indicator 3
One of several formats that an SNA TH can use. An FID3 TH is used for transferring messages between a subarea node and a PU 1, using local addresses.

FID4
format indicator 4
One of several formats that an SNA TH can use. An FID4 TH encapsulates messages between two subarea nodes that are capable of supporting virtual and explicit routes.

field-replaceable unit
See FRU.

FIFO queuing
First In First Out queuing
Classic algorithm for packet transmission. With FIFO, transmission occurs in the same order as messages are received. Until recently, FIFO queuing is the default for all router interfaces with the bandwidth greater then 2.048 Mbps.

file transfer
Popular network application that allows files to be moved from one network device to another.

File Transfer Protocol
See FTP.

File Transfer, Access, and Management
See FTAM.

filter
Generally, a process or device that screens network traffic for certain characteristics, such as source address, destination address, or protocol, and determines whether to forward or discard that traffic based on the established criteria.

FIP
FDDI Interface Processor
Interface processor on the Cisco 7000 series routers. The FIP supports SASs, DASs, dual homing, and optical bypass, and contains a 16-mips processor for high-speed (100-Mbps) interface rates. The FIP complies with ANSI and ISO FDDI standards.

firewall
Router or access server, or several routers or access servers, designated as a buffer between any connected public networks and a private network. A firewall router uses access lists and other methods to ensure the security of the private network.

firmware
Software instructions set permanently or semipermanently in ROM.

First In First Out queuing
See FIFO queuing.

fish tape
Retractable coil of steel tape used to guide cable through a wall from above or below.

flapping
Routing problem where an advertised route between two nodes alternates (flaps) back and forth between two paths due to a network problem that causes intermittent interface failures.

Flash memory
Technology developed by Intel and licensed to other semiconductor companies. Flash memory is nonvolatile storage that can be electrically erased and reprogrammed. Allows software images to be stored, booted, and rewritten as necessary.

flash update
Routing update sent asynchronously in response to a change in the network topology. Compare with routing update.

fldsup account
field service personnel account
One of the four default user accounts that are created in the factory on each LightStream 2020 ATM switch. The fldsup account is for the use of field service personnel. Its default interface is the bash shell.

flooding
Traffic passing technique used by switches and bridges in which traffic received on an interface is sent out all of the interfaces of that device except the interface on which the information was originally received.

flow
Stream of data traveling between two endpoints across a network (for example, from one LAN station to another). Multiple flows can be transmitted on a single circuit.

flow control
Technique for ensuring that a transmitting entity, such as a modem, does not overwhelm a receiving entity with data. When the buffers on the receiving device are full, a message is sent to the sending device to suspend the transmission until the data in the buffers has been processed. In IBM networks, this technique is called pacing.

FM
frequency modulation. Modulation technique in which signals of different frequencies represent different data values. Compare with AM and PAM.

FNC
Federal Networking Council
Group responsible for assessing and coordinating U.S. federal agency networking policies and needs.

FOIRL
fiber-optic interrepeater link
Fiber-optic signaling methodology based on the IEEE 802.3 fiber-optic specification. FOIRL is a precursor of the 10BASE-FL specification, which is designed to replace it.

format indicator 0
See FID0.

format indicator 1
See FID1.

format indicator 2
See FID2.

format indicator 3
See FID3.

format indicator 4
See FID4.

forward channel
Communications path carrying information from the call initiator to the called party.

forward delay interval
Amount of time an interface spends listening for topology change information after that interface has been activated for bridging and before forwarding actually begins.

forward explicit congestion notification
See FECN.

forwarding
Process of sending a frame toward its ultimate destination by way of an internetworking device.

forwarding priority
See transmit priority.

Fourier transform
Technique used to evaluate the importance of various frequency cycles in a time series pattern.

four-part dotted notation
See dot address.

fractional T1
See channelized T1.

FRAD
Frame Relay access device
Any network device that provides a connection between a LAN and a Frame Relay WAN.

fragment
Piece of a larger packet that has been broken down to smaller units.

fragmentation
Process of breaking a packet into smaller units when transmitting over a network medium that cannot support the original size of the packet.

frame
Logical grouping of information sent as a data link layer unit over a transmission medium. Often refers to the header and trailer, used for synchronization and error control, that surround the user data contained in the unit. The terms datagram, message, packet, and segment are also used to describe logical information groupings at various layers of the OSI reference model and in various technology circles.

frame check sequence
See FCS.

frame forwarding
See FF.

Frame Relay
Industry-standard, switched data link layer protocol that handles multiple virtual circuits using HDLC encapsulation between connected devices. Frame Relay is more efficient than X.25, the protocol for which it is generally considered a replacement.

Frame Relay Access Device
See FRAD.

Frame Relay Access Support
See FRAS.

Frame Relay bridging
Bridging technique, described in RFC 1490, that uses the same spanning-tree algorithm as other bridging functions, but allows packets to be encapsulated for transmission across a Frame Relay network.

frame switch
See LAN switch.

FRAS
Frame Relay Access Support
Cisco IOS software feature that allows SDLC, Token Ring, Ethernet, and Frame Relay-attached IBM devices to connect to other IBM devices across a Frame Relay network.

frequency
Number of cycles, measured in hertz, of an alternating current signal per unit time.

frequency modulation
See FM.

frequency-division multiplexing
See FDM.

from switch unit
See FSU.

front end
Node or software program that requests services of a back end.

front-end processor
See FEP.

FRU
field-replaceable unit
Hardware component that can be removed and replaced by Cisco-certified service providers. Typical FRUs include cards, power supplies, and chassis components.

FSIP
Fast Serial Interface Processor
The default serial interface processor for Cisco 7000 series routers. The FSIP provides four or eight high-speed serial ports.

FST
Fast Sequenced Transport
Connectionless, sequenced transport protocol that runs on top of the IP protocol. SRB traffic is encapsulated inside of IP datagrams and is passed over an FST connection between two network devices (such as routers). Speeds up data delivery, reduces overhead, and improves the response time of SRB traffic.

FSU
from switch unit
Subsystem of each line card on a LightStream 2020 ATM switch that accepts calls from the switch card, verifies their checksums, and passes them to the reassembly unit. The FSU selectively drops cells if the network becomes congested.

FTAM
File Transfer, Access, and Management
In OSI, an application layer protocol developed for network file exchange and management between diverse types of computers.

FTP
File Transfer Protocol
Application protocol, part of the TCP/IP protocol stack, used for transferring files between network nodes. FTP is defined in RFC 959.

full duplex
Capability for simultaneous data transmission between a sending station and a receiving station. Compare with half duplex and simplex.

full mesh
Term describing a network in which devices are organized in a mesh topology, with each network node having either a physical circuit or a virtual circuit connecting it to every other network node. A full mesh provides a great deal of redundancy, but because it can be prohibitively expensive to implement, it is usually reserved for network backbones.

function card
Line card or an NP card in a LightStream 2020 ATM switch.

function card load
See fcload.

Fuzzball
Digital Equipment Corporation LSI-11 computer system running IP gateway software. The NSFnet used these systems as backbone packet switches.

G.703/G.704
ITU-T electrical and mechanical specifications for connections between telephone company equipment and DTE using BNC connectors and operating at E1 data rates.

G.804
ITU-T framing standard that defines the mapping of ATM cells into the physical medium.

gain
The amount of increase in energy that an antenna appears to add to an RF signal. There are different methods for measuring this, depending on the reference point chosen.

gateway
In the IP community, an older term referring to a routing device. Today, the term router is used to describe nodes that perform this function, and gateway refers to a special-purpose device that performs an application layer conversion of information from one protocol stack to another. Compare with router.

Gateway Discovery Protocol
See GDP.

gateway host
In SNA, a host node that contains a gateway SSCP.

gateway NCP
NCP that connects two or more SNA networks and performs address translation to allow cross-network session traffic.

Gateway-to-Gateway Protocol
See GGP.

GDP
Gateway Discovery Protocol
Cisco protocol that allows hosts to dynamically detect the arrival of new routers as well as determine when a router goes down. Based on UDP.

generic routing encapsulation
See GRE.

Get Nearest Server
See GNS.

GGP
Gateway-to-Gateway Protocol
MILNET protocol specifying how core routers (gateways) should exchange reachability and routing information. GGP uses a distributed shortest-path algorithm.

GID
global information distribution
Process that runs on the NP of every LightStream 2020 ATM switch in a network. GID maintains a database and keeps nodes in the network apprised of changes in topology such as ports, cards, and nodes being added or removed, and trunks going up or down. This information is supplied by the ND process. Global information distribution is also known as global information distribution daemon (GIDD).

GIDD
Global information distribution daemon. See GID.

gigabit
In data communications, a gigabit is 1,000,000,000 (10^9) bits. Abbreviated Gb.

gigabits per second
Abbreviated Gbps.

gigabyte
Abbreviated GB.

gigabytes per second
Abbreviated GBps.

gigahertz
Abbreviated GHz.

GLBP
Gateway Load Balancing Protocol
GLBP is an improvement to HSRP and VRRP, allowing automatic selection and simultaneous use of multiple available gateways as well as automatic failover between those gateways. With GLBP, resources can be fully utilized without the administrative burden of configuring multiple groups and managing multiple default gateway configurations as is required with HSRP and VRRP.

global information distribution
See GID.

global information distribution daemon
See GID.

global unicast address
An IPv6 unicast address that is globally unique. It can be routed globally with no modification. It shares the same address format as an IPv6 anycast address. Global unicast addresses are assigned by the Internet Assigned Numbers Authority (IANA). Compare with local unicast address.

GNS
Get Nearest Server
Request packet sent by a client on an IPX network to locate the nearest active server of a particular type. An IPX network client issues a GNS request to solicit either a direct response from a connected server or a response from a router that tells it where on the internetwork the service can be located. GNS is part of the IPX SAP.

GOSIP
Government OSI Profile
U.S. government procurement specification for OSI protocols. Through GOSIP, the government has mandated that all federal agencies standardize on OSI and implement OSI-based systems as they become commercially available.

Government OSI Profile
See GOSIP.

grade of service
Measure of telephone service quality based on the probability that a call will encounter a busy signal during the busiest hours of the day.

graphical user interface
See GUI.

GRE
generic routing encapsulation
Tunneling protocol developed by Cisco that can encapsulate a wide variety of protocol packet types inside IP tunnels, creating a virtual point-to-point link to Cisco routers at remote points over an IP internetwork. By connecting multiprotocol subnetworks in a single-protocol backbone environment, IP tunneling using GRE allows network expansion across a single-protocol backbone environment.

ground
Electrically neutral contact point.

ground loop
Arrangement that exists when a multi-path connection exists between computers. Usually this occurs when computers are connected to each other through a ground wire and when computers are attached to the same network using twisted pair cable.

ground station
Collection of communications equipment designed to receive signals from (and usually transmit signals to) satellites.
Ground station is also known as downlink station.

group address
See multicast address.

group delay
See distortion delay.

guard band
Unused frequency band between two communications channels that provides separation of the channels to prevent mutual interference.

GUI
graphical user interface
User environment that uses pictorial as well as textual representations of the input and output of applications and the hierarchical or other data structure in which information is stored. Conventions such as buttons, icons, and windows are typical, and many actions are performed using a pointing device (such as a mouse). Microsoft Windows and the Apple Macintosh are prominent examples of platforms utilizing a GUI.

gutter
Type of wall-mounted channel with removable cover used to support horizontal cabling. Gutter is big enough to hold several cables.

H channel
high-speed channel
Full-duplex ISDN primary rate channel operating at 384 Kbps. Compare with B channel, D channel, and E channel.

H.323
H.323 allows dissimilar communication devices to communicate with each other by using a standardized communication protocol. H.323 defines a common set of CODECs, call setup and negotiating procedures, and basic data transport methods.

half duplex
Capability for data transmission in only one direction at a time between a sending station and a receiving station. Compare with full duplex and simplex.

hammer drill
Tool resembling an oversized electric drill used for drilling into masonry. As it turns the bit, it hammers rapidly.

handshake
Sequence of messages exchanged between two or more network devices to ensure transmission synchronization.

hardware address
See MAC address.

HBD3
Line code type used on E1 circuits.

HCC
horizontal cross-connect
Wiring closet where the horizontal cabling connects to a patch panel which is connected by backbone cabling to the main distribution facility.

HDLC
High-Level Data Link Control
Bit-oriented synchronous data link layer protocol developed by ISO. Derived from SDLC, HDLC specifies a data encapsulation method on synchronous serial links using frame characters and checksums.

headend
The end point of a broadband network. All stations transmit toward the headend; the headend then transmits toward the destination stations.

header
Control information placed before data when encapsulating that data for network transmission. Compare with trailer.

header checksum
Field within an IP datagram that indicates the integrity check on the header.

HELLO
Interior routing protocol used principally by NSFnet nodes. HELLO allows particular packet switches to discover minimal delay routes. Not to be confused with the Hello protocol.

hello packet
Multicast packet that is used by routers for neighbor discovery and recovery. Hello packets also indicate that a client is still operating and network-ready.

Hello protocol
Protocol used by OSPF systems for establishing and maintaining neighbor relationships. Not to be confused with HELLO.

helper address
Address configured on an interface to which broadcasts received on that interface will be sent.

HEPnet
High-Energy Physics Network
Research network that originated in the United States, but that has spread to most places involved in high-energy physics. Well-known sites include Argonne National Laboratory, Brookhaven National Laboratory, Lawrence Berkeley Laboratory, and the Stanford Linear Accelerator Center (SLAC).

hertz
Measure of frequency. Synonymous with cycles per second. Abbreviated Hz.

heterogeneous network
Network consisting of dissimilar devices that run dissimilar protocols and in many cases support dissimilar functions or applications.

hexadecimal
Base 16. A number representation using the digits 0 through 9, with their usual meaning, plus the letters A through F to represent hexadecimal digits with values of 10 to 15. The right-most digit counts ones, the next counts multiples of 16, then $16^2=256$, etc.

hierarchical routing
Routing based on a hierarchical addressing system. For example, IP routing algorithms use IP addresses, which contain network numbers, subnet numbers, and host numbers.

hierarchical star topology
Extended star topology where a central hub is connected by vertical cabling to other hubs that are dependent on it.

High-Level Data Link Control
See HDLC.

High-Order DSP
See HODSP.

High-Performance Parallel Interface
See HIPPI.

High-Speed Communications Interface
See HSCI.

High-Speed Serial Interface
See HSSI.

highway
See bus.

HIP
HSSI Interface Processor
Interface processor on the Cisco 7000 series routers. The HIP provides one HSSI port that supports connections to ATM, SMDS, Frame Relay, or private lines at speeds up to T3 or E3.

HIPPI
High-Performance Parallel Interface
High-performance interface standard defined by ANSI. HIPPI is typically used to connect supercomputers to peripherals and other devices.

HLEN
Number of 32-bit words in the header.

HODSP
High-Order DSP
NSAP address field that is used for subdividing the domain into areas. This is roughly equivalent to a subnet in IP.

holddown
State into which a route is placed so that routers will neither advertise the route nor accept advertisements about the route for a specific length of time (the holddown period). Holddown is used to flush bad information about a route from all routers in the network. A route is typically placed in holddown when a link in that route fails.

homologation
Conformity of a product or specification to international standards, such as ITU-T, CSA, TUV, UL, or VCCI. Enables portability across company and international boundaries.

hop
Term describing the passage of a data packet between two network nodes (for example, between two routers).

hop count
Routing metric used to measure the distance between a source and a destination. RIP uses hop count as its sole metric.

horizontal cross connect
See HCC.

host
Computer system on a network. Similar to the term node except that host usually implies a computer system, whereas node generally applies to any networked system, including access servers and routers.

host address
See host number.

host node
SNA subarea node that contains an SSCP.

host number
Part of an IP address that designates which node on the subnetwork is being addressed. A host number is also known as a host address.

Hot Standby Router Protocol
See HSRP.

hot swapping
See OIR and POS.

hot wire
Ungrounded lead wire that connects the transformer and electrical devices or appliances via an electrical outlet and power plug.

HSCI
High-Speed Communications Interface
Single-port interface, developed by Cisco, providing full-duplex synchronous serial communications capability at speeds up to 52 Mbps.

HSRP
Hot Standby Router Protocol
Provides high network availability and transparent network topology changes. HSRP creates a Hot Standby router group with a lead router that services all packets sent to the Hot Standby address. The lead router is monitored by other routers in the group, and if it fails, one of these standby routers inherits the lead position and the Hot Standby group address.

HSSI
High-Speed Serial Interface
Network standard for high-speed (up to 52 Mbps) serial connections over WAN links.

HSSI Interface Processor
See HIP.

HTML
hypertext markup language
Simple hypertext document formatting language that uses tags to indicate how a given part of a document should be interpreted by a viewing application, such as a WWW browser. See also hypertext and WWW browser.

hub
1) Generally, a term used to describe a device that serves as the center of a star-topology network.
2) Hardware or software device that contains multiple independent but connected modules of network and internetwork equipment. Hubs can be active (where they repeat signals sent through them) or passive (where they do not re-

peat, but merely split, signals sent through them).

3) In Ethernet and IEEE 802.3, an Ethernet multiport repeater, sometimes referred to as a concentrator.

hybrid network
Internetwork made up of more than one type of network technology, including LANs and WANs.

hypertext
Electronically-stored text that allows direct access to other texts by way of encoded links. Hypertext documents can be created using HTML, and often integrate images, sound, and other media that are commonly viewed using a WWW browser.

hypertext markup language
See HTML.

I/O
Abbreviation for input/output.

IAB
Internet Architecture Board
Board of internetwork researchers who discuss issues pertinent to Internet architecture. Responsible for appointing a variety of Internet-related groups such as the IANA, IESG, and IRSG. The IAB is appointed by the trustees of the ISOC.

IANA
Internet Assigned Numbers Authority
Organization operated under the auspices of the ISOC as a part of the IAB. IANA delegates authority for IP address-space allocation and domain-name assignment to the NIC and other organizations. IANA also maintains a database of assigned protocol identifiers used in the TCP/IP stack, including autonomous system numbers.

IBNS
Identity Based Network Services
Integrated solution combining several Cisco products that offer authentication, access control, and user policies to secure network connectivity and resources.

ICC
intermediate cross connect
IDF that connects the horizontal cross-connect to the main cross-connect. See HCC and MCC.

ICMP
Internet Control Message Protocol
Network layer Internet protocol that reports errors and provides other information relevant to IP packet processing. Documented in RFC 792.

ICMP Router Discovery Protocol
See IRDP.

Identification, Flags, Frag Offset
Field within an IP datagram that provides fragmentation of datagrams to allow differing MTUs in the internet.

Identity Based Network Services
See IBNS.

IDF
intermediate distribution facility
Secondary communications room for a building using a star networking topology. The IDF is dependent on the MDF.

IDI
initial domain identifier
NSAP address field that identifies the domain.

IDN
International Data Number. See X.121.

IDP
interdomain part
NSAP address field that consists of the AFI and IDI together. This is roughly equivalent to a classful IP network, in decimal format.

IDPR
Interdomain Policy Routing
Interdomain routing protocol that dynamically exchanges policies between autonomous systems. IDPR encapsulates interautonomous system traffic and routes it according to the policies of each autonomous system along the path. IDPR is currently an IETF proposal.

IDRP

IS-IS Interdomain Routing Protocol
OSI protocol that specifies how routers communicate with routers in different domains.

IEC

International Electrotechnical Commission
Industry group that writes and distributes standards for electrical products and components.

IEEE

Institute of Electrical and Electronics Engineers
Professional organization whose activities include the development of communications and network standards. IEEE LAN standards are the predominant LAN standards today.

IEEE 802.1

IEEE specification that describes an algorithm that prevents bridging loops by creating a spanning tree. The algorithm was invented by Digital Equipment Corporation. The Digital algorithm and the IEEE 802.1 algorithm are not exactly the same, nor are they compatible.

IEEE 802.11

IEEE specification developed to eliminate the problems inherent with proprietary WLAN technologies. It began with a 1 Mbps standard and has evolved into several other standards, including 802.11a, 802.11b, and 802.11g.

IEEE 802.11a

IEEE WLAN standard for 54 Mbps at 5 GHz.

IEEE 802.11b

IEEE WLAN standard for 11 Mbps at 2.4 GHz.

IEEE 802.11g

IEEE WLAN standard for 54 Mbps at 2.4 GHz.

IEEE 802.11h

IEEE specification that radios must comply with in order to use the 11 channels for the 802.11a standard. IEEE 802.11h includes the TPC and DFS features.

IEEE 802.11i

IEEE 802.11 specification for WPA.

IEEE 802.12

IEEE LAN standard that specifies the physical layer and the MAC sublayer of the data link layer. IEEE 802.12 uses the demand priority media-access scheme at 100 Mbps over a variety of physical media.

IEEE 802.1x

IEEE standard specifying authentication protocols, such as EAP.

IEEE 802.2

IEEE LAN protocol that specifies an implementation of the LLC sublayer of the data link layer. IEEE 802.2 handles errors, framing, flow control, and the network layer (Layer 3) service interface. Used in IEEE 802.3 and IEEE 802.5 LANs.

IEEE 802.3

IEEE LAN protocol that specifies an implementation of the physical layer and the MAC sublayer of the data link layer. IEEE 802.3 uses CSMA/CD access at a variety of speeds over a variety of physical media. Extensions to the IEEE 802.3 standard specify implementations for Fast Ethernet. Physical variations of the original IEEE 802.3 specification include 10BASE2, 10BASE5, 10BASE-F, 10BASE-T, and 10Broad36. Physical variations for Fast Ethernet include 100BASE-T, 100BASE-T4, and 100BASE-X.

IEEE 802.3i

Physical variation of the original IEEE 802.3 specification that calls for using Ethernet type signaling over twisted pair networking media. The standard sets the signaling speed at 10 megabits per second using a baseband signaling scheme transmitted over twisted pair cable employing a star or extended star topology.

IEEE 802.4

IEEE LAN protocol that specifies an implementation of the physical layer and the MAC sublayer of the data link layer. IEEE 802.4 uses token-passing access over a bus topology and is based on the token bus LAN architecture.

IEEE 802.5

IEEE LAN protocol that specifies an implementation of the physical layer and MAC sublayer of the data link layer. IEEE 802.5 uses token passing access at 4 or 16 Mbps over STP cabling and is similar to IBM Token Ring.

IEEE 802.6
IEEE MAN specification based on DQDB technology. IEEE 802.6 supports data rates of 1.5 to 155 Mbps.

IESG
Internet Engineering Steering Group
Organization, appointed by the IAB, that manages the operation of the IETF.

IETF
Internet Engineering Task Force
Task force consisting of over 80 working groups responsible for developing Internet standards. The IETF operates under the auspices of ISOC.

IFIP
International Federation for Information Processing
Research organization that performs OSI prestandardization work. Among other accomplishments, IFIP formalized the original MHS model.

IGMP
Internet Group Management Protocol
Used by IP hosts to report their multicast group memberships to an adjacent multicast router.

IGP
Interior Gateway Protocol
Internet protocol used to exchange routing information within an autonomous system. Examples of common Internet IGPs include IGRP, OSPF, and RIP.

IGRP
Interior Gateway Routing Protocol
IGP developed by Cisco to address the problems associated with routing in large, heterogeneous networks. Compare with Enhanced IGRP.

IIH
Intermediate System-to-Intermediate System Hello
Used by routers to detect neighbors and form adjacencies. In addition to the IIH, which is an IS-IS PDU, there is an ISH and an ESH, which are ES-IS PDUs.

IIN
Intelligent Information Network
Network that seamlessly supports new IP strategies, including service-oriented architecture (SOA), Web services and virtualization. It is implemented using SONA. Compare with SONA.

ILEC
Incumbent Local Exchange Carrier
Traditional telephone company. In the U.S., the Regional Bell Operation Companies (RBOCs) that were formed after the divestiture of AT and T and the Independent Operating Companies (IOCs) that usually are located in more rural areas or single cities are ILECs. In other areas of the world, ILECs are the Post, Telephone, and Telegraphs (PTTs), government-managed monopolies.

ILMI
Interim Local Management Interface
Specification developed by the ATM Forum for incorporating network-management capabilities into the ATM UNI.

IMP
Interface message processor
Former name for ARPANET packet switches. An IMP is now known as a packet-switch node (PSN).

in-band signaling
Transmission within a frequency range normally used for information transmission. Compare with out-of-band signaling.

Industry-Standard Architecture
See ISA.

infrared
Electromagnetic waves whose frequency range is above that of microwaves, but below that of the visible spectrum. LAN systems based on this technology represent an emerging technology.

infrastructure
Infrastructure mode indicates a WLAN topology where clients connect through an access point.

initial domain identifier
See IDI.

initial domain part
See IDP.

INOC
Internet Network Operations Center
BBN group that in the early days of the Internet monitored and controlled the Internet core gateways (routers). INOC no longer exists in this form.

input/output
See I/O.

Institute of Electrical and Electronics Engineers
See IEEE.

insulator
Any material with a high resistance to electrical current. See conductor.

insured burst
The largest burst of data above the insured rate that will be temporarily allowed on a PVC and not tagged by the traffic policing function for dropping in the case of network congestion. The insured burst is specified in bytes or cells. Compare with maximum burst.

insured rate
The long-term data throughput, in bits or cells per second, that an ATM network commits to support under normal network conditions. The insured rate is 100 percent allocated; the entire amount is deducted from the total trunk bandwidth along the path of the circuit. Compare with excess rate and maximum rate.

insured traffic
Traffic within the insured rate specified for the PVC. This traffic should not be dropped by the network under normal network conditions.

Integrated IS-IS
Integrated Intermediate System-to-Intermediate System
Routing protocol based on the OSI routing protocol IS-IS, but with support for IP and other protocols. Integrated IS-IS implementations send only one set of routing updates, making it more efficient than two separate implementations. Compare with IS-IS.
Integrated IS-IS was formerly known as Dual IS-IS.

Integrated Services Digital Network
See ISDN.

Intelligent Information Network
See IIN.

interarea routing
Term used to describe routing between two or more logical areas. Compare with intra-area routing.

interdomain ID
See IDI.

interdomain part
See IDP.

Interdomain Policy Routing
See IDPR.

interface
1) Connection between two systems or devices.
2) In routing terminology, a network connection.
3) In telephony, a shared boundary defined by common physical interconnection characteristics, signal characteristics, and meanings of interchanged signals.
4) The boundary between adjacent layers of the OSI model.

interface message processor
See IMP.

interface module
Combination of a line card and an access card that together allow you to connect a LightStream 2020 ATM switch to other devices.

interface processor
Any of a number of processor modules used in the Cisco 7000 series routers.

interference
Unwanted communication channel noise.

Interim Local Management Interface
See ILMI.

Interior Gateway Protocol
See IGP.

Interior Gateway Routing Protocol
See IGRP.

intermediate cross connect
See ICC.

intermediate distribution facility
See IDF.

intermediate routing node
See IRN.

intermediate system
See IS.

Intermediate System Hello
See ISH.

Intermediate System-to-Intermediate System
See IS-IS.

Intermediate System-to-Intermediate System Hello
See IIH.

International Data Number
See X.121.

International Electrotechnical Commission
See IEC.

International Federation for Information Processin
See IFIP.

International Organization for Standardization
See ISO.

International Standards Organization
Erroneous expansion of the acronym ISO. See ISO.

International Telecommunication Union Telecommunication
See ITU-T.

Internet
1) Internet. Term used to refer to the largest global internetwork, connecting tens of thousands of networks worldwide and having a "culture" that focuses on research and standardization based on real-life use. Many leading-edge network technologies come from the Internet community. The Internet evolved in part from ARPANET. At one time, called the DARPA Internet. Not to be confused with the general term internet. See also ARPANET.
2) internet. Not to be confused with the Internet. See internetwork.

Internet address
See IP address.

Internet Architecture Board
See IAB.

Internet Assigned Numbers Authority
See IANA.

Internet Control Message Protocol
See ICMP.

Internet Engineering Steering Group
See IESG.

Internet Engineering Task Force
See IETF.

Internet Group Management Protocol
See IGMP.

Internet Network Operations Center
See INOC.

Internet Protocol
1) See IP.
2) Any protocol that is part of the TCP/IP protocol stack. See TCP/IP.

Internet Research Steering Group
See IRSG.

Internet Research Task Force
See IRTF.

Internet Society
See ISOC.

internetwork
Collection of networks interconnected by routers and other devices that functions (generally) as a single network.
The term internetwork is also known as internet, which is not to be confused with the Internet.

Internetwork Packet Exchange
See IPX.

internetworking
General term used to refer to the industry that has arisen around the problem of connecting networks together. The term can refer to products, procedures, and technologies.

interNIC
Organization that serves the Internet community by supplying user assistance, documentation, training, registration service for Internet domain names, and other services.
InterNIC was formerly known as Network Information Center (NIC).

interoperability
Ability of computing equipment manufactured by different vendors to communicate with one another successfully over a network.

Inter-Switching System Interface
See ISSI.

intra-area routing
Term used to describe routing within a logical area. Compare with interarea routing.

Inverse Address Resolution Protocol
See Inverse ARP.

Inverse ARP
Inverse Address Resolution Protocol
Method of building dynamic routes in a network. Allows an access server to discover the network address of a device associated with a virtual circuit.

IOS
See Cisco IOS software.

IP address
1) 32-bit address assigned to hosts using TCP/IP. An IP address belongs to one of five classes (A, B, C, D, or E) and is written as 4 octets separated with periods (dotted decimal format). Each address consists of a network number, an optional subnetwork number, and a host number. The network and subnetwork numbers together are used for routing, while the host number is used to address an individual host within the network or subnetwork. A subnet mask is used to extract network and subnetwork information from the IP address. IP address is also known as an Internet address.
2) Command used to establish the logical network address of this interface. See also IP and subnet mask.

IP datagram
Fundamental unit of information passed across the Internet. Contains source and destination addresses along with data and a number of fields that define such things as the length of the datagram, the header checksum, and flags to indicate whether the datagram can be (or was) fragmented.

IP multicast
Routing technique that allows IP traffic to be propagated from one source to a number of destinations or from many sources to many destinations. Rather than sending one packet to each destination, one packet is sent to a multicast group identified by a single IP destination group address.

IP options
Field within an IP datagram that deals with network testing, debugging, security, and others.

IPng
Internet Protocol next generation. See IPv6.

IPSO
IP Security Option
U.S. government specification that defines an optional field in the IP packet header that defines hierarchical packet security levels on a per interface basis.

IPv4
Internet Protocol version 4
Network layer protocol in the TCP/IP stack offering a connectionless internetwork service. IPv4 provides features for addressing, type-of-service specification, fragmentation and reassembly, and security. Documented in RFC 791.

IPv6
Internet Protocol version 6
Network layer IP standard used by electronic devices to exchange data across a packet-

switched internetwork. It follows IPv4 as the second version of the Internet Protocol to be formally adopted for general use. IPv6 includes support for flow ID in the packet header, which can be used to identify flows.

IPv6 was formerly known as IP next generation (IPng).

IPv6-over-IPv4 tunnels
See 6to4.

IPX
Internetwork Packet Exchange
NetWare network layer (Layer 3) protocol used for transferring data from servers to workstations. IPX is similar to IP and XNS.

IPXWAN
Internetwork Packet Exchange
Protocol that negotiates end-to-end options for new links. When a link comes up, the first IPX packets sent across are IPXWAN packets negotiating the options for the link. When the IPXWAN options have been successfully determined, normal IPX transmission begins. Defined by RFC 1362.

IRDP
ICMP Router Discovery Protocol
Enables a host to determine the address of a router that it can use as a default gateway. Similar to ESIS, but used with IP.

IRN
intermediate routing node
In SNA, a subarea node with intermediate routing capability.

IRSG
Internet Research Steering Group
Group that is part of the IAB and oversees the activities of the IRTF.

IRTF
Internet Research Task Force
Community of network experts that consider Internet-related research topics. The IRTF is governed by the IRSG and is considered a subsidiary of the IAB.

IS
intermediate system
Router which participates in routing IS-IS information.

ISA
Industry-Standard Architecture
16-bit bus used for Intel-based personal computers.

isarithmic flow control
Flow control technique in which permits travel through the network. Possession of these permits grants the right to transmit. Isarithmic flow control is not commonly implemented.

ISATAP
Intra-Site Automatic Tunnel Addressing Protocol
Allows an IPv4 private intranet (which may or may not be using RFC 1918 addresses) to incrementally implement IPv6 nodes without upgrading the network.

ISDN
Integrated Services Digital Network
Communication protocol, offered by telephone companies, that permits telephone networks to carry data, voice, and other source traffic.

ISH
Intermediate System Hello
ISH packets are a type of a hello packet. ISH is part of the ES-IS spec 9542; similar to IRDP in TCP/IP; used for ISs and ESs to detect each other. ISH packets are sent out to all IS-IS-enabled interfaces. On LANs they are sent out periodically, destined to a special multicast address. Routers will become neighbors when they see themselves in their neighbor's hello packets and link authentication information matches.

IS-IS
Intermediate System-to-Intermediate System
OSI link-state hierarchical routing protocol based on DECnet Phase V routing whereby ISs (routers) exchange routing information based on a single metric to determine network topology. Compare with Integrated IS-IS.

IS-IS Hello
See IIH.

IS-IS Interdomain Routing Protocol
See IDRP.

ISM
Industrial, Scientific, and Medical
The 900-MHz and 2.4-GHz bands are referred to as the ISM bands.

ISO
International Organization for Standardization
International organization that is responsible for a wide range of standards, including those relevant to networking. ISO developed the OSI reference model, a popular networking reference model.

ISO 3309
HDLC procedures developed by ISO. ISO 3309:1979 specifies the HDLC frame structure for use in synchronous environments. ISO 3309:1984 specifies proposed modifications to allow the use of HDLC in asynchronous environments as well.

ISO 9000
Set of international quality-management standards defined by ISO. The standards, which are not specific to any country, industry, or product, allow companies to demonstrate that they have specific processes in place to maintain an efficient quality system.

ISO development environment
See ISODE.

ISOC
Internet Society
International nonprofit organization, founded in 1992, that coordinates the evolution and use of the Internet. In addition, ISOC delegates authority to other groups related to the Internet, such as the IAB. ISOC is headquartered in Reston, Virginia, U.S.A.

isochronous transmission
Asynchronous transmission over a synchronous data link. Isochronous signals require a constant bit rate for reliable transport. Compare with asynchronous transmission, plesiochronous transmission, and synchronous transmission.

ISODE
International Organization for Standardization development environment
Large set of libraries and utilities used to develop upper-layer OSI protocols and applications.

isotropic
An antenna that radiates its signal in a spherical pattern. Compare with dipole.

ISSI
Inter-Switching System Interface
Standard interface between SMDS switches.

ITU-T
International Telecommunication Union Telecommunication Standardization Sector
International Telecommunication Union Telecommunication Standardization Sector (ITU-T) (formerly the Committee for International Telegraph and Telephone ([CCITT]). An international organization that develops communication standards.

jabber
1) Error condition in which a network device continually transmits random, meaningless data onto the network.
2) In IEEE 802.3, a data packet whose length exceeds that prescribed in the standard.

JANET
Joint Academic Network
X.25 WAN connecting university and research institutions in the United Kingdom.

Japan UNIX Network
See JUNET.

jitter
Analog communication line distortion caused by the variation of a signal from its reference timing positions. Jitter can cause data loss, particularly at high speeds.

John von Neumann Computer Network
See JvNCnet.

Joint Academic Network
See JANET.

jumper
1) Term used for patchcords found in a wiring closet.
2) Electrical switch consisting of a number of pins and a connector that can be attached to the pins in a variety of different ways. Different circuits are created by attaching the connector to different pins.

JUNET
Japan UNIX Network
Nationwide, noncommercial network in Japan, designed to promote communication between Japanese and other researchers.

JvNCnet
John von Neumann Computer Network
Regional network, owned and operated by Global Enterprise Services, Inc., composed of T1 and slower serial links providing midlevel networking services to sites in the Northeastern United States.

Karn's algorithm
Algorithm that improves round-trip time estimations by helping transport layer protocols distinguish between good and bad round-trip time samples.

keepalive interval
Period of time between each keepalive message sent by a network device.

keepalive message
Message sent by one network device to inform another network device that the virtual circuit between the two is still active.

Kermit
Popular file-transfer and terminal-emulation program.

KERN
Kernel trap logging facility. Process that runs on each NP of every LightStream 2020 ATM switch in a network. KERN converts LynxOS kernel messages, sent to the console, into SNMP messages.

kilobit
Approximately 1,000 bits. Abbreviated kb.

kilobits per second
A bit rate expressed in thousands of bits per second. Abbreviated kbps.

kilobyte
Approximately 1,000 bytes. Abbreviated KB.

kilobytes per second
A bit rate expressed in thousands of bytes per second. Abbreviated KBps.

LAN
local-area network
High-speed, low-error data network covering a relatively small geographic area (up to a few thousand meters). LANs connect workstations, peripherals, terminals, and other devices in a single building or other geographically limited area. LAN standards specify cabling and signaling at the physical and data link layers of the OSI model. Ethernet, FDDI, and Token Ring are widely used LAN technologies. Compare with MAN and WAN.

LAN emulation
See LANE.

LAN Emulation Client
See LEC.

LAN Emulation Configuration Server
See LECS.

LAN Emulation Server
See LES.

LAN Extender
Any of the products in the Cisco 1000 series. Cisco LAN Extenders provide a transparent connection between a central site and a remote site, logically extending the central network to include the remote LAN. LAN Extender products support all standard network protocols and are configured and managed through a host router at the central site, requiring no technical expertise at the remote end. See also Cisco 1000.

LAN Manager
Distributed NOS, developed by Microsoft, that supports a variety of protocols and platforms.

LAN Manager for UNIX
See LM/X.

LAN Network Manager
See LNM.

LAN Server
Server-based NOS developed by IBM and derived from LNM.

LAN switch
High-speed switch that forwards packets between data-link segments. Most LAN switches forward traffic based on MAC addresses. This variety of LAN switch is sometimes called a frame switch. LAN switches are often categorized according to the method they use to forward traffic: cut-through packet switching or store-and-forward packet switching. Multilayer switches are an intelligent subset of LAN switches. An example of a LAN switch is the Cisco Catalyst 5000. Compare with multilayer switch.

LANE
LAN emulation
Technology that allows an ATM network to function as a LAN backbone. The ATM network must provide multicast and broadcast support, address mapping (MAC-to-ATM), SVC management, and a usable packet format. LANE also defines Ethernet and Token Ring ELANs.

LAPB
Link Access Procedure, Balanced
Data link layer protocol in the X.25 protocol stack. LAPB is a bit-oriented protocol derived from HDLC.

LAPD
Link Access Procedure on the D channel
ISDN data link layer protocol for the D channel. LAPD was derived from the LAPB protocol and is designed primarily to satisfy the signaling requirements of ISDN basic access. Defined by ITU-T Recommendations Q.920 and Q.921.

LAPF
Link Access Procedure for Frame Relay
The international draft standard that defines the structure of frame relay frames. All frame relay frames entering a frame relay network automatically conform to this structure.

LAPM
Link Access Procedure for Modems
ARQ used by modems implementing the V.42 protocol for error correction.

laser
light amplification by stimulated emission of radiation
Analog transmission device in which a suitable active material is excited by an external stimulus to produce a narrow beam of coherent light that can be modulated into pulses to carry data. Networks based on laser technology are sometimes run over SONET.

LAT
local-area transport
A network virtual terminal protocol developed by Digital Equipment Corporation.

LATA
local access and transport area
Geographic telephone dialing area serviced by a single local telephone company. Calls within LATAs are called "local calls." There are well over 100 LATAs in the United States.

latency
1) Delay between the time a device requests access to a network and the time it is granted permission to transmit.
2) Delay between the time when a device receives a frame and the time that frame is forwarded out the destination port.

LCC
line card control
Process that runs on the NP for each CLC, LSC, and MSC of a LightStream 2020 ATM switch. LCC establishes VCCs, maintains the link management protocol for the line card, continually monitors line quality on each trunk using TUD, and performs other functions.

LCI
logical channel identifier. See VCN.

LCN
logical channel number. See VCN.

LCP
link control protocol
Protocol that establishes, configures, and tests data-link connections for use by PPP.

leaf internetwork
In a star topology, an internetwork whose sole access to other internetworks in the star is through a core router.

learning bridge
Bridge that performs MAC address learning to reduce traffic on the network. Learning bridges manage a database of MAC addresses and the interfaces associated with each address.

leased line
Transmission line reserved by a communications carrier for the private use of a customer. A leased line is a type of dedicated line.

LEC
1) LAN Emulation Client. Entity in an end system that performs data forwarding, address resolution, and other control functions for a single ES within a single ELAN. A LEC also provides a standard LAN service interface to any higher-layer entity that interfaces to the LEC. Each LEC is identified by a unique ATM address, and is associated with one or more MAC addresses reachable through that ATM address. See also ELAN and LES.
2) local exchange carrier. Local or regional telephone company that owns and operates a telephone network and the customer lines that connect to it.

LECS
LAN emulation configuration server
Entity that assigns individual LANE clients to particular ELANs by directing them to the LES that corresponds to the ELAN. There is logically one LECS per administrative domain, and this serves all ELANs within that domain.

LED
light emitting diode
Semiconductor device that emits light produced by converting electrical energy. Status lights on hardware devices are typically LEDs.

LES
LAN Emulation Server
Entity that implements the control function for a particular ELAN. There is only one logical LES per ELAN, and it is identified by a unique ATM address.

Level 1 IS
Level 1 intermediate system
Provides routing within an area. It keeps track of the routing within its own area. For a packet destined for another area, a Level 1 IS sends the packet to the nearest Level 2 IS in its own area, regardless of what the destination area is.

Level 1 router
Device that routes traffic within a single DECnet or OSI area.

Level 2 IS
Level 2 intermediate system
Provides routing between Level 1 areas and form an intradomain routing backbone. It keeps track of the paths to destination areas. A level 1 must go through a level 2 IS to communicate with another area.

Level 2 router
Device that routes traffic between DECnet or OSI areas. All Level 2 routers must form a contiguous network.

Level 3 IS
Level 3 intermediate system
Provides routing between separate domains.

light amplification by stimulated emission of radiation
See laser.

light emitting diode
See LED.

lightweight access point
A lightweight access point is the type of access point used in a centralized WLAN solution where a wireless controller monitors and manages the access points.

limited resource link
Resource defined by a device operator to remain active only when being used.

line
1) In SNA, a connection to the network.
2) See link.

line card
Card on a LightStream 2020 ATM switch that, together with its access card, provides I/O services for the switch. There are four types of line cards: CLC, LSC, MSC, and PLC.

line card control
See LCC.

line code type
One of a number of coding schemes used on serial lines to maintain data integrity and reliability. The line code type used is determined by the carrier service provider.

line conditioning
Use of equipment on leased voice-grade channels to improve analog characteristics, thereby allowing higher transmission rates.

line driver
Inexpensive amplifier and signal converter that conditions digital signals to ensure reliable transmissions over extended distances.

Line Interface
See LINF.

line of sight
Characteristic of certain transmission systems such as laser, microwave, and infrared systems in which no obstructions in a direct path between transmitter and receiver can exist.

line printer daemon
See LPD.

line turnaround
Time required to change data transmission direction on a telephone line.

LINF
Line Interface
Interface card used on the LightStream 100 ATM switch. The LINF receives cells sent over a line, checks them for errors, and forwards them toward their destination.

link
Network communications channel consisting of a circuit or transmission path and all related equipment between a sender and a receiver. Most often used to refer to a WAN connection. A link is also known as a line or a transmission link.

Link Access Procedure for Frame Relay
See LAPF.

Link Access Procedure for Modems
See LAPM.

Link Access Procedure on the D channel
See LAPD.

Link Access Procedure, Balanced
See LAPB.

link layer
See data link layer.

link state routing algorithm
Routing algorithm in which each router broadcasts or multicasts information regarding the cost of reaching each of its neighbors to all nodes in the internetwork. Link state algorithms create a consistent view of the network and are therefore not prone to routing loops, but they achieve this at the cost of relatively greater computational difficulty and more widespread traffic (compared with distance vector routing algorithms). Compare with distance vector routing algorithm.

link-layer address
See MAC address.

link-local address
IPv6 uses link-local addresses to identify interfaces on a link that are meant to stay within a given broadcast domain. They may also be thought of as the "host portion" of an IPv6 address. These addresses are used for features such as stateless Autoconfiguration. Link-local addresses start with the prefix FE80::/10, and then include an interface ID. Compare with site-local unicast address.

link-state advertisement
See LSA.

link-state packet
See LSA.

link-state PDU database
See LSPD.

little-endian
Method of storing or transmitting data in which the least significant bit or byte is presented first. Compare with big-endian.

LLC
logical link control
Higher of the two data link layer sublayers defined by the IEEE. The LLC sublayer handles error control, flow control, framing, and MAC-sublayer addressing. The most prevalent LLC protocol is IEEE 802.2, which includes both connectionless and connection-oriented variants.

LLC 2
Connection-oriented OSI LLC-sublayer protocol.

LLQ
Low Latency Queueing
Brings strict priority queueing to Class-Based Weighted Fair Queueing (CBWFQ).

LM/X
LAN Manager for UNIX
Monitors LAN devices in UNIX environments.

LMI
Local Management Interface
Set of enhancements to the basic Frame Relay specification. LMI includes support for a keepalive mechanism, which verifies that data is flowing; a multicast mechanism, which provides the network server with its local DLCI and the multicast DLCI; global addressing, which gives DLCIs global rather than local significance in Frame Relay networks; and a status mechanism, which provides an on-going status report on the DLCIs known to the switch. LMI is known as LMT in ANSI terminology.

LMT
See LMI.

LNM
LAN Network Manager
SRB and Token Ring management package provided by IBM. Typically running on a PC, it monitors SRB and Token Ring devices, and can pass alerts up to NetView.

load balancing
In routing, the ability of a router to distribute traffic over all its network ports that are the same distance from the destination address. Good load-balancing algorithms use both line speed and reliability information. Load balancing increases the utilization of network segments, thus increasing effective network bandwidth.

local access and transport area
See LATA.

local acknowledgment
Method whereby an intermediate network node, such as a router, responds to acknowledgments for a remote end host. Use of local acknowledgments reduces network overhead and, therefore, the risk of time-outs.
Local acknowledgment is also known as local termination.

local bridge
Bridge that directly interconnects networks in the same geographic area.

local exchange carrier
See LEC.

local loop
Line from the premises of a telephone subscriber to the telephone company CO.

Local Management Interface
See LMI.

local termination
See local acknowledgment.

local traffic filtering
Process by which a bridge filters out (drops) frames whose source and destination MAC addresses are located on the same interface on the bridge, thus preventing unnecessary traffic from being forwarded across the bridge. Defined in the IEEE 802.1 standard.

local unicast address
An IPv6 address whose scope is configured to a single link. The address is unique only on this link and it is not routable off the link. Compare with a global unicast address.

local-area network
See LAN.

local-area transport
See LAT.

logical address
See network address.

logical channel
Nondedicated, packet-switched communications path between two or more network nodes. Packet switching allows many logical channels to exist simultaneously on a single physical channel.

logical channel identifier
See LCI.

logical channel number
See LCN.

Logical Link Control
See LLC.

Logical Link Control, type 2
See LLC2.

logical unit
See LU.

logical unit 6.2
See LU 6.2.

loop
Route where packets never reach their destination, but simply cycle repeatedly through a constant series of network nodes.

loopback test
Test in which signals are sent and then directed back toward their source from some point along the communications path. Loopback tests are often used to test network interface usability.

lossy
Characteristic of a network that is prone to lose packets when it becomes highly loaded.

Low Latency Queueing
See LLQ.

low-speed line card
See LSC.

LPD
Line Printer Daemon
Protocol used to send print jobs between UNIX systems.

LSA
link-state advertisement
Broadcast packet used by link-state protocols that contains information about neighbors and path costs. LSAs are used by the receiving routers to maintain their routing tables. Link-state advertisement is also known as link-state packet (LSP).

LSC
low-speed line card
Card on the LightStream 2020 ATM switch that can be configured as an edge or a trunk card. An LSC, in conjunction with an access card, supports eight trunk or edge ports (Frame Relay or frame forwarding) at individual port speeds up to 3.584 Mbps, or an aggregate rate of 6 Mbps per line card.

LSP
link-state packet

LSPD
link-state PDU database
Database maintained by each router running a link-state routing protocol. It provides a global view of the area itself and the exit points to neighboring areas.

LU
logical unit
Primary component of SNA, an LU is an NAU that enables end users to communicate with each other and gain access to SNA network resources.

LU 6.2
logical unit 6.2
In SNA, an LU that provides peer-to-peer communication between programs in a distributed computing environment. APPC runs on LU 6.2 devices.

LWAPP
Lightweight Access Point Protocol
LWAPP encapsulates and encrypts (with AES) control traffic between access points and wireless controllers. The data traffic between the access points and controllers is also encapsulated by LWAPP, but not encrypted.

LynxOS
Real-time, UNIX-like operating system that runs on the NP of a LightStream 2020 ATM switch.

MAC
Media Access Control
Lower of the two sublayers of the data link layer defined by the IEEE. The MAC sublayer handles access to shared media, such as whether token passing or contention will be used.

MAC address
Media Access Control address
Standardized data link layer address that is required for every port or device that connects to a LAN. Other devices in the network use these addresses to locate specific ports in the network and to create and update routing tables and data structures. MAC addresses are 6 bytes long and are controlled by the IEEE. Compare with network address.
MAC address is also known as hardware address, MAC-layer address, or physical address.

MAC address learning
Service that characterizes a learning bridge, in which the source MAC address of each received packet is stored so that future packets destined for that address can be forwarded only to the bridge interface on which that address is located. Packets destined for unrecognized addresses are forwarded out every bridge interface. This scheme helps minimize traffic on the attached LANs. MAC address learning is defined in the IEEE 802.1 standard.

MAC-layer address
See MAC address.

main cross connect
See MCC.

main distribution facility
See MDF.

Maintenance Operation Protocol
See MOP.

MAN
metropolitan-area network
Network that spans a metropolitan area. Generally, a MAN spans a larger geographic area than a LAN, but a smaller geographic area than a WAN. Compare with LAN and WAN.

managed object
In network management, a network device that can be managed by a network management protocol.

Management Information Base
See MIB.

Management Information Base collection
See MIB collection.

Management Information Base reporting
See MIB reporting.

management services
SNA functions distributed among network components to manage and control an SNA network.

Manchester encoding
Digital coding scheme, used by IEEE 802.3 and Ethernet, in which a mid-bit-time transition is used for clocking, and a 1 is denoted by a high level during the first half of the bit time.

Manufacturing Automation Protocol
See MAP.

MAP
Manufacturing Automation Protocol
Network architecture created by General Motors to satisfy the specific needs of the factory floor. MAP specifies a token-passing LAN similar to IEEE 802.4.

mask
See address mask and subnet mask.

master management agent
See MMA.

MAU
media attachment unit
Device used in Ethernet and IEEE 802.3 networks that provides the interface between the AUI port of a station and the common medium of the Ethernet. The MAU, which can be built into a station or can be a separate device, performs physical layer functions including the conversion of digital data from the Ethernet interface, collision detection, and injection of bits onto the network. Sometimes referred to as a media access unit, also abbreviated MAU, or as a transceiver. In Token Ring, a MAU is known as a multistation access unit and is usually abbreviated MSAU to avoid confusion.

maximum burst
Specifies the largest burst of data above the insured rate that will be allowed temporarily on an ATM PVC, but will not be dropped at the edge by the traffic policing function, even if it exceeds the maximum rate. This amount of traffic will be allowed only temporarily; on average, the traffic source needs to be within the maximum rate. Specified in bytes or cells. Compare with insured burst.

maximum rate
Maximum total data throughput allowed on a given virtual circuit, equal to the sum of the insured and uninsured traffic from the traffic source. The uninsured data might be dropped if the network becomes congested. The maximum rate, which cannot exceed the media rate, represents the highest data throughput the virtual circuit will ever deliver, measured in bits or cells per second. Compare with excess rate and insured rate.

maximum transmission unit
See MTU.

Mb/s
megabits per second
A megabit per second is a unit of data transfer rate equal to 1,000,000 bits per second.

MBONE
multicast backbone
The multicast backbone of the Internet. MBONE is a virtual multicast network composed of multicast LANs and the point-to-point tunnels that interconnect them.

MCA
Micro Channel Architecture
Bus interface commonly used in PCs and some UNIX workstations and servers.

MCC
main cross-connect
Wiring closet that serves as the most central point in a star topology and where LAN backbone cabling connects to the Internet.

MCI
Multiport Communications Interface
Card on the AGS+ that provides two Ethernet interfaces and up to two synchronous serial interfaces. The MCI processes packets rapidly, without the interframe delays typical of other Ethernet interfaces.

MCR
minimum cell rate
Parameter defined by the ATM Forum for ATM traffic management. MCR is defined only for ABR transmissions, and specifies the minimum value for the ACR.

MD5
Message Digest 5
Algorithm used for message authentication in SNMP v.2. MD5 verifies the integrity of the communication, authenticates the origin, and checks for timeliness.

MDF
main distribution facility
Primary communications room for a building. Central point of a star networking topology where patch panels, hub, and router are located.

media
The various physical environments through which transmission signals pass. Common network media include twisted-pair, coaxial and fiber-optic cable, and the atmosphere (through which microwave, laser, and infrared transmission occurs).
Media is also known as physical media. Media is the plural of medium.

Media Access Control
See MAC.

Media Access Control Address
See MAC address.

media access unit
See MAU.

media attachment unit
See MAU.

media interface connector
See MIC.

media rate
Maximum traffic throughput for a particular media type.

medium
See media.

medium-speed line card
See MSC.

megabit
Abbreviated Mb.

megabits per second
See Mb/s.

megabyte
Abbreviated MB.

mesh
Network topology in which devices are organized in a manageable, segmented manner with many, often redundant, interconnections strategically placed between network nodes.

message
Application layer (Layer 7) logical grouping of information, often composed of a number of lower-layer logical groupings such as packets. The terms datagram, frame, packet, and segment are also used to describe logical information groupings at various layers of the OSI reference model and in various technology circles.

Message Digest 5
See MD5.

message handling system
See MHS.

Message Queuing Interface
See MQI.

message switching
Switching technique involving transmission of messages from node to node through a network. The message is stored at each node until such time as a forwarding path is available. Contrast with circuit switching and packet switching.

message unit
Unit of data processed by any network layer.

metering
See traffic shaping.

metric
See routing metric.

metropolitan-area network
See MAN.

MHS
message handling system
ITU-T X.400 recommendations that provide message handling services for communications between distributed applications. NetWare MHS is a different (though similar) entity that also provides message-handling services.

MIB
Management Information Base
Database of network management information that is used and maintained by a network management protocol such as SNMP or CMIP. The value of a MIB object can be changed or retrieved using SNMP or CMIP commands. MIB objects are organized in a tree structure that includes public (standard) and private (proprietary) branches.

MIC
1) media interface connector. FDDI is the de facto standard connector.
2) message integrity check. MIC is a method use to overcome the exploitation of encryption keys by utilizing integrity checks.

micro channel architecture
See MCA.

microcode

Translation layer between machine instructions and the elementary operations of a computer. Microcode is stored in ROM and allows the addition of new machine instructions without requiring that they be designed into electronic circuits when new instructions are needed.

microsegmentation

Division of a network into smaller segments, usually with the intention of increasing aggregate bandwidth to network devices.

microwave

Electromagnetic waves in the range 1 to 30 GHz. Microwave-based networks are an evolving technology gaining favor due to high bandwidth and relatively low cost.

Military Network

See MILNET.

millions of instructions per second

See mips.

MILNET

Military Network
Unclassified portion of the DDN. Operated and maintained by the DISA.

minimum cell rate

See MCR.

MIP

MultiChannel Interface Processor
Interface processor on the Cisco 7000 series routers that provides up to two channelized T1 or E1 connections via serial cables to a CSU. The two controllers on the MIP can each provide up to 24 T1 or 30 E1 channel-groups, with each channel-group presented to the system as a serial interface that can be configured individually.

mips

millions of instructions per second
Number of instructions executed by a processor per second.

MMA

master management agent
SNMP agent that runs on the NP of a LightStream 2020 ATM switch. MMA translates between an external network manager using SNMP and the internal switch management mechanisms.

Mobile IP

An IETF standard for IPv4 and IPv6 which enables mobile devices to move without breaking current connections. In IPv6, mobility is built in, which means that any IPv6 node can use it as needed.

modem

modulator-demodulator
Device that converts digital and analog signals. At the source, a modem converts digital signals to a form suitable for transmission over analog communication facilities. At the destination, the analog signals are returned to their digital form. Modems allow data to be transmitted over voice-grade telephone lines.

modulation

Any of several techniques for combining user information with a transmitter's carrier signal. It is a process by which the characteristics of electrical signals are transformed to represent information. Types of modulation include AM, FM, and PAM.

modulator-demodulator

See modem.

monitor

Management tool on the LightStream 2020 ATM switch that allows a user to examine individual nodes in the network and learn the status of interface modules and power supplies. The monitor is an HP OpenView-based application that runs on an NMS.

monomode fiber

See single-mode fiber.

MOP

Maintenance Operation Protocol
Digital Equipment Corporation protocol, a subset of which is supported by Cisco, that provides a way to perform primitive maintenance operations on DECnet systems. For example, MOP can be used to download a system image to a diskless station.

Mosaic
Public-domain WWW browser, developed at the National Center for Supercomputing Applications (NCSA).

MP-BGP
Multiprotocol - Border Gateway Protocol
Used to enable BGP4 to carry information of other protocols, for example, Multiprotocol Label Switching (MPLS) and IPv6.

MPLS
Multiprotocol Label Switching
Labeling technique used to increase the speed of traffic flow. Each packet is tagged with the path sequence to the destination. This saves time by not have to do a lookup of the routing table. In another word packet switching is done at layer 2 instead of layer 3. MPLS support multiple protocols such as IP, ATM, and frame relay.

MPLS/TE
Multiprotocol Label Switching/Traffic Engineering
Provides a way to integrate TE capabilities (such as those used on Layer 2 protocols like ATM) into Layer 3 protocols (IP). MPLS TE uses an extension to existing protocols (Resource Reservation Protocol (RSVP), IS-IS, Open Shortest Path First (OSPF))to calculate and establish unidirectional tunnels that are set according to the network constraint. Traffic flows are mapped on the different tunnels depending on their destination.

MQI
Message Queuing Interface
International standard API that provides functionality similar to that of the RPC interface. In contrast to RPC, MQI is implemented strictly at the application layer.

MSAU
multistation access unit
Wiring concentrator to which all end stations in a Token Ring network connect. The MSAU provides an interface between these devices and the Token Ring interface of, for example, a Cisco 7000 TRIP.
MSAU is also abbreviated MAU.

MSC
medium-speed line card
Card on the LightStream 2020 ATM switch that can be configured as an edge or a trunk card. The MSC, in conjunction with an access card, supports two trunk or edge (UNI) ports at data rates up to T3 or E3.

MTU
maximum transmission unit
Maximum packet size, in bytes, that a particular interface can handle.

mu-law
North American companding standard used in conversion between analog and digital signals in PCM systems. Similar to the European alaw.

multiaccess network
Network that allows multiple devices to connect and communicate simultaneously.

multicast
Single packets copied by the network and sent to a specific subset of network addresses. These addresses are specified in the destination address field. Compare with broadcast and unicast.

multicast address
Single address that refers to multiple network devices. Synonymous with group address. Compare with broadcast address and unicast address.

multicast backbone
See MBONE.

multicast group
Dynamically determined group of IP hosts identified by a single IP multicast address.

multicast router
Router used to send IGMP query messages on their attached local networks. Host members of a multicast group respond to a query by sending IGMP reports noting the multicast groups to which they belong. The multicast router takes responsibility for forwarding multicast datagrams from one multicast group to all other networks that have members in the group.

multicast server
Establishes a one-to-many connection to each device in a VLAN, thus establishing a broadcast domain for each VLAN segment. The multicast server forwards incoming broadcasts only to the multicast address that maps to the broadcast address.

MultiChannel Interface Processor
See MIP.

multihomed host
Host attached to multiple physical network segments in an OSI CLNS network.

multihoming
Addressing scheme in IS-IS routing that supports assignment of multiple area addresses.

multilayer switch
Switch that filters and forwards packets based on MAC addresses and network addresses. A subset of LAN switch. The Catalyst 5000 is an example of a multilayer switch. Compare with LAN switch.

multimode fiber
Optical fiber supporting propagation of multiple frequencies of light.

multipath distortion
The echoes created as a radio signal bounces off of physical objects. Multipath distortion occurs when an RF signal has more than one path between a receiver and a transmitter. RF waves can take more than one path when going from a transmitting to a receiving antenna. These multiple signals arrive at the receiving antenna at different times and phases which causes distortion of the signal.

multiple domain network
SNA network with multiple SSCPs.

multiplexing
Scheme that allows multiple logical signals to be transmitted simultaneously across a single physical channel. Compare with demultiplexing.

Multiport Communications Interface
See MCI.

Multiprotocol BGP
See MP-BGP.

Multiprotocol Label Switching (MPLS)
See MPLS.

Multiprotocol Label Switching/Traffic Engineering
See MPLS/TE.

multistation access unit
See MSAU.

NAC
Network Admission Control
Method of controlling access to a network in order to prevent the introduction of computer viruses. Using a variety of protocols and software products, NAC assesses the condition of hosts when they attempt to log onto the network, and handles the request based on the host's condition, called its posture. Infected hosts can be placed in quarantine; hosts without up-to-date virus protection software can be directed to obtain updates, and uninfected hosts with up-to-date virus protection can be allowed onto the network.

Nagle's algorithm
Actually two separate congestion control algorithms that can be used in TCP-based networks. One algorithm reduces the sending window; the other limits small datagrams.

NAK
negative acknowledgment
Response sent from a receiving device to a sending device indicating that the information received contained errors. Compare to ACK.

name caching
Method by which remotely discovered host names are stored by a router for use in future packet-forwarding decisions to allow quick access.

name resolution
Generally, the process of associating a name with a network location.

name server
Server connected to a network that resolves network names into network addresses.

NAP
network access point
Location for interconnection of Internet service providers in the United States for the exchange of packets.

narrowband
See baseband.

Narrowband ISDN
See N-ISDN.

NAT
Network Address Translation
Only globally unique in terms of the public internet. A mechanism for translating private addresses into publicly usable addresses to be used within the public internet. An effective means for hiding actual device addressing within a private network.
Network Address Translation is also known as Network Address Translator.

National Bureau of Standards
See NBS.

National Institute of Standards and Technology
See NIST.

National Science Foundation
See NSF.

National Science Foundation Network
See NSFNET.

native client interface architecture
See NCIA.

NAT-PT
Network Address Translation - Protocol Translation
Translation mechanism that sits between an IPv6 network and an IPv4 network. The job of the translator is to translate IPv6 packets into IPv4 packets and vice versa. Compare with Stateless IP/Internet Control Message Protocol (ICMP) Translation (SIIT) algorithm and DNS ALG.

NAU
network addressable unit
SNA term for an addressable entity. Examples include LUs, PUs, and SSCPs. NAUs generally provide upper-level network services. Compare with path control network.

NAUN
nearest active upstream neighbor
In Token Ring or IEEE 802.5 networks, the closest upstream network device from any given device that is still active.

NBMA
nonbroadcast multiaccess
Term describing a multiaccess network that either does not support broadcasting (such as X.25) or in which broadcasting is not feasible (for example, an SMDS broadcast group or an extended Ethernet that is too large).

NBS
National Bureau of Standards
Organization that was part of the U.S. Department of Commerce.
National Bureau of Standards is now known as National Institute of Standards and Technology (NIST).

NCIA
native client interface architecture
SNA applications-access architecture, developed by Cisco, that combines the full functionality of native SNA interfaces at both the host and client with the flexibility of leveraging TCP/IP backbones. NCIA encapsulates SNA traffic on a client PC or workstation, thereby providing direct TCP/IP access while preserving the native SNA interface at the end-user level. In many networks, this capability obviates the need for a standalone gateway and can provide flexible TCP/IP access while preserving the native SNA interface to the host.

NCP
Network Control Protocol
In SNA, a program that routes and controls the flow of data between a communications controller (in which it resides) and other network resources.

NCP/Token Ring Interconnection
See NTRI.

ND
neighborhood discovery
Process that runs on the NP of each LightStream 2020 ATM switch in the ATM network. For call routing purposes, every node in the network needs to know about changes in network topology, such as trunks and ports going up or down. ND learns about such changes at the chassis level and forwards this information to the GID process, which sends the information throughout the network.
Neighborhood discovery is also known as neighborhood discovery daemon (NDD).

NDD
Neighborhood discovery daemon.

NDIS
network driver interface specification
Specification for a generic, hardware- and protocol-independent device driver for NICs. Produced by Microsoft.

nearest active upstream neighbor
See NAUN.

NEARNET
Regional network in New England (United States) that links Boston University, Harvard University, and MIT. Now part of BBN Planet.

negative acknowledgment
See NAK.

neighborhood discovery
See ND.

neighborhood discovery daemon
See ND.

neighboring routers
In OSPF, two routers that have interfaces to a common network. On multiaccess networks, neighbors are dynamically discovered by the OSPF Hello protocol.

NET
network entity title
NSAP with an n-selector of zero. All router NETs have an n-selector of zero, implying the network layer of the IS itself (0 means no transport layer). For this reason, the NSAP of a router is always referred to as a NET.

NetBEUI
NetBIOS Extended User Interface
Enhanced version of the NetBIOS protocol used by network operating systems such as LAN Manager, LAN Server, Windows for Workgroups, and Windows NT. NetBEUI formalizes the transport frame and implements the OSI LLC2 protocol.

NetBIOS
Network Basic Input/Output System
API used by applications on an IBM LAN to request services from lower-level network processes. These services might include session establishment and termination, and information transfer.

NetView
IBM network management architecture and related applications. NetView is a VTAM application used for managing mainframes in SNA networks.

NetWare
Popular distributed NOS developed by Novell. Provides transparent remote file access and numerous other distributed network services.

NetWare Link Services Protocol
See NLSP.

NetWare Loadable Module
See NLM.

network
1) Collection of computers, printers, routers, switches, and other devices that are able to communicate with each other over some transmission medium.
2) Command that assigns a NIC-based address to which the router is directly connected.
3) Command that specifies any directly connected networks to be included.

network access point
See NAP.

network access server
See access server.

network address
Network layer address referring to a logical, rather than a physical, network device. Compare with MAC address.
Network address is also known as protocol address.

network addressable unit
See NAU.

network administrator
Person responsible for the operation, maintenance, and management of a network.

Network Admission Control
See NAC.

network analyzer
Network monitoring device that maintains statistical information regarding the status of the network and each device attached to it. More sophisticated versions using artificial intelligence can detect, define, and fix problems on the network.

Network Basic Input/Output System
See NetBIOS.

Network byte order
Internet-standard ordering of the bytes corresponding to numeric values.

Network Control Program
See NCP.

network driver interface specification
See NDIS.

network entity title
See NET.

Network File System
See NFS.

Network Information Center
See NIC.

Network Information Service
See NIS.

network interface
Boundary between a carrier network and a privately-owned installation.

network interface card
See NIC.

network layer
Layer 3 of the OSI reference model. This layer provides connectivity and path selection between two end systems. The network layer is the layer at which routing occurs. Corresponds roughly with the path control layer of the SNA model.

network management
Generic term used to describe systems or actions that help maintain, characterize, or troubleshoot a network.

Network Management Processor
See NMP.

network management system
See NMS.

network management vector transport
See NMVT.

network number
Part of an IP address that specifies the network to which the host belongs.

network operating system
See NOS.

Network Operations Center
See NOC.

network operator
Person who routinely monitors and controls a network, performing such tasks as reviewing and responding to traps, monitoring throughput, configuring new circuits, and resolving problems.

network processor card
See NP card.

network service access point
See NSAP.

networking
Connecting of any collection of computers, printers, routers, switches, and other devices for the purpose of communication over some transmission medium.

Network-to-Network Interface
See NNI.

neutral wire
Circuit wire that is connected to an earth ground at the power plant and at the transformer.

Next Hop Resolution Protocol
See NHRP.

NFS
Network File System
As commonly used, a distributed file system protocol suite developed by Sun Microsystems that allows remote file access across a network. In actuality, NFS is simply one protocol in the suite. NFS protocols include NFS, RPC, External Data Representation (XDR), and others. These protocols are part of a larger architecture that Sun refers to as ONC.

NHRP
Next Hop Resolution Protocol. Protocol Used by routers to dynamically discover the MAC address of other routers and hosts connected to a NBMA network. These systems can then directly communicate without requiring traffic to use an intermediate hop, increasing performance in ATM, Frame Relay, SMDS, and X.25 environments.

NIC
1) network interface card. Board that provides network communication capabilities to and from a computer system. A network interface card is also known as an adapter.
2) Network Information Center. Organization whose functions have been assumed by the InterNIC. See interNIC.

NIS
Network Information Service
Protocol developed by Sun Microsystems for the administration of network-wide databases. The service essentially uses two programs: one for finding a NIS server and one for accessing the NIS databases.

N-ISDN
Narrowband ISDN
Communication standards developed by the ITU-T for baseband networks. Based on 64-kbps B channels and 16- or 64-kbps D channels. Contrast with BISDN.

NIST
National Institute of Standards and Technology
Formerly the NBS, this U.S. government organization supports and catalogs a variety of standards.

NLM
NetWare Loadable Module
Individual program that can be loaded into memory and function as part of the NetWare NOS.

NLRI
Network Layer Reachability Information
BGP sends routing update messages containing NLRI to describe a route and how to get there. In this context, an NLRI is a prefix. A BGP update message carries one or more NLRI prefixes and the attributes of a route for theNLRI prefixes; the route attributes include a BGP next hop gateway address, community values, and other information.

NLSP
NetWare Link Services Protocol
Link-state routing protocol based on IS-IS. The Cisco implementation of NLSP also includes MIB variables and tools to redistribute routing and SAP information between NLSP and other IPX routing protocols.

NMP
Network Management Processor
Processor module on the Catalyst 5000 switch used to control and monitor the switch.

NMS
network management system
System responsible for managing at least part of a network. An NMS is generally a reasonably powerful and well-equipped computer such as an engineering workstation. NMSs communicate with agents to help keep track of network statistics and resources.

NMVT
network management vector transport
SNA message consisting of a series of vectors conveying network management specific information.

NNI
Network-to-Network Interface
ATM Forum standard that defines the interface between two ATM switches that are both located in a private network or are both located in a public network. The interface between a public switch and private one is defined by the UNI standard. Also, the standard interface between two Frame Relay switches meeting the same criteria.

NOC
Network Operations Center
Organization responsible for maintaining a network.

node
1) Endpoint of a network connection or a junction common to two or more lines in a network. Nodes can be processors, controllers, or workstations. Nodes, which vary in routing and other functional capabilities, can be interconnected by links, and serve as control points in the network. Node is sometimes used generically to refer to any entity that can access a network, and is frequently used interchangeably with device.
2) In SNA, the basic component of a network, and the point at which one or more functional units connect channels or data circuits.

noise
Undesirable communications channel signals.

nominal velocity of propagation
See NVP.

nonbroadcast multiaccess
See NBMA.

non-stub area
Resource-intensive OSPF area that carries a default route, static routes, intra-area routes, inter-area routes, and external routes. Nonstub areas are the only OSPF areas that can have virtual links configured across them, and are the only areas that can contain an ASBR. Compare with stub area.

nonvolatile random-access memory
See NVRAM.

normal mode
Term used to describe problems between the hot and neutral wires on a power line.

normal response mode
See NRM.

NOS
network operating system
Generic term used to refer to what are really distributed file systems. Examples of NOSs include LAN Manager, NetWare, NFS, and VINES.

Novell IPX
See IPX.

NP card
network processor card
Main computational and storage resource for the LightStream 2020 ATM switch. Each LightStream 2020 switch has one or two NPs. The second card, if present, serves as a backup for the first. Each NP is associated with a floppy disk drive for loading software and a hard disk drive for storing software and configuration data. Each NP also has an access card that provides an Ethernet port.

NP module
On a LightStream 2020 ATM switch, the combination of the NP card, the NP access card, and the disk assembly.

NP TCS monitoring module
See NPTMM.

npadmin account
One of the four default user accounts that are created in the factory on each LightStream 2020 ATM switch. The npadmin account is for privileged users. Its default interface is the CLI.

NPTMM
network processor test and control system monitoring module
Process that runs on the NP of every LightStream 2020 ATM switch in an ATM network. NPTMM monitors the health of the system through the TCS and coordinates switch cutover when redundant switch cards are present.

NRM
normal response mode
HDLC mode for use on links with one primary station and one or more secondary stations. In this mode, secondary stations can transmit only if they first receive a poll from the primary station.

NSAP
network service access point
Conceptual point on the boundary between the network and the transport layers. The NSAP is the location at which OSI network services are provided to the transport layer. Each transport layer entity is assigned a single NSAP.

NSAP Address
network service access point address
Network-layer address for CLNS packets. An NSAP describes an attachment to a particular service at the network layer of a node, similar to the combination of IP destination address and IP protocol number in an IP packet. NSAP encoding and format are specified by ISO 8348/Ad2. NSAP address has two major parts: the initial domain part (IDP) and the domain specific part (DSP). The IDP consists of a 1-byte authority and format identifier (AFI) and a variable-length initial domain identifier (IDI), and the DSP is a string of digits identifying a particular transport implementation of a specified AFI authority. Everything to the left of the system ID can be thought of as the area address of a network node.

NSEL
network service access point selector
Part of the NSAP address field that identifies a process on the device. It is roughly equivalent to a socket or a TCP port number in TCP/IP. The NSEL is not used in routing decisions. Domain-Specific Part (DSP): comprised of the HODSP, the system ID, and the NSEL in binary format. The last byte is the N-Selector (NSEL) and must be specified as a single-byte length preceded by a '.'. A NET definition must set the N-Selector to '00'.

NSF
National Science Foundation
U.S. government agency that funds scientific research in the United States. The now-defunct NSFNET was funded by the NSF.

NSFnet
National Science Foundation Network
Large network that was controlled by the NSF and provided networking services in support of education and research in the United States, from 1986 to 1995. NSFnet is no longer in service.

NTP
Network Time Protocol
Protocol built on top of TCP that assures accurate local time-keeping with reference to radio and atomic clocks located on the Internet. This protocol is capable of synchronizing distributed clocks within milliseconds over long time periods.

null modem
Small box or cable used to join computing devices directly, rather than over a network.

NVP
nominal velocity of propagation
Speed at which a signal moves through a cable, expressed as a percentage or fraction of the speed of light in a vacuum. To calculate a cable length, a cable tester uses NVP together with the time a signal takes to return to the testing device.

NVRAM
nonvolatile RAM
RAM that retains its contents when a unit is powered off. In Cisco products, NVRAM is used to store configuration information.

NYSERNet
Network in New York (United States) with a T1 backbone connecting NSF, many universities, and several commercial concerns.

OAM cell
Operation, Administration, and Maintenance cell
ATM Forum specification for cells used to monitor virtual circuits. OAM cells provide a virtual circuit-level loopback in which a router responds to the cells, demonstrating that the circuit is up, and the router is operational.

OC
optical carrier
Series of physical protocols (OC-1, OC-2, OC-3, and so on), defined for SONET optical signal transmissions. OC signal levels put STS frames onto multimode fiber-optic line at a variety of speeds. The base rate is 51.84 Mbps (OC-1); each signal level thereafter operates at a speed divisible by that number (thus, OC-3 runs at 155.52 Mbps).

octet
8 bits. In networking, the term octet is often used (rather than byte) because some machine architectures employ bytes that are not 8 bits long.

ODA
Open Document Architecture
ISO standard that specifies how documents are represented and transmitted electronically. Open document Architecture was known as Office Document Architecture.

ODI
Open Data-Link Interface
Novell specification providing a standardized interface for NICs that allows multiple protocols to use a single NIC.

OEMI channel
See block multiplexer channel.

OFDM
Orthogonal Frequency Division Multiplexing
OFDM is a modulation technique used with IEEE 802.11g.

Office Document Architecture
See ODA.

OIM
OSI Internet Management
Group tasked with specifying ways in which OSI network management protocols can be used to manage TCP/IP networks.

OIR
online insertion and removal
Feature that permits the addition, replacement, or removal of interface processors in a Cisco router without interrupting the system power, entering console commands, or causing other software or interfaces to shut down. Online insertion and removal is also known as hot swapping.

omni-directional
This typically refers to a primarily circular antenna radiation pattern.

ONC
Open Network Computing
Distributed applications architecture designed by Sun Microsystems, currently controlled by a consortium led by Sun. The NFS protocols are part of ONC.

ones density
Scheme that allows a CSU/DSU to recover the data clock reliably. The CSU/DSU derives the data clock from the data that passes through it. In order to recover the clock, the CSU/DSU hardware must receive at least one 1 bit value for every 8 bits of data that pass through it. Ones density is also known as pulse density.

online insertion and removal
See OIR.

on-the-fly packet switching
See cut-through packet switching.

open architecture
Architecture with which third-party developers can legally develop products and for which public domain specifications exist.

open circuit
Broken path along a transmission medium. Open circuits will usually prevent network communication.

Open Data-Link Interface
Open Data-Link Interface
Novell specification providing a standardized interface for NICs that allows multiple protocols to use a single NIC.

Open Document Architecture
See ODA.

Open Network Computing
See ONC.

Open Shortest Path First
See OSPFv2 and OSPFv3.

Open System Interconnection
See OSI.

Open System Interconnection reference model
See OSI reference model.

oper account
One of the four default user accounts that are created in the factory on each LightStream 2020 ATM switch. The oper account is for general users. Its default interface is the CLI.

Operation, Administration, and Maintenance cell
See OAM cell.

Optical Carrier
See OC.

optical fiber
See fiber-optic cable.

Organizational Unique Identifier
See OUI.

Orthogonal Frequency Division Multiplex (OFDM)
A wireless modulation technique used by IEEE 802.11a-compliant wireless LANs for transmission at 6, 9, 12, 18, 24, 36, 48, and 54 Mbps.

oscillation
Secondary signal on top of the 60-Hz waveform. It has a magnitude that ranges from 15 % to 100 % of the normal voltage carried on the power line.

OSI
Open System Interconnection
International standardization program created by ISO and ITU-T to develop standards for data networking that facilitate multivendor equipment interoperability.

OSI Internet Management
See OIM.

OSI Presentation Address
Address used to locate an OSI Application entity. It consists of an OSI Network Address and up to three selectors, one each for use by the transport, session, and presentation entities.

OSI reference model
Open System Interconnection reference model
Network architectural model developed by ISO and ITU-T. The model consists of seven layers, each of which specifies particular network functions such as addressing, flow control, error control, encapsulation, and reliable message transfer. The highest layer (the application layer) is closest to the user; the lowest layer (the physical layer) is closest to the media technology. The next to lowest layer are implemented in hardware and software, while the upper five layers are implemented only in software. The OSI reference model is used universally as a method for teaching and understanding network functionality. Similar in some respects to SNA.

OSINET
International association designed to promote OSI in vendor architectures.

OSPFv2
Open Shortest Path First version 2
OSPFv2 is an IPv4 link-state, hierarchical IGP routing algorithm proposed as a successor to RIP in the Internet community. OSPF features include least-cost routing, multipath routing, and load balancing. OSPF was derived from an early version of the ISIS protocol.

OSPFv3
Open Shortest Path First version 3
Protocol implementation for IPv6. It is based on OSPF version 2 (OSPFv2), with enhancements.

OUI
Organizational Unique Identifier
The 3 octets assigned by the IEEE in a block of 48-bit LAN addresses.

outframe
Maximum number of outstanding frames allowed in an SNA PU 2 server at any time.

out-of-band signaling
1) Transmission using frequencies or channels outside the frequencies or channels normally used for information transfer. Out-of-band signaling is often used for error reporting in situations in which in-band signaling can be affected by whatever problems the network might be experiencing. Contrast with in-band signaling.
2) Out-of-band management is the use of a dedicated management channel for device management. This channel is isolated from the data channel and not vulnerable to network connectivity issues.

P/F
poll/final bit
Bit in bit-synchronous data link layer protocols that indicates the function of a frame. If the frame is a command, a 1 in this bit indicates a poll. If the frame is a response, a 1 in this bit indicates that the current frame is the last frame in the response.

pacing
See flow control.

packet
Logical grouping of information that includes a header containing control information and (usually) user data. Packets are most often used to refer to network layer units of data. The terms datagram, frame, message, and segment are also used to describe logical information groupings at various layers of the OSI reference model and in various technology circles.

packet assembler/disassembler
See PAD.

packet buffer
See buffer.

packet Internet groper
See ping.

Packet Level Protocol
See PLP.

packet line card
See PLC.

packet switch
WAN device that routes packets along the most efficient path and allows a communications channel to be shared by multiple connections. A packet switch is also known as a packet switch node (PSN), and was formerly known as an interface message processor (IMP).

packet switch exchange
See PSE.

packet switching
Networking method in which nodes share bandwidth with each other by sending packets. Compare with circuit switching and message switching.

packet-switched data network
See PSN.

packet-switched network
See PSN.

packet-switching node
See PSN.

PAD
packet assembler/disassembler
Device used to connect simple devices (like character-mode terminals) that do not support the full functionality of a particular protocol to a network. PADs buffer data and assemble and disassemble packets sent to such end devices.

paddle card
See access card.

Palo Alto Research Center
See PARC.

PAM
pulse amplitude modulation
Modulation scheme where the modulating wave is caused to modulate the amplitude of a pulse stream. Compare with AM and FM.

PAP

Password Authentication Protocol
Authentication protocol that allows PPP peers to authenticate one another. The remote router attempting to connect to the local router is required to send an authentication request. Unlike CHAP, PAP passes the password and host name or username in the clear (unencrypted). PAP does not itself prevent unauthorized access, but merely identifies the remote end. The router or access server then determines if that user is allowed access. PAP is supported only on PPP lines. Compare with CHAP.

parallel channel

Channel that uses bus and tag cables as a transmission medium. Compare with ESCON channel.

parallel transmission

Method of data transmission in which the bits of a data character are transmitted simultaneously over a number of channels. Compare with serial transmission.

parallelism

Indicates that multiple paths exist between two points in a network. These paths might be of equal or unequal cost. Parallelism is often a network design goal: if one path fails, there is redundancy in the network to ensure that an alternate path to the same point exists.

PARC

Palo Alto Research Center
Research and development center operated by XEROX. A number of widely-used technologies were originally conceived at PARC, including the first personal computers and LANs.

PARC Universal Protocol

See PUP.

parity check

Process for checking the integrity of a character. A parity check involves appending a bit that makes the total number of binary 1 digits in a character or word (excluding the parity bit) either odd (for odd parity) or even (for even parity).

partial mesh

Term describing a network in which devices are organized in a mesh topology, with some network nodes organized in a full mesh, but with others that are only connected to one or two other nodes in the network. A partial mesh does not provide the level of redundancy of a full mesh topology, but is less expensive to implement. Partial mesh topologies are generally used in the peripheral networks that connect to a fully meshed backbone.

partial sequence number PDU

See PSNP.

passive interface

A passive interface receives updates, but does not send them. It is used to control routing update. The passive-interface command can be used with all IP interior gateway protocols. That is that it can be use with RIP, IGRP, EIGRP, OSPF, and IS-IS.

Password Authentication Protocol

See PAP.

patch panel

An assembly of pin locations and ports which can be mounted on a rack or wall bracket in the wiring closet. Patch panels act like switchboards that connect workstations cables to each other and to the outside.

path control layer

Layer 3 in the SNA architectural model. This layer performs sequencing services related to proper data reassembly. The path control layer is also responsible for routing. Corresponds roughly with the network layer of the OSI model.

path control network

SNA concept that consists of lower-level components that control the routing and data flow through an SNA network and handle physical data transmission between SNA nodes. Compare with NAU.

path cost

See cost.

path name
Full name of a UNIX, DOS, or LynxOS file or directory, including all directory and subdirectory names. Consecutive names in a path name are typically separated by a forward slash (/) or a backslash (\), as in /usr/app/base/config.

payload
Portion of a frame that contains upper-layer information (data).

PBX
private branch exchange
Digital or analog telephone switchboard located on the subscriber premises and used to connect private and public telephone networks.

PCI
protocol control information
Control information added to user data to comprise an OSI packet. The OSI equivalent of the term header.

PCM
pulse code modulation
Transmission of analog information in digital form through sampling and encoding the samples with a fixed number of bits.

PCR
peak cell rate
Parameter defined by the ATM Forum for ATM traffic management. In CBR transmissions, PCR determines how often data samples are sent. In ABR transmissions, PCR determines the maximum value of the ACR.

PDAs
personal digital assistant
Handheld device. Depending on the model and version, they can offer a varying amount of features including some of the following: personal organizers, address book, calculators, clock and calendar functions, computer games, Internet access, e-mail, radio and MP3 playback, video recording, GPS, mobile phones (smartphone), web browsers or media players.

PDN
public data network
Network operated either by a government (as in Europe) or by a private concern to provide computer communications to the public, usually for a fee. PDNs enable small organizations to create a WAN without all the equipment costs of long-distance circuits.

PDU
protocol data unit
OSI term for packet. See also BPDU and packet.

peak cell rate
See PCR.

peak rate
Maximum rate, in kilobits per second, at which a virtual circuit can transmit.

peer-to-peer computing
Peer-to-peer computing calls for each network device to run both client and server portions of an application. Also describes communication between implementations of the same OSI reference model layer in two different network devices.

performance management
One of five categories of network management defined by ISO for management of OSI networks. Performance management subsystems are responsible for analyzing and controlling network performance including network throughput and error rates.

peripheral node
In SNA, a node that uses local addresses and is therefore not affected by changes to network addresses. Peripheral nodes require boundary function assistance from an adjacent subarea node.

permanent virtual circuit
See PVC.

permanent virtual connection
See PVC.

permanent virtual path
See PVP.

permit processing
See traffic policing.

Personal digital assistants
See PDAs.

PGP
Pretty Good Privacy
Public-key encryption application that allows secure file and message exchanges. There is some controversy over the development and use of this application, in part due to U.S. national security concerns.

phase
Location of a position on an alternating wave form.

phase shift
Situation in which the relative position in time between the clock and data signals of a transmission becomes unsynchronized. In systems using long cables at higher transmission speeds, slight variances in cable construction, temperature, and other factors can cause a phase shift, resulting in high error rates.

PHY
physical sublayer
One of two sublayers of the FDDI physical layer. See also PMD.

physical address
See MAC address.

physical control layer
Layer 1 in the SNA architectural model. This layer is responsible for the physical specifications for the physical links between end systems. Corresponds to the physical layer of the OSI model.

Physical layer
Layer 1 of the OSI reference model. The physical layer defines the electrical, mechanical, procedural and functional specifications for activating, maintaining, and deactivating the physical link between end systems. Corresponds with the physical control layer in the SNA model.

physical layer convergence procedure
See PLCP.

physical media
See media.

physical medium
See media.

physical medium dependent
See PMD.

physical sublayer
See PHY.

physical unit
See PU.

Physical Unit 2
See PU 2.

Physical Unit 4
See PU 4.

Physical Unit 5
See PU 5.

Physics Network
See PHYSNET.

PIM
Protocol Independent Multicast
Multicast routing architecture that allows the addition of IP multicast routing on existing IP networks. PIM is unicast routing protocol independent and can be operated in two modes: dense mode and sparse mode.

PIM dense mode
One of the two PIM operational modes. PIM dense mode is data-driven and resembles typical multicast routing protocols. Packets are forwarded on all outgoing interfaces until pruning and truncation occurs. In dense mode, receivers are densely populated, and it is assumed that the downstream networks want to receive and will probably use the datagrams that are forwarded to them. The cost of using dense mode is its default flooding behavior. Contrast with PIM sparse mode.
PIM dense mode is also known as dense mode PIM or PIM DM.

PIM DM
See PIM dense mode.

PIM SM
See PIM sparse mode.

PIM sparse mode
One of the two PIM operational modes. PIM sparse mode tries to constrain data distribution so that a minimal number of routers in the net-

work receive it. Packets are sent only if they are explicitly requested at the RP. In sparse mode, receivers are widely distributed, and the assumption is that downstream networks will not necessarily use the datagrams that are sent to them. The cost of using sparse mode is its reliance on the periodic refreshing of explicit join messages and its need for RPs. Sometimes called sparse mode PIM or PIM SM. Contrast with PIM dense mode.

pin location
A color-coded slot on a patch panel. Cable wires are punched down using a punch tool to make an electrical connection that allows the network to function.

ping
packet Internet groper
Utility to determine whether a specific IP address is accessible. It works by sending a packet to the specified address and waiting for a reply. PING is used primarily to troubleshoot Internet connections.
PING is also known as Packet Inter-network Groper

pixel
picture element
The smallest element of a display image, corresponding to a single displayed spot or color triad on a display, or to a single input spot from a camera.

plain old telephone service
See PSTN.

PLC
packet line card
Card on the LightStream 2020 ATM switch that can be configured only as an edge card. A PLC, in conjunction with an access card, supports up to eight Ethernet or two FDDI edge ports.

PLCP
physical layer convergence procedure
Specification that maps ATM cells into physical media, such as T3 or E3, and defines certain management information.

plesiochronous transmission
Term describing digital signals that are sourced from different clocks of comparable accuracy and stability. Compare with asynchronous transmission, isochronous transmission, and synchronous transmission.

PLP
Packet Level Protocol
Network layer protocol in the X.25 protocol stack.
Packet Level Protocol is also known as X.25 Level 3 or X.25 Protocol.

PLU
primary logical unit
The LU that is initiating a session with another LU.

PMD
physical medium dependent
Sublayer of the FDDI physical layer that interfaces directly with the physical medium and performs the most basic bit transmission functions of the network.

PNNI
Private Network-Network Interface
ATM Forum specification that describes an ATM virtual circuit routing protocol, as well as a signaling protocol between ATM switches. Used to allow ATM switches within a private network to interconnect.
Private Network-Network Interface is also known as Private Network Node Interface.

PoE
Power over Ethernet
PoE is the powering of network devices over Ethernet cable. IEEE 802.3af and Cisco specify two different PoE methods. Cisco power sourcing equipment (PSE) and powered devices (PDs) support both PoE methods.

point of presence
See POP.

point-to-multipoint connection
One of two fundamental connection types. In ATM, a point-tomultipoint connection is a unidirectional connection in which a single source end-system (known as a root node) connects to

multiple destination end-systems (known as leaves). Compare point-to-point connection.

point-to-point connection
One of two fundamental connection types. In ATM, a point-topoint connection can be a unidirectional or bidirectional connection between two ATM end-systems. Compare point-to-multipoint connection.

Point-to-Point Protocol
See PPP.

poison reverse updates
Routing updates that explicitly indicate that a network or subnet is unreachable, rather than implying that a network is unreachable by not including it in updates. Poison reverse updates are sent to defeat large routing loops. The Cisco IGRP implementation uses poison reverse updates.

polarization
Polarization is the physical orientation of the element on the antenna that actually emits the RF energy. All Cisco Aironet antennas are set for vertical polarization. A vertical dipole antenna is vertically polarized.

policy routing
Routing scheme that forwards packets to specific interfaces based on user-configured policies. Such policies might specify that traffic sent from a particular network should be forwarded out one interface, while all other traffic should be forwarded out another interface.

policy-based routing
See policy routing.

poll/final bit
See P/F.

polling
Access method in which a primary network device inquires, in an orderly fashion, whether secondaries have data to transmit. The inquiry occurs in the form of a message to each secondary that gives the secondary the right to transmit.

POP
point of presence
Point of presence is the point of interconnection between the communication facilities provided by the telephone company and the building's main distribution facility.

port
1) Interface on an internetworking device (such as a router).
2) In IP terminology, an upper-layer process that is receiving information from lower layers.
3) To rewrite software or microcode so that it will run on a different hardware platform or in a different software environment than that for which it was originally designed.
4) A female plug on a patch panel which accepts the same size plug as an RJ45 jack. Patch cords are used in these ports to cross connect computers wired to the patch panel. It is this cross connection which allows the LAN to function.

POS
power-on servicing
Feature on the LightStream 2020 ATM switch that allows faulty components to be diagnosed, removed, and replaced while the rest of the switch continues to operate normally. Power-on servicing is also known as hot swapping.

POST
power-on self test
Set of hardware diagnostics that runs on a hardware device when that device is powered up. On a LightStream 2020 ATM switch, for example, the NP, switch card, and line card all perform the POST.

Post, Telephone, and Telegraph
See PTT.

POTS
plain old telephone service. See PSTN (Public Switched Telephone Network).

power tray
Power supply for a LightStream 2020 ATM switch. A LightStream 2020 switch can have one or two bulk power trays. In a redundant system, the two power trays load share, but

each can power the entire system in the event that the other fails. The power tray can provide either AC or DC power to the switch.

power-on self test
See POST.

power-on servicing
See POS.

PPK
per-packet keying
Method of overcoming the exploitation of encryption keys with key hashing.

PPP
Point-to-Point Protocol
A successor to SLIP, PPP provides router-to-router and host-to-network connections over synchronous and asynchronous circuits.

PQ
Priority Queuing
Routing feature in which frames in an interface output queue are prioritized based on various characteristics such as packet size and interface type.

presentation layer
Layer 6 of the OSI reference model. This layer ensures that information sent by the application layer of one system will be readable by the application layer of another. The presentation layer is also concerned with the data structures used by programs and therefore negotiates data transfer syntax for the application layer. Corresponds roughly with the presentation services layer of the SNA model.

presentation services layer
Layer 6 of the SNA architectural model. This layer provides network resource management, session presentation services, and some application management. Corresponds roughly with the presentation layer of the OSI model.

Pretty Good Privacy
See PGP.

PRI
Primary Rate Interface
ISDN interface to primary rate access. Primary rate access consists of a single 64-Kbps D channel plus 23 (T1) or 30 (E1) B channels for voice or data. Compare to BRI.

primary
See primary station.

Primary LU
See PLU.

Primary Rate Interface
See PRI.

primary station
In bit-synchronous data link layer protocols such as HDLC and SDLC, a station that controls the transmission activity of secondary stations and performs other management functions such as error control through polling or other means. Primary stations send commands to secondary stations and receive responses.
A primary station is also known as a primary.

print server
Networked computer system that fields, manages, and executes (or sends for execution) print requests from other network devices.

priority queuing
See PQ.

private branch exchange
See PBX.

Private Network Node Interface
See PNNI.

Private Network-Network Interface
See PNNI.

process switching
Operation that provides full route evaluation and per-packet load balancing across parallel WAN links. Involves the transmission of entire frames to the router CPU where they are repackaged for delivery to or from a WAN interface, with the router making a route selection for each packet. Process switching is the most resource-intensive switching operation that the CPU can perform.

programmable read-only memory
See PROM.

PROM
programmable read-only memory
ROM that can be programmed using special equipment. PROMs can be programmed only once. Compare with EPROM.

propagation delay
Time required for data to travel over a network, from its source to its ultimate destination.

protocol
1) Formal description of a set of rules and conventions that govern how devices on a network exchange information.
2) Field within an IP datagram that indicates the upper layer (Layer 4) protocol sending the datagram.

protocol address
See network address.

protocol analyzer
See network analyzer.

protocol control information
See PCI.

protocol converter
Enables equipment with different data formats to communicate by translating the data transmission code of one device to the data transmission code of another device.

protocol data unit
See PDU.

Protocol Independent Multicast
See PIM.

protocol stack
Set of related communications protocols that operate together and, as a group, address communication at some or all of the seven layers of the OSI reference model. Not every protocol stack covers each layer of the model, and often a single protocol in the stack will address a number of layers at once. TCP/IP is a typical protocol stack.

protocol translator
Network device or software that converts one protocol into another, similar, protocol.

proxy
Entity that, in the interest of efficiency, essentially stands in for another entity.

proxy Address Resolution Protocol
See proxy ARP.

proxy ARP
Proxy Address Resolution Protocol
Variation of the ARP protocol in which an intermediate device (for example, a router) sends an ARP response on behalf of an end node to the requesting host. Proxy ARP can lessen bandwidth use on slow-speed WAN links.

proxy polling
Technique that alleviates the load across an SDLC network by allowing routers to act as proxies for primary and secondary nodes, thus keeping polling traffic off of the shared links. Proxy polling has been replaced by SDLC Transport.

PSDN
packet-switched data network. See PSN (packet-switched network).

PSE
packet switch exchange
Essentially, a switch. The term PSE is generally used in reference to a switch in an X.25 PSN.

PSN
1) packet-switched network. Network that utilizes packet-switching technology for data transfer. Packet-switched network is also known as packet-switched data network (PSDN).
2) packet-switching node. Network node capable of performing packet switching functions.

PSNP
partial sequence number protocol data unit
PSNPs are used to request one or more LSPs and acknowledge receipt of one or more LSPs.

PSTN
Public Switched Telephone Network
General term referring to the variety of telephone networks and services in place worldwide.
PSTN is also known as plain old telephone service (POTS).

PTT
Post, Telephone, and Telegraph
Government agency that provides telephone services. PTTs exist in most areas outside North America and provide both local and long-distance telephone services.

PU
physical unit
SNA component that manages and monitors the resources of a node, as requested by an SSCP. There is one PU per node.

PU 2
Physical Unit 2
SNA peripheral node that can support only DLUs that require services from a VTAM host and that are only capable of performing the secondary LU role in SNA sessions.

PU 4
Physical Unit 4
Component of an IBM FEP capable of full-duplex data transfer. Each such SNA device employs a separate data and control path into the transmit and receive buffers of the control program.

PU 5
Physical Unit 5
Component of an IBM mainframe or host computer that manages an SNA network. PU 5 nodes are involved in routing within the SNA path control layer.

public data network
See PDN.

Public Switched Telephone Network
See PSTN.

pull string
Strong, heavy string used to pull cable in multiple runs.

pulse amplitude modulation
See PAM.

pulse code modulation
See PCM.

pulse density
See ones density.

punch tool
Spring-loaded tool used for cutting and connecting wire in a jack or on a patch panel.

PUP
PARC Universal Protocol
Protocol similar to IP developed at PARC.

PVC
permanent virtual circuit
Virtual circuit that is permanently established. PVCs save bandwidth associated with circuit establishment and tear down in situations where certain virtual circuits must exist all the time. Compare with SVC.
Permanent virtual circuit is known as permanent virtual connection in ATM terminology.

PVP
permanent virtual path
Virtual path that consists of PVCs. See also PVC and virtual path.

Q.920/Q.921
ITU-T specifications for the ISDN UNI data link layer.

Q.922A
ITU-T specification for Frame Relay encapsulation.

Q.931
ITU-T specification for signaling to establish, maintain, and clear ISDN network connections.

Q.93B
ITU-T specification signaling to establish, maintain, and clear BISDN network connections. An evolution of ITU-T recommendation Q.931.

QLLC
Qualified Logical Link Control
Data link layer protocol defined by IBM that allows SNA data to be transported across X.25 networks.

QoS
Quality of Service
Measure of performance for a transmission system that reflects its transmission quality and service availability.

QoS parameters
quality of service parameter
Parameters that control the amount of traffic the source router in an ATM network sends over an SVC. If any switch along the path cannot accommodate the requested QoS parameters, the request is rejected, and a rejection message is forwarded back to the originator of the request.

Quadruple Phase Shift Keying
A modulation technique used by IEEE 802.11b-compliant wireless LANs for transmission at 2 Mbps.

Qualified Logical Link Control
See QLLC.

quality of service
See QoS.

quartet signaling
Signaling technique used in 100VG-AnyLAN networks that allow data transmission at 100 Mbps over four pairs of UTP cabling at the same frequencies used in 10BASE-T networks.

query
Message used to inquire about the value of some variable or set of variables.

queue
1) Generally, an ordered list of elements waiting to be processed.
2) In routing, a backlog of packets waiting to be forwarded over a router interface.

queuing delay
Amount of time that data must wait before it can be transmitted onto a statistically multiplexed physical circuit.

queuing theory
Scientific principles governing the formation or lack of formation of congestion on a network or at an interface.

RACE
Research on Advanced Communications in Europe
Project sponsored by the European Community (EC) for the development of broadband networking capabilities.

raceway
Wall-mounted channel with a removable cover used to support horizontal cabling.

radio frequency
See RF.

radio frequency interference
See RFI.

RAM
random-access memory
Volatile memory that can be read and written by a microprocessor.

random-access memory
See RAM.

range
A linear measure of the distance that a wireless transmitter can send a signal.

RARP
Reverse Address Resolution Protocol
Protocol in the TCP/IP stack that provides a method for finding IP addresses based on MAC addresses. Compare with ARP.

rate enforcement
See traffic policing.

rate queue
Value that is associated with one or more virtual circuits, and that defines the speed at which an individual virtual circuit will transmit data to the remote end. Each rate queue represents a portion of the overall bandwidth available on an ATM link. The combined bandwidth of all configured rate queues should not exceed the total bandwidth available.

RBHC
Regional Bell Holding Company
One of seven telephone companies created by the AT and T divestiture in 1984.

RBOC
Regional Bell Operating Company
Local or regional telephone company that owns and operates telephone lines and switches in one of seven U.S. regions. The RBOCs were created by the divestiture of AT and T. Regional Bell Operating Company is also known as Bell Operating Company (BOC).

rcp
remote copy protocol
Protocol that allows users to copy files to and from a file system residing on a remote host or server on the network. The rcp protocol uses TCP to ensure the reliable delivery of data.

rcp server
Router or other device that acts as a server for rcp.

read-only memory
See ROM.

Ready To Send
See RTS.

reassembly
The putting back together of an IP datagram at the destination after it has been fragmented either at the source or at an intermediate node.

receiver sensitivity
A measurement of the weakest wireless signal a receiver can receive and still correctly translate it into data.

redirect
Part of the ICMP and ES-IS protocols that allows a router to tell a host that using another router would be more effective.

redirector
Software that intercepts requests for resources within a computer and analyzes them for remote access requirements. If remote access is required to satisfy the request, the redirector forms an RPC and sends the RPC to lower-layer protocol software for transmission through the network to the node that can satisfy the request.

redistribution
Allowing routing information discovered through one routing protocol to be distributed in the update messages of another routing protocol.
Redistribution is also known as route redistribution.

redundancy
1) In internetworking, the duplication of devices, services, or connections so that, in the event of a failure, the redundant devices, services, or connections can perform the work of those that failed. See also redundant system.
2) In telephony, the portion of the total information contained in a message that can be eliminated without loss of essential information or meaning.

redundant system
Computer, router, switch, or other computer system that contains two or more of each of the most important subsystems, such as two disk drives, two CPUs, or two power supplies. For example, on a fully redundant LightStream 2020 ATM switch, there are two NP cards with disks, two switch cards, and two power trays. A partially redundant LightStream 2020 switch might have two NPs, one switch card, and one power tray.

reflection
Physical phenomenon which occurs when radio frequency waves bounce off objects (for example, metal or glass surfaces).

Refraction
The measure of how much a given material bends light.

Regional Bell Holding Company
See RBHC.

Regional Bell Operating Company
See RBOC.

registered jack connector
See RJ connector.

relay
OSI terminology for a device that connects two or more networks or network systems. A data link layer (Layer 2) relay is a bridge; a network layer (Layer 3) relay is a router.

reliability
Ratio of expected to received keepalives from a link. If the ratio is high, the line is reliable. Used as a routing metric.

remote bridge
Bridge that connects physically disparate network segments via WAN links.

remote copy protocol
See rcp.

remote login
See rlogin.

Remote Monitoring
See RMON.

Remote Operations Service Element
See ROSE.

remote shell protocol
See rsh.

remote source-route bridging
See RSRB.

remote-procedure call
See RPC.

rendezvous point
See RP.

repeater
Device that regenerates and propagates electrical signals between two network segments.

Request For Comments
See RFC.

request/response unit
See RU.

Research on Advanced Communications in Europe
See RACE.

reserved
Set to zero.

Reverse Address Resolution Protocol
See RARP.

Reverse Path Multicasting
See RPM.

RF
radio frequency
Generic term referring to frequencies that correspond to radio transmissions. Cable TV and broadband networks use RF technology.

RFC
Request For Comments
Document series used as the primary means for communicating information about the Internet. Some RFCs are designated by the IAB as Internet standards. Most RFCs document protocol specifications such as Telnet and FTP, but some are humorous or historical. RFCs are available online from numerous sources.

RFI
radio frequency interference
Radio frequencies that create noise that interferes with information being transmitted across unshielded copper cabling.

RIF
Routing Information Field
Field in the IEEE 802.5 header that is used by a source-route bridge to determine through which Token Ring network segments a packet must transit. A RIF is made up of ring and bridge numbers as well as other information.

RII
Routing Information Identifier
Bit used by SRT bridges to distinguish between frames that should be transparently bridged and frames that should be passed to the SRB module for handling.

ring
Connection of two or more stations in a logically circular topology. Information is passed sequentially between active stations. Token Ring, FDDI, and CDDI are based on this topology.

ring topology
Network topology that consists of a series of repeaters connected to one another by unidirec-

tional transmission links to form a single closed loop. Each station on the network connects to the network at a repeater. While logically a ring, ring topologies are most often organized in a closed-loop star. Compare with bus topology, star topology, and tree topology.

RIP
Routing Information Protocol
IGP supplied with UNIX BSD systems. The most common IGP in the Internet. RIP uses hop count as a routing metric.

RIPng
Routing Information Protocol next generation
Distance vector routing protocol with a limit of 15 hops that uses split-horizon and poison reverse to prevent routing loops. It is based on IPv4 RIP v2 and similar to RIPv2, but uses IPv6 for transport. The multicast group address FF02::9 identifies all RIPng enabled routers.(RIPng, RFC 2080)

RIPv2
Routing Information Protocol version 2
Defined in RFC 1723 and is supported in IOS versions 11.1 and later. RIPv2 is not a new protocol, just RIPv1 with some extensions to bring it up-to-date with modern routing environments. RIPv2 has be updated to supports VLSM, authentication, and multicast updates.

RJ connector
registered jack connector
Standard connectors originally used to connect telephone lines. RJ connectors are now used for telephone connections and for 10BASE-T and other types of network connections. RJ-11, RJ-12, and RJ-45 are popular types of RJ connectors.

rlogin
remote login
Terminal emulation program, similar to Telnet, offered in most UNIX implementations.

RMON
Remote Monitoring
MIB agent specification described in RFC 1271 that defines functions for the remote monitoring of networked devices. The RMON specification provides numerous monitoring, problem detection, and reporting capabilities.

ROM
read-only memory
Nonvolatile memory that can be read, but not written, by the microprocessor.

root account
1) Privileged account on UNIX systems used exclusively by network or system administrators.
2) One of the four default user accounts that are created in the factory on each LightStream 2020 ATM switch. The root account is for use by the system or network administrator only. Its default interface is the bash shell. See also bash.

root bridge
Exchanges topology information with designated bridges in a spanning-tree implementation in order to notify all other bridges in the network when topology changes are required. This prevents loops and provides a measure of defense against link failure.

ROSE
Remote Operations Service Element
OSI RPC mechanism used by various OSI network application protocols.

round-trip time
See RTT.

route
Path through an internetwork.

route extension
In SNA, a path from the destination subarea node through peripheral equipment to a NAU.

route map
Method of controlling the redistribution of routes between routing domains.

Route Processor
See RP.

route redistribution
See redistribution.

route summarization
Consolidation of advertised addresses in OSPF and IS-IS. In OSPF, this causes a single summary route to be advertised to other areas by an area border router.

Route/Switch Processor
See RSP.

routed protocol
Protocol that can be routed by a router. A router must be able to interpret the logical internetwork as specified by that routed protocol. Examples of routed protocols include AppleTalk, DECnet, and IP.

router
Network layer device that uses one or more metrics to determine the optimal path along which network traffic should be forwarded. Routers forward packets from one network to another based on network layer information. Occasionally called a gateway (although this definition of gateway is becoming increasingly outdated). Compare with gateway.

routing
Process of finding a path to a destination host. Routing is very complex in large networks because of the many potential intermediate destinations a packet might traverse before reaching its destination host.

routing domain
Group of end systems and intermediate systems operating under the same set of administrative rules. Within each routing domain is one or more areas, each uniquely identified by an area address.

Routing Information Field
See RIF.

Routing Information Identifier
See RII.

Routing Information Protocol
See RIP.

routing metric
Method by which a routing algorithm determines that one route is better than another. This information is stored in routing tables. Metrics include bandwidth, communication cost, delay, hop count, load, MTU, path cost, and reliability.
Routing metric is also known as metric.

routing protocol
Protocol that accomplishes routing through the implementation of a specific routing algorithm. Examples of routing protocols include IGRP, OSPF, and RIP.

routing table
Table stored in a router or some other internetworking device that keeps track of routes to particular network destinations and, in some cases, metrics associated with those routes.

Routing Table Protocol
See RTP.

routing update
Message sent from a router to indicate network reachability and associated cost information. Routing updates are typically sent at regular intervals and after a change in network topology. Compare with flash update.

RP
1) route processor. Processor module on the Cisco 7000 series routers that contains the CPU, system software, and most of the memory components that are used in the router. Route processor is also known as supervisory processor.
2) rendezvous point. Router specified in PIM sparse mode implementations to track membership in multicast groups and to forward messages to known multicast group addresses. See also PIM sparse mode.

RPC
remote-procedure call
Technological foundation of client-server computing. RPCs are procedure calls that are built or specified by clients and executed on servers, with the results returned over the network to the clients.

RPM
Reverse Path Multicasting
Multicasting technique in which a multicast datagram is forwarded out of all but the receiv-

ing interface if the receiving interface is one used to forward unicast datagrams to the source of the multicast datagram.

RP-TNC

A connector type unique to Cisco Aironet radios and antennas. Part 15.203 of the FCC rules covering spread spectrum devices limits the types of antennas that may be used with transmission equipment. In compliance with this rule, Cisco Aironet, like all other wireless LAN providers, equips its radios and antennas with a unique connector to prevent attachment of non-approved antennas to radios.

RS-232

Popular physical layer interface. RS-232 is known as EIA/TIA-232.

RS-422

Balanced electrical implementation of EIA/TIA-449 for high-speed data transmission. RS-422 is referred to collectively with RS-423 as EIA-530.

RS-423

Unbalanced electrical implementation of EIA/TIA-449 for EIA/TIA-232 compatibility. RS-423 is referred to collectively with RS-422 as EIA-530.

RS-449

Popular physical layer interface. RS-449 is known as EIA/TIA-449.

rsh

remote shell protocol
Protocol that allows a user to execute commands on a remote system without having to log in to the system. For example, rsh can be used to remotely examine the status of a number of access servers without connecting to each communication server, executing the command, and then disconnecting from the communication server.

RSP

Route/Switch Processor
Processor module used in the Cisco 7500 series routers that integrates the functions of the RP and the SP.

RSRB

remote source-route bridging
SRB over WAN links.

RSVP

Resource Reservation Protocol
Protocol that supports the reservation of resources across an IP network. Applications running on IP end systems can use RSVP to indicate to other nodes the nature (bandwidth, jitter, maximum burst, and so forth) of the packet streams they want to receive. Resource Reservation Protocol is also known as Resource Reservation Setup Protocol.

RTP

1) Routing Table Protocol. VINES routing protocol based on RIP. Distributes network topology information and aids VINES servers in finding neighboring clients, servers, and routers. Uses delay as a routing metric. See also SRTP.
2) Real-Time Transport Protocol. Commonly used with IP networks. RTP is designed to provide end-to-end network transport functions for applications transmitting real-time data, such as audio, video, or simulation data, over multicast or unicast network services. RTP provides such services as payload type identification, sequence numbering, timestamping, and delivery monitoring to real-time applications.

RTS

Ready To Send
EIA/TIA-232 control signal that requests a data transmission on a communications line.

RTT

round-trip time
Time required for a network communication to travel from the source to the destination and back. RTT includes the time required for the destination to process the message from the source and generate a reply. RTT is used by some routing algorithms to aid in calculating optimal routes.

RU

request/response unit
Request and response messages exchanged between NAUs in an SNA network.

run-time memory
Memory accessed while a program runs. On a LightStream 2020 ATM switch, this memory contains configuration data that is accessed while the switch operates.

safety ground wire
Circuit wire that connects to a local earth ground and the chassis of an electrical appliance or device via an electrical outlet and plug. It is used to ensure that no voltage potential exists between the chassis of the electrical device and the earth ground.

sag
Any decrease of below 80% in the normal voltage carried by a power line. A sag is sometimes referred to as a brownout.

sampling rate
Rate at which samples of a particular waveform amplitude are taken.

SAP
1) service access point. Field defined by the IEEE 802.2 specification that is part of an address specification. Thus, the destination plus the DSAP define the recipient of a packet. The same applies to the SSAP. See also DSAP and SSAP.
2) Service Advertisement Protocol. IPX protocol that provides a means of informing network clients, via routers and servers, of available network resources and services. See also IPX.

satellite communication
Use of orbiting satellites to relay data between multiple earth-based stations. Satellite communications offer high bandwidth and a cost that is not related to distance between earth stations, long propagation delays, or broadcast capability.

Sbus
Bus technology used in Sun SPARC-based workstations and servers. The SBus specification has been adopted by the IEEE as a new bus standard.

scattering
Scattering is the physical phenomenon that occurs when radio frequency waves strike an uneven surface (for example, a rough surface) and are reflected in many directions.

SCR
sustainable cell rate
Parameter defined by the ATM Forum for ATM traffic management. For VBR connections, SCR determines the long-term average cell rate that can be transmitted.

SCTE
serial clock transmit external
Timing signal that DTE echoes to DCE to maintain clocking. SCTE is designed to compensate for clock phase shift on long cables. When the DCE device uses SCTE instead of its internal clock to sample data from the DTE, it is better able to sample the data without error even if there is a phase shift in the cable.

SDH
Synchronous Digital Hierarchy
European standard that defines a set of rate and format standards that are transmitted using optical signals over fiber. SDH is similar to SONET, with a basic SDH rate of 155.52 Mbps, designated at STM-1.

SDLC
Synchronous Data Link Control
SNA data link layer communications protocol. SDLC is a bit-oriented, full-duplex serial protocol that has spawned numerous similar protocols, including HDLC and LAPB.

SDLC Transport
Cisco router feature with which disparate environments can be integrated into a single, high-speed, enterprise-wide network. Native SDLC traffic can be passed through point-to-point serial links with other protocol traffic multiplexed over the same links. Cisco routers can also encapsulate SDLC frames inside IP datagrams for transport over arbitrary (non-SDLC) networks. Replaces proxy polling.

SDLLC
Feature that performs translation between SDLC and IEEE 802.2 type 2.

SDSU
Switched Multimegabit Data Service DSU DSU for access to SMDS via HSSIs and other serial interfaces.

secondary
See secondary station.

secondary station
In bit-synchronous data link layer protocols such as HDLC, a station that responds to commands from a primary station.
A secondary station is also known as a secondary.

security management
One of five categories of network management defined by ISO for management of OSI networks. Security management subsystems are responsible for controlling access to network resources.

segment
1) Section of a network that is bounded by bridges, routers, or switches.
2) In a LAN using a bus topology, a segment is a continuous electrical circuit that is often connected to other such segments with repeaters.
3) Term used in the TCP specification to describe a single transport layer unit of information. The terms datagram, frame, message, and packet are also used to describe logical information groupings at various layers of the OSI reference model and in various technology circles.

sequence number
Number used to ensure correct sequencing of the arriving data.

Sequenced Routing Update Protocol
See SRTP.

serial clock transmit external
See SCTE.

Serial Interface Processor
See SIP.

Serial Line Internet Protocol
See SLIP.

serial transmission
Method of data transmission in which the bits of a data character are transmitted sequentially over a single channel. Compare with parallel transmission.

serial tunnel
See STUN.

server
Node or software program that provides services to clients.

Server Message Block
See SMB.

service access point
See SAP.

Service Advertisement Protocol
See SAP.

service point
Interface between non-SNA devices and NetView that sends alerts from equipment unknown to the SNA environment.

Service Profile Identifier
See SPID.

Service-Oriented Network Architecture
See SONA.

session
1) Related set of communications transactions between two or more network devices.
2) In SNA, a logical connection enabling two NAUs to communicate.

session layer
Layer 5 of the OSI reference model. This layer establishes, manages, and terminates sessions between applications and manages data exchange between presentation layer entities. Corresponds to the data flow control layer of the SNA model.

SF
Super Frame
Common framing type used on T1 circuits. SF consists of 12 frames of 192 bits each, with the 193rd bit providing error checking and other functions. SF has been superseded by ESF, but is still widely used.
Super Frame is also known as D4 framing.

SGMP
Simple Gateway Monitoring Protocol
Network management protocol that was considered for Internet standardization and later evolved into SNMP. Documented in RFC 1028.

shaping
See traffic shaping.

shielded cable
Cable that has a layer of shielded insulation to reduce EMI.

shielded twisted-pair
See STP.

Shipworm
See Teredo.

shortest path first algorithm
See SPF.

shortest-path routing
Routing that minimizes distance or path cost through application of an algorithm.

signal injector
Device used to measure attenuation of a signal on a network.

signal reference ground
Reference point used by computing devices to measure and compare incoming digital signals.

signaling
Process of sending a transmission signal over a physical medium for purposes of communication.

signaling packet
Generated by an ATM-connected device that wants to establish a connection with another such device. The signaling packet contains the ATM NSAP address of the desired ATM endpoint, as well as any QOS parameters required for the connection. If the endpoint can support the desired QOS, it responds with an accept message, and the connection is opened.

Signaling System number 7
See SS7.

SIIT
Stateless IP/ICMP Translation
Algorithm used in NAT-PT that translates the IP header fields. Compare with NAT-PT and DNS ALG.

Silicon Switch Processor
See SSP.

silicon switching
Switching based on the SSE, which allows the processing of packets independent of the Silicon Switch Processor (SSP) system processor. Silicon switching provides high-speed, dedicated packet switching.

silicon switching engine
See SSE.

Simple Gateway Monitoring Protocol
See SGMP.

Simple Mail Transfer Protocol
See SMTP.

Simple Multicast Routing Protocol
See SMRP.

Simple Network Management Protocol
See SNMP.

simplex
Capability for data transmission in only one direction between a sending station and a receiving station. Compare with full duplex and half duplex.

single-mode fiber
Fiber-optic cabling with a narrow core that allows light to enter only at a single angle. Such cabling has higher bandwidth than multimode fiber, but requires a light source with a narrow spectral width (for example, a laser).
Single-mode fiber is also known as monomode fiber.

SIP

1) SMDS Interface Protocol. Used in communications between CPE and SMDS network equipment. Allows the CPE to use SMDS service for high-speed WAN internetworking. Based on the IEEE 802.6 DQDB standard. See also DQDB.

2) Serial Interface Processor. Obsolete interface processor for Cisco 7000 series routers that provided either two or four channel-independent ports for synchronous serial connections at speeds from 2.4 Kbps to 4 Mbps. The SIP has been replaced by the FSIP. Sometimes called SX-SIP or Pre-FSIP. See also FSIP.

site-local unicast address

An IPv6 address which is very similar in function to the IPv4 private address space that includes ranges. These addresses are meant for internal communications and are not routable on the public Internet. Site-local addresses start with the prefix FEC0::/10. Compare with link-local unicast address.

sliding window

Refers to the fact that the window size is negotiated dynamically during the TCP session.

sliding window flow control

Method of flow control in which a receiver gives transmitter permission to transmit data until a window is full. When the window is full, the transmitter must stop transmitting until the receiver advertises a larger window. TCP, other transport protocols, and several data link layer protocols use this method of flow control.

SLIP

Serial Line Internet Protocol
Standard protocol for point-to-point serial connections using a variation of TCP/IP. Predecessor of PPP.

slotted ring

LAN architecture based on a ring topology in which the ring is divided into slots that circulate continuously. Slots can be either empty or full, and transmissions must start at the beginning of a slot.

slow switching

Packet processing performed at process level speeds, without the use of a route cache. Contrast with fast switching.

SMAC

Source MAC
MAC address specified in the Source Address field of a packet. Compare with DMAC.

SMB

Server Message Block
File-system protocol used in LAN Manager and similar NOSs to package data and exchange information with other systems.

SMDS

Switched Multimegabit Data Service
High-speed, packet-switched, datagram-based WAN networking technology offered by the telephone companies.

SMDS Interface Protocol

See SIP.

SMI

Structure of Management Information
Document (RFC 1155) specifying rules used to define managed objects in the MIB.

smoothing

See traffic shaping.

SMRP

Simple Multicast Routing Protocol
Specialized multicast network protocol for routing multimedia data streams on enterprise networks. SMRP works in conjunction with multicast extensions to the AppleTalk protocol.

SMT

Station Management
ANSI FDDI specification that defines how ring stations are managed.

SMTP

Simple Mail Transfer Protocol
Internet protocol providing electronic mail services.

SNA
Systems Network Architecture
Large, complex, feature-rich network architecture developed in the 1970s by IBM. Similar in some respects to the OSI reference model, but with a number of differences. SNA is essentially composed of seven layers.

SNA Distribution Services
See SNADS.

SNA Network Interconnection
See SNI.

SNADS
SNA Distribution Services
Consists of a set of SNA transaction programs that interconnect and cooperate to provide asynchronous distribution of information between end users. One of three SNA transaction services.

SNAP
Subnetwork Access Protocol
Internet protocol that operates between a network entity in the subnetwork and a network entity in the end system. SNAP specifies a standard method of encapsulating IP datagrams and ARP messages on IEEE networks. The SNAP entity in the end system makes use of the services of the subnetwork and performs three key functions: data transfer, connection management, and QOS selection.

Snapshot routing
Method of gathering routing information during an active time, taking a snapshot of the information and using that routing information for a configured length of time (referred to as the quiet time).

SNI
1) Subscriber Network Interface. Interface for SMDS-based networks that connects CPE and an SMDS switch. See also UNI.
2) SNA Network Interconnection. IBM gateway connecting multiple SNA networks.

SNMP
Simple Network Management Protocol
Network management protocol used almost exclusively in TCP/IP networks. SNMP provides a means to monitor and control network devices, and to manage configurations, statistics collection, performance, and security.

SNMP communities
Authentication scheme that enables an intelligent network device to validate SNMP requests from sources such as the NMS. A LightStream 2020 ATM switch, for example, responds only to SNMP requests that come from members of known communities and that have the access privileges required for that request.

SNMP2
Simple Network Management Protocol version 2
Version 2 of the popular network management protocol. SNMP2 supports centralized as well as distributed network management strategies, and includes improvements in the SMI, protocol operations, management architecture, and security.

SNPA
subnetwork point of attachment address
SNPA address is the point at which subnetwork services are provided. This is the equivalent of the Layer 2 address corresponding to the Layer 3, NET or NSAP, address and is therefore usually a MAC address on a LAN or Virtual Circuit ID in X.25, Frame-Relay, or ATM.

socket
Software structure operating as a communications end point within a network device.

SONA
Service-Oriented Network Architecture
Architectural framework that guides the evolution of the network to an Intelligent Information Network (IIN). It enables enterprises to optimize applications, processes, and resources to deliver greater business benefits.

SONET
Synchronous Optical Network
High-speed (up to 2.5 Gbps) synchronous network specification developed by Bellcore and designed to run on optical fiber. STS-1 is the basic building block of SONET. Approved as an international standard in 1988.

source address
Address of a network device that is sending data.

source and destination IP addresses
Field within an IP datagram that indicates the 32-bit source and destination IP addresses.

source MAC
See SMAC.

source port
Number of the calling port.

source service access point
See SSAP.

source-route bridging
See SRB.

source-route translational bridging
See SR/TLB.

source-route transparent bridging
See SRT.

Southeastern Universities Research Association Network
See SURAnet.

SP
switch processor
Cisco 7000-series processor module that acts as the administrator for all CxBus activities. Switch processor is also known as ciscoBus controller.

SPAN
1) Switched Port Analyzer. Feature of the Catalyst 5000 switch that extends the monitoring abilities of existing network analyzers into a switched Ethernet environment. SPAN mirrors the traffic at one switched segment onto a predefined SPAN port. A network analyzer attached to the SPAN port can monitor traffic from any of the other Catalyst switched ports.
2) Full-duplex digital transmission line between two digital facilities.

spanning tree
Loop-free subset of a network topology.

Spanning Tree Protocol
See STP.

spanning-tree algorithm
See STA.

spanning-tree protocol
See STP.

sparse mode PIM
See PIM sparse mode.

speed matching
Feature that provides sufficient buffering capability in a destination device to allow a high-speed source to transmit data at its maximum rate, even if the destination device is a lower-speed device.

SPF
shortest path first algorithm
Routing algorithm that iterates on length of path to determine a shortest-path spanning tree. Commonly used in link-state routing algorithms.
SPF is also known as Dijkstra's algorithm.

SPID
Service Profile Identifier
Number that some service providers use to define the services to which an ISDN device subscribes. The ISDN device uses the SPID when accessing the switch that initializes the connection to a service provider.

spike
Any power impulse lasting between .5 and 100 microseconds and possessing an amplitude over 100% of peak power line voltage.

split-horizon updates
Routing technique in which information about routes is prevented from exiting the router interface through which that information was received. Split-horizon updates are useful in preventing routing loops.

spoofing
1) Scheme used by Cisco routers to cause a host to treat an interface as if it were up and supporting a session. The router spoofs replies to keepalive messages from the host in order to convince that host that the session still exists. Spoofing is useful in routing environments such as DDR, in which a circuit-switched link is taken down when there is no traffic to be sent

across it in order to save toll charges. See also DDR.

2) The act of a packet illegally claiming to be from an address from which it was not actually sent. Spoofing is designed to foil network security mechanisms such as filters and access lists.

spread spectrum

A radio transmission technology that spreads the user information over a much wider bandwidth than otherwise required in order to gain benefits such as improved interference tolerance and unlicensed operation.

SR/TLB

source route/translational bridging
Method of bridging where source-route stations can communicate with transparent bridge stations with the help of an intermediate bridge that translates between the two bridge protocols. Compare with SRT.

SRAM

Type of RAM that retains its contents for as long as power is supplied. SRAM does not require constant refreshing, like DRAM. Compare with DRAM.

SRB

source-route bridging
Method of bridging originated by IBM and popular in Token Ring networks. In a SRB network, the entire route to a destination is predetermined, in real time, prior to the sending of data to the destination. Contrast with transparent bridging.

SRT

source-route transparent bridging
IBM bridging scheme that merges the two most prevalent bridging strategies, SRB and transparent bridging. SRT employs both technologies in one device to satisfy the needs of all ENs. No translation between bridging protocols is necessary. Compare with SR/TLB.

SRTP

Sequenced Routing Update Protocol
Protocol that assists VINES servers in finding neighboring clients, servers, and routers.

SS7

Signaling System number 7
Standard CCS system used with BISDN and ISDN. Developed by Bellcore.

SSAP

source service access point
The SAP of the network node designated in the Source field of a packet. Compare to DSAP.

SSCP

system services control points
Focal points within an SNA network for managing network configuration, coordinating network operator and problem determination requests, and providing directory services and other session services for network end users.

SSCP-PU session

system services control points - physical unit session
Session used by SNA to allow an SSCP to manage the resources of a node through the PU. SSCPs can send requests to, and receive replies from, individual nodes in order to control the network configuration.

SSE

silicon switching engine
Routing and switching mechanism that compares the data link or network layer header of an incoming packet to a silicon-switching cache, determines the appropriate action (routing or bridging), and forwards the packet to the proper interface. The SSE is directly encoded in the hardware of the Silicon Switch Processor (SSP) of a Cisco 7000 series router. It can therefore perform switching independently of the system processor, making the execution of routing decisions much quicker than if they were encoded in software.

SSID

service set identifier
The SSID is a code attached to all packets on a wireless network to identify each packet as part of that network. The code is a case sensitive text string which consists of a maximum of 32 alphanumeric characters. All wireless devices attempting to communicate with each other must share the same SSID. Apart from identifying each packet, SSID also serves to uniquely

identify a group of wireless network devices used in a given service set.

SSP

1) Silicon Switch Processor. High-performance silicon switch for Cisco 7000 series routers that provides distributed processing and control for interface processors. The SSP leverages the high-speed switching and routing capabilities of the SSE to dramatically increase aggregate router performance, minimizing performance bottlenecks at the interface points between the router and a high-speed backbone.
2) Switch-to-Switch Protocol. Protocol specified in the DLSw standard that routers use to establish DLSw connections, locate resources, forward data, and handle flow control and error recovery.

STA

Spanning Tree Algorithm
Algorithm used by the Spanning Tree Protocol to create a spanning tree.

stack

See protocol stack.

standard

Set of rules or procedures that are either widely used or officially specified.

star topology

LAN topology in which end points on a network are connected to a common central switch by point-to-point links. A ring topology that is organized as a star implements a unidirectional closed-loop star, instead of point-to-point links. Compare with bus topology, ring topology, and tree topology.

StarLAN

CSMA/CD LAN, based on IEEE 802.3, developed by AT and T.

start-stop transmission

See asynchronous transmission.

stat mux

See statistical multiplexing.

stateless autoconfiguration

Plug-and-play IPv6 feature that enables devices to connect themselves to the network without any configuration and without any servers (like DHCP servers). This key feature enables deployment of new devices on the Internet, such as cellular phones, wireless devices, home appliances, and home networks.

Stateless IP/Internet Control Message Protocol (ICMP)

See SIIT.

static electricity

Unpredictable electrical charges in the atmosphere that interfere with radio reception, computer networking, and the like.

static route

Route that is explicitly configured and entered into the routing table. Static routes take precedence over routes chosen by dynamic routing protocols.

Station Management

See SMT.

statistical multiplexing

Technique whereby information from multiple logical channels can be transmitted across a single physical channel. Statistical multiplexing dynamically allocates bandwidth only to active input channels, making better use of available bandwidth and allowing more devices to be connected than with other multiplexing techniques. Also referred to as statistical time-division multiplexing or stat mux. Compare with ATDM, FDM, and TDM.

statistical time-division multiplexing

See STDM.

STDM

statistical time-division multiplexing
Technique whereby information from multiple logical channels can be transmitted across a single physical channel. Statistical multiplexing dynamically allocates bandwidth only to active input channels, making better use of available bandwidth and allowing more devices to be connected than with other multiplexing techniques. Also referred to as statistical time-division multiplexing or stat mux. Compare with ATDM, FDM, and TDM.

STM-1
Synchronous Transport Module level 1
One of a number of SDH formats that specifies the frame structure for the 155.52-Mbps lines used to carry ATM cells.

store and forward packet switching
Packet-switching technique in which frames are completely processed before being forwarded out the appropriate port. This processing includes calculating the CRC and checking the destination address. In addition, frames must be temporarily stored until network resources (such as an unused link) are available to forward the message. Contrast with cut-through packet switching.

STP
1) shielded twisted-pair. Two-pair wiring medium used in a variety of network implementations. STP cabling has a layer of shielded insulation to reduce EMI. Compare with UTP.
2) Spanning Tree Protocol. Bridge protocol that utilizes the spanning-tree algorithm, enabling a learning bridge to dynamically work around loops in a network topology by creating a spanning tree. Bridges exchange BPDU messages with other bridges to detect loops, and then remove the loops by shutting down selected bridge interfaces. Refers to both the IEEE 802.1 Spanning-Tree Protocol standard and the earlier Digital Equipment Corporation Spanning-Tree Protocol upon which it is based. The IEEE version supports bridge domains and allows the bridge to construct a loop-free topology across an extended LAN. The IEEE version is generally preferred over the Digital version.

StreamView network management
Cisco suite of SNMP-based network management tools used in conjunction with the LightStream 2020 ATM switch. The StreamView suite includes three GUI-driven applications: a configuration program (the configurator), a network topology map (the topology map), and a node monitoring program (the monitor); and a command-line interface (CLI).

Structure of Management Information
See SMI.

STS-1
Synchronous Transport Signal level 1
Basic building block signal of SONET, operating at 51.84 Mbps. Faster SONET rates are defined as STS-n, where n is a multiple of 51.84 Mbps.

STS-3c
Synchronous Transport Signal level 3, concatenated
SONET format that specifies the frame structure for the 155.52-Mbps lines used to carry ATM cells.

stub area
OSPF area that carries a default route, intra-area routes, and interarea routes, but does not carry external routes. Virtual links cannot be configured across a stub area, and they cannot contain an ASBR. Compare to non-stub area.

stub network
Network that has only a single connection to a router.

STUN
serial tunnel
Router feature allowing two SDLC- or HDLC-compliant devices to connect to one another through an arbitrary multiprotocol topology (using Cisco routers) rather than through a direct serial link.

subarea
Portion of an SNA network that consists of a subarea node and any attached links and peripheral nodes.

subarea node
SNA communication controller or host that handles complete network addresses.

subchannel
In broadband terminology, a frequency-based subdivision creating a separate communications channel.

subinterface
One of a number of virtual interfaces on a single physical interface.

subnet
See subnetwork.

subnet address
Portion of an IP address that is specified as the subnetwork by the subnet mask.

subnet mask
32-bit address mask used in IP to indicate the bits of an IP address that are being used for the subnet address.
Subnet mask is also known as mask.

subnet mask field
The subnet mask field contains a 32-bit mask that identifies the network and subnet portion of the IP address. The addition of this field is the single most important change made to the RIP v2 message structure.

subnetwork
1) In IP networks, a network sharing a particular subnet address. Subnetworks are networks arbitrarily segmented by a network administrator in order to provide a multilevel, hierarchical routing structure while shielding the subnetwork from the addressing complexity of attached networks. Subnetwork is also known as subnet. See also IP address, subnet address, and subnet mask.
2) In OSI networks, a collection of ESs and ISs under the control of a single administrative domain and using a single network access protocol.

Subnetwork Access Protocol
See SNAP.

subnetwork point of attachment
See SNPA.

Subscriber Network Interface
See SNI.

subvector
A data segment of a vector in an SNA message. A subvector consists of a length field, a key that describes the subvector type, and subvector specific data.

Super Frame
See SF.

supernetting
Aggregating IP network addresses advertised as a single classless network address. For example, given four Class C IP networks-192.0.8.0, 192.0.9.0, 192.0.10.0 and 192.0.11.0-each having the intrinsic network mask of 255.255.255.0, one can advertise the address 192.0.8.0 with a subnet mask of 255.255.252.0.

supervisory processor
See RP (route processor).

SURAnet
Southeastern Universities Research Association Network
Network connecting universities and other organizations in the Southeastern United States. SURAnet, originally funded by the NSF and a part of the NSFNET, is now part of BBN Planet.

surge
Any voltage increase above 110% of the normal voltage carried by a power line.

sustainable cell rate
See SCR.

SVC
switched virtual circuit
Virtual circuit that is dynamically established on demand and is torn down when transmission is complete. SVCs are used in situations where data transmission is sporadic.
Switched virtual circuit is also known as switched virtual connection in ATM terminology.

switch
1) Network device that filters, forwards, and floods frames based on the destination address of each frame. The switch operates at the data link layer of the OSI model.
2) General term applied to an electronic or mechanical device that allows a connection to be established as necessary and terminated when there is no longer a session to support.

switch card
Card on the LightStream 2020 ATM switch that handles communication between the other cards on the switch. Each LightStream 2020 switch has one or two switch cards. The second card, if present, serves as a backup for the first.

Switch Processor
See SP.

switched LAN
LAN implemented with LAN switches.

Switched Multimegabit Data Service
See SMDS.

Switched Port Analyzer
See SPAN.

switched virtual circuit
See SVC.

switched virtual connection
See SVC.

Switch-to-Switch Protocol
See SSP.

SwitchVision
Cisco SNMP-based network management software, running on Microsoft Windows, that offers a powerful set of tools to manage an entire network, including switches, hubs, routers, and bridges. SwitchVision can automatically discover and map any SNMP device on the network and show the status of network devices. SwitchVision allows network administrators to set event thresholds, activate actions when error conditions occur, and set up custom tables and graphs to view critical network variables.

synchronization
Establishment of common timing between sender and receiver.

Synchronous Data Link Control
See SDLC.

Synchronous Digital Hierarchy
See SDH.

Synchronous Optical Network
See SONET.

synchronous transmission
Term describing digital signals that are transmitted with precise clocking. Such signals have the same frequency, with individual characters encapsulated in control bits (called start bits and stop bits) that designate the beginning and end of each character. Compare with asynchronous transmission, isochronous transmission, and plesiochronous transmission.

Synchronous Transport Module level 1
See STM-1.

Synchronous Transport Signal level 1
See STM-1.

Synchronous Transport Signal level 3, concatenated
See STS-3c.

sysgen
system generation
Process of defining network resources in a network.

system generation
See sysgen.

System ID
System ID is a NSAP address field that identifies an individual OSI device. In OSI, a device has an address, just as it does in DECnet, while in IP an interface has an address.

system services control points
See SSCP.

Systems Network Architecture
See SNA.

T1
Digital WAN carrier facility. T1 transmits DS-1-formatted data at 1.544 Mbps through the telephone-switching network, using AMI or B8ZS coding. Compare with E1.

T3
Digital WAN carrier facility. T3 transmits DS-3-formatted data at 44.736 Mbps through the telephone switching network. Compare with E3.

TAC
1) Terminal Access Controller. Internet host that accepts terminal connections from dial-up lines.
2) Technical Assistance Center. Cisco TACs provide technical assistance to partners and end users, and form the hub of Cisco global support.

TACACS
Terminal Access Controller Access Control System
Authentication protocol, developed by the DDN community, that provides remote access authentication and related services, such as event logging. User passwords are administered in a central database rather than in individual routers, providing an easily scalable network security solution.

TACACS+
Terminal Access Controller Access Control System Plus
Proprietary Cisco enhancement to TACACS. Provides additional support for authentication, authorization, and accounting.

tagged traffic
ATM cells that have their CLP bit set to 1. If the network is congested, tagged traffic can be dropped to ensure delivery of higher-priority traffic.
Tagged traffic is also known as discard eligible (DE).

TAXI 4B/5B
Transparent Asynchronous Transmitter/Receiver Interface 4-byte/5-byte
Encoding scheme used for FDDI LANs as well as for ATM. Supports speeds of up to 100 Mbps over multimode fiber. TAXI is the chipset that generates 4B/5B encoding on multimode fiber.

T-carrier
TDM transmission method usually referring to a line or cable carrying a DS-1 signal.

TCP
Transmission Control Protocol
Connection-oriented transport layer protocol that provides reliable full-duplex data transmission. TCP is part of the TCP/IP protocol stack.

TCP/IP
Transmission Control Protocol/Internet Protocol
Common name for the suite of protocols developed by the U.S. DoD in the 1970s to support the construction of worldwide internetworks. TCP and IP are the two best-known protocols in the suite.

TCS
test and control system
Independently-powered subsystem used to initialize, monitor, and troubleshoot the hardware on a LightStream 2020 ATM switch. The TCS consists of a hub residing on the switch card and slaves on NPs and line cards.

TCU
trunk coupling unit
In Token Ring networks, a physical device that enables a station to connect to the trunk cable.

TDM
time-division multiplexing
Technique in which information from multiple channels can be allocated bandwidth on a single wire based on preassigned time slots. Bandwidth is allocated to each channel regardless of whether the station has data to transmit. Compare with ATDM, FDM, and statistical multiplexing.

TDR
time domain reflectometer
Device capable of sending signals through a network medium to check cable continuity, length, and other attributes. TDRs are used to find physical layer network problems.

Technical Assistance Center
See TAC.

Technical Office Protocol
See TOP.

telco
Abbreviation for telephone company.

telecommunications
Term referring to communications (usually involving computer systems) over the telephone network.

Telecommunications Industry Association
See TIA.

telephony
Science of converting sound to electrical signals and transmitting it between widely removed points.

telepole
Telescoping pole with a hook at one end. It is used to get cable across a ceiling or attic quickly.

teleworker
Work arrangement in which employees enjoy limited flexibility in working location and hours. The daily commute to a central place of work is replaced by telecommunication links. Teleworking is also known as a Branch of One, telecommuting, e-commuting, telework, or working from home (WFH).

telex
Teletypewriter service allowing subscribers to send messages over the PSTN.

Telnet
Command used to verify the application layer software between source and destination stations. This is the most complete test mechanism available.

Tempest
U.S. military standard. Electronic products adhering to the Tempest specification are designed to withstand EMP.

Teredo
Teredo is a mechanism which tunnels IPv6 datagrams within IPv4 UDP. This method provides for private IPv4 address use and IPv4 NAT traversal.
Teredo was formerly known as Shipworm.

termid
SNA cluster controller identification. Termid is meaningful only for switched lines.
Termid is also known as Xid.

terminal
Simple device at which data can be entered or retrieved from a network. Generally, terminals have a monitor and a keyboard, but no processor or local disk drive.

Terminal Access Controller
See TAC.

Terminal Access Controller Access System
See TACACS.

terminal adapter
Device used to connect ISDN BRI connections to existing interfaces such as EIA/TIA-232. Essentially, an ISDN modem.

terminal emulation
Network application in which a computer runs software that makes it appear to a remote host as a directly attached terminal.

terminal server
Communications processor that connects asynchronous devices such as terminals, printers, hosts, and modems to any LAN or WAN that uses TCP/IP, X.25, or LAT protocols. Terminal servers provide the internetwork intelligence that is not available in the connected devices.

terminator
Device that provides electrical resistance at the end of a transmission line to absorb signals on the line, thereby keeping them from bouncing back and being received again by network stations.

test and control system
See TCS.

Texas Higher Education Network
See THEnet.

TFTP
Trivial File Transfer Protocol
Simplified version of FTP that allows files to be transferred from one computer to another over a network.

TH
transmission header
SNA header that is appended to the SNA basic information unit (BIU). The TH uses one of a number of available SNA header formats.

THC over X.25
Feature providing TCP/IP header compression over X.25 links, for purposes of link efficiency.

THEnet
Texas Higher Education Network
Regional network comprising over 60 academic and research institutions in the Texas (United States) area.

Thinnet
Term used to define a thinner, less expensive version of the cable specified in the IEEE 802.3 10BASE2 standard. Compare with Cheapernet.

throughput
Rate of information arriving at, and possibly passing through, a particular point in a network system.

TIA
Telecommunications Industry Association
Organization that develops standards relating to telecommunications technologies. Together, the TIA and the EIA have formalized standards, such as EIA/TIA-232, for the electrical characteristics of data transmission.

tie-wraps
Plastic ties used for holding cables together or for holding cables in place.

time domain reflectometer
See TDR.

time domain reflectometry
Technique of sending an electrical signal down a cable and then timing the signal's reflection back from the end of the cable.

Time Notify
See TNotify.

Time To Live
See TTL.

time-division multiplexing
See TDM.

time-out
Event that occurs when one network device expects to hear from another network device within a specified period of time, but does not. The resulting time-out usually results in a retransmission of information or the dissolving of the session between the two devices.

TKIP
Temporal Key Integrity Protocol
TKIP is a WPA feature used to ensure integrity in wireless data transmission.

TLV
Type, Length, Value
TLV is in the IS-IS and ES-IS PDUs that contain variable-length fields, depending on the function of the PDU. Each field contains a type code and length, followed by the appropriate values. These fields are identified by one octet of type (T), one octet of length (L) and "L" octets of value (V). The Type field indicates the type of items in the Value field. The Length field indicates the length of the Value field. The Value field is the data portion of the packet. Not all router implementations support all TLVs, but they are required to ignore and retransmit the ignored types.

TN3270
Terminal emulation software that allows a terminal to appear to an IBM host as a 3278 Model 2 terminal. The Cisco TN3270 implementation allows users to access an IBM host without using a special IBM server or a UNIX host acting as a server.

TNotify
Time Notify
Specifies how often SMT initiates neighbor notification broadcasts.

to switch unit
See TSU.

token
Frame that contains control information. Possession of the token allows a network device to transmit data onto the network.

token bus
LAN architecture using token passing access over a bus topology. This LAN architecture is the basis for the IEEE 802.4 LAN specification.

token passing
Access method by which network devices access the physical medium in an orderly fashion based on possession of a small frame called a token. Contrast with circuit switching and contention.

Token Ring

Token-passing LAN developed and supported by IBM. Token Ring runs at 4 or 16 Mbps over a ring topology. Similar to IEEE 802.5.

TOP

Technical Office Protocol
OSI-based architecture developed for office communications.

topology

Physical arrangement of network nodes and media within an enterprise networking structure.

topology map

Tool for managing a LightStream 2020 ATM switch that examines a network and displays the status of its nodes and trunks. The topology map is an HP OpenView-based application that runs on an NMS.

ToS

type of service
Field within an IP datagram that indicates how the datagram should be handled.

total length

Field within an IP datagram that indicates total length of the header plus the data.

Totally stub area

An area that does not accept external autonomous system (AS) routes and summary routes from other areas internal to the autonomous system. Instead, if the router needs to send a packet to a network external to the area, it sends it using a default route.

TPC

Transmit Power Control
TPC is an IEEE 802.11h specification which has been used in the cellular telephone industry for years. TPC sets the transmit power of the access point and the client adapter to allow for different coverage area sizes and to conserve battery life.

trace route

Program available on many systems that traces the path a packet takes to a destination. It is mostly used to debug routing problems between hosts. There is also a traceroute protocol defined in RFC 1393.

traffic management

See ControlStream traffic management.

traffic policing

Process used to measure the actual traffic flow across a given connection and compare it to the total admissable traffic flow for that connection. Traffic outside of the agreed upon flow can be tagged (where the CLP bit is set to 1) and can be discarded en route if congestion develops. Traffic policing is used in ATM, Frame Relay, and other types of networks. Also know as admission control, permit processing, rate enforcement, and usage parameter control (UPC).

traffic profile

Set of COS attribute values assigned to a given port on a LightStream 2020 ATM switch. The profile affects numerous parameters for data transmitted from the port including rate, cell drop eligibility, transmit priority, and inactivity timer.

traffic shaping

Use of queues to limit surges that can congest a network. Data is buffered and then sent into the network in regulated amounts to ensure that the traffic will fit within the promised traffic envelope for the particular connection. Traffic shaping is used in ATM, Frame Relay, and other types of networks.
Traffic shaping is also known as metering, shaping, or smoothing.

trailer

Control information appended to data when encapsulating the data for network transmission. Compare with header.

transaction

Result-oriented unit of communication processing.

transaction services layer

Layer 7 in the SNA architectural model. Represents user application functions, such as spreadsheets, word-processing, or electronic mail, by which users interact with the network. Corre-

transceiver
See MAU.

transceiver cable
See AUI.

transfer priority
See transmit priority.

transit bridging
Bridging that uses encapsulation to send a frame between two similar networks over a dissimilar network.

translational bridging
Bridging between networks with dissimilar MAC sublayer protocols. MAC information is translated into the format of the destination network at the bridge. Contrast with encapsulation bridging.

transmission control layer
Layer 4 in the SNA architectural model. This layer is responsible for establishing, maintaining, and terminating SNA sessions, sequencing data messages, and controlling session level flow. Corresponds to the transport layer of the OSI model.

Transmission Control Protocol
See TCP.

Transmission Control Protocol/Internet Protocol
See TCP/IP.

transmission group
In SNA routing, one or more parallel communications links treated as one communications facility.

transmission header
See TH.

transmission link
See link.

transmit power
A radio transmission technology that spreads the user information over a much wider bandwidth than otherwise required in order to gain benefits such as improved interference tolerance and unlicensed operation.

transmit priority
Queuing scheme in which each internal TOS of a LightStream 2020 ATM switch correlates to a relative priority in queues in the ATM network. This priority determines which traffic is serviced first in the case of contention for a network resource.
Transmit priority is also known as forwarding priority or transfer priority.

TRANSPAC
Major packet data network run by France Telecom.

Transparent Asynchronous Transmitter/Receiver Interface 4-byte/5-byte
See TAXI 4B/5B.

transparent bridging
Bridging scheme often used in Ethernet and IEEE 802.3 networks in which bridges pass frames along one hop at a time based on tables associating end nodes with bridge ports. Transparent bridging is so named because the presence of bridges is transparent to network end nodes. Contrast with SRB.

transport layer
Layer 4 of the OSI reference model. This layer is responsible for reliable network communication between end nodes. The transport layer provides mechanisms for the establishment, maintenance, and termination of virtual circuits, transport fault detection and recovery, and information flow control. Corresponds to the transmission control layer of the SNA model.

trap
Message sent by an SNMP agent to an NMS, console, or terminal to indicate the occurrence of a significant event, such as a specifically defined condition or a threshold that has been reached.

tree topology
LAN topology similar to a bus topology, except that tree networks can contain branches with multiple nodes. Transmissions from a station

propagate the length of the medium and are received by all other stations. Compare with bus topology, ring topology, and star topology.

Trivial File Transfer Protocol
See TFTP.

trunk
Physical and logical connection between two ATM switches across which traffic in an ATM network travels. An ATM backbone is composed of a number of trunks.

trunk card
Line card on a LightStream 2020 ATM switch that is configured to communicate with other ATM switches. LightStream 2020 trunk cards offer a variety of interface types. CLCs, LSCs, and MSCs can operate as trunk cards.

trunk coupling unit
See TCU.

Trunk Up-Down
See TUD.

TSU
to switch unit
Subsystem on each LightStream 2020 ATM switch line card that appends ATM routing information to outgoing cells and sends the cells to the switch card.

TTL
time to live
Field in an IP header that indicates how long a packet is considered valid.

TUD
Trunk Up-Down
Protocol used in ATM networks that monitors trunks and detects when one goes down or comes up. ATM switches send regular test messages from each trunk port to test trunk line quality. If a trunk misses a given number of these messages, TUD declares the trunk down. When a trunk comes back up, TUD recognizes that the trunk is up, declares the trunk up, and returns it to service.

tunneling
Architecture that is designed to provide the services necessary to implement any standard point-to-point encapsulation scheme.

TUV
German test agency that certifies products to European safety standards.

twisted pair
Relatively low-speed transmission medium consisting of two insulated wires arranged in a regular spiral pattern. The wires can be shielded or unshielded. Twisted pair is common in telephony applications and is increasingly common in data networks.

two-way simultaneous
See TWS.

TWS
two-way simultaneous
Mode that allows a router configured as a primary SDLC station to achieve better utilization of a full-duplex serial line. When TWS is enabled in a multidrop environment, the router can poll a secondary station and receive data from that station while it sends data to or receives data from a different secondary station on the same serial line.

Type 1 operation
IEEE 802.2 (LLC) connectionless operation.

Type 2 operation
IEEE 802.2 (LLC) connection-oriented operation.

type of service
See ToS.

Type, Length, Value
See TLV.

UART
Universal Asynchronous Receiver/Transmitter
Integrated circuit, attached to the parallel bus of a computer, used for serial communications. The UART translates between serial and parallel signals, provides transmission clocking, and buffers data sent to or from the computer.

UBR
unspecified bit rate
QOS class defined by the ATM Forum for ATM networks. UBR allows any amount of data up to a specified maximum to be sent across the network, but there are no guarantees in terms of cell loss rate and delay. Compare with available bit rate (ABR), CBR, and VBR.

UDP
User Datagram Protocol
Connectionless transport layer protocol in the TCP/IP protocol stack. UDP is a simple protocol that exchanges datagrams without acknowledgments or guaranteed delivery, requiring that error processing and retransmission be handled by other protocols. UDP is defined in RFC 768.

UL
Underwriters Laboratories
Independent agency within the United States that tests product safety.

ULP
upper-layer protocol
Protocol that operates at a higher layer in the OSI reference model, relative to other layers. ULP is sometimes used to refer to the next-highest protocol (relative to a particular protocol) in a protocol stack.

unbalanced configuration
HDLC configuration with one primary station and multiple secondary stations.

Underwriters Laboratories
See UL.

UNI
User-Network Interface
ATM Forum specification that defines an interoperability standard for the interface between ATM-based products (a router or an ATM switch) located in a private network and the ATM switches located within the public carrier networks. Also used to describe similar connections in Frame Relay networks.

unicast
Message sent to a single network destination. Compare with broadcast and multicast.

unicast address
Address specifying a single network device. Compare with broadcast address and multicast address.

uninsured traffic
Traffic within the excess rate (the difference between the insured rate and maximum rate) for a VCC. This traffic can be dropped by the network if congestion occurs.

Universal Asynchronous Receiver/Transmitter
See UART.

Universal Resource Locator
See URL.

UNIX
Operating system developed in 1969 at Bell Laboratories. UNIX has gone through several iterations since its inception. These include UNIX 4.3 BSD (Berkeley Standard Distribution), developed at the University of California at Berkeley, and UNIX System V, Release 4.0, developed by AT and T.

unnumbered frames
HDLC frames used for various control and management purposes, including link startup and shutdown, and mode specification.

unshielded twisted-pair
See UTP.

unspecified bit rate
See UBR.

UPC
usage parameter control. See traffic policing.

upper-layer protocol
See ULP.

UPS
uninterruptable power supply
Backup device designed to provide an uninterrupted power source in the event of a power failure. They are commonly installed on all file servers and wiring hubs.

Urgent Pointer
Indicates the end of the urgent data.

URL
Universal Resource Locator
Standardized addressing scheme for accessing hypertext documents and other services using a WWW browser.

usage parameter control
See UPC.

USENET
Initiated in 1979, one of the oldest and largest cooperative networks, with over 10,000 hosts and a quarter of a million users. Its primary service is a distributed conferencing service called news.

User Datagram Protocol
See UDP.

User-Network Interface
See UNI.

UTP
unshielded twisted-pair
Four-pair wire medium used in a variety of networks. UTP does not require the fixed spacing between connections that is necessary with coaxial-type connections. There are five types of UTP cabling commonly used: Category 1 cabling, Category 2 cabling, Category 3 cabling, Category 4 cabling, and Category 5 cabling. Compare with STP.

V.24
ITU-T standard for a physical layer interface between DTE and DCE. V.24 is essentially the same as the EIA/TIA-232 standard.

V.35
ITU-T standard describing a synchronous, physical layer protocol used for communications between a network access device and a packet network. V.35 is most commonly used in the United States and in Europe, and is recommended for speeds up to 48 Kbps.

V.42
ITU-T standard protocol for error correction using LAPM.

variable bit rate
See VBR.

Variable Length Subnet Masking
See VLSM.

variable-length subnet mask
See VLSM.

VBR
variable bit rate
QOS class defined by the ATM Forum for ATM networks. VBR is subdivided into a real time (RT) class and non-real time (NRT) class. VBR (RT) is used for connections in which there is a fixed timing relationship between samples. VBR (NRT) is used for connections in which there is no fixed timing relationship between samples, but that still need a guaranteed QOS. Compare with ABR, CBR, and UBR.

VC
virtual circuit
Logical circuit created to ensure reliable communication between two network devices. A virtual circuit is defined by a VPI/VCI pair, and can be either permanent (PVC) or switched (SVC). Virtual circuits are used in Frame Relay and X.25. In ATM, a virtual circuit is called a virtual channel.

VCC
virtual channel connection
Logical circuit, made up of VCLs, that carries data between two end points in an ATM network.
Virtual channel connection is also known as virtual circuit connection.

VCI
virtual channel identifier
16-bit field in the header of an ATM cell. The VCI, together with the VPI, is used to identify the next destination of a cell as it passes through a series of ATM switches on its way to its destination. ATM switches use the VPI/VCI fields to identify the next network VCL that a cell needs to transit on its way to its final destination. The function of the VCI is similar to that of the DLCI in Frame Relay. Compare to DLCI.

VCL
virtual channel link
Connection between two ATM devices. A VCC is made up of one or more VCLs.

VCN
virtual circuit number
12-bit field in an X.25 PLP header that identifies an X.25 virtual circuit. Allows DCE to determine how to route a packet through the X.25 network.
Virtual circuit number is also known as logical channel identifier (LCI) or logical channel number (LCN).

vector
Data segment of an SNA message. A vector consists of a length field, a key that describes the vector type, and vector-specific data.

VERS
Version number field with in an IP datagram.

Versatile Interface Processor
See VIP.

vertical cabling
See backbone cabling.

video on demand
See VoD.

VINES
Virtual Integrated Network Service
NOS developed and marketed by Banyan Systems.

VIP
1) Versatile Interface Processor. Interface card used in Cisco 7000 and Cisco 7500 series routers. The VIP provides multilayer switching and runs the Cisco IOS software.
2) Virtual IP. Function that enables the creation of logically separated switched IP workgroups across the switch ports of a Catalyst 5000 running Virtual Networking Services software.

virtual address
See network address.

virtual channel
See virtual circuit (VC).

virtual channel connection
See VCC.

virtual channel identifier
See VCI.

virtual channel link
See VCL.

virtual circuit
See VC.

virtual circuit connection
See VCC.

virtual circuit number
See VCN.

Virtual Integrated Network Service
See VINES.

virtual IP
See VIP.

virtual LAN
See VLAN.

virtual LAN internetwork
See VLI.

Virtual Networking Services
Software on some Catalyst 5000 switches that enables multiple workgroups to be defined across switches and offers traffic segmentation and access control.

virtual path
Logical grouping of virtual circuits that connect two sites.

virtual path connection
See VPC.

virtual path identifier
See VPI.

virtual path identifier/virtual channel identifier
See VPI/VCI.

virtual path link
See VPL.

virtual ring
Entity in an SRB network that logically connects two or more physical rings together either locally or remotely. The concept of virtual rings can be expanded across router boundaries.

virtual route
In SNA, a logical connection between subarea nodes that is physically realized as a particular explicit route. SNA terminology for virtual circuit. See also virtual circuit.

virtual telecommunications access method
See VTAM.

Virtual Terminal Protocol
See VTP.

VLAN
virtual LAN
Group of devices on a LAN that are configured (using management software) so that they can communicate as if they were attached to the same wire, when in fact they are located on a number of different LAN segments. Because VLANs are based on logical instead of physical connections, they are extremely flexible.

VLANs
virtual LAN
Group of devices on a LAN that are configured (using management software) so that they can communicate as if they were attached to the same wire, when in fact they are located on a number of different LAN segments. Because VLANs are based on logical instead of physical connections, they are extremely flexible.

VLSM
variable-length subnet mask
Ability to specify a different subnet mask for the same network number on different subnets. VLSM can help optimize available address space.

VoD
video on demand
Systems that allow users to select and watch video content over a network as part of an interactive television system. VoD systems either "stream" content, allowing viewing while the video is being downloaded, or "download" it in which the program is brought in its entirety to a set-top box before viewing starts.

VoIP
Voice over IP
The capability to carry normal telephony-style voice over an IP-based internet with POTS-like functionality, reliability, and voice quality. VoIP enables a router to carry voice traffic (for example, telephone calls and faxes) over an IP network. In VoIP, the DSP segments the voice signal into frames, which then are coupled in groups of two and stored in voice packets. These voice packets are transported using IP in compliance with ITU-T specification H.323.

VPC
virtual path connection
Grouping of VCCs that share one or more contiguous VPLs.

VPI
virtual path identifier
8-bit field in the header of an ATM cell. The VPI, together with the VCI, is used to identify the next destination of a cell as it passes through a series of ATM switches on its way to its destination. ATM switches use the VPI/VCI fields to identify the next VCL that a cell needs to transit on its way to its final destination. The function of the VPI is similar to that of the DLCI in Frame Relay. Compare with DLCI.

VPI/VCI
virtual path identifier/virtual channel identifier
See VCI and VPI.

VPL
virtual path link
Within a virtual path, a group of unidirectional VCLs with the same end points. Grouping VCLs into VPLs reduces the number of connections to be managed, thereby decreasing network control overhead and cost. A VPC is made up of one or more VPLs.

VRRP
Virtual Router Redundancy Protocol
VRRP is a vendor neutral alternative to HSRP and GLBP, providing router redundancy for traffic exiting a LAN environment. VRRP allows a group of routers to form a single virtual

router. One router is elected to handle all requests sent to the virtual IP address. A VRRP group has one master router and one or more backup routers.

VTAM

virtual telecommunications access method
Set of programs that control communication between LUs. VTAM controls data transmission between channel-attached devices and performs routing functions.

VTP

1) Virtual Terminal Protocol. ISO application for establishing a virtual terminal connection across a network.
2) VLAN Trunking Protocol. A Cisco proprietary protocol that uses Layer 2 trunk frames to communicate VLAN information among a group of switches and to manage the addition, deletion, and renaming of VLANs across the network from a central point of control.

WAN

Wide Area Network
Data communications network that serves users across a broad geographic area and often uses transmission devices provided by common carriers. Frame Relay, SMDS, and X.25 are examples of WANs.

waveform coding

Electrical techniques used to convey binary signals.

WCS

Wireless Control System
WCS allows the centralized configuration of Cisco WLAN controllers in conjunction with lightweight access points (centralized WLAN model).

WDS

Wireless Domain Services
An access point providing WDS on your wireless LAN maintains a cache of credentials for CCKM-capable client devices on your wireless LAN. When a CCKM-capable client roams from one access point to another, the WDS access point forwards the client's credentials to the new access point with the multicast key. Only two packets pass between the client and the new access point, greatly shortening the reassociation time.

Weighted fair queuing

See WFQ.

WEP

Wired Equivalent Privacy
An optional security mechanism defined within the 802.11 standard designed to make the link integrity of wireless devices equal to that of a cable.

WFQ

weighted fair queuing
Queuing method that prioritizes interactive traffic over file transfers in order to ensure satisfactory response time for common user applications.

wide-area network

See WAN.

wideband

See broadband.

Wi-Fi Alliance

The Wi-Fi Alliance offers certification for interoperability between vendors of 802.11 products. It helps to market a WLAN technology by promoting interoperability between vendors. Certification includes all three 802.11 RF technologies and WPA.

Wi-Fi Protected Access

See WPA.

wildcard mask

32-bit quantity used in conjunction with an IP address to determine which bits in an IP address should be ignored when comparing that address with another IP address. A wildcard mask is specified when setting up access lists.

window

Number of octets that the receiver is willing to accept.

window size

Refers to the number of messages that can be transmitted while awaiting an acknowledgment.

wire map
Feature provided by most cable testers. Used to test twisted pair cable installations, it shows which wire pairs connect to what pins on the plugs and sockets.

wireless controller
A wireless controller is a device used in a centralized WLAN topology which handles authentication, association, mobility, and frame translation and bridging.

wiring closet
Specially designed room used for wiring a data or voice network. Wiring closets serve as a central junction point for the wiring and wiring equipment that is used for interconnecting devices.

WLAN
wireless LAN
A WLAN a wireless local area network, which permits a network connection between two or more computers without using wires. It uses radio communication to accomplish the same functionality that a wired LAN has.

WLSE
Wireless LAN Solution Engine
WLSE is a CiscoWorks option which allows centralized configuration and monitoring of the Cisco Aironet autonomous access points and provides RF management, rogue access point detection, and interference detection. WLSE is used with autonomous access points in the distributive WLAN model.

workgroup
Collection of workstations and servers on a LAN that are designed to communicate and exchange data with one another.

World Wide Web
See WWW.

WPA
Wi-Fi Protected Access
WPA is a security model for WLANs released in 2003, based on the IEEE 802.11i standard. It is a standards-based, interoperable security enhancement that strongly increases the level of data protection and access control for existing and future wireless LAN systems. It is derived from and will be forward-compatible with the upcoming IEEE 802.11i standard. WPA leverages Temporal Key Integrity Protocol (TKIP) for data protection and 802.1X for authenticated key management.

WWW
World Wide Web
Large network of Internet servers providing hypertext and other services to terminals running client applications such as a WWW browser.

WWW browser
World Wide Web browser
GUI-based hypertext client application, such as Mosaic, used to access hypertext documents and other services located on innumerable remote servers throughout the WWW and Internet.

X.121
ITU-T standard describing an addressing scheme used in X.25 networks. X.121 addresses are sometimes called IDNs (International Data Numbers).

X.21
ITU-T standard for serial communications over synchronous digital lines. The X.21 protocol is used primarily in Europe and Japan.

X.21bis
ITU-T standard that defines the physical layer protocol for communication between DCE and DTE in an X.25 network. Virtually equivalent to EIA/TIA-232.

X.25
ITU-T standard that defines how connections between DTE and DCE are maintained for remote terminal access and computer communications in PDNs. X.25 specifies LAPB, a data link layer protocol, and PLP, a network layer protocol. Frame Relay has to some degree superseded X.25.

X.25 Level 3
See PLP.

X.25 Protocol
See PLP.

X.28
ITU-T recommendation that defines the terminal-to-PAD interface in X.25 networks.

X.29
ITU-T recommendation that defines the form for control information in the terminal-to-PAD interface used in X.25 networks.

X.3
ITU-T recommendation that defines various PAD parameters used in X.25 networks.

X.400
ITU-T recommendation specifying a standard for electronic mail transfer.

X.500
ITU-T recommendation specifying a standard for distributed maintenance of files and directories.

X.75
ITU-T specification that defines the signalling system between two PDNs. X.75 is essentially an NNI.

X3T9.5
Number assigned to the ANSI Task Group of Accredited Standards Committee for their internal, working document describing FDDI.

XID
1) exchange identification. Request and response packets exchanged prior to a session between a router and a Token Ring host. If the parameters of the serial device contained in the XID packet do not match the configuration of the host, the session is dropped.
2) See termid.

XML
eXtensible Markup Language
A standard maintained by the World Wide Web Consortium (W3C). It defines a syntax that lets you create markup languages to specify information structures. Information structures define the type of information, for example, subscriber name or address, not how the information looks (bold, italic, and so on). External processes can manipulate these information structures and publish them in a variety of formats. Text markup language designed to enable the use of SGML on the World Wide Web. XML allows you to define your own customized markup language.

XNS
Xerox Network Systems
Protocol suite originally designed by PARC. Many PC networking companies, such as 3Com, Banyan, Novell, and UB Networks used or currently use a variation of XNS as their primary transport protocol.

zero code suppression
Line coding scheme used for transmission clocking. Zero line suppression substitutes a one in the seventh bit of a string of eight consecutive zeros.

CCNA Exploration learning resources

Cisco Press, the authorized publisher for the Cisco® Networking Academy®, has a variety of learning and preparation tools to help you master the knowledge and prepare successfully for the CCENT™ and CCNA® exams.

From foundational learning to late-stage review, practice, and preparation, the varied print, software, and video products from Cisco Press can help you with learning, mastering, and succeeding!

Companion Guides

Companion Guides provide textbook-style support with additional content from leading Academy instructors.

Network Fundamentals, CCNA Exploration Companion Guide	1-58713-208-7 / 978-1-58713-208-7
Routing Protocols and Concepts, CCNA Exploration Companion Guide	1-58713-206-0 / 978-1-58713-206-3
LAN Switching and Wireless, CCNA Exploration Companion Guide	1-58713-207-9 / 978-1-58713-207-0
Accessing the WAN, CCNA Exploration Companion Guide	1-58713-205-2 / 978-1-58713-205-6

Labs and Study Guides

Labs and Study Guides provide study tools and labs, both from the online curriculum and from leading Academy instructors.

Network Fundamentals, CCNA Exploration Labs and Study Guide	1-58713-203-6 / 978-1-58713-203-2
Routing Protocols and Concepts, CCNA Exploration Labs and Study Guide	1-58713-204-4 / 978-1-58713-204-9
LAN Switching and Wireless, CCNA Exploration Labs and Study	1-58713-202-8 / 978-1-58713-202-5
Accessing the WAN, CCNA Exploration Labs and Study Guide	1-58713-201-X / 978-1-58713-201-8

Other CCNA resources

1-58713-197-8 / 978-1-58713-197-4	31 Days Before your CCNA Exam, Second Edition
1-58720-183-6 / 978-1-58720-183-7	CCNA Official Exam Certification Library, Third Edition
1-58720-193-3 / 978-1-58720-193-6	CCNA Portable Command Guide, Second Edition
1-58720-216-6 / 978-1-58720-216-2	CCNA 640-802 Network Simulator (from Pearson Certification)
1-58720-221-2 / 978-1-58720-221-6	CCNA 640-802 Cert Flash Cards Online

For more information on this and other Cisco Press products, visit www.ciscopress.com /academy

Cisco Press

Learning is Serious Business. **Invest Wisely.**